Optimal
DATABASE
MARKETING

Optimal
DATABASE
MARKETING
Strategy,
Development,
and Data Mining

Ronald G. Drozdenko
Western Connecticut State University

Perry D. Drake
Drake Direct

SAGE Publications
International Educational and Professional Publisher
Thousand Oaks ▪ London ▪ New Delhi

For information:

Sage Publications, Inc.
2455 Teller Road
Thousand Oaks, California 91320
E-mail: order@sagepub.com

Sage Publications Ltd.
6 Bonhill Street
London EC2A 4PU
United Kingdom

Sage Publications India Pvt. Ltd.
M-32 Market
Greater Kailash I
New Delhi 110 048 India

Printed in the United States of America

Library of Congress Cataloging-in-Publication Data

Drozdenko, Ronald G.
  Optimal database maketing: strategy, development, and data mining/
  by Ronald G. Drozdenko and Perry D. Drake.
      p.   cm.
    Includes bibliographical references and index.
    ISBN 0-7619-2357-8
    1. Database marketing. 2. Electronic commerce.
    I. Drake, Perry D.   II. Title.
  HF5415.126 .D76   2002
    658.8'4-dc20   2001005596

This book is printed on acid-free paper.

    03   04   05   10   9   8   7   6   5   4   3   2

Acquisitions Editor: Marquita Flemming
Editorial Assistant: MaryAnn Vail
Production Editor: Claudia A. Hoffman
Indexer: Molly Hall
Cover Designer: Michelle Lee

Contents

Preface

Contemporary direct marketing and e-commerce companies cannot exist in today's competitive environment without the use of marketing databases. Databases allow marketers to reach customers and cultivate relationships more effectively and efficiently. Although databases provide a means to establish and enhance relationships, they can also be used incorrectly, inefficiently, and unethically. Our goal in this book is to provide the reader with a complete and solid understanding of how to properly establish and use databases to help organizations maximize their relationships with customers. In fact, we have not found any other book on the market today that contains the level of detail regarding database marketing applications that this one has.

We have been involved in the direct marketing industry and academia for many years. Ron Drozdenko teaches Strategic Marketing Databases and Interactive Marketing Management and has been a consultant to many firms over the course of his career. He is currently the Chair of the Marketing Department at Western Connecticut State University. Perry Drake is an independent database marketing consultant and adjunct faculty member of New York University, where he teaches Statistics for Direct Marketers, Database Modeling, and Advanced Database Modeling in the Direct Marketing Master's Degree program.

In teaching such topics to students, we both have found little material to draw upon. As such, we were required to create our own content from our industry experience, help from peers, and published case studies. Several excellent books have been written on the topic of direct marketing. However, many of those books delve only into areas such as copywriting and media selection and place less emphasis on database marketing applications from a marketer's perspective. Our intent with this book is to focus on the marketing database and take readers systematically through the process of database strategy, development, and analysis.

We originally met each other in the summer of 1997 when we were approached by the Direct Marketing Educational Foundation (DMEF) to develop a database marketing course. The database course is one of a series

of undergraduate courses in direct marketing the DMEF developed in col-
laboration with the Marketing Department of the Ancell School of Business
at Western Connecticut State University. (You can contact the DMEF to
obtain more information about these courses.)

Our target audience for this book is both students and practitioners:
upper-level undergraduates, graduate students in an MBA program, and
entry- and middle-level direct marketers. In addition, database analysts and
statisticians fairly new to the field of direct marketing will find the book
useful. It will provide a complete overview of the analytical applications in
the field of direct marketing. Direct marketing executives will also find the
strategic elements of the book helpful for business planning.

Supplemental Material

Academic adopters of this book have access to the following support material from the authors:

- A comprehensive collection of PowerPoint slides for each chapter
- Sample exercises and solutions for each chapter
- Sample syllabi and course organization
- Sample exams and quizzes
- Sample marketing databases for case study work given in various formats (delimited text files, SAS, Excel, SPSS, etc.).

Acknowledgments

A number of people contributed directly or indirectly to the development of this book. Because the book evolved from an outline developed by an advisory board established by the DMEF, the members of the board deserve acknowledgment. In particular, Richard Montesi and Laurie Spar were instrumental in establishing the board and organizing the meetings. David Henneberry and Dante Cirilli worked with us to establish the original outline that served as the basis for the database marketing course and eventually this book. The extensive backgrounds of Dave and Dan in the direct marketing industry ensure that the book's foundation is solid.

We also wish to acknowledge the indirect contributions of a number of small and large professional associations in the direct marketing community that allowed us to examine database marketing in application. In particular, The Reader's Digest Association and Grolier Direct Marketing influenced our perspectives on database marketing.

One of our primary reasons for writing this book is to provide marketing students with a good foundation in database strategy, development, and analysis. Therefore, the feedback we obtained from our students at the Ancell School of Business at Western Connecticut State University and New York University was especially valuable in translating course materials into a coherent book. Students also read drafts of sections of the book and offered several cogent suggestions. In particular, Perry gives special thanks to some of his past students at NYU—Joe Bello, Janelle Bowleg, Eric Chism, Dean Krispin, Steve LaScala, and Bob Wiener—for their tremendous efforts in ensuring that the book content was complete, consistent, and understandable.

Industry reviewers of chapters of this book deserve our gratitude. In particular, Perry personally thanks, first and foremost, Pierre Passavant, the previous director of the NYU Direct Marketing Master's Degree program, for his support and the many opportunities he provided. Secondly, we thank Gary Coles for his significant review of Chapter 10, Rich Lawsky for his significant review of Chapter 4, and Elizabeth Colquhoun for her review of all the chapters for clarity. In addition, we thank Craig Ceire,

Mary-Elizabeth Eddlestone, Mary Halloran, Patrick Hanrahan, Jim Tucker, Henry Weinberger, and Pat Zamora for their individual contributions dealing with specific topics. We are also indebted to the following reviewers of the completed manuscript. Their comments and suggestions have helped improve the final version of the book.

Naomi Bernstein

Dante Cirilli

C. Samuel Craig

David Heneberry

Richard Hochhauser

Patrick E. Kenny

Brian Kurtz

Peter C. Mueller

Pierre Passavant

Kari Regan

Mary Lou Roberts

Thanks to the team at Sage Publications, including Marquita Flemming, MaryAnn Vail, and our copy editor, Barbara Coster, for their support and guidance.

Last, but certainly not least, our appreciation goes to our families. In addition to lending moral support, some family members provided direct contributions to the development of the book. Rita Drozdenko, Ron's wife, read several chapters and provided feedback from the perspective of a novice to the field. Rhonda Knehans Drake, Perry's wife and an accomplished database marketing consultant, made a significant contribution to the book. Rhonda wrote Chapter 16, "Analyzing and Targeting Online Customers," and also provided professional critiques of other chapters. Tarry Drake-Schaffner, Perry's sister, an avid book reader and bookstore owner, spent a tremendous amount of time editing and rewriting all the technically oriented chapters. Words cannot express the thanks that Perry has for her invaluable input in ensuring that complex topics could be understood by a beginner. As a novice to the field herself, this was not an easy task for Tarry, especially given the tight deadlines. Thank you, Tarry, for your tremendous efforts.

—Ronald G. Drozdenko
—Perry D. Drake

Foreword

With about 70 years of management and teaching experience between us, we know a superior training/reference book when we read it. This is a great one. We aren't surprised, because we both confer with the authors about the database issues of our own seminars, classes, and clients.

If you have a database, chances are you have database questions and issues: How good are the data? How complete? Are you capturing the right data? Are you using the data to the maximum advantage? Will investments in new system enhancements pay out? What steps must be followed when considering to outsource your database? What issues must be considered when examining data mining tools? How do you learn sound database management practices? How do you teach them? How do you provide intelligent leadership to database management departments that report to you?

The answers require a thoughtful examination of what is needed, how to capture it, at what cost—and some knowledge of statistics that most of us don't have. You won't find a better resource than this book. It covers all aspects of database marketing, including database design, maintenance, data usage, test design, and data analysis. In all these areas, the focus is on how to best utilize the database to optimize marketing efforts. Important current issues such as e-commerce, ethics, privacy, and globalization are also covered.

Coauthor Ronald G. Drozdenko, Ph.D., Professor and Chair of the Marketing Department at the Ancell School of Business, Western Connecticut State University, teaches Strategic Marketing Databases and Interactive/Direct Marketing Management. He was a member of the advisory board established by the Direct Marketing Educational Foundation to develop a model curriculum for direct/interactive marketing. This model program is currently being offered at the Ancell School. In his role as faculty adviser for student interns, Ron uses company feedback to enrich the program with continuing real-life applications. Ron has also accumulated more than 20 years of applied marketing experience. Both his academic and applied marketing backgrounds are reflected in the approach taken in this book.

Coauthor Perry D. Drake is currently a database marketing consultant and faculty member in the Master's of Science in Direct Marketing program at New York University. Prior to this, Perry had spent over 10 years in various database marketing roles at The Reader's Digest Association, most recently as the director of a special division within the Marketing Services group. During Perry's first year at NYU, word got around that he had a remarkable ability to make topics such as statistics and database modeling and regression understandable and interesting. In recognition of his abilities, he won the first Outstanding Master's Faculty Award. Perry's exceptional teaching skills are very evident in the chapters of this book.

The book that Ron and Perry have written tracks a character, Keri Lee, as she resolves data and database issues at every step in her advancement through the ranks, first in a technology agency servicing clients and later as a senior manager in a large publishing company. Her reasoning and her solutions to data problems of increasing complexity demonstrate the methodology of database management in all its statistics-driven splendor. Go as deeply as you need for your purpose. The practical wisdom and concrete examples make it an ideal resource for business managers, instructors, trainers, and students.

If you are a business manager, this book will help you oversee the various specialists you must work with to implement a database marketing strategy. If you are an instructor, trainer, or student, it will give you a clear picture of what actually happens in the real world of business and specific techniques used by business professionals. Keep the book at hand to resolve your next database dilemma.

—David Heneberry
Director, Direct Marketing Certificate Programs,
Ancell School of Business, Western Connecticut State University

—Pierre Passavant
Professor of Direct Marketing, Mercy College, Westchester, New York

1 Introduction to Database Marketing Concepts

It's 7:15 p.m., Keri Lee, a 29-year-old account executive for a technology company, stops at a supermarket in Southbury, Connecticut, on her way home from work. After picking up Diet Pepsi, a few tomatoes, lettuce, and a package of Swiss cheese, she goes to the express checkout line. Keri hands her store card to the clerk, who scans it prior to processing her order. Using the store card allows her to get a discount on the cheese. With her sales receipt, she also gets a $0.40 coupon for Ritz Crackers. The bill came to $6.20. Keri paid with her VISA card.

Keri picks up her mail before going into the house. There are catalogs from Bloomingdales, L. L. Bean, Macy's, and Pottery Barn. She puts the Pottery Barn catalog to the side. Her sister's birthday is in two weeks and the items in the catalog are consistent with her sister's decorating style.

In addition to the electric and VISA bills, she has a letter from the Volkswagen dealership thanking her for her recent purchase and a letter from the American Red Cross. Remembering that the Red Cross recently helped her friend who was caught in a flood, she makes a contribution by checking a box and entering her VISA number.

Keri also got the new issues of Smart Business, Business Week, *and* Self *magazines. An ad in* Business Week *about a technology conference attracts her attention, and she fills out an attached response card requesting more information.*

After dinner, she receives a phone call from an insurance company. At first, she is irritated by the call. She then remembers that her car insurance rates increased substantially since she leased her new Volkswagen and asks the person on the phone for a quote. Later that evening, she goes on the Internet to look for other insurance companies and requests three more quotes online.

Browsing the Web, she remembers that she has almost finished the book she has been reading and goes to Amazon.com. The Amazon page provides her with suggestions based on her previous purchase, A Certain Justice, *by P. D. James. A new mystery by Elizabeth George is on the suggestion list. It can be shipped within 24 hours. Keri places the book into the Shopping Cart and uses 1-Click to check out.*

Before leaving the Amazon site, she clicks on the Music tab and searches for Sarah McLachlan. She heard a new single by McLachlan on the radio and was curious about the other songs on the CD. Keri listens to five cuts from McLachlan's new CD but decides not to order yet.

At 10:00 p.m., she scans through the channels on TV and pauses at QVC when a bracelet grabs her attention. Calling QVC, she gives her account number that she used 2 months ago when she purchased a color printer. In less than 1 minute, the bracelet is ordered and she returns to scanning the channels.

Keri's daily routine is similar to the routines of millions of other people in the United States and other countries. These transactions provide us with the goods and services that are a part of our lives. In the scenario above, **databases** underlie all the transactions that Keri made. They underlie the purchases in the grocery store, catalogs, TV shopping, Internet, tele-marketing, and the charitable contributions. Databases are a collection of information related to a particular subject or purpose that are usually maintained on a computer for easy search, retrieval, and analysis. Although databases are not new, they are becoming an essential element of marketing. Organizations in consumer products, business-to-business (b-to-b), char-ities, health care, politics, media, investments, government, insurance, and so on are finding **marketing databases** essential to their survival and success. In addition, because technology has become more accessible, small businesses are finding the use of databases a cost-effective way to stay in touch with their customers.

Several changes in the business, social, and technological environments have led to the widespread use of databases in marketing. However, the one underlying reason for the adoption of databases is that they allow marketers to use information about individual customers to reach those customers and cultivate relationships more effectively and efficiently.

Databases provide a means to establish and enhance relationships, but they can also be used incorrectly, inefficiently, and unethically. Organ-izations can use databases to help customers make shopping easier and make better purchase decisions, or they can use databases to intrude into people's lives. Good marketers know that maintaining customer satisfac-tion is the key to long-term success, and using a database to flood people with unwanted promotional materials is not only wasteful but is unlikely to build productive long-term relationships with customers. One of the goals of this book is to look beyond the temptation of the quick sale and consider the long-term impact of database marketing techniques on the organization, customers, prospective customers, and society in general.

This first chapter introduces marketing database concepts. We begin by defining marketing databases and examining the environmental trends that help to explain why the use of marketing databases is growing so rapidly. Because one of the principal uses of marketing databases is in direct/interactive marketing, we examine this type of marketing, compare it to marketing through conventional retail channels, and briefly explore its advantages and disadvantages. We conclude the chapter by providing a framework for the concepts and techniques covered in this book.

What Is a Marketing Database?

A marketing database is a file containing information about individual customers or potential customers that is relevant to the marketing process. This file can be simple or sophisticated. For centuries, businesspeople recorded customer information on slips of paper or in notebooks. Some organizations still use these manual databases. In contrast, companies like American Express and Macy's have computer databases that contain millions of names. Some of these names have hundreds of pieces of information.

Whether the database uses simple or sophisticated technologies, the purpose is the same—to gain a better understanding of customers in order to increase the customer's satisfaction and the organization's objectives. Although some organizations still use paper databases, the focus of this book is on computer databases and how data about customers are stored, manipulated, and analyzed on a computer.

Where do the data about customers come from? Companies build marketing databases from a number of sources. Like Keri Lee, if you receive product offers in the mail, such as a catalog, you are on a database. Your name could have been added to the database from a telephone book list, a membership list, or lists of public notices (like a home purchase). When you respond to an offer for a product, your name usually gets added to another database.

There are companies that specialize in gathering and renting lists of customers. You might be surprised at the range and diversity of available lists. For example, as a marketer, you could rent lists of female corporate decision makers, residential pool owners, neuroscientists, serious collectors of plates, coins, and stamps, and people who have contributed to humanitarian causes. In deciding on which list to select, you would match the characteristics of these lists to your **target market**. Often the lists include detailed demographic and psychographic data.

Trends Leading to the Use of Databases in Marketing

At this point, we define some of the terms we use in the book. Note that there is ambiguity in the literature on how these terms are used; therefore, our definitions may not correspond with all others in the field. We have already defined a marketing database as a file containing information about individual customers or potential customers that is relevant to the marketing process. **Database marketing** refers to marketing activities (e.g., selecting prospective customers) that utilize a marketing database. The term *direct marketing* is often used interchangeably with *database marketing*. In this book, we discriminate between database marketing and direct marketing on the basis of the marketing activities. We view direct marketing as a broader term that includes other activities such as development of offers and advertisements that are indirectly related to the database. The **Direct Marketing Association's (DMA)** definition takes this broader view of direct marketing:

> Direct Marketing is an interactive system of marketing that uses one or more advertising media to effect a measurable response and/or transaction at any location, with this activity stored on database.

This definition implies that the marketer is obtaining specific information about the customer. Each time a customer orders a product or requests literature, this response information is recorded on the database, allowing the marketer to determine the effectiveness of specific marketing programs such as mailings or Internet promotions.

When we use the term *database marketing*, our focus is on the strategy, development, and analysis of the database for marketing purposes rather than on the broader range of activities implied in the term *direct marketing*. In addition, companies that are involved in personal selling also use database marketing, and personal selling is often not considered a part of direct marketing.

The term *interactive marketing* is often used interchangeably with *direct marketing*. However, interactive marketing sometimes refers only to Internet marketing. In this book, we use the terms interactive marketing and direct marketing interchangeably.

Direct marketing has been increasing at a rapid rate. According to the DMA (2000), direct marketing sales revenues are expected to increase by 9.6% from 2000 to 2005. This increase is greater than the expected increase of 5.4% in total U.S. sales during that same period. U.S. sales revenue attributable to direct marketing is estimated to reach $1.7 trillion in 2000 and grow to $2.7 trillion in 2005.

A readers' survey conducted by *Direct* magazine (Levey, 2001) shows database investment continuing to grow. About 48% of the respondents indicated that their company planned to increase database development/maintenance budgets in 2002. They indicated that the databases were used for a variety of purposes, including (in descending order) promotion, cross-selling products, customized offers, profiling customers, providing information to the direct sales staff, upselling products, supporting the telemarketing staff, personalizing offers, modeling customers, obtaining revenues from the sales of names, and performing **regression analysis**.

Why is database marketing increasing so rapidly? Several trends in the marketplace may provide insights. These trends include the following and are discussed below.

♦ Greater use of market segmentation
♦ Emphasis on service and customer relationship management (CRM)
♦ Changes in media
♦ Changes in distribution structure and power
♦ Lifestyle and demographic trends
♦ Accountability for marketing actions
♦ Integration of business functions
♦ Technological advances
♦ More informed customers

Market Segmentation

Market segmentation means dividing a market into smaller pieces based on demographic, psychographic, or behavioral (purchase) patterns. The marketer takes a diverse (heterogeneous) market and attempts to find similar (homogenous) groups of people or organizations. Because of intense competition and diverse customer needs, marketers have to develop products and marketing plans that are responsive to more specific groups of customers. It is almost impossible to find a market that has not been segmented. The automobile market, for example, is extensively segmented by a number of **variables** such as age, gender, income level, personality, task situation (e.g., weather conditions, off-road), lifestyle, and activities, interests, and opinions (AIO).

For example, Polk, a company offering database management and analysis services ("Full-Size Sport Utility Market," 1997), determined that there are differences between domestic and import sport utility vehicle (SUV) owners. Seventy-nine percent of Tahoe, Suburban, Yukon, and Ford Expedition owners are interested in boating and sailing, home workshop, camping and hiking, hunting and shooting, crafts, domestic travel, and fishing, compared to 40% of Land Rover, Land Cruiser, and Lexus LX450 owners. On the other hand, import owners (36%) are more interested in cultural arts and events, tennis, fashion, wines, and foreign travel, compared to domestic full-size SUV owners (23%). "Our analysis paints a clear picture of the differences between domestic and import full-size SUV owners," said Glenn Forbes, Polk's vice president of transportation. "A domestic SUV is more likely to be found with a deer strapped to its hood, while an evening at the theater might be a prime time to spot import full-size SUVs." Polk also segmented this market by demographic characteristics such as income and geography.

By specifically targeting people who share these defined characteristics, a marketer can increase the probability of reaching potential customers. A database that can be segmented according to these target characteristics can be a valuable marketing tool.

Emphasis on Service and CRM

Service offerings such as banking, airlines, and insurance have grown at a greater rate than more tangible categories of goods such as grocery items and household appliances. Services are estimated to represent about three quarters of the U.S. gross domestic product and nearly 80% of all jobs. In addition, the service element of products is becoming a more important aspect of the overall product. In the b-to-b market, for example, buyers are increasingly less concerned with a product's tangible features and technical specifications and more concerned with whether the product meets their needs. For this reason, companies like IBM now stress "solutions" rather than "boxes." IBM's Web site provides examples from different industries and business applications to guide customers and potential customers through sample solutions to business problems. IBM is concerned about selling the right combination of software, **hardware**, consulting, and ongoing support that achieves their clients' objectives.

A database allows customers' needs to be precisely documented and tracked. The increased emphasis on CRM has brought database marketing to the forefront of many organizations. When a customer calls with a question, the database allows the customer service representative or technician to get a good understanding of the situation rapidly. More responsive service increases the probability of developing long-term relationships with customers, which leads to repeat purchases. That is a major advantage to the marketer, because retaining old customers is usually more profitable and less costly than acquiring new customers.

However, CRM has become a controversial topic. Skeptics point to the hype that is associated with a concept that is not always clearly defined.

Others question the premise that it is even possible for marketers to develop true relationships with customers. Few companies actually can develop one-to-one marketing, which is the basis of any real relationship. For many companies, CRM just means increasing the probability of repurchase. (Beardi, 2001, p. 1).

In a response to CRM cynics, Ray Schultz (2001) acknowledges that true one-to-one marketing is unlikely, but customer-centric marketing (marketing that focuses on customer needs) and a two-way dialogue with customers is possible. Direct marketers, through their databases, can develop programs to establish this dialogue with customers and measure the effectiveness of these programs.

Changes in Media

Marketers have traditionally reached customers through media that are today becoming more and more fragmented. Just a few decades ago, when there were three major television networks, a marketer could reach a large audience with a single ad. Now, hundreds of cable and satellite television channels target the special interests of segments of viewers from sports to classic movies. Some of these categories have been segmented even further, such as classic sports, golf, racing, and radical sports. Some magazine categories also show increasing fragmentation. In the food category, you can subscribe to magazines that focus on home cooking, gourmet cuisine, vegetarian fare, cooking with chocolate, low-calorie cooking, and spicy-hot food, among others.

The Internet represents an extreme in fragmentation. Althoug **e-commerce** is still in the process of developing, we can be certain that more people in the future will use the Internet as a source of information. Internet communication has the potential to reach even smaller, more specialized segments of the market. Databases containing these special-interest cable viewers, magazine subscribers, and Internet site registrants provide highly targeted lists for goods and services.

Direct marketing, including mail, **e-mail**, and telemarketing, can bring targeted messages to individual consumers and business customers with very specific characteristics. Mail and telemarketing have the potential to communicate to people based on individual needs and relate these needs to the offer. Many organizations have not developed this ability to adequately and efficiently target and communicate with individual customers, and therefore resources are wasted. The challenge for direct marketers is both to increase the relevance of the communication in order to increase response to an offer and also to reduce contacts with individuals who have a low probability of responding to the offer. Databases provide the means to meet the challenge of fragmented media by focusing marketing communications on the specific needs of customers.

Changes in Distribution Structure and Power

Power in the distribution channel has shifted. No longer are manufacturers in control of distribution channels, as they were in the past. Now, with the consolidation of retailing on a regional, national, and even multinational level, one retailer has much more impact on the bottom line of a manufacturer. If Wal★Mart or Home Depot decides not to carry a manufacturer's product, the manufacturer may lose millions of dollars in sales annually. Even large manufacturers like Proctor & Gamble do not take lightly their relationships with national retailers. In fact, some manufacturers have changed their organizational structure in order to focus on these important retail customers. By establishing databases, such as the one at the supermarket that contains Keri Lee's information, retailers are gaining even more power. They now have extensive databases on the purchasing patterns of millions of customers. These customer databases can be used to locate segments that may be important to marketers such as customers loyal to specific brands, frequent purchasers, high-volume purchasers, brand switchers, and promotion-sensitive customers.

In an attempt to maintain direct contact with customers, manufacturers have developed their own databases. Often these manufacturers' databases have been used for promotions rather than direct sales. For example, Kellogg's has used databases for new product introductions, sending potential customers free samples and coupons. The objective of these database promotions is to help generate retail sales. On the other hand, some manufacturers have developed alternative distribution channels. It may not be possible to sell low margin products, like many of the products found in supermarkets, directly to consumers. However, manufacturers may be able to develop more exclusive niche products that have the potential to become profitable through direct channels. General Foods, the maker of Maxwell House Coffee, uses database marketing to sell a premium coffee directly to consumers. The brand, Gevalia Kaffee, is positioned as "fine coffees of Europe," and customers receive shipments of coffee at a regular interval. To entice customers to become members of this program, Gevalia provides a free coffeemaker and the option to drop out of the program at any time without obligation. The initial risk for Gevalia management is great, and profit is not expected until after several purchase cycles. However, over the longer term, the product can be profitable.

Some marketing experts, such as Lester Wunderman (1998), see dramatic changes in the way we think about distribution channels. Single distribution channels will become multiple-channel distribution systems. Products will be available where people want to buy them. The Internet has become a vehicle for moving rapidly to multiple distribution channels. A number of products, including cars, computers, greeting cards, books, groceries, and even M&M's (see www.ColorWorks.com), can be purchased directly on the Internet as well as through their conventional retail channels.

Proctor & Gamble, the manufacturer of many supermarket items, including Tide, Pringles, Oil of Olay, and Folgers, also markets a premium coffee direct to consumers through the mail and the Internet. Although P&G uses the Internet and other direct channels to promote its products, it offers very few directly to consumers. Expansion into direct channels can be viewed as a direct challenge to store retailers, and P&G wants to avoid any impressions of a threat ("P&G Makes AOL Debut," 1999). So even though databases allow marketers distribution channel options, a number of factors such as product category and current channel arrangements have to be considered.

Lifestyle and Demographic Trends

A number of lifestyle and demographic trends have moved consumers away from traditional retailers. Although store-based retailing is still strong, people seem to have less and less time for the process of getting into the car, driving miles to stores, searching for products, and waiting in lines to buy them. In our Keri Lee scenario, you might have noticed that she did not leave work until after 7:00 p.m. With the current pressures on businesses to perform more work with fewer employees, many people are in Keri's situation. Keri still shops at the supermarket and other retail stores, but she shops more often from catalogs, shopping channels, and on the Internet. As Internet commerce expands, consumers have more opportunities to shop for more products from home. Internet companies are delivering groceries, drugs, and general merchandise directly to homes in certain parts of the United States.

The demographic trends that contribute to the movement of shoppers away from store retailers include

- Higher percentage of women in the workforce
- Higher percentage of family members working
- More child-rearing activities that require parents' time (e.g., lessons, carpools, sports, trips)
- Increasing access to the Internet at home, which increases the chances of online shopping
- Increase in ethnic populations seeking products that may not be available from local store retailers
- Less brand loyalty, driving people to find convenient alternative sources for products

In response to these trends, marketers will make more types of products available from nonstore sources (Internet, mail, TV). As more nonstore sources become available, competition will increase, driving more consumers away from store retailers. As mentioned previously, direct marketing sales are expected to increase at a rate that is higher than sales in general. Because all forms of direct marketing are dependent on databases, the use of databases will also increase.

Accountability for Marketing Actions

Accountability for expenditures is more prevalent in business today. In publicly held companies, shareholders are becoming more sensitive to financial reports. Within the organizations, upper-level managers want to know whether expenditures on specific promotions (ad campaigns, trade promotions, etc.) yield an appropriate return on investment. It is often difficult, however, to directly relate mass media advertising to changes in sales. Marketing databases allow expenses and revenues to be tracked and evaluated.

In particular, the database can be used to track the profitability of products over time. As mentioned above, companies have to invest in customers through the costs of promotions. Sometimes these promotions include free items such as the coffeemaker that Gevalia sends new customers and free CDs offered by record clubs. Even if no incentives are used, an investment is needed in list rentals, the cost of the mailing, and overhead expenses. Often these investments are not recovered immediately. However, in the long term, these promotions may become very profitable as the customer makes additional purchases. Similarly, in the b-to-b market, marketing and other costs related to customer acquisition can be substantial and must be evaluated over a long period of time. Sometimes, return on investment may not come for several years, if at all.

With the database, a marketer can track profits from individual customers over time and further break down the effectiveness of individual marketing programs such as promotions with incentives. This long-term tracking of customers is only possible with a database. Without the long-term tracking of individual customers, a potentially profitable marketing program may be stopped prematurely.

Not only are databases important to upper management as an accountability tool, but other marketing personnel can directly benefit from them. As an account executive, Keri Lee wants to use her time productively. Part of her compensation is based on commissions. She uses a database to manage customer relationships by scheduling contacts at critical times, such as prior to contract renewals. She can also respond to customers more efficiently and effectively, because critical data on the account are easily available. She can determine who her best customers are, and she can evaluate the amount of time she spends on less productive accounts. Methods such as

lifetime value (LTV) analysis have been developed that evaluate promotional activities, customer segments, and product lines.

Integration of Business Functions

When all the functional areas of a business work together (marketing, accounting, finance, operations, human resources, information systems, etc.), the organization usually becomes more effective and efficient. In the older business model, the functional areas work almost independently. Tasks are moved from one area to another in a sequential manner. Problems often arise from this "silo" approach to business organizations. For example, Production may not be aware of marketing programs that might require increases in production levels, and Marketing may not be aware of increases in production costs that may require pricing modifications.

Today, more and more businesses seek to increase the efficiency by integrating functional areas. Databases facilitate this integration. Costs can be clearly documented, and sales levels can be more accurately forecasted and monitored to allow for adjustments in production, inventory, and staffing levels. From the financial perspective, sales revenues from individual items and product lines can be tracked more closely for better financial planning and resource allocation.

A direct marketing organization is centered on its database. The database can provide all functional areas immediate access to the progress of marketing programs, individual items, product lines, and divisions. Although technology as greatly improved the ability of manufacturers to monitor products through conventional retail distribution channels, problems getting data quickly from the many distributors and retailers still exist. Therefore, the organization that uses marketing databases well can be more responsive to internal and external changes.

Technological Advances

In recent years, the computer technology needed for developing marketing databases has decreased in price and increased in power. Consequently, more organizations have the financial resources to purchase the hardware and software necessary to develop a marketing database. In addition, because of the increasing power of low-cost PCs, smaller organizations can utilize databases. Within the organization, more people have access to technology and, therefore, can take advantage of the database. In Keri's organization, all account executives have a powerful notebook computer that allows access to the database even on the road. Through the network, the database is constantly updated, allowing all areas of the business to be aware when a transaction is made.

Software has also become more user friendly, so that people don't have to be computer experts to take advantage of the benefits of databases. Not only are there general database programs that are easy to learn and use such as Access and Paradox, but even small businesses can use sales and marketing databases such as ACT! and GoldMine. Furthermore, industry-specific database programs are available that allow small organizations to coordinate marketing and other business functions.

More Informed Customers

Consumers and business customers have access to substantially more information now than in the past. Greater product knowledge brings more critical evaluation of products and greater consideration of price. Information from marketers extends to areas outside traditional mass advertising. Sales promotion methods such as rebates, sweepstakes, contests, and coupons continue to be widely used. Event marketing that associates products with sporting, music, and other events have been used with a greater frequency in the last few years. Marketers of prescription pharmaceuticals now target patients directly, providing information about product benefits (and side effects) in an attempt to induce patient-physician discussions about the possible trial of a drug. The Internet and infomericals have provided marketers with an opportunity to present detailed information about products to consumers.

However, marketers have to compete not only with information provided by other marketers but also with information from other sources such as public interest groups, governmental agencies, journalists, and not-for-profit organizations. In our Keri Lee scenario, you may have noticed that she was able to get insurance quotes online. Furthermore, it is now common for car customers to get product information, reviews, ratings, invoice pricing, and price quotes via the Internet (see, e.g., www.edmunds.com). In addition to its magazine, Consumers Union has a Web site (www.consumerreports.org), and television news programs routinely present CU's product reviews and consumer information. Organizations such as the Center for Science in the Public Interest (www.cspinet.org) often present information that is in conflict with information given by marketers. For example, the Center opposes the marketing of products containing Proctor and Gamble's low-calorie fat, Olestra. Network programs such as *Dateline* and *20/20* frequently feature segments on consumer issues. Chat rooms allow consumers to ask questions and voice opinions about products. In addition, with the expansion of specialized cable channels and magazines, consumers are learning more about products in specific categories such as home improvement, fashion, sporting equipment, food, and health care.

Although the availability of information is increasing, some consumers feel overwhelmed and confused by the conflicting information they are receiving from various sources. For example, consumers may hear from some sources and marketers that food supplements like ginseng are beneficial and from other sources that there is no benefit from using the product.

Consequently, access to more information does not always result in more informed consumers. Access to the proper type of information is more critical. With databases, marketing communications can be more specifically targeted so that the information matches the characteristics of the consumer. For example, if a database contains information on the purchase history of potential customers of financial services, a mail campaign can be designed to communicate differently to novice versus experienced investors.

Database Marketing Versus Aggregate Marketing

In database marketing, customers are selected from a database or list to receive a marketing communication through the mail, by phone, or by e-mail. In some cases, as with direct TV or newspaper inserts, traditional mass media is used for the initial contact. Direct TV and newspaper inserts have a response mechanism (e.g., phone number or post card) that direct marketers can use for initiating and tracking a contact. Although the media used are mass (as opposed to mailing or calling an individual), it is still direct marketing because of the response mechanism that allows customer tracking. With traditional mass media, the response to the ad is not directly tracked. For example, someone sees a Burger King ad and goes out to buy something at a Burger King. We can't directly relate that purchase to the ad. On the other hand, if someone orders a diet plan after seeing an infomercial, the order and ad are linked and the transaction for the specific customer is put into a database. The customer may respond to the offer, and the marketer acts to fulfill an order or send additional information (see Exhibit 1.1). When a customer responds to an offer, the specific characteristics (e.g., date, payment, quantity) of the response are recorded on the database.

In contrast, in a traditional retail transaction, there is no feedback loop to a database, and no information on individual customers is obtained (see Exhibit 1.2). Note that the arrow goes in only one direction.

In a traditional retail environment, product success or failure is determined by aggregate sales through the distribution system (see Exhibit 1.3).

Exhibit 1.4 shows that the consumer obtains information about the product in a traditional retail environment through mass media or retailer promotions, and the marketer does not know the individual customer.

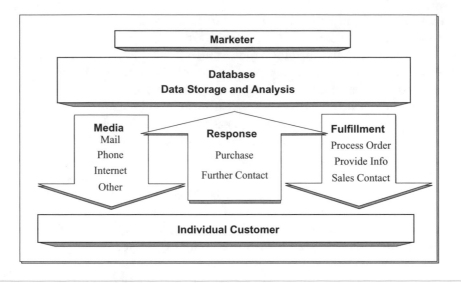

Exhibit 1.1   Transaction Flow in Database Marketing.

With **aggregate marketing,** information about the end consumer is obtained through anonymous marketing research sampling methods. Marketers can obtain information about the demographic and psychographic characteristics of customers and customer segments, but this information is not related to an individual's purchase patterns as it is with database marketing (see Exhibit 1.5).

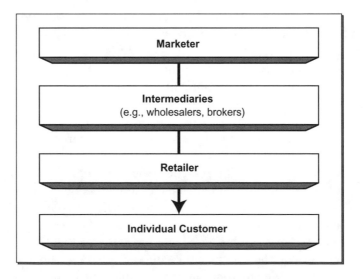

Exhibit 1.2   Transaction Flow in Traditional Retail Marketing.

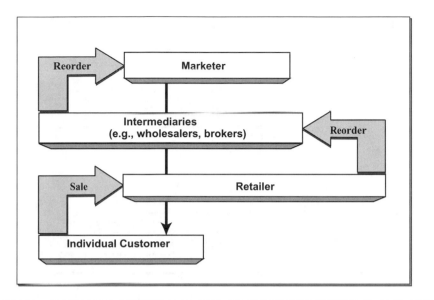

Exhibit 1.3   Customer Feedback in Traditional Retail Marketing.

Advantages of Database Marketing

The preceding discussion highlights the advantages of database marketing over aggregate or mass marketing. Aggregate marketing is based on the "average" customer, so messages cannot be tailored to individuals. With

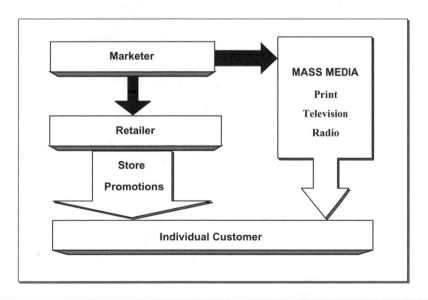

Exhibit 1.4   Flow of Marketing Information to Customers in Traditional Retail Marketing.

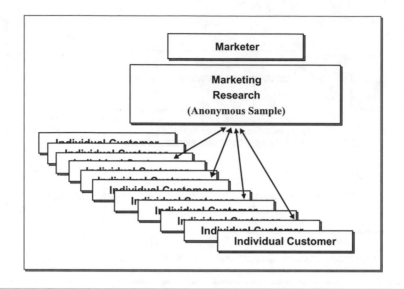

Exhibit 1.5   Research Process in Traditional Retail Marketing.

the database, the capability exists to segment down to the individual level, allowing personalized messages. Only the media limit the ability to segment markets. This can be a problem for aggregate marketers. In some circumstances, magazines, television channels, radio stations, or newspapers do not adequately reach a target segment. A direct mail or telemarketing campaign can reach people who are difficult to reach through mass media. Recording customer response (e.g., purchases, requests for information, redeeming a coupon) makes the database a powerful marketing tool, and it allows us to develop effective and efficient marketing programs.

Disadvantages of Database Marketing

Although the use of databases can increase the effectiveness and efficiency of marketing programs, some disadvantages need to be evaluated and obstacles overcome.

Cost Issues

The cost of establishing sophisticated database marketing systems can be substantial for some organizations. With database marketing, the organization requires a higher level of technical skills. Start-up costs for internal databases and order fulfillment can be high compared to traditional **brick and mortar**

retailing, and often database marketing has higher costs per contact (consider the cost of mailing a catalog versus running a print ad). For all these reasons, database marketing may not be feasible for many low-margin products. Therefore, it is important that the organization set clear objectives for the database and conduct an analysis to estimate the expected return on the investment in the database. In the next chapter, we outline a process for evaluating how the database might fulfill organizational objectives.

In addition, although the costs of database technologies have generally decreased, some printing and mailing costs have increased. In response to these cost increases, marketers have developed strategies and tactics to reduce costs. One method is exploring e-commerce and communicating through the Internet. Other methods include automated dialing for telemarketing and sorting for postal discounts. Some of these methods require performing analyses on the database to determine which customers are most likely to respond.

Global Markets

The use of marketing databases presents special challenges to companies doing business internationally. Many U.S. corporations are experiencing more growth in foreign markets compared to domestic markets. As markets have become more saturated at home, companies have been expanding into both developed and developing countries. For database marketers, global expansion is limited by technology, the legal and political environment, and cultural factors. In some developing countries, support systems for technology are not readily available, and it is difficult or impossible to acquire lists of potential customers. Even where the technology and support systems do exist, the legal and political environment may be more restrictive. For example, there are more stringent regulations on the use of personnel information in most European countries than in the United States. In the final chapter, we discuss factors in the global environment that have an impact on database marketing.

Competition From Traditional Retailers

Traditional brick and mortar retailers (i.e., retailers who have physical locations) have become more effective and efficient. In some product categories, it is difficult, if not impossible, for direct marketers to compete on price with traditional retailers, at least in the near future. What may emerge is a greater use of integrated multichannel marketing. For example, a customer may order a product online and pick it up at a local retailer.

Negative Perceptions

One of the greatest threats to database marketing is the generally negative attitude of consumers and politicians. People commonly refer to mailings from direct marketers as junk mail and disdain telemarketers. Consumers are also concerned about how their personal data are used. In particular, public interest groups have initiatives to protect medical data and information on children. With the expansion of Internet commerce, debates go on in Congress and in the Federal Trade Commission about how to protect consumers making online transactions. The industry wants to establish self-regulation, whereas many public interest groups want mandated regulation. In response to such concerns, one important objective of database marketers is to develop strategies and techniques to contact only those individuals who may be interested in their product.

Framework for This Book

This book starts by covering general concepts and examples of marketing databases and then moves on to more specific techniques. To facilitate learning, we use examples and short cases to illustrate concepts and explain techniques. We have also made use of tables and diagrams whenever appropriate. Our objective is to build on previous knowledge in sequential steps.

We have already examined the factors that have led to the widespread use of databases and how marketing with databases is different from brick and mortar marketing. In the next chapters, we provide examples of databases and take a strategic view of database development. It is important to consider if and how an organization could benefit from developing a marketing database.

We then start to examine more technical aspects of the database. We explore how databases are developed, enhanced, and maintained. We also examine the basics of database technology. Our objective for these chapters is to provide fundamental concepts about database technology that can assist you in using databases in marketing.

One of the most important aspects of database marketing is the extensive capability to understand customers through data analysis (also known as **data mining**). Starting with the fundamental concept of segmentation, we explore how databases are partitioned to isolate the "best" customers and track them over an extended period of time to determine profitability. The discussion of data analysis expands to cover statistical techniques that help predict which customers are most likely to respond to a particular offer. We also examine testing alternative marketing programs as a method to increase effectiveness and efficiency. Our objective with these chapters on data analysis is not to train marketers to become statisticians but rather to facilitate an understanding of the concepts and techniques that enhance the marketing process. We have also included two chapters on databases in Internet marketing. Chapter 15 points out the differences between Internet marketing and other database marketing methods. Chapter 16 provides an introduction to data analysis on the Internet.

The book concludes with a discussion of important current topics related to database marketing: ethics, the global marketplace, and future trends. After you have finished reading this book, you should have obtained a good general understanding of the strategic use of marketing databases and the techniques that are used to help realize the database's potential in achieving organizational objectives.

Chapter Summary

In this chapter, we introduce marketing database concepts and define some common terms. The marketing environment has changed dramatically in recent years, and we discuss those trends leading to the use of databases in marketing. We compare database marketing with conventional aggregate marketing and point to potential advantages and disadvantages. The chapter concludes with a description of the framework of the book.

Review Questions

1. In the vignette about Keri Lee, how have databases benefited her life? Are these benefits substantial or superficial?

2. What is a marketing database, and why are databases important to marketers?

3. What are some of the trends that have led to the utilization of marketing databases?

4. How is database marketing different from aggregate marketing?

5. What are some of the advantages and disadvantages of database marketing compared to traditional brick and mortar marketing?

6. What do you think about the concerns some consumers have about database marketing? How would you respond to those concerns?

2 Strategic Database Development in the Marketing Planning Process

Keri Lee works for Diversified Software Inc. (DSI), a company that develops and markets a wide range of graphics software. When DSI was established in the late 1970s, they had few customers and served the b-to-b market exclusively. Originally, the company did not have a customer database. A sole salesperson recorded all information about customers on paper.

As sales expanded and more salespeople were hired, the company decided that it was necessary to have a more structured system of keeping track of customers. Because it was possible for several salespeople to contact a single customer or for the customer to contact more than one salesperson, a database of customer contacts was developed. For example, an internal salesperson might call a purchasing agent in a company to check on a reorder, and an external salesperson might demonstrate a new product to the information systems manager in the same company. Having all customer contacts recorded in the database allowed DSI to understand their customers' needs better and determine who were their best customers.

When Keri joined the company in 1997, the database had been upgraded. Keri was given a notebook computer that was configured to access the database on the company's network by modem. Keri is in charge of several accounts, and every time she contacts a customer, she records the time, date, and comments into the database. She is also able to check purchase history, any promotions the company received, and the current status of orders. In the database, Keri can enter personal information about her customers (e.g., birthdays, hobbies, names of spouses and children, favorite restaurants). Keri found that for some customers, developing more personalized relationships is important for maintaining a good business relationship. Keri can also enter a future date to contact a particular customer. This helps her to keep current with all her customers and stay ahead of the competition. Keri finds the database a valuable sales tool, because she can have full account information whenever she contacts a customer or whenever a customer contacts her.

Although there is an expense associated with the development and maintenance of the database, DSI management has seen clear benefits. Since the database has been implemented, customer retention has increased by 30%. Because mailings and other marketing programs can be tested and tracked for effectiveness, the response to these marketing efforts has improved by 15%. Overall, profitability has increased by about 18% since the implementation of the database, and management recovered its investment after about 2 years.

*Before implementing the database, DSI embarked on strategic and **marketing planning**. The decision to upgrade and invest in new database technologies was based on a comprehensive analysis of internal and external factors. These factors included potential target markets, competition, company resources, and the current technological advancements. DSI's upper management was aware that developing new database technology was not an end in itself but a means to achieve organizational objectives. The database would be used to implement and monitor specific marketing programs.*

This chapter focuses on the strategic considerations related to marketing database development. We consider the critical factors when evaluating the potential utility of databases in achieving a range of objectives within an organization. We examine some basic examples of marketing databases and compare customer databases with other types of databases used by marketers. Strategic marketing planning is a process that is intended to help the organization achieve its objectives. We examine the need for strategic planning, provide alternative marketing strategies, and outline the common elements of the marketing planning process, emphasizing database applications.

In the last chapter, we provided a general definition of a marketing database. We said it is a file containing information about customers or potential customers that enhances marketing functions. The goal in establishing the database is to allow customer information to be accessed and manipulated rapidly and accurately in order to meet customer needs and organizational objectives. We have to keep in mind that although a database may be large and use sophisticated technology, it is only valuable to the organization if it helps achieve objectives, like increasing profits. Before we discuss complex databases, let's look at a simple one that accomplishes organizational objectives.

Think of a food vendor who serves busy businesspeople in a city's commerce area. Although the vendor may serve dozens of customers on a given day, he gets to know many of them by name because they frequent his small stand. For example, when a particular customer walks up to his stand, he knows her first name, how she takes her coffee, and how much cream cheese to put on her raisin bagel.

The food vendor has developed a "mental" customer database. Retaining this information helps him serve his customers more personally and quickly so that they can get to work on time. These customers are more likely to be satisfied and consequently more likely to return to his stand in the future rather than going to his competitors. The vendor may adjust his product assortment based on sales trends he notes. People may be buying more bagels and less Danish pastry, or he may notice more people requesting decaffeinated coffee. He may reward his regular customers by occasionally giving them a free cup of coffee with a sandwich order. He realizes that the success of his business is dependent on repeat customers. He listens to his customers in order to improve his business and notes their characteristics such as age, gender, ethnicity, and occupation. He may also segment customers by when they purchase (e.g., morning, noon, evening) or the types of things they purchase. To increase business in the morning, he may add breakfast sandwiches to compete with a nearby chain restaurant. He'll keep a mental note of the success of these new offerings.

Problems arise with a mental database when the customer base increases. With thousands of customers and many customer characteristics, it becomes impossible to hold their characteristics in memory. Paper databases have been used for many years to record customer characteristics. A hairstylist may record customer names, addresses, phone numbers, appointment dates, coloring and treatment formulations, and hair care product purchases on index cards or a Rolodex. Again, this information helps the organization serve customers better. As the hair stylist's business grows and she hires other stylists, she may decide to store this information in a computer database rather than use paper records. Database software has been developed for specialized businesses like hair stylists to help them function more efficiently and effectively. Remember that the fundamental rationale for developing the database is to help to achieve organizational objectives. If the database does not accomplish this or hampers interaction with customers, as might occur with some small businesses, then there is no reason to implement it.

Computerized Databases

Although mental or paper databases may work adequately for some organizations, our objective is to explore computerized databases and how they may be used to achieve organizational objectives. In a simple form, a computerized customer database can be visualized as spreadsheets, with each row representing the record of one customer. The columns represent

NAME	ADDRESS	LAST PURCHASE	AMOUNT
P. James	4 Oak Lane	Pappagallo-162	129.50
K. Lang	7 Maple St.	Easy Spirit-200	68.90
⋮	⋮	⋮	⋮
T. Clark	3 Pine Drive	MootsieTootsie-87	48.88

Exhibit 2.1   Hypothetical Database for a Retailer

customer **attributes** or characteristics (often referred to as fields). Exhibit 2.1 shows a portion of a hypothetical database for a shoe retailer.

What other types of information might be valuable to the shoe retailer? Of course, we would need complete address information so the customers could be contacted. In addition to recording the last purchase, it would be valuable to have a more comprehensive record of purchase history. This would help us determine the best customers over a number of years. If we were sending a catalog or were engaged in Internet commerce, it would be valuable to link specific purchases to these marketing programs in order to evaluate effectiveness. Knowing demographic (e.g., age, gender, ethnicity, occupation) and psychographic (e.g., activities, interests, and opinions) characteristics of customers may help in developing new products and finding lists of potential customers with similar characteristics. As you can see, the more relevant information we can obtain about customers, the better we can understand who they are and predict what they might purchase.

Customer Databases Versus Other Marketing Databases

In this book, we are primarily concerned with databases that contain information about individual customers. That is, the customer database allows us to reach customers directly. **Prospecting databases** also contain data on individuals, but these individuals are not customers. When individuals from the prospecting database respond to an offer, their names are moved to the customer database.

Marketers also develop databases that contain summarized data such as sales by product line, territory, and salesperson. Internet marketers routinely collect data on the number of visitors to their Web site, most popular pages on the site, and other aggregate data. Although these databases are also useful for marketing planning, they do not allow us to analyze customers and develop systematic direct marketing programs to the same degree as customer databases. Knowing that 3,250 customers purchased shoes during a sale is not as valuable as having the names, contact information, and specific purchases of each of these customers. With the latter data, these customers could be contacted for a number of marketing programs. These programs could range from a simple thank-you note to help bond the relationship, to alerting these customers of the arrival of new products.

The Need for Strategic Planning

Marketing database development should start with some type of strategic plan. The strategic plan provides a guide for database development and defines how it will assist in achieving organizational objectives in the near and distant future.

Nonetheless, there has been discussion in recent years on the value of strategic planning in a rapidly changing marketplace. Some of the criticisms of developing a formal strategic plan revolve around the issue of lack of flexibility and timeliness. That is, if an organization is committed to following a plan, opportunities might be missed. This is a particularly cogent argument for entrepreneurs. However, even advocates of eliminating the formal strategic plan still believe in the importance of "strategic thinking." Carl Long (2000), for example, includes many of the elements of strategic planning (e.g., knowledge of customers, capabilities, competitors, markets) as requirements for strategic thinking for entrepreneurs, even though he doubts the usefulness of a formal plan. Although adopting a strategic thinking rather than a strategic planning approach may work for entrepreneurs and small businesses, a lack of a formal plan has disadvantages for larger organizations. The plan helps communicate the organization's direction to employees. A more formalized plan provides the following advantages:

- Points to potential and existing problems, opportunities, threats in the market environment
- Defines organizational strengths and weakness
- Plots the acquisition and use of resources
- Details methods to obtain goals and objectives
- Assists in implementation of strategies
- Regulates growth
- Establishes roles and functions of departments and individuals
- Makes better use of resources
- Establishes tasks and timing
- Helps achieve personal goals of individual employees
- Stimulates thinking and communication within the organization

The last advantage of a formal planning process should not be overlooked. When the plan is written and distributed, the organization can take advantage of the valuable input of its employees. Indeed, a good strategic planning process incorporates the input of employees at several levels within the organizations. Furthermore, a strategic plan should not be a static document followed without revision or question. Rather, periodic review of both the marketing environment and marketing programs is essential. Organizations in rapidly changing market environments need to have more frequent reviews of their plans. Michael Porter, arguably the leading authority on strategy management, states that many successful companies in the "New Economy" do have a strategic focus. Porter says that these companies have a "clear sense of what they're trying to do and of how to do it" (Surowiecki, 1999, p. 135). Porter (2001) argues that companies in the New Economy actually have more of a need for a strategy that will distinguish them from competitors. The Internet tends to weaken profitability when low pricing policies and competitive emulation are pursued. Strategic planning allows competitive strengths such as unique products, superior product knowledge, and superlative service to be realized.

Developing a Systematic Plan for Using Marketing Databases

Now that we have covered basic database and strategic planning concepts, our next step is to examine how the organization might evaluate the need for the database and develop a plan for implementation. Planning occurs at several levels within the organization and originates from the organization's strategic plan. This corporate strategic plan sets the general direction for the organization, and all other planning should be consistent with this corporate plan.

Corporate strategic plans commonly include a mission statement, a market analysis, overall objectives, and general strategies. Exhibit 2.2 shows the levels of planning that might occur within a large organization.

Note that not all organizations will have divisional planning. Divisional planning may apply to organizations that are operating in more than one market. One example is General Electric, which is in a wide range of markets, including consumer appliances, financial services, and jet engines. Functional planning refers to plans developed for the areas of the business such as marketing, finance, operations, human resources, and product development. In our discussion, we focus on marketing, which may also develop plans at the operating levels of advertising, product development, research, distribution, sales, and so on. Finally, some organizations develop plans for individuals or teams.

It is important for a marketing manager to keep the levels of planning in perspective throughout the planning process. To get upper management to buy into the plan, marketing personnel need to clearly express how their

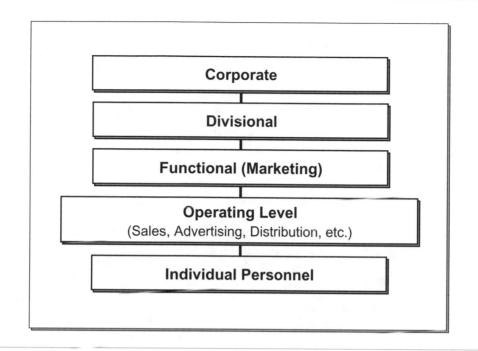

Exhibit 2.2   Levels of Organizational Planning

proposed marketing plan helps the organization achieve its primary objectives. This management buy-in is particularly important when the plan includes the development of a marketing database, because the resources dedicated to such a project are often substantial.

The Marketing Planning Process and Database Implementation

We examine the marketing planning process as it applies to decision criteria for databases. At the beginning of the marketing planning process, marketing managers must first review the corporate strategic plan to determine if the development of a marketing database is consistent with organizational objectives and resources. Alternatively, in the process of developing the annual marketing plan, the marketing manager may determine that a customer database might help achieve objectives. The follow types of questions may be addressed:

- Does the company have the human and financial resources to support a database system?
- Are the financial objectives of the organization compatible with developing a customer database that will take 5 years before a return on investment is realized?

♦ Is the development of a customer database consistent with the corporate strategy? For example, the development of an extensive database to increase penetration in current markets may not be totally consistent with a corporate strategy of diversification into new markets with new products.

If database development is found to be consistent with the corporate plan, marketing management will proceed through the marketing planning steps. We should emphasize that marketing planning is a continual process that requires constant review. It is not a static document but rather an interactive tool for enhancing the marketing process. Following is a common basic model used in marketing planning:

♦ Perform **situational analysis**
♦ Specify objectives
♦ Develop strategies
♦ Implement marketing programs (tactics)
♦ **Monitor and control**

For organizations that are using or are planning to use direct distribution or promotion systems, the use of some sort of database system is a foregone conclusion. For example, marketers who promote directly to customers via mail, phone, TV, catalogs, or the Internet need to have a database to enter and fulfill orders. Therefore, the question for these organizations is not whether a database system should be employed but rather whether to define the database system according to organizational and customer needs. Car companies often use mailings to bring customers to dealerships. They can adopt a limited or outsourced database system to implement this mail program. On the other hand, a clothing cataloger or Internet drugstore that does not have physical retail locations is highly dependent on the database system, as it is the primary means to maintain contact with customers.

As companies integrate across multiple promotion and distribution channels, developing strategic database systems will become more essential. Organizations will have to assess the return for developing resource-intensive database technologies that allow customers to access the company from multiple channels. We discuss integrated database systems in Chapter 15.

Situational Analysis

An analysis of the marketing situation is the starting point for marketing planning. Before developing a marketing plan for a new organization or making changes to an existing marketing plan, it is necessary to carefully examine all market factors relevant to the organization. These might include

- General environmental factors: global, cultural, economic, legal, political, social, demographic, technological, and so on
- Internal resources: technology, human resources, marketing, production, etc.
- Present and future markets: evolving and established segments
- Target market characteristics: **demographics, psychographics,** purchase patterns
- Competitors' characteristics: direct and indirect

The strengths, weaknesses, opportunities, and threats of the organization are evaluated within the context of the environment. For example, an organization may be aligned to expand in a existing market (strength) but currently may not have the resources to remain competitive in another market (weakness). A new technology developed by a competitor may pose a threat to an organization, whereas an organization's rapid product development capabilities provide an opportunity to move quickly into a new market niche.

If database development is a consideration, we can begin to access the feasibility of developing the database within organizational objectives by examining each variable of the situational analysis. For example, growing competition for a product at the retail level may be affecting a company's growth. An analysis of the competition and the purchasing habits of the target market may point to an opportunity for using direct channels of promotion and distribution, which implies that a database has to be developed. Then we examine if the organization has the capabilities to develop the database with current technology and personnel. In some cases, the organization uses external contractors to develop and maintain the database, which may reduce initial financial risk, but the trade-off is some loss of control.

Establishing Marketing Objectives

After performing a situational analysis, an organization has enough information to establish its **marketing objectives**. General marketing objectives can reflect sales revenues, profitability, gross margins, price targets, and marketing share. Examples of marketing objectives might be to increase sales volume by 10% in the next year or increase net profits to 30% by 2005. Quantification of objectives is necessary for evaluation and control. Saying that your objective is to increase sales is inadequate. This objective could be satisfied with a 1% increase over 10 years. Most organizations would consider that accomplishment dismal.

The advantage of implementing databases is that they allow clear, quantitative, and continual tracking of objectives. Tracking sales through a complex distribution system with many retailers can be difficult. With database marketing, individual sales can be recorded immediately, and the effectiveness of marketing programs relative to objectives can be tracked continually.

Strategy Development

Strategy is the longer-term direction for interacting with markets to achieve marketing objectives. It involves developing products to meet customer needs and **positioning** products (i.e., communicating about benefits) to target segments. The situational analysis provides a guide to strategy development. Market segments, potential targets, competition, internal resources, and so on need to be considered when developing strategies. Strategy development is complex, and we do not examine it here in detail. But to show the importance of relating database development to **marketing strategy**, we do examine some general strategies in marketing. They include **market penetration, market development, product development,** and **diversification**. These strategies are shown in the grid in Exhibit 2.3 developed by Ansoff (1988, p. 109). Examples of the use of databases in these strategies follow.

Market Penetration Strategy. Involves increasing product use for existing customers or targeting potential customers who possess characteristics similar to those of existing customers. Products are not modified with market penetration strategy. Customer relationship programs fit into this strategy category. By developing long-term relationships with existing customers, the organization is attempting to increase repeat purchases.

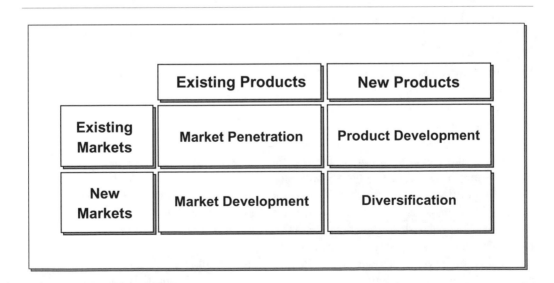

Exhibit 2.3   Product/Market Strategy Grid

A database may assist in reaching existing customers more efficiently and effectively. Promotions can be more specifically targeted to existing customers based on a better understanding of their potential needs.

Furthermore, the database can be analyzed to specify the critical characteristics of existing customers in order to find new ones. For example, many publishers of magazines develop profiles of their customers based on demographic, purchase history, and psychographic data to determine what types of mailing lists to rent. A substantial portion of this book is dedicated to examining the analysis process in detail.

Market Development Strategy. Involves offering the organization's existing products to new markets. For example, a producer of an industrial cleaner that primarily sells to manufacturing organizations could acquire lists of customers in other industries such as health care or hospitality. The list could be the foundation for a customer database. When these potential customers respond to the company's offer, additional information is recorded in the database. Here is another example of a market development strategy: A company that sells clothing domestically primarily through brick and mortar retailers could acquire a list of customers in another country and establish database marketing techniques. This strategy would reduce the risk of developing traditional distribution channels in a foreign country.

Product Development Strategy. Involves developing new products for existing markets. A company that markets educational books for children and then develops educational software for those same customers is adopting a product development strategy. The database can help in product development through the use of systematic analysis and testing paradigms. Discovering that their current customers have certain hobbies or are involved in certain activities may provide clues for product development. Techniques for expanding our knowledge of current customers, called **data enhancement**, are discussed in Chapter 4.

Furthermore, the database allows us to use valuable testing methods. For example, new products can be evaluated through "hypothetical" direct mail offerings, or **dry testing** and does not require the investment that is normally required for product testing through brick and mortar retailers. Chapters 13 and 14 are dedicated to database testing methods.

Diversification Strategy. Occurs when organizations move into new markets with new products. Diversification strategy is usually the riskiest, because the organization is moving away from markets and products they know. For example, an organization that sells commercial ovens may be interested in developing products for the home gourmet kitchen. A database of potential customers could be developed based on variables such as subscriptions to gourmet magazines and recent home purchases. Database methods could reduce diversification risk by using a direct distribution channel. Also, similar to the product development strategy, testing the new products on a selected list of potential customers in the consumer market is a way to reduce diversification risk.

Strategy Development, Targeting, and Product Positioning

Although the product/market grid illustrated in Exhibit 2.3 is useful for evaluating potential strategies and setting direction for an organization, marketers must bring strategy down to another level. This level specifically focuses on the target group. The process starts with market segmentation, which is the process of breaking a larger market into smaller groups based on certain characteristics such as demographics, psychographics, and past purchase behavior. (See Chapter 8 for more information on market segmentation.) After the market has been segmented, the marketer selects one or several segments to target. The selection of the target group is based on a number of factors such as market demand characteristics, competition, and the organization's strengths and weaknesses. In some cases, a marketer pursues a smaller segment or niche because it has been rejected or ignored by larger companies. However, the niche needs to have an appropriate return on investment potential for a particular organization.

Once the target market is selected, the product or product line needs to be positioned. Product or brand positioning is a complex area in marketing, and we consider only the basic concepts here. The marketer wants to position the product to take advantage of the needs of the target group. Positioning refers to how the customers or potential customers perceive the product relative to competitors on dimensions that are important to the target group. For example, online investment companies might want to position their services for specific types of investors. The important product characteristics for novice online investors might be basic investment advice, ease of use, and risk reduction. In contrast, experienced investors might prefer to make their own decisions and seek easy access to data for their own analysis, and they are more likely to want to make timely investments and a greater number of them than novice investors. Therefore, they are concerned with how quickly orders are placed and how the transactions are recorded and reported to them.

To position the investment services properly to a target market, the marketer has to incorporate the desired characteristics into the product and communicate these characteristics properly. Marketers often use product positioning maps to examine how customers or potential customers perceive a company's product relative to the competition. Sometimes marketers see a discrepancy between the desired positioning and the way the target market actually perceives the product. For example, a catalog marketer of inexpensive household convenience items wants to expand into a niche market of more affluent customers who have an interest in gardening. A new catalog contains more exclusive and expensive crafted items for the garden. The cataloger has to develop the appropriate assortment of products for this target segment to meet their needs and establish the perception that the catalog is "for them." In some cases, marketers may have to change the brand name to dissociate it from existing brand perceptions that are inconsistent with a new target group. For example, to reach a more affluent market with different tastes, marketers of coffee and chocolates have developed new brands, because the old brands are deeply entrenched in a less exclusive positioning.

Note that in the past, direct marketers focused on the offer and response to the offer and were not generally concerned with establishing a brand positioning. More recently, however, direct marketers have seen the value in establishing a strong brand positioning. This shift in strategy is a result of increasing competition and the realization that customer loyalty is critical for success. Consumers are flooded with offers, and many consumers just filter out most of them, so direct marketers often don't get the consumer to focus on the offer. However, if a direct marketer does break through to the consumer and satisfies that consumer, it is now important to use that past satisfaction to break through to customers in the future. Strong brand recognition can do this. Therefore, when a catalog, phone call, e-mail, or other direct marketing communication is associated with a brand that a customer likes, these communications are more likely to elicit a favorable response.

Marketing Programs

Marketing programs (also called **marketing tactics**) are the specific means to implement the marketing strategy. In practice, these programs should be well detailed and include timelines for implementation. Each relevant element of the marketing mix (promotion, price, distribution, product) should be carefully considered. For example, a market penetration strategy might be implemented by increasing distribution or promotion to the existing target market.

Database marketers have several advantages when programs are implemented. Because response to programs is fed back into the database, performance can be tracked rapidly and accurately. This also allows a quicker response to problems. In addition, testing of direct marketing programs can be more extensive and less expensive relative to mass marketing testing. Some marketers have used database marketing for product introduction and then expanded to mass distribution channels as the product becomes established. In the following sections, we provide examples of how databases can be used in marketing programs.

Distribution

Distribution systems are the means by which products get to customers. With a database, a marketer can target new customers by directly contacting a list of potential customers. These potential customers may not currently have easy access to an existing retail channel or are looking for alternative ways to purchase products. The databases that are being developed for Internet commerce are a response to this need for alternative ways to purchase products. A database system can also be used to track the performance of channel members. Marketing programs directed at channel members can be customized and evaluated. For example, incentive programs directed at specific retailers can be evaluated in terms of return on investment. The distribution program should include details on how the databases will be developed. If lists are used, the program should include information on how the lists will be selected, accessed, and tested for effectiveness.

Promotion

Promotion is the element of marketing that focuses on communicating information about products to customers. Promotion can be straightforward (e.g., a table of technical specifications) or provocative (e.g., emotional advertising or sweepstakes). Basic promotion goals are to inform, remind, and persuade. With a database, a marketer can develop relevant communications based on the benefits a specific target group is seeking. For example, a new target segment may be more responsive to the durability of a product than to the fashion orientation of current customers. In addition, communications can be adapted depending on other information in the database. The time since last purchase, specific products purchased, and other data in the customer's record are used to personalize communications. In other words, relationship programs that reward customers based on past purchases require a database to maintain a proper record of transactions and rewards.

Testing marketing communications is an ongoing process with database marketers. Although it is beyond the scope of this book to examine direct marketing communications in detail, we do examine the analysis process of testing database marketing programs. Be aware that direct marketers have developed many processes and techniques for marketing communications. Direct marketing experts like Stone (1996) have noted that certain techniques such as sweepstakes promotions or free gift offers increase response rates.

Because the database can provide a more personalized message to individuals in a target group, it possesses a competitive advantage. Compared to mass advertising, in which a marketer immediately reveals marketing strategies and tactics to competitors, communicating with individuals in the database is more private. Therefore, a database marketer has the opportunity to maintain an exclusive product positioning or unique communication technique for a longer time.

Price

Pricing is the value attached to a product, and this element of marketing directly has an impact on profits. Setting pricing levels is complex; lower prices don't necessarily increase demand. With a complex distribution system, the marketer may lose some control over pricing as wholesalers and retailers modify pricing to meet their objectives. But pricing levels in database marketing can be systematically tested and controlled by the marketer. Offers can be varied based on customer characteristics and associated costs. Discounts and other price incentives can be provided to special groups of customers such as first-time buyers or large quantity purchasers.

Product

The product element of the marketing mix embodies all the tangible and intangible aspects of goods and services. Most customers cannot easily discriminate the more tangible aspects of a product from the less tangible aspects. For example, a consumer's perception of coffee is not only affected by the taste, but it is also affected by the price, packaging, advertising, and where the product is purchased. A low-cost coffee purchased at a discount chain with an "economy" positioning is perceived as inferior by many consumers, regardless of the tangible quality of the coffee.

The customer service element of the product has recently gained more prominence, prompting a focus on customer management and customer loyalty programs. Customer satisfaction or dissatisfaction with product selection assistance, usage advice, and return policies is usually perceived by customers to be part of the total product package rather than separate components. Many marketers believe that they lose more customers because of nonresponsive customer service than because of product failure or dissatisfaction. Therefore, it is important for most marketers to establish customer service policies and practices that are responsive to the needs of the target market.

We have already noted the product testing advantages that a database provides to a marketer. With this capability, the marketer can fine-tune product development strategies and develop programs to offer customers new products based on an analysis of their characteristics. For example, a company currently selling golf equipment performs an analysis of the database, and the analysis reveals that many of these customers are also interested in travel. A company with a product development strategy might begin to implement the strategy by testing various golf-oriented travel packages.

Monitor and Control

Marketers must constantly monitor marketing programs. Performance is compared to objectives. If performance does not reach objectives at specific milestones, the program or strategy may need to be modified. Performance deficits may occur due to improper analysis, overoptimistic objectives, inappropriate strategy, or poor implementation. We have already indicated that database marketers can track performance rapidly and accurately, allowing a quicker response to problems. In addition, testing of database programs is more extensive and less expensive relative to mass marketing through physical retail channels.

Databases and the Planning Process

Ideally, database development or expansion should be considered at all levels of the planning process. However, some organizations are not strategically oriented, or a database may be developed to solve an immediate tactical problem without much consideration of longer-term strategies or objectives. For example, a database may be developed to support a specific promotional campaign for product introduction. The reuse of the database after the promotion is not anticipated. Although the temporary use of a database may help achieve some short-term objectives, the real power of databases is in their ability to track and evaluate customers over the long term. Databases can help develop relationships between the customer and marketer by making the marketer aware of changing needs. From a performance perspective, databases can be used to evaluate marketing programs over time and determine the LTV of the customer to the organization.

The marketing planning model we have presented here is intended to provide a perspective on how a marketing database can help an organization market more effectively and efficiently. The model uses commonly accepted planning elements available from a number of sources. However, marketers use other planning models as well. Exhibit 2.4 outlines a model for direct marketing program planning presented by Roberts and Berger (1999). Note that this model for direct marketing program planning should be based on a strategic plan that defines marketing objectives, target markets, competition, and so on.

Exhibit 2.4 The Direct Marketing Program Planning Process

Establish Communications Objectives Based on Stated Marketing Objectives

Evaluate the Marketplace
   Business Environment
   Competition
   Customer Market Segments
   Product/Market Fit

Evaluate Past Experience and Performance in Similar Programs

Develop The Communications Strategy
   Target Market(s)
   Positioning/Desired Brand Personality
   Key Selling Proposition(s)
   Offer Strategy
   Media/List Strategy
   Message Strategy

Specify Database Development, Use, and Enhancement Requirements

Determine the Program Budget

Establish the Implementation Timetable

Develop Creative Prototypes

Establish Evaluation Rules and Methods

Direct Marketing Management, 2/E by Mary Lou Roberts and Paul D. Berger. Reprinted by permission of Pearson Education, Inc., Upper Saddle River, NJ.

Chapter Summary

In this chapter, we attempt to emphasize the importance of determining the fit between organizational objectives and database development. A database has to be designed from the perspective of achieving organizational objectives, and we present a marketing planning model as a means to determine how the database can help to achieve these objectives. We describe how the database can provide an advantage in understanding customer characteristics, developing new products, determining optimal pricing levels, communicating more personally, and maintaining more control of product distribution.

We consider other organizational issues in our discussion of the process of database development in Chapter 5. In particular, we examine how the marketing department must be able to properly communicate with technical personnel in order to develop an effective and efficient database. In addition, as we progress through the chapters, we show more specifically how the databases can help achieve organizational objectives through analysis techniques.

Review Questions

1. What is the primary purpose of a marketing database?

2. What is the difference between a customer database and other types of marketing databases?

3. Why is it important to examine the marketing environment and organizational resources before proceeding to develop a marketing database?

4. How are database marketing strategies different from marketing programs?

5. What advantages do databases provide to marketers for implementing marketing programs?

6. Provide an example of how tactical database implementation is different from strategic database implementation.

3

Defining Customer Data Requirements

Keri Lee had mixed emotions when she received the news that her application for a new position at DSI was approved. Although she enjoyed her job selling software to customers in the b-to-b market, she was seeking a change. The constant travel required in the sales position was reducing the time Keri wanted to spend with family and friends. She also wanted to be part of a team that was more directly involved in developing marketing strategies and programs. Her new position, as associate product manager in DSI's consumer's division, would present this challenge. The consumer division was new, and they were in the process of developing a database to achieve marketing objectives.

Keri's new supervisor had extensive experience in database marketing, coming to DSI from a major direct marketer of computer hardware. Keri realized there would be much to learn. However, she was confident that with her academic background—she was a marketing major and an information systems minor—and previous work experience, she would succeed.

At her first meeting in the consumer division, Keri discovered that database development had only just started. There was some customer information housed in various company files and databases, but this information was incomplete and scattered throughout several departments. DSI had just developed a very basic Web site, and some data were also being collected there.

After DSI analyzed the opportunities and structure of the consumer graphics software market, they decided to use direct marketing approaches. The goal was to establish a database of nonbusiness users of graphics software programs so that the company could develop targeted promotions for their product lines. Because the development of graphics software is very dynamic, DSI felt that they could gain a competitive advantage in responding to customers' needs through a database. One of Keri's first tasks was *to gather all usable internal data and explore external data sources. She would be working with the marketing manager and the information systems manager on this project.*

As we discussed in Chapter 2, the process of building a marketing database begins with a definition of what the database is expected to achieve in both the short and long term from a marketing perspective. A review of the organizational objectives and marketing plans must first be conducted in order to set the foundation for database development. Once determined, the details of the database can be outlined.

In particular, the following steps must be taken in the development of the database to ensure that marketing objectives will be met:

+ Determine the data requirements needed to meet the marketing objective
+ Establish guidelines for database maintenance and program coding
+ Evaluate the database structure, including hardware/software requirements
+ Determine whether the database will be built and maintained inside the organization or outsourced

This chapter discusses the first step—determining the data requirements. Subsequent steps are discussed in Chapters 4 and 5.

Data Needs Determination

Database development begins by determining the types of data attributes (fields) required to support the marketing objectives. The amount of data residing on a database can vary greatly from company to company depending on needs and how the database will be used to meet the marketing objectives. For instance, a food company might wish to use a database only to introduce a new line of organic breakfast cereals. To promote the cereal to a group of health enthusiasts, the company might use a mail-in response card in a diet and nutrition magazine. Responders will get a free sample of the new cereal. Because the product will be sold only in supermarkets, the company will not be able to establish a database that includes historical sales data. After the product is introduced, the database's utility will be limited to a consumer loyalty program (e.g., coupons).

On the other hand, the direct marketer of a series of home improvement books might be striving to establish long-term relationships with customers. Customer retention and product development are important goals for the database. Therefore, an extensive database is needed to record and analyze the ongoing transactions of customers.

Fulfillment, Marketing, and Prospecting Databases

Before proceeding any further, you need to know the difference between a marketing database and fulfillment and prospecting databases.

Any direct marketer currently taking and fulfilling orders of any kind must have, at the very least, a fulfillment database or **fulfillment file**. In all likelihood, this file is managed and maintained by an outside vendor. The sole purpose of this file is to preserve information on customers about their order, product shipment, and billing information and status. Most fulfillment files do not maintain historical data. As such, they cannot be used to conduct analyses of past customer purchase behavior.

A marketing database, on the other hand, is structured for efficiency and does maintain a history of all customer transactions over time. These databases are derived from the customer information in a fulfillment database. How often the fulfillment data feed the marketing database depends on the enterprise's needs. This is discussed in greater detail in Chapter 4.

Marketing databases allow direct marketers to more easily obtain quick counts on active customers, select names for future promotions across the various divisional product lines, and track customer performance over time. This book focuses solely on the use of a marketing database.

Prospecting databases are a type of marketing database but comprised solely of noncustomers. They are usually kept as a separate file because they have limited information on these noncustomers. Once prospects order and become a customer, their information will be transferred from the prospecting database to the marketing database.

Data Residing on the Marketing Database

To be successful, a direct marketer must know not only which data elements to keep on the customer file but also how to use the data most effectively. The types of data residing on a marketing database can be classified as either internal or external, as shown in Exhibit 3.1.

Internal or House Data

Internal or house data are obtained from a number of sources within the organization. Accounting, customer service, sales, research, and information systems departments can have data relevant for marketing purposes. Even within those departments, several different databases can exist. Marketers should be aware that the incompatibilities of existing databases can pose

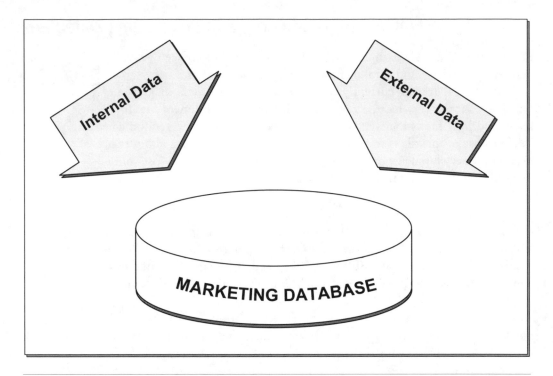

Exhibit 3.1   Sources of Data in the Marketing Database

problems when a database specialist attempts to consolidate data from various sources within the organization. A current concern for many marketers is integrating Internet databases with older **legacy systems** (Internet **database integration** issues are discussed in Chapter 15). Problems with incompatibility can result in project delays.

The types of customer data available from internal sources can vary widely, and the format and degree of completeness of these data will vary from organization to organization. The data include

- ◆ Previous contact information
- ◆ Past purchase records
- ◆ Product returns data
- ◆ Customer service data
- ◆ Responses to internal surveys
- ◆ Voluntary customer registration data (e.g., warranty cards, Internet site registration)

Internal or house customer data found on a marketing database can be classified as either fulfillment, marketing, or customer contact data.

Fulfillment Data

Fulfillment data are basically raw or transactional-level data and are primarily used for billing and fulfilling orders. However, a marketer also wants to use such data. For example, the data field "Last Bill Effort Sent" is used by a marketer as an indicator of how quickly a customer pays.

Marketing Data

Marketing data are any piece of customer information used by marketers for the purpose of increasing the effectiveness or efficiencies of marketing activities. This includes data that can help marketers promote customers, develop relationships with customers, and establish marketing strategies and programs. For example, most past purchase information will be used by the marketing division to help predict a customer's future purchase behavior. Most marketing data elements are based on summarized and "rolled-up" fulfillment data. For example, past information on customer payment patterns might be helpful for segmenting the best customers in the database.

In general, house marketing data can be classified into three types:

1. **Recency data** are related to the recency of a customer's last promotion, order, payment, and so on. Examples of recency data created and maintained on marketing databases include time in months since a customer's last order and time in months since a customer's last payment.

2. **Frequency data** are related to a customer's total number of promotions, orders, payments, etc. Examples of frequency data created and maintained on marketing databases include total number of promotions sent to a customer and total number of product returns by a customer.

3. **Monetary data** are related to a customer's total dollar value of orders placed, payments made, etc. Examples of monetary data created and maintained on marketing databases include total dollars written off for a customer due to nonpayment.

Recency data are the strongest of the three data elements. As a result, the predictive strength of frequency and monetary data elements can be amplified by incorporating an element of recency in their definition. For example, the total number of orders placed by a customer is a strong predictor of a customer's likelihood to order in the future, but the total number of orders placed by a customer *within the past 12 months* is an even stronger predictor.

If appropriate, bringing in an element of affinity to any of the above three classifications of data elements will also make these data elements even more relevant. For example, the total amount of money spent by a customer on investment books in the past 24 months is a very strong indicator of the customer's likelihood of ordering investment books in the future.

According to *Direct* magazine's 2000 subscriber survey, at least 75% of consumer and 52% of b-to-b direct marketers maintain standard recency, frequency, and monetary (RFM) indicators. Only 48% maintain promotional history, and only 35% keep track of promotional nonresponses—both of which are quite important in allowing a marketer to be effective in cross-selling and reactivating customers.

Customer Contact Data

Customer contact data are the foundation of the database. The marketer must have a means to reach customers. Basic contact information includes name, address, zip code, phone and fax numbers, and e-mail address. Marketing efficiency and effectiveness is greatly affected by the quality of the contact information. The required contact information must correspond to the organization's marketing communication vehicle. A telemarketer must have an accurate telephone number, a mail marketer must have an accurate mailing address, and an Internet marketer must have an accurate e-mail address. Therefore, the strategy for developing and maintaining the database should encompass the importance of the information for marketing purposes (see Chapter 4).

Smaller organizations often have poorly organized information about customers. For example, the sales staff of a small b-to-b marketer can have customer information on their PCs or in paper files. Centralization of marketing information in a common database will help to facilitate and coordinate marketing efforts. In the b-to-b market, redundant sales contacts can be avoided and interaction with multiple personnel in the organization can be documented to get a better idea of customer needs.

In an attempt to streamline the management of the sales process, some companies require salespeople to use Internet-based programs. This allows real-time updates on the time and location of their next appointment. In addition, the database provides the salesperson with market profiles and intelligence on customers and prospective customers. Although some salespeople were initially reluctant to use the Internet database for account management, they have found it reduces account maintenance tasks. With account maintenance task reductions, salespeople can spend more time on commission-generating activities. (Dana, 1999). Larger organizations with existing databases for nonmarketing purposes (e.g., operations, accounting) may need to restructure the database to make it suitable for marketing purposes. For example, existing databases may have customer contact and purchase transaction information. However, it can be difficult or impossible to relate specific purchases to a particular marketing program such as a mail or direct TV campaign. Remember that the goal for the organization is to develop a structured and systematic method of not only contacting customers but also tracking the individual account. Integration across functional areas of the business is a necessity for an optimal marketing database. Strategic priorities for developing the database should be placed on those areas that translate into effective and efficient customer contact and tracking.

External or Enhancement Data

External or enhancement data are information about a direct marketer's customers obtained from a third party or vendor. This type of data is generally purchased by direct marketers to supplement their own house customer data to learn more about their customers. The marketers can then more effectively

♦ Determine current and future customer needs
♦ Enhance advertising
♦ Increase response rates
♦ Acquire new customers
♦ Extend appropriate credit

External data can be classified into three categories:

1. **Compiled list data**
2. **Census data**
3. **Modeled data**

How enhancement data are collected and how they can be used has recently become a topic of much debate due to privacy concerns of many citizens and the ease by which such information can be obtained via the Internet. For example, the Fair Credit Reporting Act forbids the sale of consumer credit report information to direct marketers unless authorized for specific purposes. The Driver's Privacy Protection Act recently stopped the sale of all DMV (Department of Motor Vehicles) data. This was the single most accurate source of age information available. States must now obtain written permission from licensed drivers before selling the data to third-party marketers.

Compiled List Data

Compiled list data are individual-level data collected by list service bureaus or list vendors such as Polk, infoUSA, Experian/Metromail, Acxiom, and

Trans Union to sell it to direct marketers. It can be gathered from a variety of sources: telephone directories, voter registration files, birth records, housing purchase records, membership rosters, etc.

The information on compiled lists can be categorized as either demographic or psychographic. Examples of the types of data elements you can purchase are shown in Exhibit 3.2.

Assume a major men's shoe chain is considering expanding by selling upscale athletic shoes and exercise apparel. They have no information on their customer database that indicates who might be most interested in this new product line. Currently, they sell only expensive men's dress and casual shoes. Before expanding, they would like to gauge demand for this new product line from their current customer base by determining what percentage of their customers are interested in fitness and exercise. What information could they use to enhance their customer database that would help them determine the demand?

The shoe marketer might consider some of the following enhancement data elements:

♦ Members of health clubs
♦ Recent purchasers of exercise equipment
♦ Respondents who checked "enjoy exercising" on a questionnaire or warranty card
♦ Recent purchasers of exercise clothing
♦ Readers of exercise and fitness magazines

Assuming that a high percentage of their current customer base shows an interest in fitness and exercise, the shoe chain can use this enhancement data to help them select names from the database for a special promotion.

Direct marketers can also collect their own demographic and psychographic data via questionnaires. Nordstrom, the upscale department store chain, recently augmented the information in its cardholder database from

Exhibit 3.2 Demographic and Psychographic Data Elements

Demographic	*Psychographic*
Income	Hobbies
Age	Reading interests
Gender	Exercising habits
Marital status	Music preferences (rock, country, etc.)
Education level	Movie preferences (action, drama, etc.)
National origin, ethnicity	Political orientation
Family size	Social (opinions on the environment, education, family, health care, etc.)
Occupation	
Credit information	Donor (the arts, health sciences, etc.)

a survey mailed to its 5 million cardholders. The survey has provided them with critical information for targeting purposes, including spending habits and price sensitivity (DM News, 2000b).

Census Data

Census data are obtained from the U.S. Census Bureau from **geo-demographic data** (zip code, block group, census track, etc.) It is not available at an individual level as compiled list data. Rather, census data represent the average measurement of residents within the geo-demographic region. For example, people residing in zip code 12345 have an average income of $56,345. This income value will be appended to those residents on the database in zip code 12345.

Census tracts are subdivisions of counties. Today, there are approximately 50,000 census tracts. **Block groups** are subdivisions of census tracts formed by grouping blocks (streets). There are approximately 225,000 block groups. Being too fine a split, some sensitive economic and personal data are not reported at the block group level; however, it is reported at a census tract or zip code level. This is because doing so can provide individual information if, for example, it was known that in a block group only one family of a particular ethnic group resides.

However, it should be noted that with the 2000 U.S. Census, marketers have access to more than 63 single-race or multirace categories down to the block level. This segmentation can be valuable to marketers desiring to target certain racial groups by modifying marketing communications or offers to the needs of particular groups.

The U.S. government gathers census data every 10 years, reestimating some data such as population growth estimates between updates. Census data available within a geo-demographic region include

- Median income
- Average household size
- Average home value
- Average monthly mortgage
- Percentage ethnic breakdown
- Percentage married
- Percentage college educated
- And even such measures as average daily commuting time

Exhibit 3.3 shows census information for three very demographically distinct census tracts. If you were to promote an expensive children's book series and could only market to the names within one of the three census tracts, which would you choose and why?

Exhibit 3.3   Census-Level Data Pertaining to Three Tracts

Area	Median Household Size	Median Age	Median Monthly Mortgage	Median Household Income	Percentage with Undergraduate or Graduate Degree
Chappaqua, NY 10514 (Block Group 2, Census Tract 013102, FIPS Code 36119)	4.1	37.2	$2,000	$148,649	38.5
Affton, MO 63123 (Block Group 1, Census Tract 219800, FIPS Code 29189)	2.7	37.2	$661	$41,579	22.4
West Frankfort, IL 62896 (Block Group 3, Census Tract 040900, FIPS Code 17055)	2.2	40.9	$490	$12,636	3.7

When lacking an abundant amount of individual-level data pertaining to customers, a direct marketer often relies on census-level data. The premise in using this type of data for determining a product's target market, when no other data are available, is that all individuals living within a geo-demographic region are similar to one another. Although this is true in some cases, it certainly is not in others.

For example, it might be true that most people living in Beverly Hills, California, are quite wealthy and drive expensive cars, but the majority of these residents will not have the same interests in reading, music, or hobbies.

Head-to-head, census-level data will never be as powerful as individual-level data in predicting customer behavior. However, as previously mentioned, when no other information is available, it will and can play a fairly strong role depending on your applications. Consider the following examples:

- Census data indicating a customer's financial status (average income levels, average home value, average number of cars owned) will play a fairly strong role in helping determine who to promote with a free trial offer, ensuring a minimal number of written-off accounts.
- Census data indicating a customer's financial status can also play a strong role in determining the customers most likely to respond to promotions from such companies as Lexus, BMW, KitchenAid Appliances, and Neiman Marcus Department Stores.

♦ Using census-level data to help determine the customers most likely to purchase a general reference coffee table book will be much more difficult. Selecting more educated and literate areas for promotion would be weak at best. In this case, the best bet is to append individual-level lifestyle data from a compiled list source.

Direct marketers can obtain free census data to target their mailings from the data collection company SRC by logging on to their Web site at www.FreeDemographics.com.

Modeled Data

Modeled data are generated from statistical analysis such as customer clustering. These data are often used to classify or segment customers based on purchase patterns, demographics, and psychographics. On the basis of certain geographic data, for example, income or educational levels can be predicted.

Claritas, a company that analyzes and develops databases, offers a classification scheme called PRIZM. PRIZM is based on the premise that people with similar lifestyles tend to live near one another. PRIZM describes every U.S. neighborhood in terms of 62 distinct lifestyle types, called clusters. Clusters have been given names such as Second City Elite, Upward Bound, Boomtown Singles, Starter Families, Smalltown Downtown, Pools & Patios, Country Squires, God's Country, Greenbelt Families, and Middle America. Each cluster has certain characteristics. For example, the Elite Exurban Family cluster is aged 45 to 64, professional, and has a median household income of $89,000. This PRIZM cluster is most likely to go cross-country skiing, bank online, own a fax machine, watch *Frasier* on TV, and read *Forbes*. The Elite Exurban Family cluster live in neighborhoods such as Prospect, Kentucky, New Fairfield, Connecticut, and Belle Mead, New Jersey. Marketers of cross-country skiing equipment or home fax machines can enhance their database with this cluster information or rent such names for promotion.

The use of this data to segment customers is discussed in more detail in Chapter 8.

Lists Versus Data

Names residing on lists can also be rented for promotions or purchased and added to a direct marketer's prospecting database. Either way, the sole purpose is to acquire new customers. Depending on the agreement made with the list owner, you may or may not be able to promote the names multiple times. Typically, contracts are set for a one-time use or a one-year agreement with unlimited use. Outside intermediaries such as list brokers or managers often handle list rentals and maintenance for an organization.

Regarding names found on compiled lists, the main issue is that they are not proven direct mail responsive. Remember, these names came from various sources such as questionnaires, registration lists, and warranty cards.

Acxiom, a major provider of compiled lists, offers InfoBase, a large collection of U.S. consumer, business, and telephone data for prospecting or enhancement. A few of their offerings include names and lists dealing with

- New movers
- Young families
- Active seniors
- Working mothers
- High-tech industry
- Banking industry

INSOURCE is a composite of the independent databases of Metromail and Experian. INSOURCE enhancement data include the following information from various sources:

- A broad range of demographics
- Consumer interests and lifestyle
- Telephone numbers
- Mail order responsiveness indicators
- Automotive ownership
- Real estate holdings
- Segmentation and clustering systems
- Census geo-demographics

There are many vendors of compiled lists and data, many of which advertise in industry publications such as *DM News* and *Direct* magazine.

Response lists are lists of names or businesses put on the market by direct marketers for rent by other direct marketers. They are called response lists because they have responded to past offers from, for example, mail order catalogs, magazine subscriptions, or charities. Response lists have a higher potential response rate than compiled lists because past behavior is a good predictor of future behavior. Therefore, marketers seek response lists composed of purchasers (or donors) in the same or a similar category to their own.

Some lists are further specified as being comprised of recent purchasers. These are called **hot-line lists,** and individuals on these lists are often more likely to purchase. Direct marketers can retain any name of a person who orders or responds in some manner (e.g., makes a purchase or requests more information). However, the use of the names of the people on the response list who did not respond is restricted by the rental agreement.

The Reader's Digest Association offers more than 30 million of their names for rent. You can select names based on recency of order in addition to various demographic and psychographic attributes. They also offer response models and "best customer" models as other options in selecting names from their file that will be most responsive to your offer (Levey, 2000).

You cannot enhance your file with names rented from a response list or add them to your prospecting database. You rent the name for a one-time use only—a promotion. When you rent a response list, you first match it to your **house file**. This allows you to eliminate any name on the response list that matches a name on your house file that, for example, already ordered the product or service you will be offering or currently owes you money. In addition, when you match the response list to your house file, a certain portion of the matches will be to your older inactive customers. Therefore, the response list provides you with valuable information for some of your older inactives. This valuable piece of information tells you which of your older inactives are active on the list owner's file. Take advantage of this information and promote these names. However, remember, you cannot retain this data on your customer file indicating that they matched the list owner's file unless you have made such an arrangement with the list owner in advance.

Applying and Using Enhancement Data

If direct marketers wish to have enhancement data (census, compiled, or modeled) overlaid on their customer file, they often follow these steps:

1. The direct marketing company makes a copy of their customer file (or whatever portion they wish to enhance) and sends it to the to the enhancement service.

2. The service bureau matches their file to the direct marketing company's file using a name and address-matching algorithm (Chapter 4).

3. Once matched, the service bureau appends the desired information (e.g., age, income, lifestyle indicators) to the copy of the file given to them.

4. The direct marketing company matches the file back to their database (via a unique customer number) and appends the enhancement data to their file for future use.

Match rates from a single source vary, depending on the makeup and size of the customer file and the specific data elements being appended.

To get better coverage on age enhancement data, for example, consider going to several sources. You can usually work out appropriate net name/match arrangements with vendors when pursuing multiple sources of the same data field.

We end this chapter with three case studies illustrating the use of enhancement data.

Case Study 1: A Tire Manufacturer

Company: A leading manufacturer of tires, automotive parts, and services with retail locations throughout the United States.

Situation Analysis: With a proprietary cardholder base of 1 million customers, the company wanted to capture consumers in the growing segment of the female marketplace: women purchasing automotive accessories and services.

Objective: Widen existing customer base to include more female consumers.

Strategy: Using INSOURCE, the retailer overlaid demographic and automotive information onto its credit card member file, creating a more complete picture of its customer base. Focusing on the retailer's female cardholders, a profile was developed. This was used to select a compiled list of prospects who closely resembled what the retailer now identified as its female "best customer." This list was run against the client file, removing names duplicated on the database. A customized, direct mail campaign was developed with offers designed specifically for the above audience. To enhance response rates, customized offers were ink-jetted onto direct mailers in regions where retail locations were offering discounts.

Result: The manufacturer generated an 18 percent response rate from the promotion and converted 45 percent of those respondents into cardholders.

Source: http://www.experian.com/direct_marketing/products/direct.html#insource

---

Case Study 2: A Direct Marketer of Sporting Goods

Company: A major direct marketer of sporting goods.

Situation Analysis: Learn more about customer product needs.

Objective: Expand product lines.

Strategy: This company currently has all necessary information to contact customers (name, address, phone) and past purchase information. They want to learn more about the customers for the purpose of product development. They will send a questionnaire to customers as well as enhance the customer file with information pertaining to sporting and lifestyle activities.

Result: The sporting goods marketer determined what additional products to offer their current customers based on an assessment of their needs and lifestyles via questionnaire and enhancement data.

Case Study 3: A Magazine Publisher

Company: A magazine publisher.

Situation Analysis: Profile subscriber base.

Objective: Increase advertising revenue.

Strategy: Using demographic and psychographic data overlays, the publisher created a profile of their current subscriber base. In particular, they appended information regarding age, income, household composition, car ownership, and occupation. Profile reports were generated for the advertising sales staff to assist them in their efforts.

Result: By profiling the subscriber base, the advertising team was successful in obtaining new accounts and renewing old accounts. As a result, advertising revenue increased over the prior 12-month period by more than 19 percent.

Chapter Summary

Defining data requirements is an important early step in the development of a marketing database. Marketers have to determine what information about customers is necessary to achieve their objectives. To optimize the utility of a customer database, marketers gather data from a number of internal and external sources. Internal sources can provide data on transactions and any other information collected on individuals by the company. External sources can enhance this internal or house data by providing demographic, psychographic, and **transaction data**. There are also external lists of potential customers based on demographics, psychographics, and actual responses to offers. Some of these lists are compiled from sources such as telephone directories, birth records, and membership rosters. Response lists are distinguished from complied lists because individuals or businesses on response lists have previously responded to some type of offer. Data from the U.S. Census Bureau can be used to specify the characteristics (e.g., median income, household size, racial group, education level) of people living within geographic segments of the country. Modeled data generated from statistical analyses classify individuals in certain geographic areas by lifestyle categories such as Starter Families and Upward Bound. The chapter concludes with examples of how enhancement data are used to reach organizational objectives.

Review Questions

1. What are some of the sources of data that can be included in the database?

2. Give some examples of demographic and psychographic data elements.

3. How are compiled lists different from response lists?

4. Why are house files (internal databases) enhanced with supplemental data?

5. Describe how marketers can use U.S. Census Bureau data.

6. What steps are involved in using an outside service to enhance a house file?

4

Database
Maintenance and Coding

While carefully reviewing a draft proposal of the marketing department's database requirements, Keri noted that the section on database maintenance was incomplete. She met with her marketing manager to discuss the omissions. Keri incorrectly assumed that the Information Systems (IS) department would know which fields in the database to update as promotional campaigns were run and purchases were made. To avoid miscommunications, Keri and her boss decided to systematically review all updating and maintenance requirements. They started the systematic review by examining how the fields in an individual record should change as they are entered into the database, sent promotional materials, placed an order, made purchases, or returned products. They wanted to make sure the effectiveness of lists and ad campaigns could be tracked through codes on the individual records. Whether the customer entered the database from a response to an ad in a computer magazine, filled out a form on the Web site, or came from any other medium, Marketing wanted to be able to track and evaluate the source. Customer contact information also needed to be updated as addresses, telephone numbers, and e-mail addresses changed. After Keri documented the potential updating and maintenance requirements, she was surprised at the extent of these ongoing tasks. She also realized that without periodic and accurate database maintenance, they would not be able to maximize marketing effectiveness.

Keri remembered her past experiences with improperly maintained databases. When the database was modified in DSI's b-to-b division, sales were lost because client data were not updated properly. Keri also recalled getting irrelevant information from marketers of consumer products. For example, she received an e-mail notifying her that the manufacturer was recalling her car. She did not own that model but had only requested information about it. She also received letters welcoming her as a new catalog customer, even though she had spent hundreds of dollars over the course of several years with the company. Keri was hoping to avoid these types of problems, caused by improper database maintenance, at DSI.

Databases must be maintained and updated regularly to maximize marketing effectiveness and efficiency. This chapter considers aspects of databases that need to be maintained, examines the importance of maintaining database fields, and provides examples on how maintenance procedures are accomplished. Database maintenance also involves developing codes for records in the file. These codes help track marketing programs and eliminate inefficiencies.

Technical aspects of the database also need to be maintained. For example, IS must routinely back up data, update programs, and run tests on computer components and operating systems. Marketing may request that new versions of programs such as statistical packages be installed as they are issued. Marketing also routinely requests that IS make copies of house files for the purpose of data enhancement by external organizations. Although these types of technical maintenance procedures are important, our discussion focuses on those particular fields of the database that need routine maintenance in order to enhance the marketing process.

Standard Database Maintenance Routines

Several standard maintenance routines must be performed to keep the names and all information on the database relevant from a promotional point of view. Although software is available for many of these routines, skilled technicians are required to maintain and operate such software. The standard database maintenance routines discussed in this chapter include

- **Deduping the customer file**
- **Householding the customer file**
- Purging old customer records
- Changing contact information (address, phone number, e-mail)
- Standardizing addresses
- Removing names on databases at consumer's request
- Identifying customers with **match coding**

In addition, we discuss the following procedures:

- **Merge/purge processing**
- Coding source and promotional offers
- Adding **decoy records** (**salting** the customer file)
- Identifying credit risks and frauds
- Field updating rules

- Reporting summary and aggregate level information
- Database storage and security
- Database maintenance schedules
- Technical aspects of database maintenance

Deduping the Customer File

Occasionally, customers receive duplicates of a mailing. For example, they might receive two of the same offer for a credit card. If you review the name and addresses on the duplicate offers, there is most likely a difference. These duplicate mailings are an unnecessary expense for the marketer. Therefore, you have to dedupe your customer file.

Duplicate names on a marketing database can occur for a number of reasons:

- The customer's name and/or address appeared different on an external list versus the house file
- For a particular order, the customer used a different mailing address
- The direct marketer confused the bill to/ship to addresses in the system

For example, if a marketer is mailing to current customers along with potential customers from three response lists of magazine subscribers, it is possible that some of the names on the lists and on the house file will be the same. Some may subscribe to several magazines. If names on these various lists and the house file are not properly deduped, the customer database will have duplicate customer records. To avoid this situation, a marketer performs a merge/purge process to the mailing file prior to sending the names to the letter shop. (This is discussed in more detail later in this chapter.)

Unfortunately, not all duplicate instances can be caught. As a result, duplicates will appear on the marketing database. Direct marketers should regularly clean up duplicate records on their database. The frequency is determined by the costs and savings.

Exhibit 4.1 Costs Associated With Duplicate Records

	Total Number of Records		
Percentage Duplication	50,000 Records	100,000 Records	1,000,000 Records
5	$1,250	$2,500	$25,000
10	$2,500	$5,000	$50,000
15	$3,750	$7,500	$75,000
20	$5,000	$10,000	$100,000

As the percentage of duplicate records in the file increases, so does the associated expense. Exhibit 4.1 shows the costs of different levels of duplicates in files of various sizes, assuming the cost of mailing is $500 per thousand or $0.50 for each piece mailed.

Should marketers *always* attempt to remove duplicates from the file? The answer depends on a number of factors such as the number of duplicates in the file and the cost of the mailing piece itself. The cost to remove duplicates is normally minimal. Most vendors charge $0.002 per record processed for deduping. Because the cost to dedupe is minimal, you might decide to use multiple matching steps to remove duplicates.

Although there can be situations in which it is *not* profitable for a direct marketer to reduce waste, it might not be viewed as a good practice from a customer service or social point of view. Should the direct marketer send a mailing with a known level of duplicates that will end up in landfills or recycling centers even though they have the capacity to remove them? Will the customer become upset at receiving multiple copies of the same catalog over and over again?

If you do decide to clean the duplicate records off your database, you must put in place various rules that allow you to combine the account information of the dupes. You do not want to lose valuable information by simply eliminating one of the duplicate accounts.

Householding the Customer File

Similar to deduping a customer file, householding a customer file means examining the database for two different customers at the same address. When multiple contacts at one address are not desirable, as in the case of mailing a large annual catalog, direct marketers should identify multiple household accounts at a single address and thereby obtain promotional efficiencies and effectiveness. This allows them to avoid sending duplicate mailings to the same address. For example, both Mr. and Mrs. Jones are on the customer file. Their accounts will be identified as a "household" match, and one name will be promoted. Who is promoted from the household may depend on the individual characteristics of each member. For example, if the offer is for a cookbook, Mrs. Jones can be the best candidate.

In addition, when mailing out different offers to your customers for the same product in a single campaign, it is equally important to household the file. Not doing so can result in two people in the same household receiving two different offers. Consider the following real-life example:

Coauthor Perry Drake and his wife, Rhonda Knehans-Drake, each received a promotion approximately 2 years ago from a major credit card company at their home. Perry and Rhonda have been customers of this credit card company since 1986. This company was offering each of them the opportunity to sign up for a new credit card. Rhonda was offered the incentive of two free round-trip tickets to anywhere within the continental United States. Perry received no incentive. How do you think this made Perry feel, given that he had been a customer of this major credit card company just as long as his wife?

Be aware that customer servicing issues can also arise with householding. For example, consider the situation in which adult children are still living with their parents or where the home has mother-in-law quarters.

How household duplicates are identified is discussed later in this chapter.

Purging Old Customer Records

On a yearly basis, direct marketers should **purge** old inactive customers and customers whose addresses they can no longer confirm. Direct marketers should also strive to remove names of the deceased from their files to minimize the occurrence of negative reactions from consumers. Solicitations naming the deceased can be very disturbing to relatives. For example, a health insurance company in Florida experienced negative feedback from relatives of deceased individuals when offers were addressed to the deceased.

Purging old and undeliverable customer records off the database makes the database more efficient to use because fewer records have to be searched when going against the database for counts or selects. Examples of names to purge include

- Inactive for the past 3 years
- No promotions sent to the customer for the past 3 years
- Unable to confirm address for over 2 years
- Lack of external verification
- Deceased
- Nondeliverable

The details of purging rules vary from company to company. Some companies maintain two files: an active file and a purged/inactive file. A company can hold the purged/inactive file for the purpose of reactivation promotions. As we discuss in the next section, in some cases a physical address can get a response even if the current occupants have moved.

Changing Contact Information

Approximately 43 million people in the United States change addresses annually, according to the U.S. Postal Service (USPS). Nondeliverable mail (sometimes called **nixies**) should be removed from your database to eliminate this unnecessary expense. A service that helps to eliminate nixies is **NCOA** (National Change of Address) processing, which is licensed by the USPS. The source of the NCOA data is Permanent Change of Address forms filed by relocating postal customers. On average, NCOA contains approximately 108 million permanent change-of-address records, and the changes are kept on file for 3 years from the effective date of the move.

When a marketer sends a file to an NCOA service provider, addresses on the marketer's file are compared with "old" addresses on the NCOA file. If a match is made, all available new addresses are returned to the marketer's file. Approximately 13% of the records on the NCOA do not include a forwarding address. The USPS requires that NCOA maintenance be conducted in order to qualify for certain postal rate discounts. For more information on the exact requirements, visit the USPS small business Web site at www.usps.com/smallbiz and click on "How can I find and reach my target audience?" and then Business Mail 101.

Some services also check address changes against magazine publishing and credit agency data in addition to the USPS NCOA data. One reason for the additional address checks is that people may neglect to file a change of address form with the USPS when they move, but they may notify magazine publishers in order to continue to receive their subscriptions. Another reason is that NCOA matching is very strict.

Although external services are available for address and phone number updating, an organization also needs an internal updating system. Many direct marketers give customers the opportunity to provide information about change of address or phone numbers. This information should be updated on a regular basis. The address changes of an organization's customers can be updated using NCOA services, but internal data sent directly by the customer can be more timely. According the DMA List Database Council/Research Department's 19th Annual List Usage Survey, only 61% of responding companies use NCOA processing.

Names of people who have recently moved are called chadds in the industry. In general, chadds respond very well to promotions. Consider a selection of these recent chadds in your next promotion. Most direct marketers find that they can profitably promote all chadds on a regular basis.

The old address of a chadd is typically called a ghost record in the industry. The address of a ghost record is valid, but the current occupant is unknown. Some direct marketers keep the address of the ghost record along with relevant data about purchases by the prior occupants. For example, if the prior resident at some address purchased several gardening books from you, it is likely this address has a nicely landscaped yard. Perhaps the new, unknown resident at this same address would also be interested in purchasing garden books by way of a "current resident" promotion. In this way, the ghost record can also point you to the current address.

Telemarketers should remove disconnected numbers from the database, as the cost of an average telemarketing effort can range between $1.50 and $2.50 per completed call effort. In addition to internal purging of these disconnected numbers as they occur, you can use outside services that will remove the disconnects from the database.

Removing undeliverable e-mail addresses, though costing substantially less than mail and telemarketing, still should be considered. E-mails that are repeatedly flagged as undeliverable should be removed from the database to help reduce standard database maintenance and processing costs.

Standardizing Addresses

Address quality is the key to any successful mailing project. By processing your list or file to meet USPS regulations, you can save money and stabilize postal rates. It also improves matching for purposes of deduping or householding the customer file.

The process of cleaning up a mailing list is known as address validation and standardization and is performed with CASS (USPS Coding Accuracy Support System)-certified software. This process checks each address on a list for compliance with the USPS preferred format and, when possible, converts the address to this format. It will also make changes to incorrect or missing address information on your list and add valuable postal information such as carrier routes and delivery point bar codes.

An actual example of an address before and after **address standardization** follows:

Address before standardization	Address after standardization
6B	214 East 168th Street, Apt. B6
214 168	Bronx, NY 10456
Bronx, NY 10456	

Again, to qualify for certain postal rate discounts, the USPS requires that address standardization be conducted on a set schedule. For more information on the exact requirements, visit the USPS Web site at www.usps.com and search for Business Mail 101 information.

Removing Names From Databases at Consumer Request

The Direct Marketing Association Inc. (DMA, found at www.the-dma.org) maintains a file of people who requested that their names be removed from mail, telephone, and e-mail databases. These consumers do not want unsolicited offers from direct marketers. The DMA programs called **Mail Preference Service (MPS)**, **Telephone Preference Service (TPS)**, and **E-Mail Preference Service (E-MPS)** are used by many national marketers to purge their files of these names. The DMA updates the MPS and TPS listings quarterly. Identifying people from the house file that do not want to be contacted saves the cost of a very low probability contact and also avoids negative consumer perceptions about a company and the industry. Here are some important things to remember regarding the preference services:

- Given the lead times in preparing for a mailing campaign, a consumer can still be contacted by a participating organization for a period of time after the receipt of a removal request.
- Not all direct marketers use the preference services, so other direct marketers might still contact a particular consumer.
- The preference services are typically "all or none." However, there are exceptions. For example, a magazine publisher will still fulfill issues and ask for renewals even if the customer is on the preference list.
- When people on the preference list have responded to an offer, they can possibly receive future contacts from that organization.

Direct marketers are also required to remove names from databases when they receive direct requests from mail or phone call recipients. This is covered by law, and direct marketers must be aware of these federal and state laws regarding contacting customers and prospects. You can be fined for noncompliance with these regulations. For example, the Telephone Consumer Protection Act was passed in 1991. The Federal Communications Commission's rules and regulations implementing the act went into effect on December 20, 1992. One of the provisions of the act specifies that marketers must maintain a "do not call list" and honor any request to not be called again. A person's name must be kept on the do not call list indefinitely. One error is allowed in a 12-month period. Subsequently, the soliciting companies are subject to penalties.

Identifying Customers With Match Coding

The importance of removing duplicate records at the same address has been discussed. Match coding helps in the process of removing duplicate records. Duplicate records of the same customer can occur in the house file for a number of reasons. For instance, names can be written in different ways in different databases that are being merged. The following is an example of different database presentations of coauthor Ron Drozdenko's name:

- Ronald Drozdenk (full first name and misspelled last name)
- R. G. Drosdenko (first and middle initials and misspelled last name)
- Dr. Ronald G. Drozdenko (title, full first name, middle initial, and last name)

Another reason is that association lists might include a full name, whereas lists based on reply cards might have only initials, because people often fill them out in haste or there is a lack of space on the card. In addition, names are sometimes misspelled when they are transcribed into the database, and some consumers intentionally use variations of their names and addresses to track the sources of mailings they receive.

Match coding involves taking elements of the name and address to develop a unique identifier of an individual. Exhibit 4.2 is an example of match coding for a fictitious person living on a fictitious street in New York City.

The **match code** method will vary, based on organizational needs, and is typically derived internally. For some organizations, it is sufficient to code only by address and last name. Furthermore, some organizations might only be concerned with addresses if they know it is not a multiple-household dwelling. One catalog per household might be sufficient for some organizations, but other organizations may want to target specific individuals within a household. For example, some political and professional organizations want to contact specific members of the household individually with application forms.

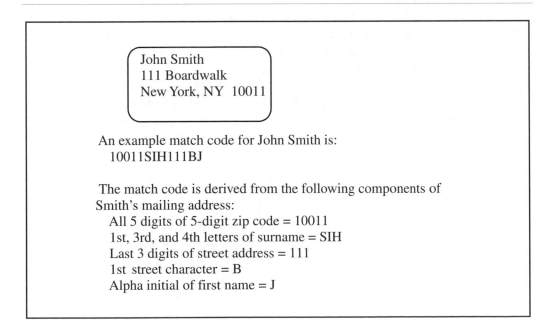

Exhibit 4.2   Match Code Example

A direct marketer can also use different levels of match code precision. A "tight" match requires that all or almost all characters of the code correspond, and a "loose" match requires fewer characters to correspond. Each method of matching has advantages and disadvantages. Tight code matching yields fewer matches but more are likely to be duplicates, whereas loose code matching yields more matches of which fewer are likely duplicates. Your specific needs will determine whether you need tight or loose match coding. For example, if you want to determine how much credit to extend to someone for a preapproved home equity loan, you want to apply tight match coding against the credit bureau's file to ensure that you properly match the name to be promoted, or sent an offer, to the proper credit history data.

If the contact is costly relative to the expected return, the marketer should take measures to reduce duplicates. For example, some b-to-b organizations send customers and potential customers mailings with advertising specialty items ("gifts" such as pens, cups, calendars, key chains) that are often costly; therefore, duplicates should be avoided. A loose match code will reduce duplicates for these marketers. For less expensive contact methods, such as self-mailers to establish consumer awareness of a new retailer, reducing duplicates is less of a concern.

Merge/Purge Processing

Merge/purge is the process of deduping mailing lists associated with an outside list campaign. For example, two outside lists, with no duplicates in them, can be merged together and then purged of duplicates between the two lists prior to sending out the promotion. This happens because within each list individually, there are no duplicates, but when the lists are merged, there could be duplicates. For example, List A = R, S, T, and U, and List B = U, V, W, and X. Neither List A nor List B has duplicates, but if you merge them, the duplicate item will be U. The lists are merged, duplicates identified via matching algorithms, and finally one record will be eliminated from the mailing file prior to promotion.

As was the case with deduping the customer file mentioned earlier in this chapter, the most important reason for performing a merge/purge prior to mailing outside lists is the significant cost savings that can result from reduced printing and postage costs. In addition, it enhances compliance to industry regulations by minimizing the likelihood of promoting to consumers who have requested that the DMA remove their name from DMA members' lists.

For example, in September 2000, coauthor Perry Drake, who is an adjunct faculty member at NYU, received a credit card promotion from a major credit card company that assumed he was a student. Perry has been a cardholder of this credit card company since 1986. How did this happen? Perry's name must have accidentally been placed on an NYU student list. The credit card company must have then rented this list for promotion and decided not to apply merge/purge processing against their database of current cardholders. Perhaps the company felt that the percentage of matches would be so low that the savings in reduced mail quantities would not outweigh the cost of merge/purge processing. Unfortunately, they failed to realize the hidden cost of treating a long-time customer as a noncustomer and misidentifying his occupation.

Coding Source and Promotional Offers

Companies add unique codes to customer records to track the performance of the customers' actions by various in-house marketing programs. Exhibit 4.3 is a mailing label that contains codes used by a company. Note the key, I.D., and media codes associated with the customer.

The catalog marketer uses these codes to monitor marketing programs and assist in order fulfillment and file maintenance.

A variety of marketing programs such as different mailing packages, media, offers, and pricing can all be uniquely coded on the customers' record to determine which marketing programs individuals have received. The codes can also be used in tests to identify which variation of a program has the best response.

Some organizations call this key coding, and some have both **key codes** and media codes. There is no standard method of coding in the industry,

```
                                           BULK RATE
                                           U.S POSTAGE
                                           PAID
                                           EDDIE CREW

******************* ECRLOT **         Key Code
R-004                                 3357231
Laura Martin
487 Old Kettle Rd                     I.D. Code
Waterbury, MA  02798-3241             853000922

                                      Media Code
                                      E
```

Exhibit 4.3 Catalog Mailing Label

and there are a number of reasons why different coding systems are used. For example, to save space on a database file, some companies use complex codes to record a number of marketing programs (e.g., specific offers for new or existing products) that individuals have received over time. Other organizations add additional fields for new programs.

For maximum evaluation and control, each marketing activity should be identified in the database. For example, a company that markets CDs, videotapes, and books wants to relate each order to a specific mailing, direct response TV campaign, or magazine insert.

Organizations use other codes based on their needs. For example, a marketer may develop codes for a specific offer, catalog, test, payment method (credit card, check, money order, etc.), ordering method (phone, mail, Internet), list identification, and ad.

A direct marketer also wants to capture the source of new customers. The source field in the database indicates how a record originally entered the file. We have already discussed how an individual might enter a database (e.g., through rented lists, response to specific advertisements, cards filled out at a retailer, or request for information filled out on a Web site). The source is used to evaluate the performance of the method that acquired a record. Poor performing lists or promotions could be eliminated or modified. Lists or promotions that perform well could be used as models for future list acquisitions or marketing programs.

The cost of the source must also be considered in the evaluation of source performance. A higher-responding source may have an associated higher cost that does not yield a comparable return relative to a lower-responding, lower-cost source. Furthermore, the performance of sources should be evaluated over time. Some sources may have a high initial response rate but show low retention of customers over time, whereas other lower responding sources may retain more of their initial responders. These issues are discussed further in Chapter 12 in the section on Lifetime Value Methodologies.

Salting Files and Decoy Records

Owners of databases often include names in the file that are not real customers. This is referred to as salting the file with decoy records, and organizations do it to

- Check the performance and security of outside service bureaus that are responsible for mailing the promotional offer or fulfilling orders.
- Monitor delivery of packages for timed programs.
- Verify adherence to the list rental agreement (e.g., one-time or limited use). For organizations that rent their lists to other organizations, the

decoy names on the list can be used to detect if the list was used more times than specified in the agreement.

Mail monitoring can be outsourced. For example, U.S. Monitor offers a service that allows companies to monitor mail delivery in 100 cities in the United States. This service documents the delivery of mail pieces sent to the unique decoy names, allowing organizations to verify mail delivery, determine the length of delivery time to specific locations, and check for unauthorized use of lists.

Identifying Credit Risks and Frauds

National credit services such as Trans Union and The Credit Index flag or remove individuals from files who are considered poor credit risks. Trans Union's national consumer credit information file includes public record information and accounts receivable data from national, regional, and local credit grantors. This detailed information is incorporated into a credit report that provides the consumer's history of payment on financial obligations. If authorized under the Fair Credit Reporting Act, a direct marketer can use such data to extend credit, for example. The Credit Index is a co-op database compiled from various direct marketing companies that report customers who have not paid for products. This file is not strictly regulated by law, because it is compiled and shared by direct marketers about their own customers. However, The Credit Index does have its own restrictions to ensure there is no misuse of the data by direct marketers.

The Postal Bulletin (the official source of updates to USPS policies and procedures) also lists "high-risk" addresses from time to time. Direct-mailers should verify if they have these addresses and mark accordingly.

Field Updating Rules

Every time a promotion is sent to an individual on a house file and every time an individual responds to an offer, the record must be updated. Every house data item (field or variable) residing on a database has rules regarding how it should be maintained. For example, when a promotion is sent, various fields are updated on the marketing database:

+ The customer is marked as being promoted for the specific offer.
+ The "date of last promotion" field is updated.
+ The "total number of promotions sent" field is updated.
+ Any other fields derived from the core promotional fields are also updated.

Exhibit 4.4   Jones Customer Status as of May 15, 2000

Name	Address	Last Order Date	Last Promotion Date	Time Since Last Order in Months	Total Dollars Paid	Total Number of Paid Products	Total Number of Promotions Sent
Jones	Main Street	2/15/00	3/25/00	3	$334.56	10	62

Exhibit 4.5   Jones Customer Status as of July 15, 2000

Name	Address	Last Order Date	Last Promotion Date	Time Since Last Order in Months	Total Dollars Paid	Total Number of Paid Products	Total Number of Promotions Sent
Jones	Main Street	6/15/00	5/16/00	1	$360.51	11	63

When payment for the product arrives, the following fields are also updated:

- "Total dollars paid"
- "Total products paid"
- "Date of last payment"
- Any other fields derived from the core payment fields

Assume a promotion for a new cookbook was sent to customer Jones on May 16, 2000 and Jones ordered the cookbook on June 15, 2000 and sent full payment of $25.95 on July 5, 2000. If no other promotions were sent, orders received, or payments received on the Jones account between May 16, 2000 and July 5, 2000, how would the data elements shown in Exhibit 4.4 reflecting Jones's status as of May 15, 2000 change as of July 15, 2000? Exhibit 4.5 shows the updated Jones customer record.

Reporting Summary/Aggregate-Level Information

In addition to updating individual records, **summary/aggregate data** for reporting purposes are also necessary for accurate decision-making purposes. These reports are used for marketing planning, evaluation, and control and can be updated and generated daily, weekly, monthly, and so on. Usually these reports are generated by third-party systems that are fed transactional data from the main marketing or fulfillment database in some manner. Examples of summary/aggregate fields include the following:

- Total mailings, calls, Web site hits
- Total purchases

- Total orders
- Total orders by source, key, media, and so on
- Cost per order
- Sales per thousand contacts
- Profit per thousand contacts
- Average lifetime value

Summary/aggregate reports can be used for comparing lists, comparing offers, evaluating the customer lifetime value by source, and so on, that is, if the reports are easy to read and accurate. If you are considering the purchase of a campaign reporting software package, the three most important features you should look for are real-time data access, data accuracy, and system flexibility.

For example, IMT (Integrated Marketing Technology, found at www.imtnetwork.com) has produced a software package that provides real-time campaign reporting, projection, ROI calculations, and **lifetime value analysis**, to name a few. By linking into a direct marketer's customer database, the IMT reporting software will roll up marketing information across a company's enterprise and display it as you require. In addition, IMT will even assist you in establishing new data definitions as required to ensure that the reports produced by their software are as accurate as possible.

Examples of summary-level reports generated by the IMT system are shown in Exhibits 4.6 and 4.7. Exhibit 4.6 is a report summarizing the

Source by Campaign

New Business Report / Campaign Analysis

	Mail Qty	Gross Subs	Gross Sub %	Net Subs	Net Sub %	Cash Sub %	Credit Sub %
Title: The New Economy							
Source Category: DTP							
Source: Direct Mail							
1999-06 DM: Summer - 6/1/1999	750,000	17,648	**2.35%**	5,703	**0.76%**	0.3%	99.7%
1999-12 DM: Winter - 12/17/1999	732,158	30,669	**4.19%**	11,934	**1.63%**	0.6%	99.4%
2000-03 DM: Spring - 2/28/2000	1,000,000	34,017	**3.40%**	13,210	**1.32%**	0.3%	99.7%
2000-06 DM: Summer - 6/13/2000	1,668,365	32,283	**1.94%**	7,873	**0.47%**	0.3%	99.7%
TOTAL: Direct Mail	**4,150,523**	**114,617**	**2.76%**	**38,720**	**0.93%**	**0.4%**	**99.6%**
Source: Insert Cards							
2000-01: 1/1/2000	437,832	5,316	**1.21%**	4,197	**0.96%**	5.5%	94.5%
2000-02: 2/1/2000	277,269	8,827	**3.18%**	7,119	**2.57%**	3.6%	96.4%

Exhibit 4.6 IMT Campaign-Level Summary Report

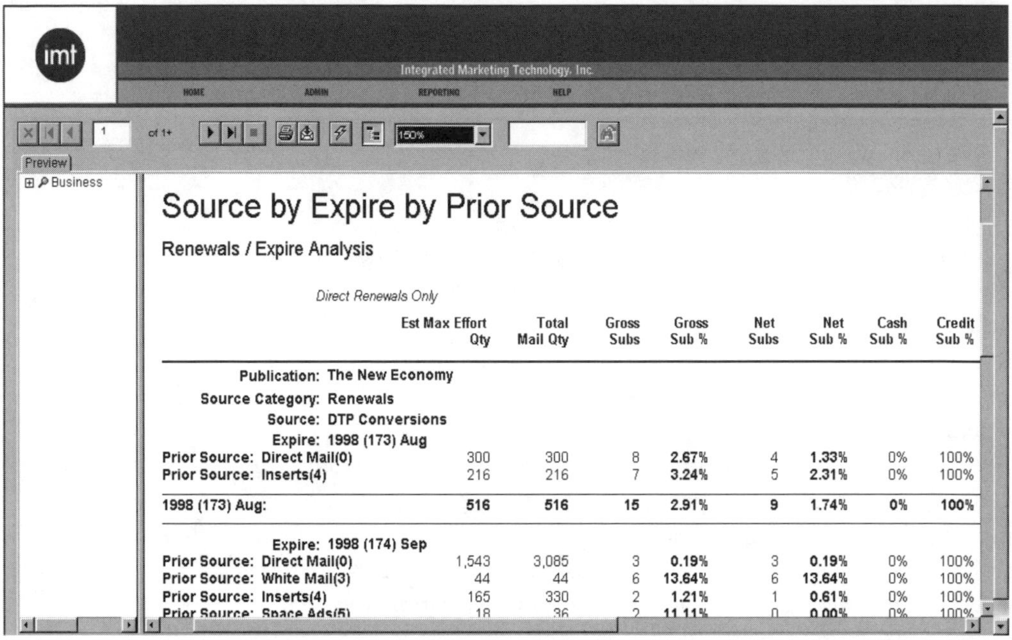

Source by Expire by Prior Source

Renewals / Expire Analysis

Direct Renewals Only

	Est Max Effort Qty	Total Mail Qty	Gross Subs	Gross Sub %	Net Subs	Net Sub %	Cash Sub %	Credit Sub %
Publication: The New Economy								
Source Category: Renewals								
Source: DTP Conversions								
Expire: 1998 (173) Aug								
Prior Source: Direct Mail(0)	300	300	8	**2.67%**	4	**1.33%**	0%	100%
Prior Source: Inserts(4)	216	216	7	**3.24%**	5	**2.31%**	0%	100%
1998 (173) Aug:	**516**	**516**	**15**	**2.91%**	**9**	**1.74%**	**0%**	**100%**
Expire: 1998 (174) Sep								
Prior Source: Direct Mail(0)	1,543	3,085	3	**0.19%**	3	**0.19%**	0%	100%
Prior Source: White Mail(3)	44	44	6	**13.64%**	6	**13.64%**	0%	100%
Prior Source: Inserts(4)	165	330	2	**1.21%**	1	**0.61%**	0%	100%
Prior Source: Space Ads(5)	18	36	2	**11.11%**	0	**0.00%**	0%	100%

Exhibit 4.7 IMT Renewal Summary Report

results of various new business campaigns by source. With this information, a direct marketer can determine which sources are the most profitable. Additional information such as lifetime value can be added to the report.

Exhibit 4.7 displays renewal information by source, expire date, and prior source for a magazine publisher. Additional calculations, views, or data can be added, depending on user needs. In addition, graphical representations of the data can also be generated.

Remember, you will base critical marketing decisions on this data. You have spent the money testing new campaigns and sources, so make sure you get the most out of reading the results properly by implementing reporting software appropriate for your particular situation.

Database Storage and Security

The survival of direct marketing organizations is dependent on the database. Therefore, it is essential to protect it. Database files should be backed up regularly. Backup files should be stored in a safe location (often off site) to protect them from possible damage such as fire and water. Organizations should also limit the number of personnel who are authorized to permanently modify the database. In addition, safeguards are placed in database software to reduce the chances of permanently removing data inadvertently. **Encryption** techniques are used to protect files from unauthorized use by internal or external sources. These encryption techniques make a file useless if unauthorized personnel access it.

Internet security is also an important concern. Organizations must have policies and procedures in place to protect and maintain the integrity of

Exhibit 4.8   Ross-Simons's Security Statement

Ross-Simons' Security Statement

Ross-Simons understands your concerns regarding Internet security. The Ross-Simons secure software encrypts all of your personal information including credit card number, name, and address, so that it cannot be read as the information travels over the Internet.

Ross-Simons has never had an Internet customer file a fraud complaint!

The Internet is as secure as using your credit card in a store or over the phone. However, in the event of any unauthorized use of your credit card, most banks either cover all charges that result from the unauthorized use, or may limit your liability to just $50.00.

Here is how the Secure Server Works

1. Starting Your Order

Every order at www.ross-simons.com is secure. All data submitted via the checkout form is encrypted using SSL (Secure Sockets Layer) encryption.

2. Making a Positive ID

After you've selected items to purchase, you'll be prompted to continue your order by clicking on "Place Your Order" or "Place Order." At this point, your browser looks for a "site certificate" to confirm that it is communicating with www.ross-simons.com. Once a positive ID is made, your order continues.

3. Entering "Secure Mode"

At this point, your computer and our server begin communicating in secure mode, sending data back and forth in an encrypted format. We are ready to ask you for your credit card information. The encryption features of browser software are exceptionally powerful and ensure the security of this data as it is transmitted to our server.

4. Your Order Is Complete

What Happens Next? The credit card numbers are placed in the SQL database on the Ross-Simons web server. A user must have login privileges on the web server (requiring a password) to be able to access the database, which also requires a password. Order information, including the credit card numbers, is retrieved by the staff at Ross-Simons through a web interface. This interface challenges the user for a password twice, and then "expires" the session after ten minutes, requiring the user to login again. All communications during these sessions are encrypted again using SSL. No credit card numbers are ever sent via email, due to the fact that email is not secure.

How can you tell if you're in Secure Mode?

The standard, unsecured URL address begins "http://". When you enter secure mode, the beginning of the URL address will change to "https://"; the "s" stands for secure. Most browsers in secure mode also display a blue line along the top of the browser window. Netscape Navigator (versions 3.0 and earlier) display a broken key symbol in the lower left corner of your browser window when you are not viewing a secure page of a site. This key will become solid when you enter secure mode. Netscape Communicator 4.0 uses a padlock, in the same location as the key, to indicate if you are in standard or secure mode. The padlock is open in standard mode and closed in secure mode. In Microsoft's Internet Explorer, you'll see a padlock symbol at the bottom of your browser window when the browser is in secure mode.

Source: www.ross-simons.com/custom/security.html

customer data. Customers are more likely to purchase online if they feel transactions are secure. Exhibit 4.8 is an example of how an online business, Ross-Simons, is attempting to reassure consumers that transactions are secure. This company sells fine jewelry, tableware, gifts, and collectibles, with many items costing thousands of dollars; therefore, making customers feel safe is important. Many customers are also concerned about personal data being accessed and used; privacy issues are discussed in Chapter 17.

Database Maintenance Schedules

There is a cost to database maintenance. Merging and purging names, flagging credit risks, updating file fields, backing up files, and so on require processing and human resource time. Therefore, maintenance should be performed at intervals that minimize maintenance costs while optimizing marketing efficiency and effectiveness.

Aging data on the database have a deteriorating impact on marketing effectiveness and efficiency. All house data elements should be routinely updated. How often direct marketers update the customer promotion, order, and payment fields residing on a marketing database will depend on how often they select names from the database for promotion. Major direct marketers with weekly campaigns update the customer data at least once per week. Others, having only one or two campaigns per month, require a monthly update.

You should update enhancement data a minimum of once per year. Lifestyle and demographic data about a customer can change quickly. Over the course of a year, a person can become a new parent, take on a new and higher paying job, take up golf, or decide to become involved with a charitable organization. Depending on how valuable you find this type of data in helping you better understand your customers' needs and target them with promotions, you might decide to update it twice per year. Your needs define the frequency of your updates.

Exhibit 4.9 gives some guidelines commonly used in the direct mail industry for the maintenance schedule of other routines.

Exhibit 4.9 Standard Maintenance Schedules

Process	Common Schedule
NCOA processing	Monthly or quarterly for large mailers; two times per year for others
Address standardization & customer file deduping	As needed for legal and postal compliance
Householding of the customer file	Annually for clean-up of duplicate records
Application of DMA do-not-promotes	As needed or quarterly. The MPS and TPS are updated quarterly by the DMA

_____ Some Technical Aspects of Database Maintenance

The best time to establish database maintenance rules and procedures is when the database is developed. The **data fields** that are to be updated when promotions are sent, orders are placed, or payments are made should be determined during the database planning stage. However, it is often impossible to anticipate all the variables that might be useful for data analysis. In some situations, the main database will not contain all the updated variables. Other files are extracted from the main database for analysis purposes, and these files will contain new variables that the analyst feels might be useful for decision making.

Depending on the database system, various techniques are used to maintain and update files. Most **relational databases** are manipulated with **structured query language** (SQL) programs. SQL is flexible and relatively easy to use. Older database systems use COBOL programming language. Despite the fact that this program is decades old, COBOL programming language is still commonly used by database marketers. Some newer applications programs such as data miners use graphical interfaces that make data manipulation and analysis easier.

_____ Chapter Summary

Customer databases are constantly changing in marketing-focused organizations. The database needs to be updated as new customers come onto the file, existing customers change addresses, promotions are delivered, orders are placed, and payments are made. Marketers also have to remove names of individuals from lists who do not wish to be contacted. Improperly maintained databases can reduce marketing efficiencies and effectiveness. Although there are costs associated with database maintenance, greater costs are usually incurred when they are not maintained. In addition, the effectiveness of marketing programs can be tracked by entering codes into the database. These codes tell marketers about the effectiveness of promotions, lists, media, offers, and so on. Because databases require substantial investments and represent a critical asset to the organization, procedures should be in place that secure the database from accidental or intentional misuse.

_____ Review Questions

1. What are some of the reasons for routinely maintaining the database?

2. What is meant by merge/purge?

3. What are some of the codes marketers place on individual records, and how are they used?

4. Why would a marketer put decoy records on a database?

5. When and how is a database updated? Give examples of some of the fields that would be routinely updated.

6. Why is database security important to both consumers and marketers?

5

Basic Database Technology, Organizational Considerations, and Database Planning

Keri Lee understood that the development of DSI's consumer database involved two processes. One process was developing the marketing specifications. The other process was technical development. Technical development involved determining the computer hardware and software that would be required for the marketing specifications. Because Keri graduated with a minor in management information systems (MIS) and had a good working knowledge of DSI's b-to-b database, DSI's marketing manager decided that Keri would be a representative from Marketing on the database development team. The development team was cross-functional and was comprised of people from MIS, Marketing, Finance, Accounting, Human Resources, and Operations. DSI's CEO was also a member of the team.

At the first meeting of the team, Marketing submitted their database specifications. These specifications included the potential size of the database in terms of records and fields, the data fields initially needed, updating requirements, and formulas for new variables derived from the data fields. In addition, Marketing wanted the database to be flexible so that new fields could be added easily and routine information could be extracted from a product manager's workstation quickly for monitoring and controlling marketing programs. Keri's supervisor, who is experienced in database analysis, also insisted that the database must be designed to allow easy access to data for transporting into statistical analysis programs.

The other issue that was critical to Marketing was Internet commerce. Because DSI's target market is computer savvy, Marketing wanted an integrated, interactive database in which customer data could be tracked across mail, phone, and Internet transactions. Marketing felt there was great potential for upgrading, upselling, and cross-selling with an Internet database. Customers could be prompted on new products and upgrades

*through e-mail or timed messages in DSI's programs that would refer them
to the company's Web site.*

*MIS immediately recognized that existing technological resources at DSI
were inadequate to meet these requirements and that new hardware and
software would have to be purchased. MIS would study Marketing's
requirements and develop a proposal for technical development. Because
new resources would be needed, the VP of Finance would also be involved
with proposal development. Because resources were limited, Marketing
might need to consider accepting some compromises. Furthermore, DSI's
corporate goal was to develop a database that was integrated across all
business functions. The other departments also would submit their
database requirements. Because DSI had a strong customer focus in their
mission statement, the CEO indicated that Marketing's specifications
would have a high priority.*

*The meeting ended at 6:45 p.m. As Keri left the building for the day, she
realized that the task of developing the database was substantial. There
might be tension among the departments, and she anticipated many more
long meetings. She already had some ideas on what types of hardware and
software might be able to meet Marketing's requirements. Keri knew that a
relational database offered the needed flexibility, but she was not sure
which software package would be ideal for the specifications of all the
departments. She was anxious to see MIS's proposal. The development of
the database would be the start of the career challenge Keri was seeking.*

In most organizations, Marketing is not responsible for establishing the
technical specifications of the database or for maintaining the database.
However, marketing personnel should have a basic understanding of database technology. This knowledge is important because it helps marketers
contribute to database system design from an applications perspective.
Knowing general concepts of database technology provides the marketer
with insights to opportunities and limitations of certain database systems.
If marketers understand these opportunities and limitations, they will be
better able to establish marketing specifications for the database that are
reasonable and will maximize effectiveness. In addition, marketers who
understand the basics of database technology are better able to interact
with MIS professionals.

In some smaller organizations, marketing personnel may have primary
responsibility for establishing the customer database. The technological
considerations are less of a problem when organizations plan to build a
relatively small database housed on a PC. If marketing personnel have
a good working understanding of PCs, they should be able to establish a
simple relational database using one of a number of user-friendly database

programs. As the complexity of the database increases, however, people with more technical knowledge of database development should be consulted.

In this chapter, we discuss computer software and hardware available on the market today, options for database organization, query languages available for pulling customers and customer information from the database, and other issues that must be addressed to ensure success. In addition, we discuss in detail how to select and manage a database provider if you decide to outsource the building of your customer database.

Computer Hardware and Software

Modern marketing databases require computer hardware and software. Hardware is the physical equipment that holds the database. It includes processors, storage devices, input and output devices, and components that link devices together in networks. The term server refers to hardware that links devices in a network, such as PCs, storage devices, Internet communication devices, and printers. Exhibit 5.1 is a simplified diagram of a **computer network**.

Networks can be limited to one location or link several locations. In addition, servers can link the company with customers and employees through the Internet. The challenge for many companies is to develop

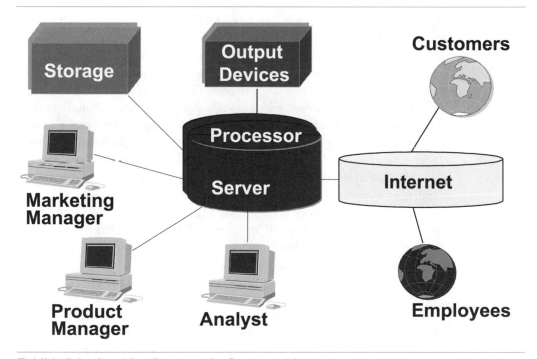

Exhibit 5.1   Simplified Diagram of a Computer Network

database systems that have the capability to handle the transition to Internet commerce.

Software comprises the programs of instructions to the hardware that allow data to be filed, sorted, analyzed, input, and output. Hardware and software have to be compatible. Therefore, it is advantageous to develop databases as a system rather than purchase hardware and software independently.

IBM and other companies offer preconfigured systems for specific purposes. These preconfigured systems can be valuable for companies that are concerned about compatibility problems. For example, IBM combines S/390 server technology with database, data mining, and operating system software. IBM also provides technical support on the system. This system will facilitate the database marketer's ability to store and analyze customer data (IBM, 2001).

In contrast, some companies prefer to configure their own systems. Although this takes more time and more expertise, it has advantages. The company can select hardware and software from a number of vendors to optimize the system for their specific needs. Recently, hardware and software manufacturers have been more cooperative in developing products that are compatible. This means that it is easier to find optimal components for database systems that are compatible.

Database Hardware

Database hardware currently can be divided into three categories: (1) mainframe, for large databases, (2) midrange, for medium to large databases, and (3) PC, for small to medium databases.

The specifications of these categories change as new generations of computer technology are developed. Computers have been able to handle larger and larger databases. Powerful midrange computers can handle databases that previously required mainframes, and PCs can handle databases that previously required midrange computers. However, as technology has advanced, so has the need for more extensive databases. Internet commerce and the global linking of databases require more powerful technology. Consequently, the predicted demise of the mainframe computer never occurred.

Mainframe computers, such as the IBM 390 series, can hold millions of customer records and are still important for large database marketers. Physically, newer mainframe computers have been reduced in size due to technological innovations. Older mainframes can span several hundred square feet and weigh more than 30,000 pounds. Newer mainframes can be less than 60 square feet and weigh a few thousand pounds. The newer mainframes also cost less, are more energy efficient, and generally are faster. Mainframe computers are also called enterprise servers and superservers because they are used for large client/server networks and high-volume Internet commerce sites. First Union Corporation, for example, uses an

Amdahl mainframe system. First Union provides financial services to more than 16 million customers throughout the East Coast and other parts of the United States. First Union needed a highly reliable system for its customers who rely on the bank for cash from its ATMs. In addition, customers want to be able to do banking any time of the day, either in person or over the Internet. The requirements of First Union's system warranted the use of powerful mainframes ("First Union," 2001).

Midrange Computers

Midrange computers, also called minicomputers, are used by many organizations that don't need the computing power of mainframes. The IBM AS/400 is an example of a midrange computer. Midrange computers have also been used as network servers to manage Internet Web sites and internal and external networks. In some applications, midrange computers interact with mainframes.

Tiffany & Company, noted for its jewelry and home décor items, is an example of a company that uses several midrange computers. Tiffany has retail stores around the world and a catalog business. A primary objective was to allow managers to easily access data in order to understand and respond to changing customer needs. The system is integrated across functional business areas and provides a unified decision-support system ("Tiffany & Company," 2001).

PCs

PCs, also called microcomputers, have evidenced a tremendous advance in technology in the past few years. PCs now have power that exceeds the mainframes of previous computer generations. The range of PCs is quite wide, varying from desktop units to notebooks to handheld units. A number of companies manufacture PCs, including Dell, IBM, Gateway, Compaq, and Hewlett Packard. Many companies now produce customized computers for individual customers. Interactive Web sites (e.g., www.dell.com) allow customers to configure and order a computer. Customers can select components such as processors, memory, disk storage, modems, sound cards, video boards, monitors, and keyboards. Software such as operating systems and business application programs can also be selected and loaded into the computer.

PCs can hold more than a million database records at this time, and their capacity continues to grow. They are often linked with mainframes and midrange computers in a network. There are substantial advantages to using network systems for marketing databases. Many midsized and large companies house the database on mainframe or midrange computers and use PCs to access data for manipulation and analysis. Product managers and other marketers can analyze and track the performance of marketing programs from their PCs.

Databases housed on PCs are very common. For example, single location retailers of all types develop customer databases on PCs. In addition to handling accounting functions, suites of programs for retailers also allow the small business owner to analyze customer databases and link the databases to other software used for mailings. Recently, small businesses have been able to establish e-commerce sites with PC-based software. One of the concerns is the ability of the database software to be upgraded as the company grows. Therefore, more vendors of small business database software are making their programs compatible with other software and hardware.

Hardware Decision Factors

When hardware from a particular vendor is evaluated, a number of factors must be considered. These include cost, performance in terms of speed and capacity, reliability, compatibility, and service support. In addition, it is desirable to have hardware that can be expanded and upgraded easily and can handle the demands of a wide range of users and their processing requirements.

MIS professionals have to consider both current and future needs of the organization. Lower-cost hardware may have limitations for future expansion as the organization's processing needs grow. Changing hardware and software is expensive and disruptive to the organization, so expandability is a high priority for many companies. Some companies with larger databases have faced (and are still facing) a long conversion process as they upgrade older mainframe systems (legacy systems). This conversion process can take years and cost millions of dollars.

Database Software

To run a database, several software programs are required. Operating systems software, like Windows NT and UNIX, provide a user interface and manage computer resources, tasks, and files. Other programs such as peripheral controllers, virus protection, and data security programs are also necessary to support the information system.

Database software controls the storage, organization, analysis, and interfaces between people and databases. Smaller organizations that run their businesses on PCs can use general-purpose relational databases like Microsoft Access (see Exhibit 5.2) and Lotus Approach.

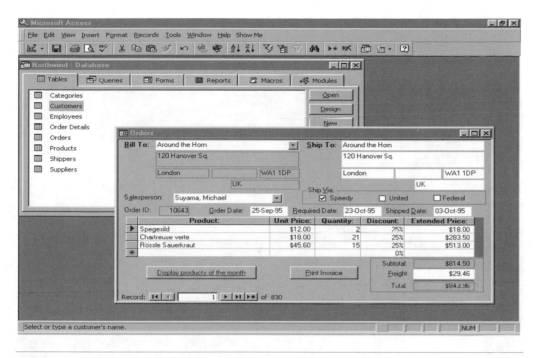

Exhibit 5.2   A Screen From Microsoft Access

These programs are easy to use and are adaptable to various business applications. Specialized database software such as ACT! (see Exhibit 5.3) and GoldMine allow small- to medium-sized businesses to manage customer relationships. Some of these customer contact programs allow multiple users and interfacing to Web sites for e-commerce.

Larger organizations that have more complex databases and run on mainframe or midrange-based systems often have database administrators and support staff that manage the database for the entire organization. These organizations have database management systems (DBMS) (see Exhibit 5.4), which are a set of computer programs that control the development, maintenance, and use of the database.

Oracle, SAP, Sybase, and DB2 are database programs used by larger organizations. Oracle, for example, offers database programs for a wide range of business applications. These programs are adaptable to many different business functions and industries. Oracle Marketing is a suite of applications designed to aid in the planning, execution, and analysis of marketing campaigns. Oracle also offers a suite of programs for Internet commerce applications. Companies like Amazon, eBay, and E*TRADE are reported to use Oracle software.

Because there are several producers of reliable and adaptable database programs, there are fewer reasons for companies to write database

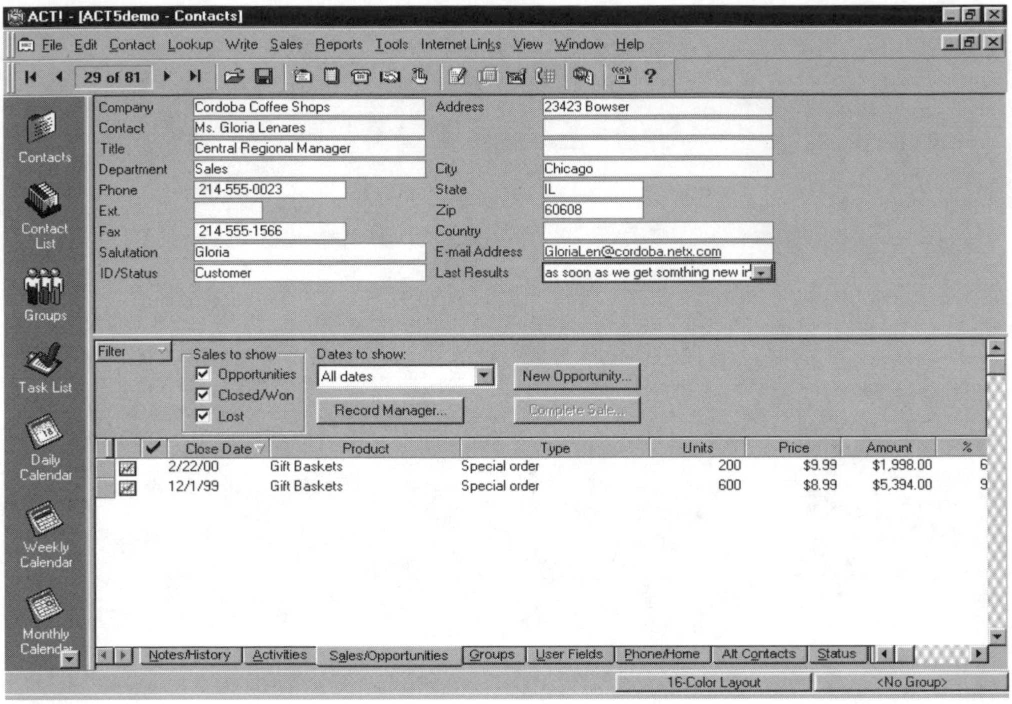

Exhibit 5.3   A Screen From ACT!

programs from scratch. Developing database software for large business applications is a complex and time-consuming process. The major database producers possess the expertise and support staff to continually improve and expand the database applications. In addition, they are constantly obtaining feedback from the companies that are using their software. Therefore, it would be difficult for a single organization to match this level of database development expertise.

It should be noted that many direct marketing organizations have developed their own database programs over the course of many years. This was a common practice before the widespread availability of commercial database programs. These companies have been constantly upgrading their databases using in-house programmers. As the business evolves, the company modifies the database programs or adds other programs to increase access or analysis capabilities. Therefore, these companies have a large investment in their current database, and regardless of the advantages of new technologies, it is not beneficial for them to change database systems. Some of these companies will upgrade in small steps to reduce the impact on daily operations.

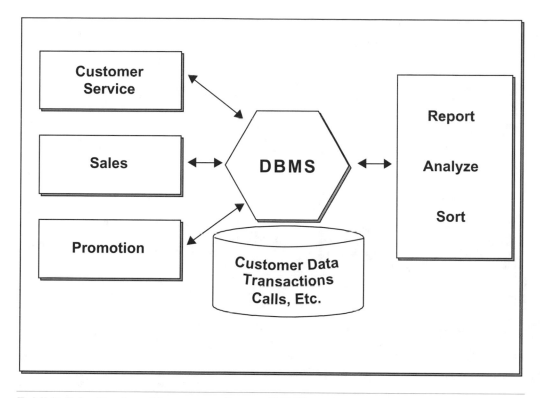

Exhibit 5.4   Database Management System (DBMS)

Database System Organization

Database systems must be organized in some manner to allow data to be retrieved. These systems can be categorized as either structured or relational, depending on how the data are stored. Data in **structured databases** come from a single source, whereas data from relational databases come from multiple sources called tables. Recently developed marketing databases are usually relational. However, some larger marketing databases that were developed in the past on mainframes still have a structured design.

Structured Databases

Structured databases can be further classified as flat, hierarchical, or network. In flat files, data are accessed in a sequential manner, and it is difficult to add new data fields. For example, to access the customer John Smith in a flat file that is organized alphabetically, you have to pass all customers with names ending with A, B, C, D, and so on. Flat files can have fixed or variable formats. With fixed formats, all customer records are of the same length, and data input to fields is limited by the space allocated. For example, if the

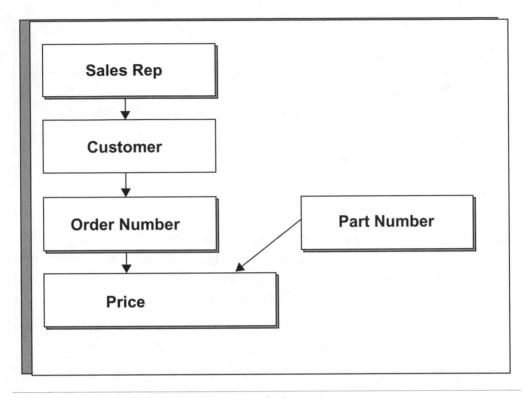

Exhibit 5.5 Example of Network Structure Paths

field for a last name is fixed at 15 spaces, all last names longer than 15 characters will have to be truncated or somehow abbreviated. The number of fields are also limited in a fixed format database. For some database applications, it becomes impractical to use the fixed format. If you expect a large variation in purchase activity, a variable file format is more efficient than a fixed format. Using the fixed format, sufficient space needs to be allocated on each record to anticipate the largest number of transactions possible. With the variable format, the size of the field adjusts according to the number of transactions. Indexed flat files are linked together by a unique customer code. The index reduces the time needed to search through the file.

Hierarchical databases use a tree structure for searching data. Each data element is related to only one element above it, so the relationships between the data items are called one-to-many. Although hierarchical databases use a predetermined path, access to data is quicker, because the data items are linked in a meaningful way.

Network structures still use predetermined paths to access data. However, they allow many-to-many relationships. That is, there may be two or more paths to access a data item. In the network structure in Exhibit 5.5, the data item "price" can be accessed through two paths. In a hierarchical structure, there would be only one path to access "price."

Exhibit 5.6   Application of Structured Versus Relational Database

Structured	Relational
Data relationships form a natural order or hierarchy	Flexibility to examine complex relationships
Data items do not change much over time	Ability to look at the big picture
Fine-tuning important	Storage efficiency important
Computer power conservation important	Development speed important

Source: Adapted from Jackson & Wang, from *Strategic Database Marketing* (1997, p. 128).

Relational Databases

Relational databases have become the database of choice for most organizations that are developing new databases systems. Relational database programs are available for PCs, midrange, and mainframe computers. No predetermined structural relationships between data items are needed to access information. Data are organized into tables that can interact with each other. For integrity of data, similar data items in different tables are linked to each other. Changes in one item must be accompanied by changes in the corresponding item(s). Relational databases offer a high degree of flexibility compared to structured databases.

Multidimensional databases are a variation of relational databases. Instead of using tables that are two-dimensional, multidimensional databases are structured on many dimensions. This is useful for some analytic procedures in which dimensions could represent product category, region, distribution channel, and time.

Comparison of Structured and Relational Databases

Although relational databases have some distinct advantages for flexibility, there are still reasons to consider structured databases. In the past and for some current larger systems, run time to update relational databases would be excessive compared to structured flat file architecture. However, as processing speed continues to increase and the cost of computer memory decreases, the advantages of structured databases will diminish. Exhibit 5.6 summarizes when to use structured or relational databases.

Structured Query Language (SQL) and Data Analysis

Data analysis is an essential element of strategic database marketing. Some software programs make the extraction of names for promotion and analysis easier and more reliable. SQL is a widely used programming language for relational databases. In contrast to third-generation programming languages like COBOL, SQL is relatively easy to use. It allows data to be extracted from large databases for promotion and analysis. For example, with just a few SQL commands, customers who have been sent a specific promotion can be easily selected. Once these customers are extracted from the database, additional analysis can be performed.

Statistical analyses are commonly performed on database files. Because of the availability of reliable statistical analysis programs, few organizations write their own statistical programs. **SAS** is an example of a statistical analysis program that is widely used by database marketers. SAS procedures are usually performed on portions of the database, so data extraction and conditioning is necessary before an analysis can be performed. SAS is often used for modeling, which allows the marketer to determine who the best customers are, based on certain characteristics. In Chapters 6 to 14, we examine statistical procedures in more detail.

Organizational Considerations in Technical Database Design

As we discussed, marketing professionals will not have primary responsibility in most organizations for selecting the hardware and software that will be used in a database. In most large organizations, the IS department (sometimes referred to as IT, information technology) is responsible for the technical development. Often a cross-functional development team is established to develop the database. Members of the development team should have a common goal: to develop an effective and efficient database that can be used to achieve organizational objectives.

In practice, this is not an easy goal to achieve. Marketing and IS people have different perspectives and sometimes different definitions of key objectives. As part of this cross-functional team, marketing professionals should strive to look at the database development process from the perspective of the IS professionals, and the IS professionals should strive to look at the process from the perspective of marketing professionals. Stephen Belfer (1998) pointed to the different perspectives that marketing and IS professionals possess based on their backgrounds. Marketers tend to be "project" people. Marketing programs must be changed in order to respond to changing market forces. As one marketing campaign ends, another begins. In contrast, IS professionals are much more "process" oriented, because their role is to maintain and enhance the overall information technology infrastructure of the company.

Individual hardware or software projects are only components of the ongoing development of the greater information system. Therefore, Marketing has to understand that IS has to consider not only Marketing's immediate needs but also how specific hardware and software decisions affect the entire information system in the long term. In addition, because IS may be working within the constraints of existing hardware and software, it may not be feasible for them to simply purchase and install a commercially available database program.

Another difference in perspectives involves defining the characteristics of an ideal database system. IS would tend to be biased in the direction of developing systems that are technically efficient. That is, the goal is to minimize storage and processing requirements. On the other hand, Marketing sees the ideal system as flexible and readily accessible. Flexible and accessible systems tend to be less efficient.

To facilitate the development process, Marketing should clearly specify the following:

- Number of records and fields required
  Present and future needs should be considered.
- How and when the records and fields need to be updated
  The required cycle for database maintenance should be specified.
- How data or records will be entered or updated
  This should consider data from external sources such as lists and determine if customer data come from multiple sources such as phone, mail, and Internet.
- How and by whom the database will be accessed
  For example, product managers and analysts should have access to the database from their PCs. Internet and other remote access capabilities should also be considered.
- Data analysis requirements
  This should include sorting and selection capabilities, statistical analysis packages, and periodic reporting requirements.
- Data security considerations
  Specify who within the organization should have access to data. Data manipulation privileges may also need to be restricted. With Internet commerce, the issue of security becomes more complex. This must be resolved through consultation with data security experts.

When IS receives these requirements from Marketing, they will determine what software and hardware will be required. On the basis of their background and personal experience, some marketing personnel may be able to suggest or require certain software programs. For example, because certain marketers or analysts are familiar with the SAS statistical package, Marketing may want to design the analysis capabilities of the database around SAS.

Outsourcing: The Process
to Select a Database Provider

In Chapter 3, we discussed customer data requirements. When examining the customer data requirements, an assessment of corporate information needs is conducted. When corporate data needs relative to the customer base are assessed and the associated data sources are identified, a corporation must make a decision: build and manage the database in house or outsource to an external vendor. This decision will be influenced largely by the number and complexity of data feeds required to build the database. A company with a single data feed may opt to build and manage the database development internally. A company with a dozen data feeds may opt to place the database maintenance and development in the hands of experts. In addition, if the situation is to create a marketing database for the first time, a company would be well served to hire a consultant because of the complexities and time-consuming nature of planning for a corporate database.

The advantages to **outsourcing** the building and management of the database include the following:

♦ The organization does not need to maintain the staff to administer the technological or data processing support for the marketing database.
♦ Existing IT staff can perform their functions with minimum disruption.
♦ The task of building and maintaining a database is placed with experts.
♦ External vendors are more conversant with cutting-edge technology for management and analysis of data than internal staff.

Because many organizations consider the marketing database a key asset of the organization and database marketing activities as a strategic advantage, there are important disadvantages to outsourcing:

♦ Loss of direct control of database management and functioning
♦ Outsourced techniques are not guaranteed to be proprietary
♦ Possible uncertainty of the long-term stability (change of management and personnel, mergers, solvency, etc.) of the database management vendor

Considering these advantages and disadvantages, the organization may opt to contract with a database management vendor to house and update their database. This relationship works best when both the client and the vendor are very clear on the parameters of their respective responsibilities. The recommended process to select an external database provider is shown below:

- Assess internal needs (required whether or not the database build is outsourced)
- Formalize needs into a specification for a proposal
- Distribute project specification to qualified vendors
- Evaluate proposals versus corporate needs and budget
- Make selection

Internal Needs Assessment

In this phase, all constituents must be interviewed to determine how a database might serve them. This interview process will help evaluate who the end users of the database will be. In particular, functional areas of Marketing (Advertising/Circulation in a publishing environment), Finance, Corporate Planning, Customer Service, Fulfillment, List Marketing, and Online Marketing should be interviewed to identify the

- Data used in each department as part of the job function and its source
- Frequency of data update required to perform their job

Once interviews have been conducted, an assessment of the various data sources should be made to determine which data sources used in the organization are specific to customer activity and belong in a customer-level database.

The first step is to identify the needs of all areas. Within the needs assessment, it is vital to know what data are used and how they are used. The usage of the information is particularly important, because time-saving efficiencies may be realized as a byproduct of the compilation of data and should be recognized in calculating the database's ROI (return on investment).

Following this data assessment, the size and number of data feeds can be ascertained. Companies with large IT departments may decide they have the ability to bring the requisite data feeds and information together. Other companies may decide that the information feeds are too varied and they lack the staff to manage the process of building a database on a routine basis.

All constituents should understand that a marketing database is not designed to fully meet the data needs of all departments but rather to be a repository that provides the best view of customer behavior and attribute information. For instance, if a finance function is to assess returns quarterly and this information is provided by reports from the product warehouse via fulfillment, a database can provide this information as well. Both database and warehouse reports should reflect the same level of returns monthly. But a database will provide additional information so that a return profile can be developed for a customer. Conversely, warehouse reports will show total returns and the proportion returned to stock, important from a finance perspective, which may not be captured on a database.

Formalize Needs Into a Specification for a Proposal. To gather external vendor proposals for a specific business needs, a detailed specification must be written and distributed to external vendors. A detailed document designed to aid in the development of proposals is called a request for proposal (RFP). A detailed assessment of database needs is essential or the specification will be out of sync with the actual database requirements.

In addition to identifying all the data sources accessed by information users, it is important to communicate

- The size in terms of number of records
- Types of records from each data feed (e.g., fulfillment, mail files, Internet, list enhancement, internal surveys)
- How data from various feeds relate to each other
- Specific tables that will require maintenance (e.g., product tables, offer tables, list tables)
- Timing of data flow
- Changes in business (as it relates to information feeds, e.g., increased circulation, cancellation cycles)
- Requirements for file maintenance such as NCOA

In a specification document, it is important to outline in detail exactly what data will be processed, how they should be processed, and with what frequency they will be processed. In addition, you should specify the analytic needs associated with your database.

Many database vendors have proprietary analytic packages that are used with their database structures. Other database designs are generic enough so that off-the-shelf analytic packages can be used with the database architecture. It is important to include in the specification document the type of analyses required with the database. The proposal from the vendor should therefore address the analytic needs.

Distribute Project Specifications to Qualified Vendors. Following a comprehensive development of specifications, the RFP document is distributed to vendors. The selection of vendors to provide proposals should be dictated by the following guidelines:

- Familiarity with the company based on reputation or industry word of mouth
- Vendor's experience with industry (catalog, Internet, publisher, retail, b-to-b, etc.)
- Particular strength in an area of importance to your project
- Breadth of services available from a larger organization

For example, if a company marketing upscale products is seeking a database vendor, it makes sense to include a database provider who is affiliated with a list company that specializes in the affluent market. The client who markets upscale products will receive synergies not available from a provider who lacks resources in marketing to the affluent market.

Evaluate Proposals Versus Corporate Needs and Budget. When all proposals are returned, they should be compared to each other and the original specification document for completeness and soundness in project planning. Points of comparison include the following:

◆ Timing
◆ Cost
◆ Technology
◆ Software
◆ Service levels
◆ Support team expertise (years, industry, related projects, etc.)
◆ Client training programs
◆ Performance guarantees
◆ Response time to requests
◆ References by existing clients

Attributes of all bidders should be compared side by side and discussed by the management committee charged with making the decision. The vendor proposals should contain all the information requested in the specification. The organization of each proposal will be unique, however, so it may be time consuming and confusing for a nontechnical person to read. A consultant can be a worthwhile resource in providing comparisons across the various dimensions among all vendors.

Make a Selection. In general, the proposals are evaluated and finalists are selected (i.e., some group of proposals are eliminated and others representing a better fit are retained for further consideration). Vendor companies whose proposals are retained may be invited to formally present their results. In this case, a dialogue can occur to identify any questions relative to the proposals. Following this stage, a company should have enough information to select a vendor.

Phases of Database Development

Whether built in-house or outside the organization, database development can be complex and time consuming. To expedite development and increase the probability of successful completion, a systematic process has been proposed. Jackson and Wang (1997, pp. 146–148) recommend the following four phases of database development:

1. System Design: User and data requirements, systems, implementation, costs

2. System development: Physical development and testing

3. System implementation: Live testing in final form

4. Ongoing management

In the initial stage, system requirements are gathered from Marketing and other departments. At that point, IS can propose a system that will meet the requirements and estimate implementation schedules and costs. Marketing must make sure that the requirements they submit are clear and complete.

Once the proposal is approved, the needed hardware and software are configured and tested. Smaller working models or prototypes may be used to test the system. Depending on the organization, Phase 2 may require major acquisitions of hardware and software or only minor modifications to existing systems.

Transition from prototypes to full working systems is the next phase. For new database systems, this transition phase provides an opportunity to evaluate the system with real data and usage situations. This "live" testing of the system is even more critical for organizations that currently have large database systems in place. A disruption to database processing during the transition phase could result in a substantial loss in revenues. Therefore, organizations will continue to run the old system along with the new system until all aspects of the new system are checked. During this phase, Marketing should systematically check as many aspects of the system as possible that have an impact on their functioning. Analysis, reporting, access, data updating, coding, tracking, and so on, should be evaluated and reported to IS.

The final phase, ongoing management, is never completed. As we discussed, many aspects of the database need to be updated on a regular basis. The schedule of maintenance should correspond to the system requirements in Phase 1. As the database system evolves over time or business conditions change, new updating requirements may be needed. For example, to meet customer needs in an increasingly competitive environment, more frequent data updating may be required than originally specified.

Comments on Technological Development of the Database

The process of database development can be expedited if there is cooperation among the functional areas of the business. People from other functional areas often remark that marketing personnel are not sympathetic to the challenges and limitations of the other functional areas. Marketers could make similar remarks about the other functional areas. Although conflicts between functional areas are often unavoidable, the degree of disruption can be mitigated. Marketers, by clearly defining their database requirements and being receptive to IS's perspective, should be able to help expedite the development process.

Chapter Summary

Although marketers usually don't have primary responsibility for the technical development of a database system, they should be aware of basic technology concepts. A range of hardware and software options allows database systems to be adapted to an organization's requirements. Within these options are certain limitations and advantages that affect how the database is used. Marketers usually want database systems that allow maximum flexibility to add fields as new marketing programs are initiated and allow easy extraction of selected data for timely analysis. The organizational considerations in database systems development can be complex and often require a multidisciplinary team to optimize the process. In many organizations, Marketing's role in database development focuses on detailing their requirements for the system. Therefore, Marketing should strive to provide a clear definition of not only present needs but also anticipated future needs. In addition to detailing the specification for the database system, the organization has to determine who will be responsible for database development. Outsourcing some or all of the development is an option for many organizations. Regardless of the database specifications and development responsibilities, database systems should be implemented in systematic stages in order to minimize disruptions to the organization and allow sufficient testing of elements of the system.

Review Questions

1. What is Marketing's primary role in database development? Provide an example of an organization where Marketing's role in database development might be more extensive.

2. What are some hardware options for a database system?

3. What are the advantages and disadvantages of using commercial database software packages versus developing database programs from scratch?

4. How is a structured database different from a relational database? What are the advantages and disadvantages of each?

5. What are some of the organizational and cross-functional factors in database development? Consider outsourcing options.

6. Discuss the implications of phasing in a new or upgraded database system.

6 The Analysis Sample

Having spent the past year helping build DSI's new consumer database, Keri Lee was ready for a change. She accepted a new job as senior product manager at Inside Source, a 3-year-old magazine covering the political scene in Washington, D.C. Although she was sad to leave DSI, she knew this was the right career move.

*In her new position at Inside Source, Keri would be responsible for all mailing campaigns to house names. Her first assignment was to better target ex-subscribers for reactivation. In the past, Inside Source had simply applied **manual selects** to the universe of ex-subscribers for promotional purposes.*

To meet her goal, she first had to determine if appropriate samples existed of ex-subscribers promoted in the past. She will need to analyze these past samples to determine the exact target market for reactivation promotions.

Direct marketers have an advantage over retailers and other marketers in that they can quickly test new marketing strategies and validate the results, if they have a well-maintained database. The test is only as good as the customer data available for name selection and analysis. A poorly maintained database will result in poor decisions, which in turn will cost the enterprise through missed opportunities.

New direct marketing product or promotional tests (format, creative, price) begin with obtaining a **sample** of the names from your database or list broker. This sample of names is then sent the test promotion, product, or offer. Once results of the test are final, this sample will be analyzed to determine, for example, the percentage of responders, the payment rate, or the unique characteristics separating responders from nonresponders.

This chapter discusses how to properly select names for testing, the components comprising the analysis sample, the importance of the "point-in-time" data residing on the analysis sample, and the purpose of splitting the sample into two parts: one for analysis and the other for validation.

How We Sample

A sample is a subset of customer records and a random selection from the universe of interest on the direct marketer's database. For example, ACME Direct, a direct marketer of books, music, videos, and magazines, is interested in testing a new book concept. The universe of interest is the most active book buyers residing on their database; therefore, the sample will be comprised of names selected from this universe. A random and **representative sample** of names from its most active book buyer segment will be test promoted (see Exhibit 6.1).

Representative Samples

To be meaningful, the sample must be representative of the entire population of interest. A representative sample is a sample accurately reflecting the population of interest from which the direct marketer draws inferences. For a sample to be representative, no members of the population of interest are purposely excluded from the sample. To determine the effectiveness of a new format test sent to a specific segment of customers residing on the database, for example, the direct marketer cannot restrict the sample to only those names living in New York. If this new format is sent only to New Yorkers, the expected results will not be representative of the entire population, but only that of New Yorkers. Some direct marketers overlook this very important concept and assume they can apply test results from one population to another. This may work in some cases, but not always. Be careful.

Typically, the only names that should be eliminated from testing are names eliminated in **rollouts** such as

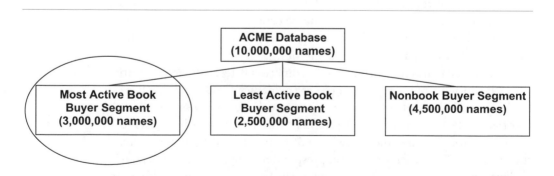

Exhibit 6.1   The Customer Segment to Be Sampled for the New Book Test Promotion

- ◆ DMA do-not-promotes
- ◆ Frauds
- ◆ Credit risk accounts

When testing new promotions, some direct marketers also consider eliminating

- ◆ Names recently promoted for other marketing tests
- ◆ States or cities such as Washington, D.C., known to have strict promotional restrictions. This is especially important if the new test promotion has not yet been fully reviewed by legal counsel.

Random Samples

A sample not taken randomly yields biased and misleading results. A **random sample** is one in which every member of the sample is equally likely to be chosen, ensuring a composition similar to that of the population. Pulling names one after another from the beginning of a geographically sequenced customer database will result in a geographically biased sample. In this case, depending on the size of the sample being drawn in comparison to the size of the total population, some regions may not be represented in the sample.

To ensure random samples, many direct marketers utilize what is called **nth selects**. For example, ACME Direct maintains a database of 10,000,000 names. To test a new format to a random sample of 10,000 names from their entire database, the direct marketer begins by selecting one name on the database, choosing every 1,000th (10,000,000/10,000) name thereafter. The result is a random sample of 10,000 names representative of the entire population or database.

A programmer in your company's marketing services group or service bureau can program nth selects. Most companies have an nth select computer program requiring the user to simply enter the sample size required and the size of the universe to be sampled. The program selects the starting name, selects every nth name thereafter, and outputs names for the test. If your company does not have such a routine, contact a direct marketing service bureau for assistance. Many are listed in trade journals such as *DM News* or *Direct* magazine.

Sample Usage

Testing is the foundation upon which direct marketing is built. With correct test planning, a direct marketer can

- Evaluate new product offerings
- Gauge the reaction to price changes by measuring the associated increase or decrease in response rates
- Determine the impact of a new promotional format change on response, payment, or conversion rates
- Identify the target market for a new product test, for example, by reviewing the characteristics (based on internal and external data) of the responders to the product offering for any patterns that might explain why some people responded and others did not
- Gain insight about specific customer groups or segments based on customer profiles using any internal and external customer data

Creation of the Analysis Sample

To determine the unique characteristics that separate responders from nonresponders of a new product offering or promotion, you will need a **frozen file**. At the exact time customers are selected for a test promotion, a special file must be created containing all customers selected for the promotion along with their customer data residing on the database. This includes their name, address, unique customer identification number, plus all internal **RFM (recency, frequency, and monetary) data elements** (promotion, purchase, and payment history), and all enhancement information (external data elements). By doing so, you will have created a file that is reflective of the customer's status at the point in time of the promotion. Think of this file as a **snapshot** of each customer's record prior to sending the promotion. This snapshot is also referred to as a frozen file.

You cannot conduct an analysis for determining the unique characteristics that separate responders from nonresponders without such a frozen file. In other words, you cannot create such a file for analysis after the fact by pulling the customer information off the database at a later time. It will not be reflective of what the customers looked like at the time they made their purchase decision. Basing decisions on such data yields misleading results.

To illustrate why point-in-time customer data are important in making sound marketing decisions, consider the following example:

> One year ago, you sent to 10,000 names from the database a special Club Med vacation package known to be of interest only to young married couples *without* children. If you examine the sample today (1 year later) to determine the characteristics that uniquely separated responders from nonresponders and use the customer characteristics as of today, you may be misled about what a responder looks like. Some responders to the test promotion may have had a baby since the

time of the original test (1 year ago). As a result, you will erroneously conclude that people with babies also are interested in this vacation package. This is false, because at the time of the promotion, when the couple made their decision to order the vacation package or not, they were childless.

The process to create a frozen file for analysis purposes is as follows:

1. Select names (including all customer data) to be test promoted

2. On the database, using a unique key code (see Chapter 4), mark the names that were selected for this test promotion

3. Create a file of the selected names with their address and customer ID information only and send it to the letter shop for promotion

4. Create a file of the selected names with all customer data for later analysis (the frozen file)

5. Once customer responses come in,

   ♦ Update the customer records on the database with response information, using the unique key code

   ♦ Update the frozen file with response information

You are now ready to conduct the analysis to determine the characteristics that separate responders from nonresponders based on the frozen file updated with response information.

Frozen files should be created for all product and list tests. These files will be needed to determine the target market definitions for large-scale rollouts.

Whether or not you should create frozen files for creative, format, or pricing tests really depends on your capacity to save such files and the likelihood that they will be needed. Many direct marketers do not. Why? When you conduct these types of tests, your only interest is in assessing the response rates to determine test winners. In other words, most direct marketers are not interested in analyzing the customer data at an individual level but rather at a summary aggregate level by promotion key (see Chapter 4).

We recommend that frozen analysis files for *all* tests (creative, format, price, product, and list) be saved, if at all possible. This allows the direct marketer to be in a position to determine the reason for any skewed results. For example, a creative test panel shows an abnormally high (or low) response rate. A saved frozen file allows the direct marketer to determine whether or not the names selected for the promotion were representative of the population of concern. Perhaps some inactive customers were accidentally selected and promoted, whereas only active customers were desired. Again, to determine this, you must have a frozen file showing what the customer looked like at the time they were selected.

Methods of Saving Point-in-Time Sample Data

Saving a snapshot of all customer data for every test sample promoted is expensive and costly. Depending on the size of the direct marketer's testing program, this can quickly create major computer storage capacity issues.

To circumvent this problem, some smaller direct marketing companies save an entire copy of their marketing database regularly (e.g., quarterly). When they require analysis of a product promotion, they create an analysis sample on the fly by identifying the names promoted for the test (and who responded) via a unique key code residing on the database. Once the names are identified on the database, customer data from the frozen customer file closest but prior to the actual promotion date are merged and an analysis sample created. This process is illustrated in Exhibit 6.2.

The danger in this method is that the customer data to be appended to the test names may not reflect the customers' status near the time of the promotion. In Exhibit 6.2, the appended data come from 2 months prior to the actual promotion date. Ideally, the customer data should represent the customers' status as close to the actual promotion date as possible. As a result, it is preferable to save a snapshot of the customer data with each test sample. However, if your company cannot do this due to data storage capacity issues, this is the preferred alternative. Do not merge a promotion file with a version of the customer database reflecting the customers' status after the date of the promotion. All customer promotion data would have been updated to reflect the test promotion for those in the sample. This would be misleading.

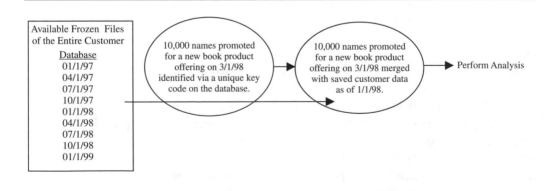

Exhibit 6.2   Merging Saved Customer File Data With Test Names in Preparation for Analysis

Analysis and Validation Samples

Before analysis of any sample is performed, the sample is typically split in two. The analysis is often performed on two thirds of the sample and the results validated or calibrated on the remaining one third of the sample.

A sample is just that—a sample—and samples have a certain level of error associated with them. The validation sample is used to ensure that the analyst does not make erroneous conclusions based on the error variance associated with the sample. For example, an analysis sample may suggest that a high proportion of responders to a particular offer have blue eyes. However, when the validation sample is considered, the correlation between ordering and having blue eyes cannot be confirmed with any statistical significance. Creating an analysis and validation sample is a very important step in the analysis process flow. We will address fully the importance of the validation sample in Chapter 11.

Application of Analysis Findings

Once the target market is defined, based on the analysis of a frozen file, you are ready to select names from the entire database meeting your criteria. When you prepare to select names from the entire database based on an analysis of a frozen file, ensure that the data residing on the customer database are current. For example, suppose an analysis determined that "being married with no children" is the target market for a particular product offering. When you go to the database to actually select names based on the criteria, all data residing on the database should be current. If not, you risk selecting, for example, a person previously married but now divorced or not selecting a person previously single but now married. Make sure you are selecting the correct names by keeping the information residing on the database fresh and relevant.

Chapter Summary

Assessing new product or promotional tests involve the taking of proper samples of customers. If the sample is not representative of the population of concern, the results will not be projectable. In addition, if the sample is not randomly taken, the results will be misleading and biased. When interest revolves around building response models for certain product tests to determine the target market, a frozen file must be taken. Such a file contains the status of all customers as they looked at the time the promotion was sent. Analyzing a sample that contains customer data not frozen at the time of the promotion will yield misleading results about the definition of the target market. Because every sample has a certain amount of error associated with it, analysis samples are often split in two prior to any analysis. The analysis is often performed on two thirds of the sample and the results validated on the remaining one third of the sample.

Review Questions

1. What does it mean for a sample to be representative?

2. How do direct marketers select names to ensure that they are taken randomly?

3. What is a frozen file and why is it important?

4. If a direct marketer does not have the necessary resources to create frozen files for every test sample promoted, what other option is available to create such a file for analysis purposes?

5. Why is it important to set aside a portion of the sample prior to analysis for validation?

7

Analyzing and Manipulating Customer Data

Although Keri Lee found that no saved analysis samples existed at Inside Source, they did save snapshots of the entire customer file on a quarterly basis for back-up purposes, as discussed in Chapter 6. As a result, Keri and her analyst were able to construct an analysis sample on the fly by using these saved snapshots of the entire customer file. On these saved files, they identified, via unique key codes, the customers who were sent various promotions, and they reconstructed a point-in-time sample for analysis purposes.

Once constructed, Keri and her analyst identified all available customer data. In viewing what is typically called the data dictionary, they counted some 235 different pieces of customer data available for analysis purposes, ranging from age information to the number of years on the database to zip-level information pertaining to income and home value.

Next, they ensured that they had a solid understanding of what each data element was measuring, how it was defined, and the maintenance rules for updating. Once they understood this, they created tabulated views of the 235 data elements using a software package to help them identify those data elements that most correlated with response. In addition, they further massaged and manipulated the data to create even more powerful predictors of response. In other words, they squeezed every bit of predictive strength out of the data by creating and assessing data interactions, ratios, and time series variables. They left no stone unturned. After all, this was Inside Source's first attempt at properly defining a target market based on an analysis, and they wanted to be successful in their efforts.

Having tested a new product or promotional offer to a random sample of names from the database, the direct marketer is now ready to determine what characteristics separate responders from nonresponders in order to help define the target market in preparation for a large-scale rollout.

Before we can begin the discussion of building the target definition or target model, we must first discuss how to examine the customer data that are ultimately used in the definition or model. This involves a solid under-standing of the customer file and the data it contains, which greatly assists in the development of (a) the strongest target definition or model for determining who to promote and not promote for an upcoming campaign and (b) the most effective segmentation scheme in which to implement your marketing campaigns.

Once we have an understanding of the data residing on the customer database, we are ready to view and manipulate the customer data to determine what characteristics best separate responders from non-responders. In particular, we discuss important techniques of data manipu-lation. Once learned, these data manipulation techniques will help you define better selects, maximize the effectiveness of your segmentation of the database, or choose variables as input to a regression response model.

Getting to Know Your Data

A direct marketing professional new to a company must develop an intimate knowledge of the company's customer data prior to any attempt to develop a name selection methodology for purposes of promotion or treatment. It is a time-consuming exercise but integral to ensuring that erroneous and costly assumptions are avoided during the analysis and modeling phases. The familiarization process should include meeting with the staff responsible for creating and maintaining the marketing data as well as those responsible for applying data updating rules. A detailed comprehension of the logic of the customer file and the rules for updating each piece of information on the file is crucial for analysis. Questions to ask may include the following:

- Does a partial payment for a product order update (increment) the "Total Products Paid" field?
- If a partial payment for a product order increments the "Total Products Paid," does it do so for all product lines? What are the exceptions?
- If a member of the company's music club orders a CD rack from the club's monthly catalog, does payment for that order update the "Total Music Club Dollars Paid" field? If not, in what field is this payment recorded?
- If a customer orders and pays and then immediately cancels, is the order in the "Total Products Paid" field eliminated? Is the "Total Products Ordered" field adjusted?

The criteria for selecting names for a product promotion is only as good as the data residing on the database. For example, a direct marketer may select customers having "Total Products Paid ≥ 5 Within the Last 24 Months," assuming these customers have paid in full for at least five products within the last 24 months. Given the data field name, this reasonable assumption may drive a further assumption that these customers are good payers. But are they? Or does this company also update this field with partial product payments? Does this mean a direct marketer may be selecting customers who have never paid in full for a product? This simple example demonstrates how easily direct marketers can arrive at a wrong conclusion when they are not in possession of the facts. When customer data elements are improperly maintained or updated inconsistently, or if rules are illogically inconsistent from one product line to another, the error rate grows exponentially.

Investigate the data capture, maintenance, and update rules for your customer data. Recommend changes if you find inconsistencies between product lines or errors in the logic. We guarantee that regardless of how good a direct marketing firm thinks they are at maintaining their customer data, errors and inconsistencies are present. The odds are, the longer the direct marketing firm has been in business and the more product lines present, the more errors and inconsistencies exist.

The Analysis

Numerous methods are available to help you assess the customer data residing on a frozen file for determining your target market for a particular product offering. These techniques include the assessment of

+ Univariate tabulations
+ Cross-tabulations
+ Logic counter variables
+ Ratio variables
+ Longitudinal variables

These various techniques to viewing and manipulating customer data help you determine which variables are the most important in terms of defining your target market.

Whether defining your target market, building a response model, or segmenting the customer file, 50% to 75% of an analyst's time should be spent on data preparation using the techniques we previously mentioned. This is true even when using a data mining tool. If the data are not well prepared and understood prior to feeding them into such a piece of software, the analysis will yield suboptimal and potentially misleading results. Many direct marketers erroneously believe data mining tools are magic boxes into which raw customer data are fed and the answer is produced. Nothing is further from the truth. Inputting garbage data into a data mining tool will produce garbage results. We discuss data mining tools further in Chapter 10.

Univariate Tabulations

Univariate analysis is the most commonly used form of analysis for determining a select, building a target model, or segmenting a customer file. Unfortunately, it is all too often the only form of analysis used. A univariate analysis involves the tabulation and viewing of the categories of a single variable or data element. In the case of a product offer test, a univariate tabulation produced on an analysis sample (see Chapter 6) will display the percentage of responders and nonresponders to the offer for the various categories of each data element. Univariate analysis, for example, will help you determine if customers over the age of 50 respond at a higher rate than customers under the age of 50 or if customers with 10 or more product purchases pay at a higher rate than customers with less than 10 product purchases. This analysis enables the analyst to determine which data elements have a strong relationship with the customer behavior of concern (ordering, paying, renewing, etc.).

Assume ACME Direct test promoted a new music CD collection titled Pop Rock USA (PRUSA) to 20,000 customers selected from the segment "Customers with 5+ paid orders in the past 24 months," as shown in Exhibit 7.1. All customer characteristics on the sample were frozen point-in-time of the promotion (see Chapter 6). The resulting test response rate received was 2.5%.

The sample was split 50/50—10,000 names for analysis and 10,000 names for validation (see Chapter 6). The analyst was asked to examine various univariate tabulations produced on the analysis segment to determine if any data elements appeared to distinguish responders from nonresponders for this particular offer. The analyst examined an age indicator, an indicator of past music purchase activity, the total number of orders placed by each customer, and the total number of promotions sent to each customer.

In the real world, analysts have hundreds, perhaps even thousands, of data elements (internal and external) to consider, depending on the amount of information housed on the customer database. For purposes of this book, we assume the analyst has only four data elements to consider.

Starting with the analysis of age, an example of a typical univariate tabulation is Exhibit 7.2. This tabulation displays how PRUSA orders break out by various age categories. The categories can vary, depending on how you decide to view the data. You can have as many age categories as you like; however, keep in mind that if you break out the variable into too

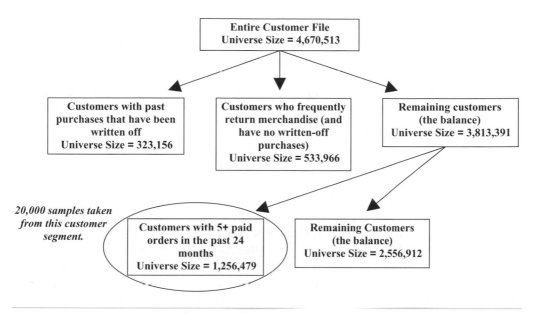

Exhibit 7.1   Segment Test Promoted "Pop Rock USA"

Exhibit 7.2   Univariate Tabulation of "Head of Household Age"

Head of Household Age	Number	Percentage of Sample	Number of Orders	Response Rate (%)	Index to Total
30 and under	1,529	15.29	67	4.38	175
31–40	1,775	17.75	63	3.55	142
41–50	1,879	18.79	46	2.45	98
51–60	2,054	20.54	29	1.41	56
61 and over	1,785	17.85	18	1.01	40
No age info. available	978	9.78	27	2.76	110
Total	10,000	100.00	250	2.5	100

many categories, it may result in sparse data. Too few names in any one category will not allow you to assess the response rates with much confidence. As a result, you may get erroneous conclusions. A rule of thumb is to assess only those categories having at least 500 names falling into them. If you end up with categories having fewer than 500 names, consider collapsing categories. In this example, age is broken down into six categories, and each category has more than 500 names.

These tabulations were produced using SAS, a statistical analysis software package, and imported into Excel. SAS is the most widely used statistical software package by data analysts in the direct marketing industry and is available for both the PC and mainframe environments. More information can be found by visiting the SAS Institute Inc. Web site at www.sas.com.

The column titled "Number" represents the number of names in the sample of 10,000 falling into each age category. For example, in this sample, 1,529 people out of 10,000 are 30 years of age and under. The "Percentage of Sample" represents the percentage of the corresponding "Number" as it relates to the total sample size. In this case, 1,529 represents 15.29% of the total.

The "Number of Orders" column represents how many of the total 250 orders for this particular product offer fell into each category. In this example, 67 of the 250 total orders for this product were placed by individuals 30 years of age and under. The response rate to this product offer is 4.38% (67/1,529) for those customers 30 years of age and under. The index value associated for those customers 30 years of age and under is calculated by taking the response rate of this group and dividing it by the response rate for the entire sample and multiplying by 100. An index value of 175 for this group tells you that the response rate for this age group is 75% higher than the response rate for all names. In other words, by promoting only those who are "30 and under," you will obtain a response rate 75% higher than if you promoted the entire sample (4.38% vs. 2.50%). This 75% figure is called the gain in response. The index value of 40 associated with the "61 and over" group implies that their response rate is 60% lower than the response rate for all names (1.01% vs. 2.50%).

Assuming the breakeven for this particular product offering is a response rate of at least 3%, which names could the product manager profitably promote using age information alone? (See Chapter 13 for a fuller explanation of breakeven.) Examining the tabulation in Exhibit 7.2, the product manager can profitably promote the "30 and under" group and the "31–40" group, because both have a response rate greater than 3%.

If the goal of this promotion is to generate 5% profit after overhead, and the resulting response rate required to generate this profit level is found to be 4.25%, which names can the product manager promote, ensuring that the goal is met? In this case, only the "30 and under" group can be promoted. Doing so would ensure that all names promoted would generate a minimum 5% profit after overhead.

Note that the "selection" criteria depends on the objective of the promotion. For name acquisition promotions, a direct marketer may actually be willing to lose money on the initial promotion in order to generate customers. Publishers, having a subscriber rate base[1] to meet, will promote as many names as needed to meet their rate base, the goal being to promote the best names. Publishers may actually lose up to $10 or more per subscriber to meet its rate base, offsetting the loss with advertising revenue.

Next, the analyst examines the customers in the sample to determine if their resulting action when promoted for last year's Rock and Roll Party (RRP) CD collection is a strong indicator of their action relative to the current product offering. That is, the analyst is interested in determining if customers who purchased last year's RRP are more likely to order PRUSA or less likely to order it. If so, then the analyst will certainly want to promote previous purchasers of RRP for PRUSA. The tabulation of this data element is shown in Exhibit 7.3. This tabulation displays how PRUSA orders break out by the various customer actions taken when promoted last year for RRP.

Applying the same breakeven criteria of 3%, the analyst successfully identified a group of customers on this sample that can be promoted (i.e., anyone who purchased RRP last year). This group represents 8.77% of this segment, with an estimated order rate for PRUSA of 5.82%, which is 133% higher than the response rate of the entire sample (5.82% vs. 2.50%). This certainly makes sense, because both music collections are comprised of rock music.

Customers who were promoted for RRP last year but did not order (the second category in Exhibit 7.3) have a PRUSA response rate below the response rate of the entire sample (2.34% vs. 2.50%). Why? These are customers ACME tried promoting once before with a rock music package (RRP), and they did not order. Therefore, it should be no surprise that these same names do not order PRUSA, also a rock music collection, at a rate greater than that of the entire sample.

In addition, customers "Not promoted" for RRP last year have a PRUSA response rate even lower than customers "Promoted and not ordered" (1.87% vs. 2.34%). Why? These are customers that, for whatever reason, ACME decided not to promote for RRP last year. Most likely the decision to not promote was because ACME did not think they would order the product. Therefore, because ACME did not think they were likely candidates for a rock music package in the past (namely RRP), it stands to reason they are not likely candidates for a different rock music package today either.

Who exactly are the customers identified as "Not available" in Exhibit 7.3? These are new-to-file customers and were not on the customer file last year when the RRP promotion was sent. In general, you can expect this group to have a slightly higher response rate than the total due to their newness to the ACME Direct database (2.65% vs. 2.50%).

Exhibit 7.3 Univariate Tabulation of Prior Purchase Behavior for "Rock and Roll Party"

Action to Last Year's Rock and Roll Party (RRP)	Number	Percentage of Sample	Number of Orders	Response Rate (%)	Index to Total
Promoted & ordered	877	8.77	51	5.82	233
Promoted & not ordered	3,967	39.67	93	2.34	94
Not promoted	3,911	39.11	73	1.87	75
Not available	1,245	12.45	33	2.65	106
Total	10,000	100.00	250	2.50	100

Exhibit 7.4   Univariate Tabulation for "Total Number of Orders Ever"

Total Number of Orders Ever (all product lines)	Number	Percentage of Sample	Number of Orders	Response Rate(%)	Index to Total
0	0	0.00	0	0.00	0
1–5	3,312	33.12	62	1.87	75
6–10	3,074	30.74	68	2.21	88
11–15	2,205	22.05	64	2.90	116
16+	1,409	14.09	56	3.97	159
Total	10,000	100.00	250	2.50	100

Next, the analyst examines "Total Number of Orders Ever" across all product lines (see Exhibit 7.4). This tabulation displays for the analyst how PRUSA orders break out by various categories relative to each customer's count of past orders placed. The categories can vary and depend on how you decide to view the data. For this example, we created five categories.

Assuming the product manager decides to promote any category meeting the breakeven of 3%, which names can be profitably promoted? On the basis of this univariate tabulation, the only category the product manager can profitably promote is the "16+ " category. This category represents 14.09% of the total segment and with an estimated response rate to the product offer of 3.97%.

As seen in Exhibit 7.4, the response rates increase as the number of orders increases. This is a pattern we like to see for such counter variables; however, this is not always the case. Some tabulations may reflect a slight bouncing of the response rates, but a pattern should be obvious. If a pattern is not present for such a counter variable, the direct marketer must proceed with caution, as there may be a problem with the sample or the variable or both.

In the final step, the analyst examines the univariate tabulation of "Total Number of Promotions Ever" across all product lines (see Exhibit 7.5). On the basis of promotional data, can the product manager find a group to profitably promote? It appears that the product manager can promote

Exhibit 7.5   Univariate Tabulation for "Total Number of Promotions Ever"

Total Number of Promotions Ever (all product lines)	Number	Percentage of Sample	Number of Orders	Response Rate (%)	Index to Total
1–5	0	0.00	0	0.00	0
6–10	768	7.68	16	2.08	83
11–20	2,544	25.44	57	2.24	90
21–30	3,563	35.63	108	3.03	121
31+	3,125	31.25	69	2.21	88
Total	10,000	100.00	250	2.50	100

anyone with "21–30" promotions and meet the breakeven criteria of a 3% response rate or higher, but should this be done?

When examining promotional counter variables on their own, it is important to keep in mind that they can be very misleading. This univariate tabulation is missing important key information such as how long a customer has been on file and how many orders were generated with those promotions. Knowing only the number of promotions is not adequate information on which to base a decision. In general, you should never use a promotional counter variable on its own in determining who to promote and not promote for a particular offer because (a) you might think that those with a lot of promotions will be your best customers (but keep in mind that this group will contain some bad customers who were once good and are therefore no longer being promoted) and (b) in addition, you might think that those with few promotions will be your worst customers (but keep in mind that this group will contain some "new-to-file" customers for which you have had little opportunity to promote yet). And as we all know, new-to-file customers are good responders to offers.

Another way to look at this issue is this way: If you think those customers with "21–30" promotions are your best customers, then why not promote everyone on your database enough times so that all customers fall into the "21–30" promotions category? Obviously, this does not make sense. Remember, a promotion is something you as a direct marketer do to a customer; it is not something a customer does. Customer actions (orders, returns, payments, etc.) are the predictors of future actions. This is why you will typically not see the response rate monotonically (i.e., smoothly) increasing or decreasing, as was the case for the variable "Total Number of Orders Ever." Additional information is needed to use this promotional counter variable safely.

How can you further exploit and use this promotional counter data? Employing **cross-tabulations** allows you to effectively evaluate such data. In particular, consider cross-tabulating this information with information pertaining to the number of products ordered or the length of time the customer has been on file.

Such information is typically used alone only for setting up promotional "resting policies" regarding how often to promote customer (see Chapter 12, Monitoring Promotional Intensity).

Cross-Tabulations

Cross-tabulations are a means of viewing two or more data elements in combination. Cross-tabbing highlights the interrelationships between variables. It can take a relatively weak data element, in terms of its predictive strength, and change it into a powerful predictor.

Continuing with our example, the analyst cross-tabulates the "Total Promotions Ever" counter field with the "Total Orders Ever" counter field (see Exhibit 7.6). This tabulation displays for the analyst how the PRUSA orders break out by various combinations of the univariate historical order and promotion categories.

The cross-tabulation presented in Exhibit 7.6 was created in SAS and is read as follows:

♦ The "Total" for each row represents the univariate figures for that variable. In this case, these values match the response rate figures on the univariate tabulation for "Total Number of Orders Ever" (see Exhibit 7.4).

♦ The "Total" for each column represents the univariate figures for that variable. In this case, these values match the response rate figures on the univariate tabulation for "Total Number of Promotions Ever" (see Exhibit 7.5).

♦ Cells not associated with the "Total" row and "Total" column represent the intersection of these two pieces of information. For example, the data highlighted in bold in Exhibit 7.6 denote that 491 names in the sample of 10,000 have "1–5" orders and "6–10" promotions. This same group yielded 8 of the 250 total orders for an order rate of 1.63% (8/491).

With SAS, you can have whatever statistics you desire placed in each cell of the cross-tabulation: response rates, counts, index values, and so on. For

Exhibit 7.6   Cross-Tabulation of "Total Number of Promotions Ever" Versus "Total Number of Orders Ever"

| Total Orders Ever | Total Promotions Ever | | | | | |
	1–5	6–10	11–20	21–30	31 plus	Total
0	0.00% (0/0)	0.00% (0/0)	0.00% (0/0)	0.00% (0/0)	0.00% (0/0)	0.00% (0/0)
1–5	0.00% (0/0)	**1.63% (8/491)**	1.76% (17/967)	2.34% (20/856)	1.60% (16/998)	1.87% (62/3,312)
6–10	0.00% (0/0)	2.89% (8/277)	1.85% (14/756)	2.51% (29/1,154)	1.80% (16/887)	2.21% (68/3,074)
11–15	0.00% (0/0)	0.00% (0/0)	3.03% (14/462)	3.03% (29/956)	2.67% (21/787)	2.90% (64/2,205)
16+	0.00% (0/0)	0.00% (0/0)	3.35% (12/359)	5.03% (30/597)	3.53% (16/453)	3.97% (56/1,409)
Total	0.00% (0/0)	2.08% (16/768)	2.24% (57/2,544)	3.03% (108/3563)	2.21% (69/3,125)	2.5% (250/10,000)

this cross-tabulation, only the response rate, number of orders, and total names (orders plus nonorders) were requested to be calculated for each cell.

On the basis solely of the data field for "Total Number of Orders Ever" in Exhibit 7.4, the product manager was able to promote only those names with 16+ orders (assuming a breakeven response rate of 3%). By cross-tabulating this data field with "Total Promotions Sent," the product manager can additionally promote those with "11–15" orders if the number of promotions sent does not exceed 30. This will increase the number of names the product manager can promote in rollout from 14.09% (1,409/10,000) to 28.27% ([1,409 + 462 + 956]/10,000), based on the data in Exhibit 7.6.

By cross-tabulating two data fields, the product manager was able to double the number of names that can be promoted and still meet the breakeven criteria.

Logic Counter Variables

When you have several data elements measuring the same customer "dimension," consider the creation of a logic counter variable. For example, if you have several data elements on your database, all measuring the customer's interest in cooking, consider combining them and creating a logic counter variable. The resulting variable will be, in most cases, stronger than the independent component variables and help you better assess a customer's true interest in cooking (or whatever it is you are trying to measure).

Three reasons to create logic counter variables are

1. It provides a means of data reduction

2. By combining similar data elements into one, it provides a means of strengthening the predictive power of low-coverage data elements such as some enhancement data

3. Logic counter variables serve an important role in the development of a parsimonious and stable regression model (this topic is discussed in greater detail in Chapter 10)

Suppose you enhance your database with the following five pieces of information from an outside vendor relating to cooking interests:

1. Hobby cooking? (which takes on 2 values: 1 if yes, 0 otherwise)

2. Buy cookbooks? (which takes on 2 values: 1 if yes, 0 otherwise)

3. Enjoy wine? (which takes on 2 values: 1 if yes, 0 otherwise)

4. Have a vegetable garden? (which takes on 2 values: 1 if yes, 0 otherwise)

5. Subscribe to cooking magazines? (which takes on 2 values: 1 if yes, 0 otherwise)

You could examine each variable separately via univariate tabulations or combine them into a logic variable. To create this "cooking logic" variable, you simply count the number of yes responses to these five questions for each customer. A logic variable is nothing more than a counter variable. In this case, it tells you the degree of interest each customer has in cooking based on the number of yes responses. The more yes responses, the stronger the customer's interest in cooking.

What is the range of possible values that this new logic variable can take on? In this case, each customer on the database could have responded yes to none or all of the five questions. Therefore, the range of possible values any one customer can have for this cooking logic variable is 0 to 5.

This is the best method of reducing the hundreds of enhancement data elements residing on the database that you may have purchased from an outside vendor.

You can also create logic counter variables from internal product purchase information, assuming they are related in some manner. For example, suppose over the past 3 years, ACME Direct offered four different rock music CD collections for sale: Rock and Roll Party, The Soul of Rock and Roll, Early Rock Legends, and Easy Listening Rock

You could examine each product variable separately via univariate tabulations or combine them into a logic counter variable. To create this rock music logic variable, you simply count, for each customer, how many of these four rock titles they purchased. In this case, the logic counter variable will tell you the degree of interest each customer has in rock music based on how many different rock music CD collections they purchased. The more rock music CD collections purchased, the stronger their interest in rock music.

What is the range of possible values that this new logic counter variable can take on? In this case, each customer on the database could have purchased none or all four of the music products. Therefore, the range of possible values any one customer can have for this "rock music logic" is 0 to 4.

These new variables can be programmed (coded) and used to select customers for an upcoming promotion. For example, in preparation for an upcoming cookbook promotion, ACME Direct might select anyone from the database that responded yes to three or more of the five cooking questions. Or in preparation for a new rock music CD collection promotion, ACME Direct might select anyone from the database that purchased at least two of the past rock music CD collections offered.

Exhibit 7.7 displays three customers selected at random from the analysis sample of 10,000 customers test promoted for PRUSA. What are the values of the new rock music logic variable (last column) for each of these three customers?

S. Jones purchased two of the four titles; therefore, Jones's value for this variable is 2. B. Smith purchased three of the four titles; therefore, Smith's

Exhibit 7.7   Creation of the New Rock Logic Variable for Three Customers

Customer Name	Customer Address	Total $ Paid	RRP	TSRR	ERL	ELR	Rock Music Logic
S. Jones	123 Main	356.34	PD	PNO	PNO	PD	?
B. Smith	8th Ave.	643.22	PNO	PD	PD	PD	?
K. Brown	45 Oak St.	264.98	NP	NP	PNO	PD	?

Product Title Legend: RRP = Rock and Roll Party; TSRR = The Soul of Rock and Roll; ERL = Early Rock Legends; ELR = Easy Listening.

Rock Action Legend: PD = Paid; PNO = Promoted but not ordered; NP = Not promoted.

value for this variable is 3. K. Brown purchased one of the four titles; therefore, Brown's value for this variable is 1.

Once everyone's value on the sample for this new rock music logic variable is determined, analysts can display the results by running a univariate tabulation in SAS. Doing so will allow analysts to determine this new variable's strength in terms of distinguishing responders from non-responders for PRUSA (see Exhibit 7.8).

The product manager has identified 21.44% (9.45% + 6.33% + 3.65% + 2.01%) of this sample with an estimated response rate above the breakeven of 3%. By combining past related purchase behavior, a strong logic counter variable has been created.

Considering RRP past purchase information alone (see Exhibit 7.3), the product manager was able to identify only 8.77% of this segment with a response rate above breakeven. By combining this purchase information with other past rock titles, a strong variable was created, allowing identification of additional names to consider for promotion.

It is not always obvious which data elements are related to one another. In such cases, one can run a **factor analysis** to determine which data elements are correlated with one another. Once determined, the correlated data elements can be combined into a logic counter variable. Factor analysis will be discussed in more detail in Chapter 8.

Exhibit 7.8   Univariate Tabulation for the New Rock Music Logic Counter Variable

Rock Logic: (RRP, TSRR, ERL, ELR)	Number	Percentage of Sample	Number of Orders	Response Rate (%)	Index to Total
Purchased 0	7,856	78.56	118	1.50	60
Purchased 1	945	9.45	47	4.97	199
Purchased 2	633	6.33	40	6.32	253
Purchased 3	365	3.65	27	7.40	296
Purchased 4	201	2.01	18	8.96	358
Total	10,000	100.00	250	2.50	100

Product Title Legend: RRP = Rock and Roll Party; TSRR = The Soul of Rock and Roll; ERL = Early Rock Legends; ELR = Easy Listening Rock.

Ratio Variables

Ratio variables are the result of dividing one data element by another. They can be easily programmed in SAS or any spreadsheet application. The data elements comprising the ratio variable must be continuous in nature. Exhibit 7.9 contains examples of ratio variables created from data on ACME Direct's customer file.

Exhibit 7.10 is a partial printout of three customers from the 10,000-name analysis sample tested for PRUSA. On the basis of "Total Orders" information alone, which of the three customers is most likely to respond to this offer? Looking at order information only, T. Bluestone appears the most likely responder and J. Jackson the least likely.

On the basis of "Total Promotions" information alone (see Exhibit 7.11), who is more likely to respond to this offer? If the product manager was forced to make a selection based on this information alone, she would in all likelihood choose T. Bluestone again, due to the fact that Bluestone has been promoted the most and must be a good customer. However, as previously mentioned, using promotion data alone to determine those most likely to respond to an offer is not a good idea.

Consider the ratio of "Total Orders" to "Total Promotions" for each customer and determine who is more likely to respond to this offer. The creation of the ratio variable is shown in Exhibit 7.12.

It is now apparent that J. Jackson—who, when looking at the individual variables, looked like the weakest candidate—is actually the

Exhibit 7.9 Examples of Ratio Variables

Ratio Variable	Measurement of
Total Products Paid for each customer divided by Total Products Ordered	Estimate of average payment rate for each customer
Total Book Products Paid divided by Total Products Paid	Strength of the book affinity as opposed to others (music, videos, gifts, etc.)
Total Orders divided by Total Promotions Sent	Overall responsiveness · to all promotions
Total Music Paid Orders divided by Total Music Promotions Sent	Estimate of average paid response rate for music orders

Exhibit 7.10 Customer Order Information

Customer Name	Customer Address	Total Orders
T. Bluestone	555 Maple	10
R. Stewart	56 South Main	7
J. Jackson	111 Rocky Rd.	2

Exhibit 7.11   Customer Promotion Information

Customer Name	Customer Address	Total Promotions
T. Bluestone	555 Maple	84
R. Stewart	56 South Main	55
J. Jackson	111 Rocky Rd.	12

Exhibit 7.12   Creation of Ratio Variable

Customer Name	Customer Address	Total Promotions	Total Orders	Ratio of Orders to Promotions (%)
T. Bluestone	555 Maple	84	10	10/84 = 11.90
R. Stewart	56 South Main	55	7	7/55 = 12.73
J. Jackson	111 Rocky Rd.	12	2	2/12 = 16.67

strongest. J. Jackson's average order rate is 16.67%, whereas T. Bluestone's is 11.90% and R. Stewart's is 12.73%.

Given what you have learned so far in this chapter, can you think of another way that the product manager could have combined these two pieces of data other than a ratio variable? These two pieces of data could have been combined into a cross-tabulation similar to that shown in Exhibit 7.6. You now have two methods of combining data elements—cross-tabulations and ratio variables. But remember, ratios can only be created for data of a continuous nature. This is not a requirement for cross-tabulations.

Longitudinal Variables

Longitudinal variables allow direct marketers to view a particular data element for each customer across time. Conceptually, they are similar to time-series variables and can be quite difficult to implement. Longitudinal variables are based on the premise that the best predictor of customers' responses to a future promotion is a review of their most recent past responses and reactions to promotions. Exhibit 7.13 displays some examples of longitudinal/time-series variables.

Exhibit 7.14 displays information on three customers taken from the ACME Direct database. The information relates to customer responses and reactions to the last three promotions they received from ACME Direct in addition to their overall "Ratio of Total Paid Products Ever to Total Promotions Ever."

On the basis of the "Ratio of Total Paid Products Ever to Total Promotions Ever," who would you select for an upcoming promotion? On the basis of this ratio alone, the likely choice is P. Johnson, because Johnson has the highest average response rate historically.

Exhibit 7.13   Examples of Longitudinal Variables

Longitudinal Variable	Measurement of
Customer's response (order, pay, silent, etc.) to their last 3 promotions sent	Estimate of customer's action on next promotion sent
Customer's action (pay, return, bad-debt) to their last 3 orders placed	Estimate of customer's performance on next order placed
Customer's last 3 product affinity shipments for the music club (rock, pop, country, etc.)	Estimate of customer's most current music interests

Exhibit 7.14   Ratio of "Total Paid Products Ever to Total Promotions Ever" for Three ACME Direct Customers

Customer Name	Ratio of Total Paid Products Ever to Total Promotions Ever
A. Flintstone	0.2546
P. Johnson	0.3796
X. Wesley	0.1408

If you considered the three most recent actions taken by these customers (see Exhibit 7.15), who would you select for an upcoming promotion?

On the basis of this longitudinal information, X. Wesley now appears to be the strongest. Out of last three promotions sent to Wesley, the last two were paid orders. Although it appears that Wesley historically is not the strongest of the three customers in terms of overall responsiveness, Wesley is the strongest when considering his or her most recent actions. On the basis of this data, we can say Wesley is the most likely to bite on the next offer sent (knowing nothing else about these three customers).

Of the remaining two customers, A. Flintstone and P. Johnson, who would you select for an upcoming promotion? Of the last three promotions sent, both were paid orders for exactly one promotion. However, because A. Flintstone's single order was more recent than P. Johnson's, Flintstone will be the most likely to order on the next promotion sent (again, knowing nothing else about these two customers).

These types of variables also allow a direct marketer to examine which customers are becoming weaker or stronger over time. For example, a customer with a history of ordering products at a high rate may suddenly become nonresponsive to offers. By identifying change (for the better or

Exhibit 7.15   Last Three Actions for Three ACME Direct Customers

Customer Name	Two Promotions Ago	One Promotion Ago	Latest Promotion
A. Flintstone	Nonresponse	Nonresponse	Order and pay
P. Johnson	Order and pay	Nonresponse	Nonresponse
X. Wesley	Nonresponse	Order and pay	Order and pay

the worse) in customer behavior via longitudinal variables, direct marketers are in a good position to implement various customer relationship management (CRM) programs to either reward or combat such changes in behavior.

Time Alignment of Key Events

Direct marketers who regularly communicate with customers due to the continuous nature of their business may require the time alignment of key events to best leverage the customer data. Such businesses include

- Clubs (e.g., music, video)
- Continuities or collectible marketers (e.g., books)
- Frequent buyer clubs
- Frequent travel services
- Banking and financial services
- Telecommunications and cable companies

For example, club direct marketers cannot compare customers who joined the club at different points in time and be in a position to make proper decisions about how to treat such customers. To say one customer is better than another in this environment requires the direct marketer to ensure that both customers joined the club at or around the same point in time or came into the club with the same offer or from the same source. This allows the direct marketer to control for variables that may have a direct influence on loyalty and attrition.

To develop predictors defining your best customers in a club environment, you may be well advised to first group all customers on the date of the initial enrollment in service. Doing so will take into account any difference in offers made over time and allow for accurate customer evaluation. Once done, the following predictors can be built as a measure of quality:

- Days to order first product following enrollment
- Longitudinal variables measuring the ratio of dollars paid to total number of promotions
- Counter variables representing the total number of promotions with no activity

In addition, you may be well advised to align your customers on the first up-sell purchase. If so, the following predictors can be built as a measure of quality:

- Time to pay for the first up-sell product
- Acceptance/nonacceptance of the first up-sell event

Failing to align customers on the first up-sell could result in comparing the "time to pay for the first up-sell product" for customers who were given different up-sell offers (where some of the up-sell offers may have been better than others).

A direct marketer can also align customer accounts based on life-stage events and develop predictors to assist them in future marketing efforts. For example, a financial direct marketer may group all customers who initiated a mortgage within the same time period and create such predictors as "the ratio of the dollars paid on the home mortgage to the total months of home ownership" or "the cross-tabulation of household income versus total home equity." How can a financial direct marketer use such information? Having such information can help a financial direct marketer cross-promote home equity loans or other extended lines of credit. This data, along with other indicators such as age, can also help a financial direct marketer to predict the time to the customer's next key life event such as retirement, purchasing a second home, or purchasing a new car.

Reducing the Amount of Customer Data to a Manageable Set via Correlation Analysis

As previously mentioned, many direct marketers have hundreds or thousands of data elements (internal and external) residing on their database. To individually assess the strength of each one every time a target definition is to be determined would be costly in terms of time expended. Prior to beginning the analysis, many direct marketers run a **correlation analysis** for each variable of a continuous nature to determine which variables are the most correlated with the action to be predicted (order, payment, renewal, etc.). This helps subset the list of candidate variables to be examined to a more manageable number. Once subset, techniques previously discussed such as univariate and cross-tabulation analyses are conducted.

Correlation analysis can answer questions such as

- Is the data element "total number of books purchased in the past 12 months" positively correlated with a customer's likelihood of ordering a new video series?
- Is income level positively correlated with the amount a customer spends on a catalog promotion? In other words, do customers with higher incomes spend more on catalog orders?

The measure of correlation is a value between −1 and +1 that reflects both the strength and the direction of the relationship:

+ **Positive Correlation:** When two variables are said to exhibit a positive correlation, this implies that higher values of one variable are associated with higher values of another variable. The closer the number is to $+1$, the stronger the positive relationship.
+ **Negative Correlation:** When two variables are said to exhibit a negative correlation, this implies that higher values of one variable are associated with lower values of another variable. The closer the number is to -1, the stronger the negative relationship.
+ **Zero Correlation:** When two variables are said to exhibit zero correlation, this implies that higher values of one variable are associated with all values of another variable, and vice versa. In other words, no association exists between the two variables.

Continuing with the example, Exhibit 7.16 displays the correlation coefficients associated with various data elements versus the likelihood of ordering PRUSA. Also displayed are p values.[2] p values tell you if the observed sample correlation for each variable is significantly different from zero. If the p value is less than 0.10 (<0.10), you will conclude with 90% or greater probability (one minus the p value) that the observed sample correlation is different from 0. If the p value is greater than 0.10 (>0.10), you will conclude that the observed sample correlation is no different from a 0 correlation, implying that the data element is in all likelihood a poor predictor of a customer ordering PRUSA. All values were calculated with the correlation procedure in SAS.

Notice the low correlations associated with each variable and ordering. This is common when correlating continuous data against a response variable that takes on only one of two values ($1 =$ order, $0 =$ nonorder).

Exhibit 7.16 Correlation Analysis for *Pop Rock USA*

Data Element	Correlation Coefficient with Ordering	p Value
Total promotions sent ever	0.01	0.2534
Total promotions sent in the past 36 months	0.02	0.1443
Total products paid ever	0.12	<0.0001
Total products paid in the past 36 months	0.17	<0.0001
Total dollars paid ever	0.13	<0.0001
Total dollars paid in the past 36 months	0.18	<0.0001
Total number of contemporary music albums purchased ever	0.19	<0.0001
Total number of cookbooks purchased ever	0.10	0.0004
Total number of classical music products purchased ever	-0.09	0.0436
Household annual income	0.01	0.1274
Individual age	-0.13	<0.0001

Consider the following questions regarding this correlation analysis:

- Why is "Total products paid in the past 36 months" positively correlated with ordering the music title PRUSA? Because past behavior is the best predictor of future behavior. In this instance, the more products customers bought in the past, the more likely they are to buy again in the future.
- Why does "Total products paid in the past 36 months" have a slightly higher positive correlation with ordering PRUSA than "Total products paid ever"? Because of the recency factor.

   Although knowing how many products have been purchased in the past is a great indicator of future behavior, knowing what the customer did most recently will strengthen its predictive power.
- Why does "Total number of contemporary music albums purchased ever" have a much higher positive correlation with ordering PRUSA than "Total products paid ever"? Because it measures the customers' affinity or their most relevant purchase history. Other products purchased may have no relationship whatsoever to contemporary music.
- Why does "Total number of cookbooks purchased ever" have a moderately positive correlation with ordering PRUSA? Because it is a measure of purchasing behavior.
- Why does "Total number of classical music products purchased ever" have a moderately negative correlation with ordering PRUSA? Because, on average, classical music lovers are not rock 'n' roll lovers.
- Why does "Individual age" have a moderately negative correlation with ordering PRUSA? Because the older customers are (the higher the value of this variable), the less likely they are to order a rock 'n' roll music package.
- Which data elements show no relationship (either positively or negatively) with ordering PRUSA? The data elements that have a p value greater than 0.10, implying no significant correlation with ordering PRUSA, are "Total promotions sent ever," "Total promotions sent in the past 36 months," and "Household annual income."
- What can be done to boost the predictive strength of the "promotion counter" fields? You can cross-tabulate this data element with the number of total orders placed.

In addition to SAS, correlation analysis can also be run in Excel. However, Excel will not generate the p values associated with each comparison.

For those interested, we show the formula for calculating the correlation coefficient in the next section.

Statistical Background—Correlation Analysis

The strength of the linear relationship between two variables is assessed by using correlation analysis. For example, are age and income somehow related? In other words, employ correlation analysis when interested in asking, "Do older people have higher incomes on average than younger people?"

Two variables can be positively correlated, negatively correlated, or exhibit no correlation.

Positive correlation. When two variables are said to exhibit a positive correlation, this implies that higher values of one variable are associated with higher values of another variable. Ten customers were selected at random from the ACME Direct database. We note their ages and income levels via enhancement data (see Exhibit 7.17 and Exhibit 7.18, which is a scatter plot of the data in Exhibit 7.17 created in Excel).

In this example, age and income are positively correlated. That is, as age increases, so does income.

Negative correlation. When two variables are said to exhibit a negative correlation, this implies that higher values of one variable are associated with lower values of another variable. Ten customers were selected at random from the ACME Direct database. We note their total number of classical/opera and country music CD packages purchased in the past (see Exhibit 7.19 and Exhibit 7.20, which is a scatter plot of Exhibit 7.19).

In this example, classical and country music purchases are negatively correlated. That is, those who have purchased many classical/opera music CD packages from ACME Direct were found to have purchased fewer country music CD packages and vice versa.

Zero correlation. When two variables are said to exhibit zero correlation, it implies that higher values of one variable are associated with all values of another variable, and vice versa. In other words, no association exists between the two variables.

Exhibit 7.17   Age and Income Levels for 10 ACME Direct Customers

Age	59	32	19	22	45	55	47	36	25	51
Income	$92,000	$43,000	$27,000	$24,000	$41,000	$65,000	$60,000	$62,000	$41,000	$85,000

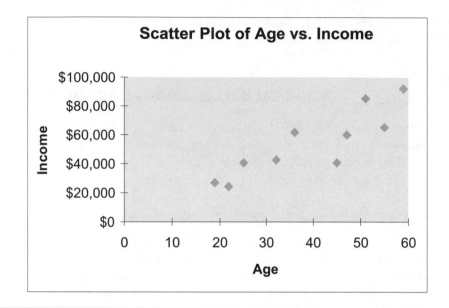

Exhibit 7.18   Scatter Plot of Age Versus Income for 10 ACME Direct Customers

Exhibit 7.19   Classical/Opera and Country Music Purchases for 10 ACME Direct
Customers

Classical/Opera Purchases	6	3	1	2	5	8	7	4	2	1
Country purchases	1	4	7	4	2	0	1	2	5	4

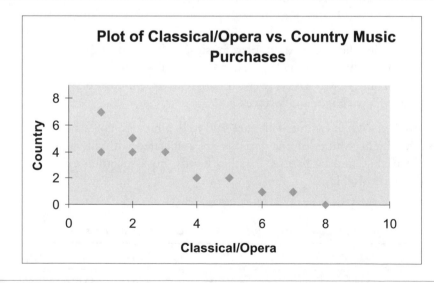

Exhibit 7.20   Plot of Classical/Opera Versus Country Music Purchases

Ten customers were randomly selected from the ACME Direct database. We note their ages and total cookbook purchases to date (see Exhibit 7.21 and Exhibit 7.22, which is a scatter plot of the data in Exhibit 7.21).

Exhibit 7.21   Age and Cookbook Purchases for 10 ACME Direct Customers

Age	21	33	76	45	61	23	66	55	51	42
Cookbook purchases	3	5	7	2	5	7	3	3	6	5

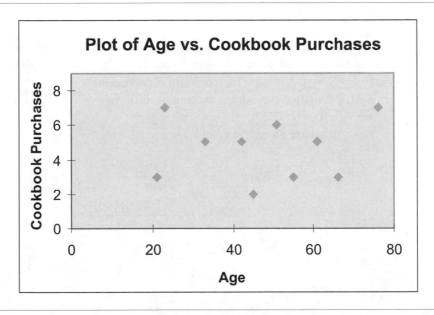

Exhibit 7.22   Scatter Plot of Age Versus Cookbook Purchases for 10 ACME Direct Customers

In this example, we say that age and cookbook purchases exhibit zero correlation. That is, the number of cookbook purchases placed with ACME Direct does not appear to be higher (or lower) for any particular age group.

To determine the degree to which two variables are correlated (either positively or negatively), we calculate what is called the correlation coefficient (denoted as r and called rho). The correlation coefficient r is a value between -1 and $+1$ that reflects both the strength and the direction of the relationship.

The formula to determine the correlation coefficient is

$$r = \frac{(SSxy)}{\sqrt{(SSxy)(SSyy)}}$$

Where

$$SSxy = \Sigma xy - \frac{[(\Sigma x)(\Sigma y)]}{n}$$

$$SSxx = \Sigma x^2 - \frac{(\Sigma x)^2}{n}$$

$$SSyy = \Sigma y^2 - \frac{(\Sigma y)^2}{n}$$

and
Σ means "the sum of"

On the basis of the data presented in Exhibit 7.17, we determined that age and income are positively correlated. The degree of this correlation is determined by calculating the correlation coefficient.

First, calculate the products and the sums of these products for the x and y data (see Exhibit 7.23).

Next, calculate $SSxy$, $SSxx$, and $SSyy$:

$$SSxy = \Sigma xy - \frac{[(\Sigma x)(\Sigma y)]}{n}$$

$$= 23,677 - \frac{[(391)(540)]}{10}$$

$$= 23,677 - 21,114$$

$$= 2,563$$

$$SSxx = \Sigma x^2 - \frac{(\Sigma x)^2}{n}$$

Exhibit 7.23   Data for Calculating the Correlation Coefficient by Hand

Age (x)	Income in Thousands (y)	x^2	y^2	xy
59	92	3,481	8,464	5,428
32	43	1,024	1,849	1,376
19	27	361	729	513
22	24	484	576	528
45	41	2,025	1,681	1,845
55	65	3,025	4,225	3,575
47	60	2,209	3,600	2,820
36	62	1,296	3,844	2,232
25	41	625	1,681	1,025
51	85	2,601	7,225	4,335
$\Sigma = 391$	$\Sigma = 540$	$\Sigma = 17,131$	$\Sigma = 33,874$	$\Sigma = 23,677$

$$= 17{,}131 - \frac{[(391)(391)]}{10}$$

$$= 17{,}131 - 15{,}288.1$$

$$= 1{,}842.9$$

$$SSyy = \Sigma y^2 - \frac{(\Sigma y)^2}{n}$$

$$= 33{,}874 - \frac{[(540)(540)]}{10}$$

$$= 33{,}874 - 29{,}160$$

$$= 4{,}714$$

And calculate r:

$$r = \frac{SSxy}{\sqrt{(SSxx)(SSyy)}}$$

$$= \frac{2{,}563}{\sqrt{(1{,}842.9)(4{,}714)}}$$

$$= \frac{2{,}563}{\sqrt{8{,}687{,}430.6}}$$

$$= \frac{2{,}563}{2{,}947.4}$$

$$= 0.87$$

Therefore, the correlation coefficient between income and age is $+0.87$. This value is very close to $+1$, thus indicating that a very strong positive relationship between these two variables exists.

Chapter Summary

A primary objective of direct marketers is to determine what differentiates people who respond to offers from those who don't respond. This chapter examines some basic analysis techniques for understanding the characteristics of customers. Prior to conducting any analysis, it is essential to check the data file. Outdated files or files with numerous errors can yield inaccurate results. Tabulation techniques can be useful for determining the characteristics of customers (e.g., age, income, previous purchases) that are more likely to respond. Depending on the characteristics of the available data, combining variables might be useful for classifying customers. Correlation is also discussed as a commonly used technique to determine the extent of the relationship between variables in the database. The concepts of correlation set the background for other analysis techniques examined in the following chapters.

Review Questions

1. Discuss the importance of becoming familiar with the characteristics of the customers in the databases and how the database tracks customer actions.

2. Explain how tabulation techniques are used to understand customers.

3. Provide an example of the proper application of a ratio variable technique.

4. What advantage does a longitudinal variable have in classifying customers?

5. Discuss how direct marketers use correlation analysis.

6. Using direct marketing variables, give examples of positive and negative correlations.

Notes

1. The rate base for a magazine publisher is the number of paid subscribers being guaranteed for advertisers.
2. We do not discuss the derivation of the p value and its statistical properties, which can be found in any intermediate statistics book.

8

Segmenting the Customer Database

Due to the successful completion of her last project, defining the target market for reactivation promotions, Keri Lee received a well-deserved promotion to marketing director. Her first challenge in this new role was to oversee the implementation of a new corporatewide segmentation scheme to the entire customer database for Inside Source.

After reviewing the project with her team, she knew that this effort would not be easy and could take several months to complete. First, the goal of the segmentation scheme was determined: maximize the effectiveness of the various acquisition, reactivation, and retention marketing efforts. To accomplish this goal, several segmentation schemes would be required.

As was the case with defining a target market, Keri first had to identify several appropriate samples of names promoted in the past in which the analysis to define the most optimal splits (segments) could be conducted.

With the assistance of her analyst, Keri decided to try several analysis techniques to determine the most optimal segmentation scheme. In particular, cross-tabulation analysis, formal RFM analysis, CHAID analysis and cluster analysis were considered. Cluster analysis was first employed as a data reduction technique. Next, CHAID was employed to help determine the optimal data splits. Last, various two- and three-way cross-tabulations were constructed in conjunction with a more formal RFM analysis.

Keri knew that if constructed properly, the various segmentation schemes would last for several years, allowing for proper customer tracking and migration.

Segmentation is an essential component in marketing planning. Segmenting the customer file allows a direct marketer to more effectively and efficiently market products and services to consumers or other businesses. In fact, according to the DMA List Database Council/Research Department's 18th and 19th Annual List Usage Survey, use of segmentation was cited by 41% of respondents as one reason for more efficient mailings.

Segmentation of the customer file can also assist in product and promotion testing, determining future customer needs and desires, estimating future demand for a current product base, and long-range strategic planning via customer tracking. A company can have several segmentation schemes with individual objectives. For example, a company may have one segmentation scheme to help maximize the effectiveness of product promotions and another to help in determining the future needs of customers via market research. Depending on the objective at hand, different customer information may be used for the actual segmentation. For example, customer activity data (RFM) may be used for product promotion segmentation, and demographic and lifestyle data may be used for market research segmentation.

This chapter reviews the importance and basic concepts of segmentation and then explores how databases are segmented. In particular, you will discover the types of segmentation schemes typically employed and the appropriate analysis techniques utilized for implementing each as well as issues to keep in mind when preparing to implement any segmentation scheme.

Defining Your Segmentation Objective

The underlying premise for segmentation of your database is that not all customers residing on the database are alike and therefore should not be treated alike. Segmentation is the process of dividing the total market into groups of people with similar needs and desires based on their characteristics and past purchase behavior. "One product for all" rarely works in today's market. It is a challenge to find a market today that has not been segmented. Exhibit 8.1 shows the process of segmenting a market starting with the total population and breaking the market into successively smaller groups or segments. As the segments become smaller, we are able to develop marketing programs that are more specific to the needs of the segment. For example, the needs of female business travelers are different from the female population in general and females within a specific age range. In addition, the needs of frequent business travelers may be different from occasional business travelers. For example, a women who is a frequent business traveler would be more likely to pay a premium price for sturdy, lightweight carry-on luggage that can accommodate business and personal items.

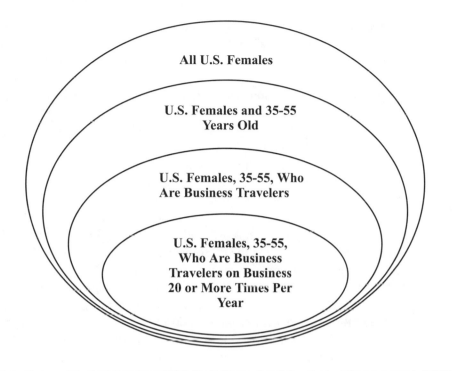

Exhibit 8.1   Segmentation for Female Business Travelers

Segmenting the customer database into submarkets will allow you to more effectively market various products, services, and offers. However, a number of conditions must be met to properly implement a segmentation scheme effectively. They include the following:

- Customers' needs in the market must be heterogeneous. In the previous example on female business travelers, we know that the needs of this group for certain products are different from the general population.
- There must be customer information on the database that reflects the heterogeneous needs of the overall market so that the market can be divided into segments. In many cases, a set of variables are used to identify and differentiate a segment (e.g., frequent, female, business travelers).
- There must be a way to measure the transactions or potential transactions of this group in order to forecast revenue from the segment.
- There must be an economical way to reach the segment with marketing programs. For example, a newly established immigrant group might be a potential segment for certain specialized foods. However, because of language barriers and lack of contact with mainstream media, it may be difficult to promote to them. Or the segment may be so small in number that from a cost perspective, it is not economical to promote this segment separately.

Segmentation starts a strategic process in marketing that leads to targeting and positioning. In selecting a target market, the organization evaluates its internal and external environments to determine the potential success in pursuing that target. For example, a software company may determine that it does not have the resources to compete in consumer and large business segments. Consequently, they might select the small retailer segment because of particular strengths of their personnel and lack of entrenched competition in the segment. After a target market is selected, a positioning strategy is developed. Positioning refers to the process of establishing and maintaining a certain image of a company's product, relative to competitors, in the customer's mind. A software company might position itself as having the turnkey solution for nontechnical small retailers.

The trend in segmentation is toward smaller and more specific groups of customers to allow for the customization of product and offer. Proctor & Gamble has developed mass merchandised cosmetics for different segments. The Cover Girl, Oil of Olay, Max Factor, and Ellen Betrix lines are Proctor & Gamble products that appeal to different segments in the global market. Recently, Proctor & Gamble established a business unit that offers customized beauty products on the Internet (www.reflect.com). Personal characteristics of customers are determined by an online survey. The survey includes questions concerning skin type, color, how the cosmetics will be used, and lifestyle and personal preferences. The objective is to offer products that fit as closely as possible to customer needs. The personal information is stored in a database that is used to customize the Web site and products for individual consumers (see Exhibit 8.2).

A company like L. L. Bean may have several million customers in its house file. L. L. Bean has catalogs in a number of categories, including women's clothing, children's clothing, fly fishing, hunting, travel, home furnishing, and corporate products. It would be inefficient to send all individuals on the house file every catalog. Therefore, a marketer will use customer data such as past purchases, gender, and sporting interests to segment the file, allowing for more effective and efficient targeting of its various catalogs.

Weber-Stephens Products Co., the company that produces food grills, uses database segmentation. The bulk of its sales come from the high-endline that is targeted to nine segments of Weber-Stephens's 1.7 million customer database. Weber-Stephens uses segmentation to target marketing communications. On the basis of the segmentation, print ads are run in publications such as Departures, Gourmet, and Robb Report, which target different aspects of luxury lifestyles. This segmentation also helps to describe the customer base to employees and retailers (Krol, 1998).

Other reasons for segmenting the database include new product development and risk assessment. For example, financial institutions have developed new products based on transaction patterns of customers. They also

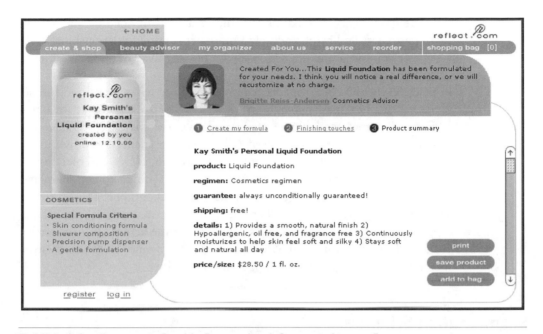

Exhibit 8.2   Proctor & Gamble Personalized Cosmetic Line, reflect.com

segment customers by the probability of defaulting on a loan based on past credit information in the database. Book marketers break down their databases by family life-cycle characteristics. For example, if there is a segment of parents that have girls in the 3- to 5-year age category, products will be developed for these children as they grow older. In addition, books can be developed for home improvement as the family moves from renting an apartment to purchasing their first home.

B-to-b marketers have segmented their databases on variables such as specific products purchased, industry category, size of customer (e.g., in income, employees, branches), geographic area, and purchasing cycles. This information can be useful in allocating sales personnel resources and integrating personal selling programs with other promotional programs and channels.

Airline Hydraulics, a company that produces pneumatic tools and accessories for the airline industry, segments their database, which is comprised of both active customers and prospects. They use a customer database program (GoldMine) that allows them to generate a list of targeted customers based on key interests for different products. The company then promotes to this segment via fax broadcasting (GoldMine, 2001).

Many b-to-b organizations use the database to move segmentation to a new realm: developing marketing approaches for individual customers. They record detailed information on the personal contacts within the organization. This may include birth dates, family information, hobbies, and favorite foods. This information is gathered as part of ongoing interactions with customers and helps to develop more personalized relationships.

Regardless of the specific reason for segmenting the database, the ultimate objective is to develop more personal and responsive relationships with customers. Segmenting Internet commerce databases provides new opportunities and challenges for marketers. One of the challenges is integrating data across channels (Internet, mail, phone, etc.). We discuss these issues in Chapter 15.

Another challenge on the Internet is to bring segmentation down to the level of the individual. For example, Netzero.com, a free **Internet service provider**, displays **banner ads** that are consistent with customer characteristics. Data are collected on demographic and psychographic characteristics of subscribers. When a subscriber logs on for the free service, banner ads appear in a window that occupies a portion of the screen. If a subscriber indicated an interest in charitable organizations, a banner ad for an environmental protection group may appear in the window.

Segmentation Schemes

As clearly revealed in the case studies previously mentioned, the customer file can have several overall segmentation schemes depending on the objective to be attained. In general, they can be classified into three main categories: (1) promotional product offerings, (2) life-stage marketing, and (3) market research.

Segmentation for Promotional Product Offerings

The main type of segmentation is designed for promotional product offerings. Typically, house customer data are used for this type of segmentation scheme. Two basic levels of segmentation are employed, each serving a unique purpose: (1) corporate-level segmentation and (2) product line-specific segmentation.

Corporate-Level Segmentation

Corporate-level segmentations, sometimes referred to as corporate-level eliminations, are concerned with issues that are common across all product lines within a corporation. The purpose is to inspect the entire file for names you do not want to pass along to any product line or division for promotional purposes.

For example, common segments of names isolated at this level for direct marketing firms include DMA do-not-promotes, **opt-outs**, frauds, and

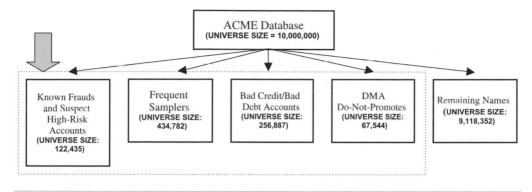

Exhibit 8.3   Corporate-Level Elimination Segments

suspect high-risk accounts. Exhibit 8.3 displays how ACME Direct segments their customer file of 10 million customers at a corporate level. Each group illustrated is unique and homogenous. With the names grouped according to a unique common qualifier, ACME Direct can communicate or not communicate with each group of names as they see fit.

Product Line-Specific Segmentation

Once corporate-level eliminations/segments have been identified, the next step is to determine how to segment the remaining names for each product line within the organization (see Exhibit 8.4). Each product line will segment the "Remaining Names" to best meet their objectives. The most important data elements for segmenting the file for the individual product lines are RFM values.

Typically, a product line segmentation scheme divides the "Remaining Names" (typically called promotable names) into groups generically

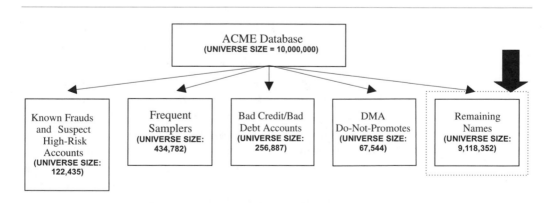

Exhibit 8.4   Names Remaining for Product Line Segmentation

defined as the primary, secondary, tertiary, and finally, the conversion segment. These divisions are based on RFM data related to the product line of concern.

The primary segment is considered the most profitable and generally consists of the most recently active customers for a given product line. The secondary segment is somewhat less profitable than the primary segment but, again, is fairly active for a given product line. Product managers employ various marketing tactics to move these names into the primary segment. The conversion segment is the group of customers who have never purchased products within the product line of interest. Product managers will employ conversion tactics to move these names into the primary segment. Tertiary and subsequent segments will have progressively lower profitability potentials.

Defining the names that belong in the conversion segment is easy. These are the people who have never purchased a product from the product line of interest. Defining the primary, secondary, tertiary, and so on markets is a more complex process that requires the analysis of RFM customer data using the techniques learned in Chapter 7. In addition, the application of formal RFM analysis, **CHAID** analysis, and cluster analysis segmentation techniques (to be discussed shortly) should be used.

For direct marketers with only one product line, the names within the conversion segment will be called prospects. They are noncustomers and are typically never included as a part of the marketing database. Usually, such names are placed in a separate database called the prospect file (see Chapter 3).

An example of how the ACME Direct video product line might segment the "Remaining Names" at a high level is shown in Exhibit 8.5. Unique marketing strategies can now be employed for each segment.

Segmentation for Life-Stage Marketing and Research

Life-stage segmentation divides the file in a way that considers primarily demographic and psychographic data. This enables marketers to develop, market, or advertise more relevant products and offers on the basis of their customers' life stages. Segmenting a customer file in this manner also allows direct marketers to understand the future needs of their customers via research.

Data used for these types of segmentation schemes typically include individual-level demographic and psychographic data as well as geo-demographic-level data such as the PRIZM clusters discussed in Chapter 3.

Life stages can be modeled using a multitude of internal and external lifestyle data. Life-stage segments residing on a customer database might include

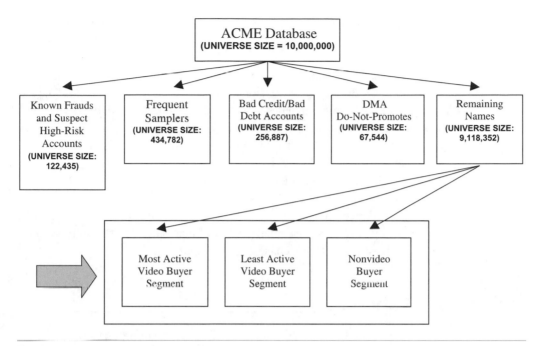

Exhibit 8.5   Product Line Segmentation

- Young families with children
- Newly moved
- Professional 25- to 40-year-olds, no children
- Entering the retirement years
- Children 2 to 5, 6 to 8, 9 to 12
- Adolescents
- College students
- Empty nesters
- New grandparents

These segments can be used to determine the future needs of your customer base through research, enabling you to promote appropriate and relevant promotions, offers, products, or services. For example, a direct marketer may decide to first determine the potential size of an "empty nesters" segment by enhancing the file with data to identify such households. Next, focus groups or surveys may be conducted to these individuals if their needs are not truly understood. Depending on the results of such research, a marketing strategy might be put in place to sell such households specific products or services or both. For example, it is a well-known fact that in the financial services industry, "empty nesters" are great prospects for annuities and that "young families with children" are good candidates for insurance.

Other examples of how such data can be utilized in segmentation is as follows:

- The *New York Times* might wish to highlight in their promotional copy "sports" coverage to professional males and "home and fashion" coverage to professional females based on demographically defined segments.
- A magazine publisher wishing to increase advertising sales revenue might use such data to develop unique demographically based segments for targeted advertising.
- The PRIZM clusters defined in Chapter 3 can be used by retailers for determining where to place stores.
- Performance data by Trans Union as discussed in Chapter 4 can be used by creditors to segment the customer base into those most likely and least likely to purchase a home equity loan.

Segmentation Techniques

Four analysis methods are commonly used for segmenting a customer file for promotional product offers, life-stage marketing, or market research purposes:

1. Univariate and cross-tabulation analysis
2. Formal RFM analysis
3. CHAID analysis
4. Factor and cluster analysis

In segmenting your customer file, you can employ several of these techniques simultaneously to determine the best scheme for your customer file. For example, CHAID analysis in combination with a more informal analysis of univariate and cross-tabulations can produce an excellent product line segmentation scheme.

Prior to segmenting your customer file, however, you must have a clear objective of the purpose of the segmentation. If properly undertaken, these segments can be used for several years to track your customers, market products to your customers, and communicate with them on a daily basis. If segment definitions are constantly changing, it is impossible for you as a marketer to forecast response rates or track customer migration.

Univariate and Cross-Tabulation Analysis

RFM measures play a key role in segmenting your customer file for promotional purposes. Recency of purchases is without a doubt the single most powerful predictor of future purchasing behavior, followed by frequency of purchases and monetary value (amount spent).

You can segment the customer file based on any one or all of these elements. To develop a segmentation scheme based on these three data elements, you can create two- or three-way cross-tabulations and divide the file, based on an analysis of historical response data in conjunction with your marketing assumptions.

To segment your customer file based on a cross-tabulation analysis of RFM data, you will need access to past product promotion history information. The steps involved are

1. Create a large sample comprised of past product promotions to the group of customers you wish to segment. Each sample used must reflect the customer's characteristics at point-in-time of the promotion (see Chapter 6). In addition, if you sell one-shot items such as books or music, you will want to include samples representing an array of product offerings across the various genres. For example, in preparing to segment the video product line, the ACME Direct analyst created a large analysis sample by combining several past video product samples representing the various genres (cooking, history, classic movies, exercise, etc.).

2. Create a two- or three-way cross-tabulation on RFM values and display the response rates, index values, and percentages falling into each cell.

3. Define the segments by looking for natural breaks in response rates that are meaningful with respect to the profitability of your product line. The number of segments depend on the size of your database. The smaller your database, the fewer the segments you will want.

4. To confirm, you will test the final segmentation scheme on past product promotion samples not used in the analysis.

Suppose the current segmentation scheme for the video product line at ACME Direct looks as shown in Exhibit 8.6. The product manager must determine a more effective method for promoting those customers within the "video buyers" segment. As a result, the product manager has asked the analyst to study past video product promotion samples to determine how best to classify these "video buyers" as excellent, good, average, and poor.

The analyst will perform the segmentation analysis by developing and examining a two-way cross-tabulation of recency and frequency indicators, using past video product samples.

The final sample used for the analysis is a combined sample of 250,000 names comprised of several past video product promotion samples representing an array of the types of videos being sold. Each sample is random

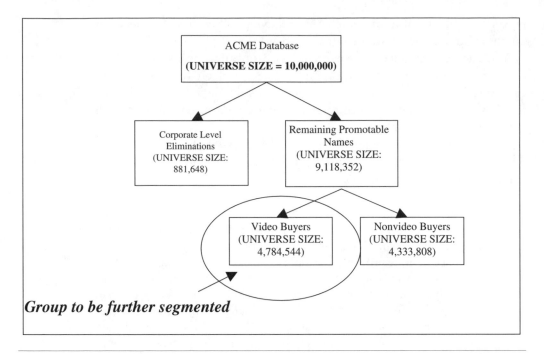

Exhibit 8.6   Current Video Segmentation Scheme

and representative of the universe of concern ("video buyers"). The overall response rate for this combined sample was 5.02%.

The resulting two-way cross-tabulation of recency and frequency indicators generated in SAS is shown in Exhibit 8.7. Displayed within each cell is the response rate, index to total (in parentheses), the number of orders, and total names (orders and nonorders). How should the analyst combine the cells based on an examination of the index values to create the four segments required by the product manager: Excellent Responders, Good Responders, Average Responders, Poor Responders?

Exhibit 8.8 illustrates how the product manager might combine the cells to create four segments based on index values.

The analyst defined these segments as follows:

- Excellent Responders = Names with an index to total above 175
- Good Responders = Names with an index to total greater than 100 but less than 175
- Average Responders = Names with an index to total greater than 85 but less than 100
- Poor Responders = Names with an index to total less than 85

Remember, the response rate of 5.02% for this combined analysis sample is really meaningless, as it is a response rate for a combination of many

Exhibit 8.7 Cross-Tabulation of Recency and Frequency Data

		Last Purchase Date				
Number of Past Purchases	0–3 Months Ago	3–6 Months Ago	6–9 Months Ago	9–12 Months Ago	12+ Months Ago	Total
0–1 Purchases	RR = 5.34% (106) Ord = 285 Tot = 5,337	RR = 4.58% (91) Ord = 383 Tot = 8,354	RR = 3.75% (75) Ord = 428 Tot = 11,420	RR = 2.98% (59) Ord = 488 Tot = 16,391	RR = 1.45% (29) Ord = 139 Tot = 9,568	RR = 3.37% (67) Ord = 1,723 Tot = 51,070
2–4 Purchases	RR = 7.54% (150) Ord = 361 Tot = 4,789	RR = 6.57% (131) Ord = 945 Tot = 14,376	RR = 4.98% (99) Ord = 1,098 Tot = 22,040	RR = 4.35% (87) Ord = 1,314 Tot = 30,203	RR = 2.79% (56) Ord = 721 Tot = 25,838	RR = 4.56% (91) Ord = 4,439 Tot = 97,246
5–10 Purchases	RR = 11.23% (224) Ord = 76 Tot = 677	RR = 9.44% (188) Ord = 192 Tot = 2,033	RR = 6.45% (128) Ord = 801 Tot = 12,426	RR = 5.45% (109) Ord = 1,418 Tot = 26,018	RR = 4.48% (89) Ord = 809 Tot = 18,051	RR = 5.57% (111) Ord = 3,296 Tot = 59,205
11+ Purchases	RR = 14.71% (293) Ord = 20 Tot = 136	RR = 11.46% (228) Ord = 77 Tot = 672	RR = 8.82% (176) Ord = 792 Tot = 8,981	RR = 7.01% (140) Ord = 1,448 Tot = 20,554	RR = 6.34% (126) Ord = 763 Tot = 12,036	RR = 7.30% (145) Ord = 3,100 Tot = 42,479
Total	RR = 6.78% (135) Ord = 742 Tot = 10,939	RR = 6.28% (125) Ord = 1,597 Tct = 25,435	RR = 5.68% (113) Ord = 3,119 Tot = 54,867	RR = 5.01% (100) Ord = 4,668 Tot = 93,266	RR = 3.71% (74) Ord = 2,432 Tot = 65,493	RR = 5.02% (100) Ord = 12,558 Tot = 250,000

Exhibit 8.8 Creation of the Four Segments

Number of Past Purchases	Last Purchase Date					
	0–3 Months Ago	3–6 Months Ago	6–9 Months Ago	9–12 Months Ago	12+ Months Ago	Total
0–1 Purchases	RR = 5.34% (106) Ord = 285 Tot = 5,337 C1[b]	RR = 4.58% (91) Ord = 383 Tot = 8,354 C2[c]	RR = 3.75% (75) Ord = 428 Tot = 11,420 C3[d]	RR = 2.98% (59) Ord = 488 Tot = 16,391 C4[d]	RR = 1.45% (29) Ord = 139 Tot = 9,568 C5[d]	RR = 3.37% (67) Ord = 1,723 Tot = 51,070
2–4 Purchases	RR = 7.54% (150) Ord = 361 Tot = 4,789 C6[b]	RR = 6.57% (131) Ord = 945 Tot = 14,376 C7[b]	RR = 4.98% (99) Ord = 1,098 Tot = 22,040 C8[c]	RR = 4.35% (87) Ord = 1,314 Tot = 30,203 C9[c]	RR = 2.79% (56) Ord = 721 Tot = 25,838 C10[d]	RR = 4.56% (91) Ord = 4,439 Tot = 97,246
5–10 Purchases	RR = 11.23% (224) Ord = 76 Tot = 677 C11[a]	RR = 9.44% (188) Ord = 192 Tot = 2,033 C12[a]	RR = 6.45% (128) Ord = 801 Tot = 12,426 C13[b]	RR = 5.45% (109) Ord = 1,418 Tot = 26,018 C14[b]	RR = 4.48% (89) Ord = 809 Tot = 18,051 C15[c]	RR = 5.57% (111) Ord = 3,296 Tot = 59,205
11+ Purchases	RR = 14.71% (293) Ord = 20 Tot = 136 C16[a]	RR = 11.46% (228) Ord = 77 Tot = 672 C17[a]	RR = 8.82% (176) Ord = 792 Tot = 8,981 C18[a]	RR = 7.01% (140) Ord = 1,448 Tot = 20,654 C19[b]	RR = 6.34% (126) Ord = 763 Tot = 12,036 C20[b]	RR = 7.30% (145) Ord = 3,100 Tot = 42,479
Total	RR = 6.78% (135) Ord = 742 Tot = 10,939	RR = 6.28% (125) Ord = 1,597 Tot = 25,435	RR = 5.68% (113) Ord = 3,119 Tot = 54,867	RR = 5.01% (100) Ord = 4,668 Tot = 93,266	RR = 3.71% (74) Ord = 2,432 Tot = 65,493	RR = 5.02% (100) Ord = 12,558 Tot = 250,000

a. Excellent Responders.
b. Good Responders.
c. Average Responders.
d. Poor Responders.

142

past video product samples. What is meaningful is the index in response of one group in relation to another group. Therefore, in our example, the analyst assessed the index values in relation to current video promotional strategies to determine what constitutes the best to worst customer groups. For example, the analyst knows, based on experience, that groups of customers with an index value less than or equal to 85 can never be promoted profitably from the video product lines point of view. Therefore, the Poor Responders group was defined as any cell containing names with an index value less than or equal to 85. For another direct marketer or even a different division within ACME Direct, such a Poor Responders group may be defined differently. It all depends on the cost and revenues associated with your particular business and division.

With the new segmentation scheme defined, the ACME Direct product manager applies the new segmentation scheme to the database as shown in Exhibit 8.9.

On the basis of the cross-tabulation shown in Exhibit 8.8, how many names of the 4,784,544 video buyers can the product manager expect to fall within the Excellent Responders segment? On the basis of the combined analysis sample, this segment (comprised of cells C11, C12, C16, C17, and

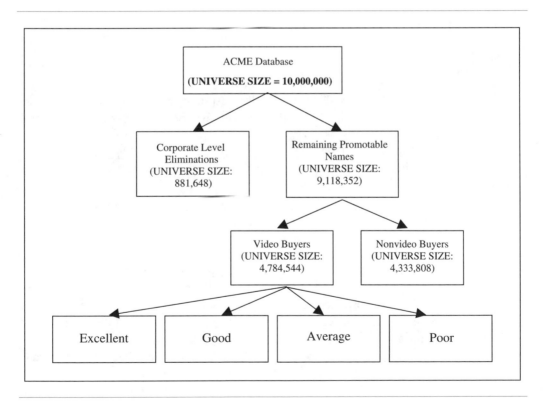

Exhibit 8.9 New Video Segmentation Scheme

C18) represents 12,499 names (677 + 2,033 + 136 + 672 + 8,981). Of the total analysis sample of size, 250,000, this represents 5% (12,499/250,000). Because the analysis sample was comprised of video buyers, the product manager can use information based on this sample to make statements about the entire set of video buyers. Therefore, the product manager should expect 239,227 (0.05 × 4,784,544) names to fall within the Excellent Responders segment. The same approach is taken to determine the expected number of names to fall within the other three segments.

What is the "index to total" value for the Excellent Responders segment? That is, how much higher is the Excellent Responders segment expected to respond versus all video buyers? To answer this question, you must first calculate the combined response rate for the five cells comprising this segment, based on the analysis sample as follows:

Excellent Responders response rate

$$= \frac{(\text{total orders in C11} + \text{C12} + \text{C16} + \text{C17} + \text{C18})}{(\text{total names in C11} + \text{C12} + \text{C16} + \text{C17} + \text{C18})}$$

$$= \frac{(76 + 192 + 20 + 77 + 792)}{(677 + 2{,}033 + 136 + 672 + 8{,}981)}$$

$$= \frac{1{,}157}{12{,}499}$$

$$= 9.26\%$$

Once computed, you can calculate the index to total for this segment by dividing the Excellent Responders response rate by the response rate for the entire sample of all video buyers and then multiplying that figure by 100:

$$\text{Excellent Responders index to total} = \frac{(\text{Excellent Responders response rate})}{(\text{response rate of total sample})} \times 100$$

$$= \frac{9.26}{5.02} \times 100$$

$$= 1.84 \times 100$$

$$= 184$$

Therefore, this group of Excellent Responders is expected to have a response rate 84% higher than all video buyers.

Assume the product manager tested a new exercise video to the segment of all video buyers last year and received a response rate of 4.45%. If, in rollout, the product manager decides to promote only those video buyers who fall within the Excellent Responders segment, what response rate can be expected?

To determine this, the product manager will index up the response rate of this test by 84%. Doing so will yield an expected response rate of 8.19% (4.45% × 1.84 = 8.19%).

How many orders can the product manager expect to receive if all 239,227 Excellent Responders are promoted for this new exercise video? The product manager can expect to receive 19,593 orders (0.0819 × 239,227).

A cross-tabulation analysis is not restricted to the use of RFM data. You can use data deemed appropriate for your particular needs.

Note that as will be seen shortly, the use of CHAID analysis in combination with a cross-tabulation analysis will help you determine which data elements best serve the segmentation and where to make the divisions for each data element used. For example, a CHAID analysis will determine if the "2–4 Purchases" and "0–3 Months Ago" cell should be combined with the Excellent Responders group or the Good Responders group, based on statistical testing.

Formal RFM Analysis

Another approach to segmenting your customer file is with a formal RFM segmentation analysis, based on an algorithmic analysis of customer behavior: recency of orders/purchases, frequency of orders, and monetary value of orders.

The main advantage of formal RFM analysis is that it is simple to implement. However, don't mistake simplicity for effectiveness. Formal RFM analysis has many drawbacks and will not produce a segmentation scheme as powerful as a cross-tabulation analysis or a CHAID analysis, which can take advantage of all available customer data and not simply RFM counter variables. Arthur Hughes, author of *The Complete Database Marketer*,[1] proposes two formal RFM segmentation approaches.

The traditional method, sometimes called hard coding, creates a weighted score for each individual record. The weighted score is based on each customer's RFM values. Those with the highest weighted score are the most desirable, and those with the lowest weighted score are the least desirable. An example of a hard-coding technique is presented later in this section.

The other method, which Hughes advocates, sorts the file into five equal parts on each of the RFM variables from most recent orderers to oldest, most frequent buyers to least frequent, and highest dollars spent to lowest dollars spent. The customers with most recent, most frequent, and highest monetary values are in the most desirable segment, whereas the customers with the oldest order, least frequent purchase history, and lowest dollar amount spent are in the least desirable segment. We will not discuss this method in this book.

Although Hughes agrees that statistical modeling techniques that use more variables can outperform formal RFM analyses, he notes that statistical modeling costs more. It is often necessary for organizations to hire analysts or outside consultants to perform the modeling. For this reason, there may not be an adequate return on investment for the increased precision that might occur if statistical modeling techniques are used instead of the more simplistic RFM techniques discussed here. Therefore, the Hughes techniques may be more appropriate for small or new direct marketers.

We now consider an example of employing the hard-coded RFM methodology (adapted from Baier & Martin, 1996). With this method, the RFM values are first recoded based on their raw values. The rules for this recoding are outlined in Exhibit 8.10.

Exhibit 8.10   Recoding Rules

Variable	Recode Rules
Recoded recency value =	20 points if last order was placed within the past 3 months
	10 points if last order was placed within the past 6 months
	5 points if last order was placed within the past 9 months
	3 points if last order was placed within the past 12 months
	1 point if last order was placed within the past 24 months
Recoded frequency value =	Number of purchases within the past 24 months $\times$ 4 points (maximum = 20 points)
Recoded monetary value =	Dollars spent within the past 24 months $\times$ 0.10 (maximum = 20 points)

Once recoded, a relative importance or weight is multiplied by each recoded value determined in the prior step. The weights are shown in Exhibit 8.11.

Exhibit 8.11   Weighting Rules

Variable	Weight/Multiplier
Recency value	5
Frequency value	3
Monetary value	2

Finally, the three weighted values are summed for the final weighted RFM score. Those customers with the highest score will be the most desirable in terms of promotion responsiveness.

Exhibit 8.12 displays raw data for three customers chosen at random from the ACME Direct database. Assuming today's date is October 2001, determine the weighted RFM score for each customer and rank them from most desirable to least desirable in terms of promotion responsiveness.

Exhibit 8.12   Raw Data Table

Customer	Recency Last Purchase Date	Frequency (last 24 months)	Monetary Value (last 24 months)
Smith	09/2001	10	$322
Jones	10/2000	2	$ 25
Johnson	10/1999	4	$120

First, recode each value as shown in Exhibit 8.13.

Exhibit 8.13   Recoded Data

Customer	Recoded Recency Value	Recoded Frequency Value	Recoded MonetaryValue
Smith	20	20	20
Jones	3	8	2.5
Johnson	1	16	12

Next, apply weights as shown in Exhibit 8.14.

Exhibit 8.14   Weighted Values

Customer	Weighted Recency Value	Weighted Frequency Value	Weighted Monetary Value
Smith	$20 \times 5 = 100$	$20 \times 3 = 60$	$20 \times 2 = 40$
Jones	$3 \times 5 = 15$	$8 \times 3 = 24$	$2.5 \times 2 = 5$
Johnson	$1 \times 5 = 5$	$16 \times 3 = 48$	$12 \times 2 = 24$

Last, the weighted RFM values are summed as shown in Exhibit 8.15.

Exhibit 8.15   Calculation of Final Weighted RFM Scores

Customer	Weighted Recency Value	Weighted Frequency Value	Weighted Monetary Value	Weighted RFM Scores Value
Smith	$20 \times 5 = 100$	$20 \times 3 = 60$	$20 \times 2 = 40$	$100 + 60 + 40 = 200$
Jones	$3 \times 5 = 15$	$8 \times 3 = 24$	$2.5 \times 2 = 5$	$15 + 24 + 5 = 44$
Johnson	$1 \times 5 = 5$	$16 \times 3 = 48$	$12 \times 2 = 24$	$5 + 48 + 24 = 77$

Which customer is the most desirable? Customer Smith is the most desirable, followed by customer Johnson and finally customer Jones.

The disadvantages of using RFM analysis over cross-tabulation analysis in segmenting your customer file are numerous:

♦ Either method of formal RFM segmentation analysis mentioned in this section considers no other customer data in determining how to segment the customer file other than straight RFM counter variables. On the other hand, a cross-tabulation analysis examines any piece of customer data in the final segmentation scheme. For example, a cross-tabulation analysis can consider "total number of promotions since a customer's last order" in addition to any demographic or psychographic data. In a formal RFM analysis, you cannot consider using such data.

- The recoding instructions and weights associated with the hard-coded RFM segmentation methodology are arbitrary and are not statistically based. As such, they will not and cannot guarantee maximum separation of customers in terms of their responsiveness to future promotions.
- Regarding the RFM ranking methodology (not discussed here), the division of names as well are not statistically based and as such will not and cannot guarantee maximum separation of customers in terms of their responsiveness to future promotions.
- In addition, with the RFM ranking methodology, it is difficult to track customer movement between customer segments. Under this method of segmentation, customers can move to a less desirable segment not because of something they did or did not do but simply because another customer on the database suddenly did something more desirable.

Formal RFM segmentation has been successfully employed for many years and is still considered valuable for many smaller direct marketers. However, one should keep in mind that larger direct marketers have so many more variables available to them today and as a result have the luxury of creating more sophisticated and powerful segmentation schemes. The bottom line: If you want the best possible segmentation scheme, you need to spend the time analyzing your customer file and becoming intimate with the data. A quick algorithm cannot do it for you. Do not rely on one approach. Test the various methods and decide on the segmentation scheme that best meets your objectives.

CHAID Analysis

CHAID is an acronym for chi-squared automated interaction detection, sometimes referred to as a tree algorithm. The main benefit of performing a CHAID analysis is that it can assist you in determining statistically meaningful splits in your data. For example, it can tell you if the four segments defined in Exhibit 8.8 are statistically significant. That is, do those segments maximize the separation of customers with respect to response? Most statistical programs such as SAS can run CHAID analysis.

The output of a CHAID analysis will result in what is typically called a spider chart or tree diagram. All splits will be statistically meaningful in terms of maximizing separation in the data with respect to the customer action of concern (response, payment, renewal, etc.). The statistical details of how this is accomplished will not be discussed in this book. The purpose of this book is not to teach the statistics but rather show you the various applications for statistics as they relate to the field of database marketing.

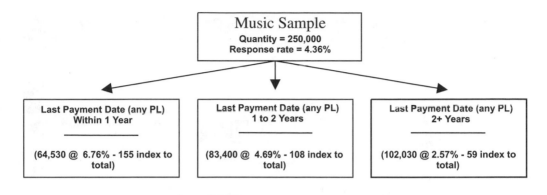

Exhibit 8.16 First-Level Split of CHAID Analysis

Consider the following example in which ACME Direct required a new segmentation scheme for the music product line in order to be more effective and efficient in their marketing efforts. To develop this new segmentation scheme, they decided to perform a CHAID analysis. The sample used to perform the CHAID analysis was one comprised of several past music product test samples. The final sample size was 250,000.

A CHAID analysis begins by examining every variable available on the sample, identifying the one variable that will most significantly maximize the separation in response rates. In this example, CHAID determined that the variable "Last Payment Date" (named "LSTPAYDT" on the sample) best discriminated between music orderers and nonorderers. In particular, three categories were generated for this variable: within 1 year, 1 to 2 years, and 2+ years. Exhibit 8.16 displays the three groups as defined by the CHAID analysis, ensuring maximum and significant separation in response rates.

Displayed in each cell of Exhibit 8.16 is the number of names, the response rate, and the index to total. In this example, the most responsive group is those with a last payment date within 1 year. This group represents 26% (64,530/250,000) of the total, with an index to the total of 155. The least responsive group to music promotions defined by CHAID are those with a last payment date 2 or more years ago. This group represents 41% (102,030/250,000) of the total, with an index to the total of 59.

The actual screen print of the SAS output showing this first level of the tree is displayed in Exhibit 8.17.

Next, CHAID examines each group at this first level individually to determine if further significant splits in the data can be made. In particular, CHAID examines the names contained in the first group, "Last Payment Date Within 1 Year," to determine if there is any other variable that will help further maximize the separation in response rates for these names. In this example, CHAID determined that it could further maximize separation

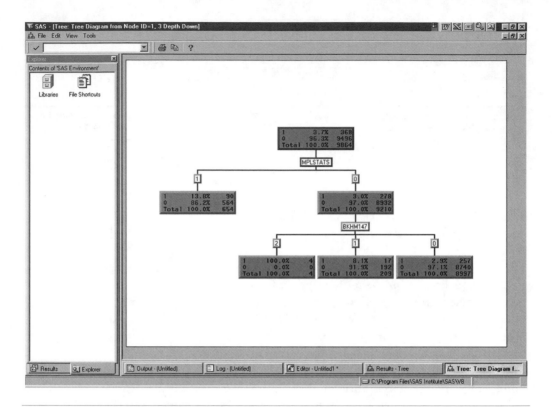

Exhibit 8.17   SAS Output of Tree

in response for these names by using the variable "Number of Music Purchases." Two categories were generated: "1–6 Music Purchases Ever" and "7+ Music Purchases Ever."

The resulting output is shown in Exhibit 8.18.

CHAID then examines the names contained in the second group, "Last Payment Date 1 to 2 Years," to determine if there is another variable that will further maximize the separation in response rates for these names. In this example, CHAID determined that it could further maximize separation in response for these names by also using the variable "Number of Music Purchases." However, in this case, the categories created were slightly different: "1–5 Music Purchases Ever" and "6+ Music Purchases Ever," as shown in Exhibit 8.19. It is not required that CHAID use the same variable in this step; however, in this example, it was determined to be the best for further segmenting this group of names also.

CHAID then examines the names contained in the third group, "Last Payment Date 2+ Years," to determine if there is another variable that will further maximize the separation in response rates for these names. In this example, CHAID was unable to find another variable that could further maximize separation for this group.

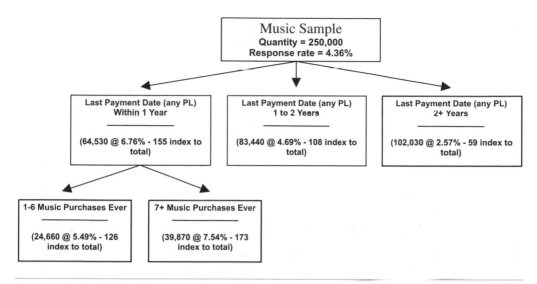

Exhibit 8.18 Additional Split for "Last Payment Date Within 1 Year" Group Based on CHAID Analysis

With the second level now fully defined, CHAID examines each group at this level individually to determine if further significant splits in the data can be made. In our example, no further splits were made by CHAID, meaning that no other variables could be found to further the separation in response rates for any of the groups at this third level.

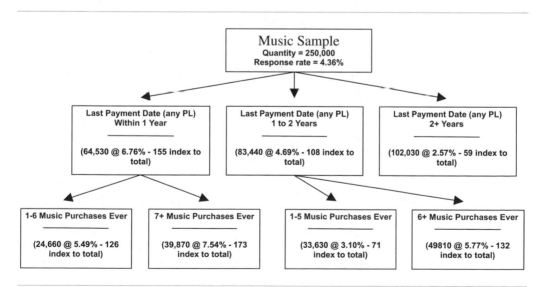

Exhibit 8.19 Additional Split for "Last Payment Date Within 1 to 2 Years" Group Based on CHAID Analysis

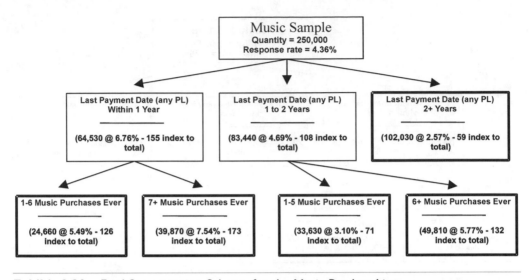

Exhibit 8.20   Final Segmentation Scheme for the Music Product Line

The resulting segmentation scheme produced by CHAID can be seen in Exhibit 8.20. The last node or box (shown in bold) on each branch represents the final segments for consideration.

For this example, the CHAID analysis created five segments. Each segment or group was determined so that the separation in response between segments to music promotions was maximized and significant.

1. Last Payment Date Within 1 Year and 1–6 Music Purchases Ever

2. Last Payment Date Within 1 Year and 7+ Music Purchases Ever

3. Last Payment Date Within 1 to 2 Years and 1–5 Music Purchases Ever

4   Last Payment Date Within 1 to 2 Years and 6+ Music Purchases Ever

5. Last Payment Date 2+ years

The variables used by CHAID vary, depending on the business application at hand. In this case study, only "Last Payment Date" and "Music Purchases" were found to be useful for our purposes. In the telecommunications industry, for example, CHAID may consider and utilize "total services contracted" or "average monthly call volume."

Assume the product manager in charge of the music product line decides to apply this segmentation scheme to the entire universe of 9,118,352 promotable names. How many names can be expected to fall within Segment 1?

On the basis of the analysis sample, first determine the percentage of names that fall into this segment:

$$\frac{24,660}{250,000} = 9.86\%$$

Next, apply this percentage to the total universe size:

$$0.0986 \times 9,118,352 = 899,070$$

The product manager can expect Segment 1 to represent a total of 899,070 names.

Assume the music product manager test promoted a new music title last spring to 10,000 names selected at random from the entire promotable universe of 9,118,352 names and received a 3.25% response rate. How many orders can the music product manager expect to receive from Segment 1 if all 899,070 of them are promoted?

First, determine the expected response rate for this title when promoted to names only within Segment 1. Segment 1 has a response rate 26% higher than the total (126 index) based on the combined analysis sample. Therefore, simply increase 3.25% by 26%:

$$3.25\% \times 1.26 = 4.10\%$$

To determine the number of orders we can expect to receive from this segment if promoted in total, multiply this figure by the estimated size of this segment:

$$0.0410 \times 899,070 = 36,862$$

Therefore, if the product manager promotes all 899,070 names falling within Segment 1, 36,862 orders can be expected.

Factor and Cluster Analysis

Factor and cluster analysis are more sophisticated segmentation techniques used by savvy direct marketers for segmenting the customer file. Both techniques are exploratory in nature. Often these techniques are used together to create the most powerful segmentation scheme available.

Factor Analysis

Factor analysis often reveals unusual and not readily apparent relationships in the customer data. This technique helps to determine the relationships among various data elements in an attempt to summarize predictors into fewer data elements. It is often considered an extension or form of principal components analysis (PCA).

The use of this technique requires a serious knowledge of statistics and is not meant to be undertaken by the novice marketer. There are many different methods and options that must be considered to get meaningful results from such an analysis. In addition, factor analysis can be sensitive to data elements that take on vastly different ranges in values. As such, our discussion of this topic will be at a relatively high level, again simply highlighting the value of this analysis technique in the field of database marketing.

As previously mentioned, factor analysis is often used as a data reduction technique. It provides a way to reduce large numbers of data elements to fewer, more powerful data elements for input to a target model or for the development of a segmentation scheme. Factor analysis can be run by most statistical software packages, including SAS and **SPSS**.

Factor analysis reduces the data elements by creating various linear combinations or groupings of them based on patterns seen in the data. It does not consider response information. This analysis is performed only on **predictor variables**. It searches the database for relationships (intercorrelations) in the customer data. For example, are the majority of customers interested in wine also interested in cooking?

In an attempt to determine new dimensions in their current customer base, ACME Direct purchased enhancement data and conducted a factor analysis. The enhancement data elements to be examined for patterns include the following:

- ◆ Household size
- ◆ Household income in thousands
- ◆ Age of head of household in years
- ◆ Child present under 1 yr (yes/no)
- ◆ Apartment renter (yes/no)
- ◆ Cooking interest (yes/no)
- ◆ Wine interest (yes/no)
- ◆ Home improvement interest (yes/no)
- ◆ Car repair interest (yes/no)
- ◆ Own investment portfolio (yes/no)
- ◆ Have retirement account (yes/no)

As previously mentioned, factor analysis can be sensitive to data elements that have vastly different ranges in values. Therefore, prior to performing the analysis, we would be wise to convert age, income, and household size to binary (0/1) variables to be more in line with the ranges in values for the other variables.

Exhibit 8.21 displays the results of the factor analysis run in SAS based on a sample of 100,000 names taken randomly from the ACME Direct customer database. In this example, the factor analysis found two unique dimensions (or **factors**) in the customer database based on this enhancement data. The numbers in Column 2 are the factor loadings or weights associated with the first dimension. Variables with a loading near zero implies it is not important in the final linear combination (factor). The numbers in Column 3 are the factor loadings associated with the second dimension. Depending on your customer set, many dimensions may result. In our example, only two meaningful dimensions resulted.

Exhibit 8.21   Resulting Factors on a Sample of 100,000 ACME Direct Names

	Factors	
Variable/Data Element	Factor 1 Loadings	Factor 2 Loadings
Household size = 2	0.85	−0.01
Household income = $80,000+	0.89	0.14
Cooking interest = yes	0.56	0.13
Wine interest = yes	0.44	0.03
Home improvement interest = yes	0.05	0.78
Car repair interest = yes	−0.06	0.76
Age of head of household = 30–35	0.56	0.62
Own investment portfolio = yes	0.92	0.20
Have retirement account = yes	0.94	0.23
Children present = under 1 year	0.11	0.89
Rent apartment = yes	0.02	0.95

To interpret each dimension or factor, first determine the important data elements by eliminating those with weights close to 0. Once determined, the remaining data elements will yield a unique customer dimension.

Important data elements in Factor 1, eliminating those with weights close to 0, include:

♦ Household size = 2
♦ Household income = $80,000+
♦ Cooking interest = yes
♦ Wine interest = yes
♦ Age of head of household = 30–35
♦ Own investment portfolio = yes
♦ Have retirement account = yes

Important data elements in Factor 2, eliminating those with weights close to 0, include:

♦ Home improvement interest = yes
♦ Car repair interest = yes
♦ Age of head of household = 30–35
♦ Children present = under 1 yr.
♦ Rent apartment = yes

What types of customers are these two factors identifying on the ACME Direct database?

♦ Factor 1 data elements appear to be describing a "2-person household with high income and expensive tastes."
♦ Factor 2 data elements appear to be describing a "young struggling family"—nonhomeowners with a newborn and a do-it-yourself lifestyle perhaps necessitated by a need to stretch income.

Exhibit 8.22   Jones and Smith Customer Records

Customer	Home Improvement	Car Repair	Age of Head of Household	Children Present= Under 1 Year	Rent Apartment
Jones	No	Yes	33	Yes	Yes—Rent
Smith	Yes	Yes	37	No	No—Own

Using these unique linear combinations, ACME Direct can identify who on their customer file is like a "2-person household with high income and expensive tastes" or a "young struggling family." They will do this by **scoring** each customer on these factors (linear combinations). The steps to score a particular customer on a factor are as follows:

1. The customer's initial score on the factor will be 0.

2. For each important variable in the factor, determine if the name meets the criteria. For example, does the customer have an interest in home improvement? If so, increment (or decrement) the score by the value of the loading associated with that variable. If they do not meet the criteria, their score is unchanged.

Customers with a higher overall score on Factor 1 relative to other customers' scores on this same factor are considered to be more similar to a "2-person household with high income and expensive tastes." Customers with a higher score on Factor 2 relative to other customers' scores on this same factor are considered to be more similar to a "young struggling family."

Assume the Jones and Smith customer records are as shown in Exhibit 8.22. Using only the most important variables relating to Factor 2, determine who is most like a "young struggling family."

The scores for Jones and Smith are shown in Exhibit 8.23. It appears that customer Jones is more likely to be a "young struggling family" than customer Smith.

Exhibit 8.23   Resulting Factors Scores for Customers Jones and Smith

Factor 2 Variables	Jones	Jones Score	Smith	Smith Score
Home improvement	no	0	yes	0.78
Car repair	yes	0.76	yes	0.76
Age of head of household = 30–35	yes	0.62	no	0
Children present = under 1 year	yes	0.89	no	0
Rent apartment	yes	0.95	no	0
Total		3.22		1.54

Direct marketers can also use this information in a select. That is, they can identify customers on their database that are considered to be a "young struggling family" by selecting names meeting all criteria determined important for that factor. For example, direct marketers will identify such names via a select by choosing those names on their database or on an outside list that are

- Interested in home improvement
- Interested in car repair
- Between the ages of 30 and 35
- Have a child less than 1 year old
- Rent an apartment

Having identified this segment, direct marketers can promote those customers most like a "young struggling family" with special products or services or both or conduct special research.

Direct marketers can also use this information to create a "young struggling family" logic counter variable (see Chapter 7). This new data element can then be used in a response model.

These two factors can also be displayed graphically to aid in their interpretation (see Exhibit 8.24). Upon examination of this graph, you will notice that the data elements group together to reveal the two distinct groups of customers as previously discussed: "young struggling family" and "2-person household with high income and expensive tastes."

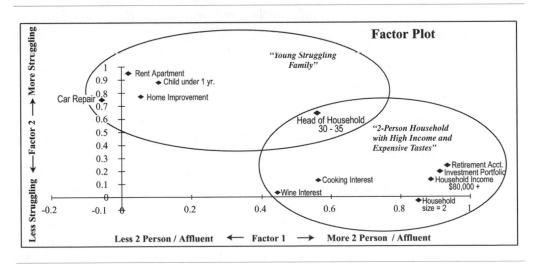

Exhibit 8.24   Graphical Presentation of Factor 1 and Factor 2

Cluster Analysis

Cluster analysis, as opposed to factor analysis, groups populations (people, bank accounts, office branches, zip codes, countries, etc.) together, based on similarities in the data. It is used to obtain subset segments that can be marketed to and treated differently, based on different needs.

Analysts often first run a factor analysis to reduce the available data elements to fewer and more meaningful descriptors. These factors are used in the cluster analysis.

How does this analysis technique know when observations (e.g., customers or zip codes) are similar enough to be grouped? It calculates a statistical measure of distance similar to the actual distance between two points on an X/Y axis. The axes become the variables or factor scores, and the observations become the points on the axes. The cluster analysis algorithm then calculates the total distance between all the points and groups the observations together in clusters, based on their distance to each other.

Be forewarned that cluster analysis is not for the novice. It requires an in-depth understanding of statistics. Like factor analysis, cluster analysis also has many different methods and options that must be considered to get meaningful results. In addition, cluster analysis is extremely sensitive to the levels of measurement, to the data scales, and to the algorithmic approach used. As such, our discussion of this topic will be at a relatively high level, again simply highlighting the value of this analysis technique in the field of database marketing.

So, how does it work? For each cluster solution, some way is needed to start the process by initially partitioning the sample of cases (e.g., customers or zip codes) into the desired number of clusters. For example, for a two-cluster solution, the total sample somehow must be partitioned into two groups as a first step, even though we know these initial groups are not likely to be the most homogeneous ones that could be formed.

How is this most commonly done? The computer routine selects two observations (seeds) from the data set at random for a two-cluster solution. After this, the routine assigns each of the remaining observations in the data set to one of the two initial clusters—the ones they are closest to, based on the key descriptors (e.g., age, income, genders) being considered.

Once the initial two clusters are created and all observations assigned, the initial seed values are replaced by the cluster centroids (the averages of all observations in each cluster). An iterative process now begins, and each observation is reevaluated to determine if it is in the correct cluster by examining the distance from the other clusters based on the key descriptor values. After several iterations, the final clusters result.

Consider the following example. A population of 40,000 customers is to be grouped into two clusters based on age and income (in thousands)

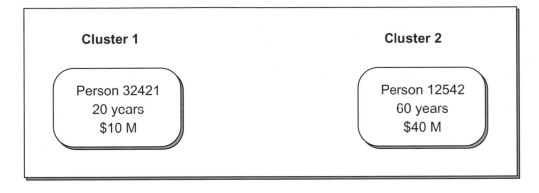

Exhibit 8.25   Two Initial Seeds Are Selected for a 2-Cluster Solution

information. Two customers (seeds) are initially selected to create the two clusters as shown in Exhibit 8.25.

With the two clusters initially established, the remaining customers are assigned to one of the two clusters one at a time. In Exhibit 8.26, the routine must decide into which cluster Person 9483 should be placed. The routine assesses whether this person is more like Cluster 1 or more like Cluster 2, based on a distance calculation.

To determine whether this person is more like Cluster 1 or more like Cluster 2, the routine calculates the distance that they lie from each cluster. First, the routine calculates the squared distance of Person 9483 from the centroid (average) of Cluster 1 and then does the same for Cluster 2 (see Exhibit 8.27).

Because the squared distance is less for Cluster 1, we assign Person 9483 to Cluster 1, as shown in Exhibit 8.28.

The routine now goes to the next person in the sample still to be assigned to a cluster. In this case, Person 342, as shown in Exhibit 8.29.

The calculations of squared distances for Person 342 is shown in Exhibit 8.30.

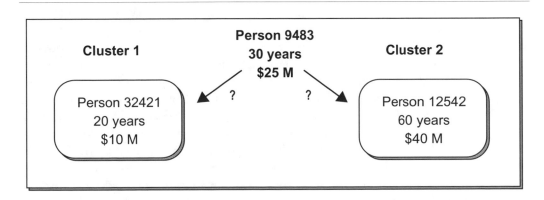

Exhibit 8.26   Determining Where to Assign Person 9483

Exhibit 8.27   Calculating Distances from Clusters for Person 9483

Person 9483	Cluster 1			Cluster 2		
	Centroid	Difference	Difference Squared	Centroid	Difference	Difference Squared
Age 30	20	10	100	60	− 30	900
Income 25	10	15	225	40	− 15	225
Total distance			325			1,125

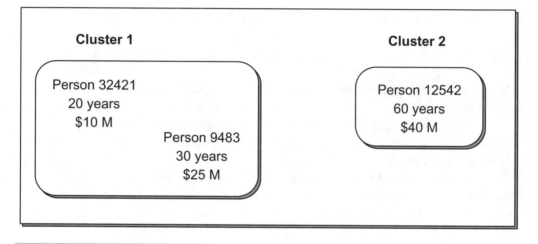

Exhibit 8.28   Assignment of Person 9483 to Cluster 1

Because the squared distance is less for Cluster 2, Person 342 is assigned to Cluster 2, as shown in Exhibit 8.31.

This process continues until all 40,000 names are assigned to one of the two clusters. Once everyone is assigned, new cluster centroids are calculated by determining the averages based on all observations within each cluster, and the process begins all over again. This process is continued for several iterations. Once complete, the final clusters are revealed. You also have another option, called the drift option, for assigning names to clusters. For the drift option, you do not wait until every observation is assigned to one of the clusters before recalculating the cluster centroids. Rather, you update the cluster centroids (averages) after each new observation is assigned to a cluster and before the next observation is to be assigned.

One method is not generally accepted as being better than the other. In fact, both methods give very similar results.

So, how do we determine the appropriate number of clusters? Unfortunately, the routine will not tell us this. You must tell the routine

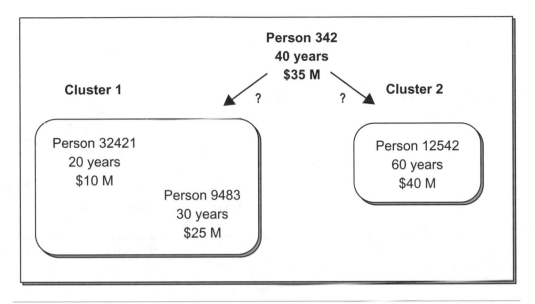

Exhibit 8.29   Determining Where to Assign Person 342

Exhibit 8.30   Calculating Distances from Clusters for Person 342

Person 342	Cluster 1			Cluster 2		
	Centroid	Difference	Difference Squared	Centroid	Difference	Difference Squared
Age 40	20	20	400	60	−20	400
Income 35	10	25	625	40	−5	25
Total distance			1,025			425

how many clusters you desire, and it will produce them for you, based on the above squared distance algorithm. In our previous example, it was necessary to tell the routine that a two-cluster solution was desired. We could have also told the routine to consider a three-, four-, or even eight-cluster solution.

Determining the number of clusters is the most difficult part of this type of analysis. It often requires running various cluster solutions and interpreting each for appropriateness. Remember, this is an exploratory analysis technique.

The basic rules for determining the appropriate number of clusters are listed below. But please be aware that none of these rules clearly point toward one best solution. Experience in interpreting the output will be your best guide.

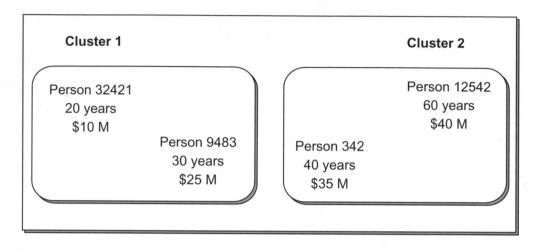

- ◆ The Sample size (if you only have 10 observations you are trying to cluster, you would not be looking for a 10-cluster solution)
- ◆ The size of each cluster (a final cluster of only one person may indicate an outlier in your data)
- ◆ Your knowledge of the business question at hand
- ◆ Cluster profiles that make the most sense, given your business knowledge

We recommend that you try several different cluster solutions and determine which best suits your needs. Some solutions may result in clusters that do not add value or do not make sense, given your objectives.

An excellent example of the rewards of employing cluster analysis can be seen at Proflowers.com, an Internet flower company, which used to implement its marketing programs by following traditional RFM segmentation analysis as discussed earlier in this chapter. Executives at Proflowers.com wanted a better understanding of who was buying and why, in order to create more personalized and effective marketing communications. Using cluster analysis, they created new customer segments and tested various messages to them. As a result, Proflowers.com was able to gain a thorough understanding of their customer base and increase response rates. In addition, this analysis also revealed new business development opportunities based on the various segments' demographics profiles, allowing Proflowers.com to partner with companies like Omaha Steaks and the Bombay Company ("Cluster Analysis Helps Proflowers," 2001).

As this case study clearly shows, factor and cluster analysis can be quite effective in revealing new knowledge about a direct marketer's customer base, which can then fuel more effective communications and opportunities.

For those requiring a more in-depth statistical understanding of factor and cluster analysis, consider reading *Multivariate Data Reduction and Discrimination with SAS Software* by Ravindra Khattree and Dayanand N. Naik, which includes many case studies and examples. Another excellent reference is *Segmentation and Positioning for Strategic Marketing Decisions* by James H. Myers.

Issues to Consider Regarding Segmentation Implementation

Although segmentation is an essential element of marketing, issues may arise with its use.

Promotional Intensity

Segmentation almost always is used to partition out "good" customers. As we have seen, "good" is typically defined as customers with high past transaction levels. Promotions are then directed to the good customers, while the "bad" (less active) customers are ignored. The continual concentration of marketing efforts on the good customers can have negative effects. With repeated contacts, customers may begin to ignore offers if they have no current need for the products. Furthermore, a high contact rate may degrade the customer perception of an organization. For example, a not-for-profit marketer may segment the database, and donors who have recently contributed a large amount of money would be targeted for subsequent contacts. The response of the customer might be, "Why are they bothering me, I just gave them money?" In the process of increasing response rates by targeting good customers, it is also possible that some of these customers will be alienated. Resting policies can be employed to minimize the promotional intensity of your "best" customers. Therefore, it is important to understand the characteristics of customers with regard to purchase or donation cycles. Alternatively, segmentation methods can be used to thank contributors and reward good customers with premiums.

Although segmentation techniques are often directed toward good customers, it can be unwise to ignore bad customers. A bad customer that ranks low on a segmentation scheme may actually be a brand loyal customer who has a longer purchase cycle or a lower overall need for a company's products. For example, an outdoor clothing company may have customers that have consistently purchased high margin products, but they only order every other year. With most segmentation schemes involving the use of recency and frequency information, they would be contacted soon after their purchase, when they don't need products from the company. As they move closer to their 2-year purchase cycle, the likelihood decreases that the company will promote to them because they have since shifted to a less active segment. If the customers do not receive an offer (e.g., catalog) when they are ready to purchase, the probability increases that the customers will be enticed by competing products. Purchase cycles of customers can be revealed through longitudinal analyses of customers.

Too Many Products

From the consumer's perspective, highly segmented markets that result in a proliferation of products can be confusing. For example, major camera manufacturers such as Canon and Nikon offer numerous models of cameras. Each produces more than 20 models of 35 mm cameras with varying features. The purchase decision is even more complex when we consider dozens of interchangeable lenses. The cameras and lenses are roughly targeted toward different needs of amateurs, advanced amateurs, and professionals. Several of the cameras overlap photographer categories, further complicating the decision process.

Other product categories such as athletic shoes, computers, and consumer electronics can be similarly confusing to the consumer, due to the wide range of product offerings. Although people who are experienced or highly involved in the product category prefer the selection, less experienced or less motivated consumers may become frustrated and postpone the purchase.

Cannibalism

In marketing, the term *cannibalism* refers to the situation in which a company's new product takes sales away from existing products. As the company develops more products in response to emerging market segments, the probability of cannibalism increases. If the new product is more profitable for the company and steals customers from the company's less profitable products, then cannibalism can have a beneficial impact on overall profitability. On the other hand, if a company "down lines" to appeal to a younger, less affluent segment, the danger exists that some potential customers of more expensive (and profitable) models will move down to the new, less expensive model.

Database marketers have a particular problem with cannibalism. It is common for customers in the house file to be segmented by various characteristics. New products are offered to customers based on demographic and psychographic characteristics. For example, a direct marketer of books offers educational books, spiritual books, and books with popular characters and themes. A customer may be in several segments and therefore may receive several product offerings. Because financial resources are generally limited for most consumers, accepting a new offer may reduce the chances of a repeat offer in another category. The goal for developing new products for new or existing segments is to draw sales from competitors, not from other products of the company.

Overgeneralization

Marketers must be careful not to overgeneralize the results of a segmentation analysis. This overgeneralization might limit the perceived valuation of a segment to the marketer. By focusing only on broad demographic categories such as age, gender, national origin, or ethnicity, direct marketers might be overlooking a potentially lucrative subsegment. For example, according to the U.S. Census Bureau, African Americans and Hispanics on aggregate earn less than Caucasians. However, there are fast-growing moderate- and high-income subsegments within these ethnic groups. Similarly, income levels of 18- to 24-year-olds and people over 65 are lower than other age categories. Despite the lower aggregate incomes of these groups, their purchasing power is enormous and represents a large proportion of certain product categories.

In database segmentation, similar precautions should be taken. Using crude segmentation schemes may misdirect marketing efforts. Database marketers have the advantage of being able to perform segmentation analyses relatively easily. The analytical techniques previously discussed in this chapter allow database marketers to focus in on responsive segments by using a combination of variables. For example, looking only at an aggregate breakdown of age categories, database marketers might conclude that the older customers on their database are not interested in gourmet foods. However, when the analysis includes other variables, such as frequency of international travel and education level, there may be many older customers who could be classified as good prospects for a gourmet food offering.

Ethical and Public Policy Issues

Targeting customers based on certain psychographic or demographic variables (e.g., children, smokers, ethnic groups) can result in reactions from public interest groups. There is no question that the public is opposed to direct and indirect targeting of children for products such as liquor and cigarettes that are intended for adults. However, there are less obvious circumstances in which targeting certain groups has elicited public response. For example, Nike was criticized in the past for targeting inner-city youths. Some community leaders said that Nike was socially irresponsible for attempting to sell these youths expensive athletic shoes. Nike responded by establishing programs for inner-city children.

Database marketers have also been criticized for targeting certain groups. In particular, telemarketers who target the elderly have been scrutinized because of the fraudulent practices of some organizations, and database marketers who sell children's products must handle their databases carefully. There is further discussion of ethical and public policy issues in Chapter 17.

Chapter Summary

Segmentation is one of the most important concepts in modern marketing. Without it, marketers are less likely to reach potential and existing customers efficiently and effectively. Segmentation can be based on a number of variables, including demographic, psychographic, and transaction data. A goal for the marketer is to select variables that help to partition customers or potential customers by purchase probability. Segmentation can be performed on a corporate-level, product line-level, or customer life stage. Database marketers utilize a number of methods for segmenting the house file, including cross-tabulations, RFM analysis, CHAID analysis, and cluster analysis techniques. Marketers should be aware that there are potential advantages and disadvantages of the various segmentation methods. More simplistic techniques may yield less than optimal results, but more sophisticated methods may be difficult for some organizations to implement and interpret. Although segmentation is an essential element of marketing, there are several important considerations for its application. For example, contacting the "good" customers too often may eventually have a negative impact on their perception of the organization. In addition, methods that focus on customers with high transaction levels may ignore customers that have reliable, although less frequent, purchase cycles.

Review Questions

1. What is the importance of segmentation to marketing, and how is it used in database marketing?

2. What variables might be used in database segmentation?

3. Describe how tabulation techniques are used to segment a database.

4. What is RFM and how is it used to segment a database? What are the limitations of formal RFM techniques?

5. How is factor analysis and cluster analysis used to segment a database? What are the advantages and limitations of the technique?

6. Discuss some of the potential problems with the application of segmentation methods to database marketing.

Note

1. Additional information on these methods is available in a paper published by Hughes at www.dbmarketing.com/articles/Art160.htm (address is case-sensitive).

9 An Introduction to Simple Linear Regression Modeling

At a staff meeting, Keri Lee's analyst discussed the possibility of employing multiple regression modeling versus manual selects for their next major marketing campaign. According to her analyst, multiple regression models are the most effective means of selecting names for promotional consideration.

Interested in learning more about this topic, Keri first learned about simple linear regression modeling. Once she understood it, Keri knew she would more easily understand the use of multiple regression models.

We learned about customer data and how to manipulate that data in Chapter 7. Now it is time to discuss the use of that data in building models for purposes of determining who to promote for an upcoming marketing campaign or determining who is likely to cancel out of a club. Employing simple "selects" is certainly one method of picking customers for a promotion or special treatment. For example, you select anyone from a list who is "over 35" for promotion, or you identify anyone from the database with "10+ paid orders" as your best customers for targeting with a special discount offer. However, you will be most successful by considering not just one or two pieces of customer information by way of a simple select but rather by considering multiple pieces of customer information (called predictors) simultaneously (e.g., age, income, RFM data elements). The more information you take into consideration, the higher the likelihood of your being successful in whatever you are trying to predict (e.g., responders, LTV, likelihood of canceling).

To incorporate multiple pieces of customer information into a select is difficult and will be weak in comparison to other methods of defining your target market. The best way to incorporate multiple pieces of customer information for purposes of identifying your target market is by way of **multiple regression** models. These models allow you to predict those customers with the highest LTV, those most likely to cancel, or those most likely to respond to a promotion, because you consider all available customer information simultaneously. The resulting model contains only those attributes deemed most important in predicting whatever it is you are trying to model.

Before embarking on a discussion of multiple **regression modeling**, we must begin with a discussion of **simple linear regression** (SLR) modeling. An SLR model is nothing more than a multiple regression model with only one predictor variable (e.g., age only). Starting with SLR modeling will help lay the foundation for making the discussion on multiple regression modeling (see Chapter 10) easier to understand.

The Simple Linear Regression Model

An SLR model is nothing more than a linear mathematical equation/line that defines the best linear relationship between two variables. Call them x and y:

$$y = a + bx$$

Where
y is the response variable, or what you are predicting (e.g., catalog expenditures, LTV)
x is the "predictor" variable (e.g., age, income)
a is a constant numerical value and denotes the y intercept when x takes on a value of 0
b, also a constant numerical value, is the slope of the regression line

Consider ACME Direct, our direct marketer of books, music, videos, and magazines. Assume the ACME Direct analyst selected 10 customers at random from the ACME Direct database that were new-to-file 1 year ago, noting their income levels and total ACME Direct expenditures to date (see Exhibit 9.1).

In an attempt to first determine if a relationship exists between income (x) and 1-year expenditures (y), the analyst created a scatter diagram of the data using the ChartWizard feature of Excel (see Exhibit 9.2).

On the basis of this scatter diagram, it appears that a relationship does exist between customers' income and their ACME Direct expenditures. In particular, it appears that as customers' income increases, so do their

Exhibit 9.1 Income and 1-Year LTV Data for 10 ACME Direct Customers

Income in Thousands (x)	58	42	24	76	33	69	31	46	51	38
1-Yr. LTV (y)	76	45	26	102	42	97	33	49	52	40

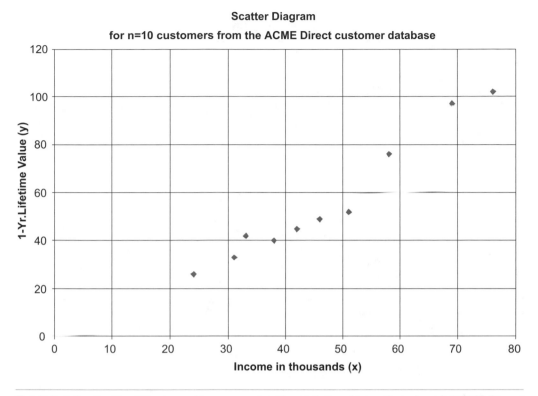

Exhibit 9.2   Scatter Diagram of Income and 1-Year Lifetime Value Data for 10 ACME Direct Customers

expenditures with ACME Direct—a positive correlation. The analyst could have also answered this question by calculating the correlation coefficient between these two variables (see Chapter 7).

The purpose of simple linear regression modeling is to define the relationship observed between two variables by fitting a straight line through the data points. In this example, simple linear regression modeling provides an estimate of expected LTV at various income levels—a valuable piece of information for ACME Direct.

How is the regression line determined? The regression line is the line that best fits the data (see Exhibit 9.3).

The line that best fits the data is the one that minimizes its predictive error, as shown in Exhibit 9.4.

Using the Analysis ToolPak feature of Microsoft Excel, you can run a simple linear regression model. Exhibit 9.5 displays the regression output from the Excel regression procedure for the data shown in Exhibit 9.1. This model could have also been run using SAS. The output is quite similar.

At this time, the only concern is with two values presented in this output: the coefficient associated with the "intercept" (the value of a), and the

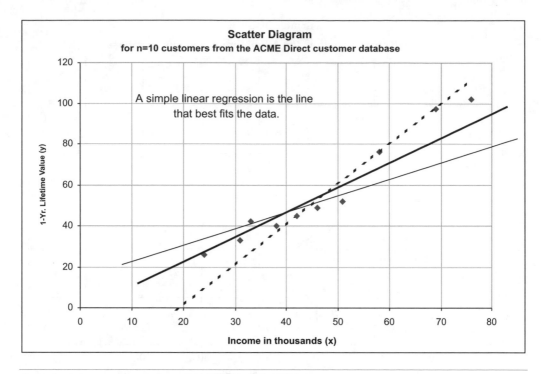

Exhibit 9.3   Fitting the Best Line to the Data Points

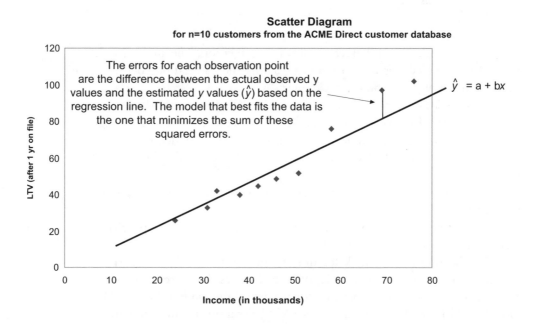

Exhibit 9.4   A Simple Linear Regression Model Fits the Line to the Data That Minimize the Error

SUMMARY OUTPUT

Regression Statistics	
Multiple R	0.976025389
R Square	0.952625559
Standard Error	6.090305274
Observations	10

	Coefficients	Standard Error	t Stat	P-value
Intercept	−15.39504236	5.964310304	−2.581194	0.0325558
Income (in Thousands)	1.529808597	0.120615476	12.683352	1.404E-06

Exhibit 9.5 A Simple Linear Regression Model Fits the Line to the Data that Minimizes the Error

coefficient associated with "income" (the value of b). Using this information, we can write the simple linear regression model as follows:

$$\hat{y} = -\$15.39 + 1.53x$$

Note that a caret (^) is now placed over y in our final regression model to signify that this is an estimated value of y for a given value of x. We read it as "y hat."

As previously mentioned, the values for a and b are derived to minimize the predictive error of this model. In other words, no other values for a and b exist that will, given one's income level, predict LTV as well. We call the values of a and b the least squares estimates because they are the values that minimize the sum of the squared errors as displayed in Exhibit 9.4.

For those interested, the exact formulas for calculating the least squares estimates a and b are shown later in this chapter.

How is the slope 1.53 interpreted? The slope signifies that for each one unit ($1,000) increase in income (x), ACME Direct 1-year expenditures (y) will increase on average by $1.53.

What is the expected 1-year value to ACME Direct of a new customer with an income of $35,498? To determine this, replace x with $35.498:

$$\hat{y} = -\$15.39 + 1.53(\$35.498)$$

$$= -\$15.39 + \$54.31$$

$$= \$38.92$$

In other words, customers with an income of $35,498 are expected to spend, on average, $38.92 with ACME Direct during their first year as a customer. This is the average expenditure at this particular income level.

Is it possible to predict the 1-year value of a new customer with an income of $20,000? No, because a value this low was not included in the development of the model. Using a regression model to predict y values based on x values outside the range of values considered in the development of the model is called extrapolation. The range of income (x) values used to develop this model was between $24,000 and $76,000. Therefore, trying to predict the LTV of any customer with an income outside this range is considered extrapolation and must be done with extreme caution. Extrapolating is not advised.

The Coefficient of Determination

As we previously learned, the parameters of the SLR model (a and b) were derived to ensure that the regression line minimizes the predictive error of the model. However, this does not mean that the fit of the regression line is good; it is merely the best one possible. To determine how well the line fits the data, you must examine the **coefficient of determination** denoted as R^2.

The coefficient of determination tells the amount of variation in the response variable y explained by the introduction of the predictor variable x.

The coefficient of determination (R^2) can take on any value between 0 and 1.

- The closer R^2 is to 1, the better the regression line or model fits the data.
- A value of 1 implies that a perfect linear relationship was found between x and y. (When plotted, all data lie exactly on a straight line.)
- A value of 0 implies that no line could be fit to the data other than one with a slope of 0 and a y intercept equal to the mean of the y data. (When plotted, data did not show a pattern.)

Does the definition of the coefficient of determination sound familiar? The coefficient of determination is merely the correlation coefficient (see Chapter 7) squared. It is squared in this case because we are not concerned with the direction of association (positive or negative), only the strength of association. In other words, we are concerned with how well the linear regression line fits the data without regard to whether it is a negative or positive slope.

Exhibits 9.6, 9.7, and 9.8 are scatter diagrams illustrating an R^2 value of 1, 0.5, and 0, respectively.

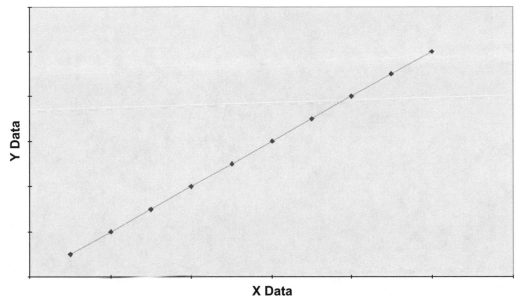

Exhibit 9.6 A Perfect Linear Relation ($R^2 = 1$)

So, what is the coefficient of determination for the regression model previously built predicting a 1-year LTV as a function of income level? Examining the Excel output in Exhibit 9.5, we note that the R^2 value is 0.9526.

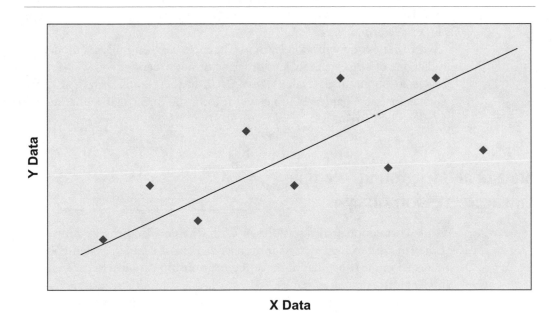

Exhibit 9.7 A Relationship With $R^2 = 0.50$

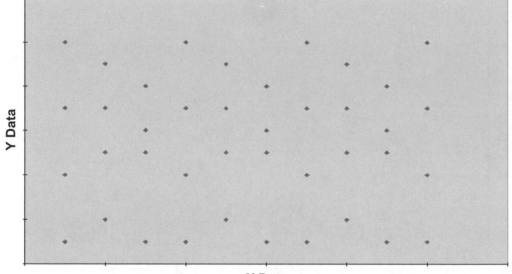

Exhibit 9.8   No Relationship ($R^2 = 0$)

How do we interpret this value? We say that 95.26% of the observed variation in 1-year LTV figures are explained by a customer's income level. This value is very close to 1, implying that income well explains the observed variation in a customer's 1-year expenditures. In other words, this is an excellent model.

Note that as you will soon learn in Chapter 10, when building models to predict one of two events such as ordering or not ordering, you will be hard pressed to obtain an R^2 value above 0.10. In these applications, it is the gains chart (see Chapter 11) that will inform the direct marketing analyst of the model's strength.

Statistical Background—Simple Linear Regression Analysis

We use correlation analysis as presented in Chapter 7 to provide a measure of the strength of linear association between two variables. When you are interested in the exact definition of the relationship between two variables, SLR analysis is required.

As previously mentioned at the beginning of this chapter, an SLR model is nothing more than a linear mathematical equation/line that defines the best relationship between two variables, call them x and y:

$$y = a + bx$$

Where

y is the response variable, or what you are predicting (e.g., catalog expenditures, LTV)

x is the "predictor" variable (e.g., age, income)

a is a constant numerical value and denotes the y intercept when x takes on a value of 0

b, also a constant numerical value, is the slope of the regression line

The values for a and b are determined such as to minimize the predictive error of the model, as previously shown in Exhibit 9.4.

The resulting formulas for the slope (b) and y intercept (a) that minimizes the predictive error are

$$b = \frac{SSxy}{SSxx} \quad \text{and} \quad a = \bar{y} - b\bar{x}$$

Where

$$SSxy = (\Sigma xy) - \frac{(\Sigma x)(\Sigma y)}{n}$$

$$SSxx = (\Sigma x^2) - \frac{(\Sigma x)^2}{n}$$

$$\bar{y} = \frac{(\Sigma y)}{n}, \text{ or the average of the } y \text{ data}$$

$$\bar{x} = \frac{(\Sigma x)}{n}, \text{ or the average of the } x \text{ data}$$

and

Σ means "the sum of."

We call these parameter estimates a and b the least squares estimates.

The easiest way to determine the values of a and b for the data previously presented in Exhibit 9.1 is to first calculate the products and the sums of these products for the x and y data (see Exhibit 9.9).

To calculate SSxy and SSxx:

$$SSxy = (\Sigma xy) - \frac{[(\Sigma x)(\Sigma y)]}{n}$$

$$= 30,202 - \frac{[(468)(562)]}{10}$$

$$= 30,202 - 26,301.6$$

$$= 3,900.4$$

Exhibit 9.9   Data for Calculating the Regression Model

Income in Thousands (x)	1-Yr. Lifetime Value (y)	x^2	y^2	xy
58	76	3,364	5,776	4,408
42	45	1,764	2,025	1,890
24	26	576	676	624
76	102	5,776	10,404	7,752
33	42	1,089	1,764	1,386
69	97	4,761	9,409	6,693
31	33	961	1,089	1,023
46	49	2,116	2,401	2,254
51	52	2,601	2,704	2,652
38	40	1,444	1,600	1,520
$\Sigma = 468$	$\Sigma = 562$	$\Sigma = 24,452$	$\Sigma = 37,848$	$\Sigma = 30,202$

$$SS = (\Sigma x^2) - \frac{(\Sigma x)^2}{n}$$

$$= 24,452 - \frac{[(486)(486)]}{10}$$

$$= 24,452 - 21,902.4$$

$$= 2,549.9$$

The slope is then calculated:

$$b = \frac{SSxy}{SSxx}$$

$$= \frac{3,900.4}{2,549.6}$$

$$= 1.5298$$

And the intercept as

$$a = \bar{y} - b\bar{x}$$

$$= \frac{562}{10} - (1.5298)\left(\frac{468}{10}\right)$$

$$= 56.2 - (1.5298)(46.8)$$

$$= 56.2 - 71.59464$$

$$= -15.3946$$

The final regression model is

$$\hat{y} = -\$15.39 + 1.53x$$

Chapter Summary

Database marketers attempt to select customers from the databases that have a higher probability of responding, paying, renewing, or canceling. Simply selecting customers that fit into a higher probability category such as "35+ years of age" is one way to segment and better target customers. However, this method of simple selects is limited. If implemented properly, more powerful techniques such as regression are better at predicting behavior. This chapter presents an introduction to regression model building by examining simple linear regression. Using one predictor variable such as age, income, or product affinity, simple linear regression attempts to predict a response such as ordering or paying for an order. Linear regression predicts customer response by calculating a straight line equation that best fits that relationship between the predictor and response. Simple linear regression techniques yield this line equation and also statistics that indicate the strength of the relationships between predictor and response variables. If we examine this simple linear regression model, the foundation is set for multiple regression techniques that increase the probability of selecting the "right customers" by using several predictor variables.

Review Questions

1. Compare the use of simple selects versus regression analysis for choosing the customers on the house file most likely to respond in a certain way to an offer.

2. What is the basic mathematical concept behind simple linear regression?

3. What is extrapolation and why should it be used with caution?

4. Give an example of a potential linear relationship that a direct marketer may examine and attempt to estimate.

5. What is the coefficient of determination and how is it used in model building?

6. Describe the scatter plots for a low R^2 and a high R^2 relationship.

10

Multiple Regression Modeling

After reading about simple linear regression models, Keri Lee was excited at the prospect of employing multiple regression modeling techniques to help identify likely responders to their next promotion.

Due to the issues surrounding the building and use of such statistically based models, she knew that this was not something she should try on her own. In particular, certain statistical properties must be adhered to in the creation of such a model. If these properties are violated, the model will be weak and unstable.

In preparation for the next campaign, Keri and her analyst created a sample of customers test promoted last year with the same creative format to be used for this year's campaign. Next, the analyst analyzed and manipulated the data using the techniques discussed in Chapter 7. Once complete, the analyst developed a multiple regression model to help identify those customers most likely to respond to the promotion.

Keri was shocked by the fact that the final model contained 14 different pieces of customer data. The old manual selects employed by Inside Source contained at most only 2 different pieces of customer data. The model, she was told by her analyst, took into account all interactions between customer characteristics that would be virtually impossible to identify through the simple manual select methodology. He also told her that each piece of customer data used in the final model was weighted according to its overall importance in identifying responders—again, something that would not be possible to do with simple manual selects.

Given the success of the modeling exercise, Keri decided to employ models for all campaigns. In addition, she discussed with her team the possibility of creating attrition models to help identify those subscribers most likely *not to renew. If she could identify such customers, she could send them a special offer to help retain them.*

Concerned with workload, Keri's analyst immediately began to explore some data mining tools to help streamline his efforts.

Now that you have obtained an understanding of how a simple linear regression (SLR) model works, it is time to discuss multiple regression models. A more sophisticated modeling technique, multiple regression models predict customer behavior based on the use of many attributes simultaneously in the modeling process as opposed to the *single* attribute used in SLR modeling. Multiple regression models are used by savvy direct marketers to build powerful target models that predict which customers are most likely to respond, pay, renew, cancel, and so on. Multiple regression models are also used to help predict customer LTV to a direct marketing corporation.

Although more and more direct marketers are embracing **response modeling** to be more effective and efficient in their marketing efforts, they are still in the minority. On the basis of *Direct* magazine's 2001 subscriber survey, only 31% (up from 27% from the prior year) of consumer and b-to-b database marketers employ such techniques. We have a long way to go to educate direct marketers on the power of regression modeling. Perhaps it tells us there is a shortage of qualified modelers or that direct marketers are not capturing data appropriately to leverage in this way.

Defining Your Marketing Objective

As previously mentioned, with the use of regression modeling, a direct marketer can more effectively and efficiently identify customers or prospects for various treatments or promotions. The process begins with the definition of the business objective. For direct marketers, this is usually to increase response, payment rates, retention, and so on.

First, you must define the universe of customers or prospects you wish to model. It must be sizable, otherwise the costs associated with the development and application of the model are not offset by the benefits. In addition, the universe must be relatively data rich, that is, it must have an adequate amount of predictive customer information such as RFM and enhancement data as defined in Chapter 3. The more appropriate customer data available for consideration by the model, the greater the odds of the model being successful.

The customer behaviors that direct marketers typically wish to predict and model include

- An order
- A bad debt/account write-off (for those direct marketers extending free trial offers)
- A return/cancel to the initial offer
- A paid order (a combined order and payment model)
- A renewal the next year out (for publishing, communications, and insurance industries)
- Subsequent shipments (for clubs and continuities)
- Catalog expenditures
- Attrition/cancellation of relationship (for credit card companies, clubs, or continuities)

Modeling such customer behaviors allows a direct marketer to make informed decisions about who to promote or not promote for a particular product offer or treatment. For example, in determining who to promote for an upcoming wireless telecommunications offer, a direct marketer may decide to build several models predicting how likely someone is to order the service, how likely someone is to *not* cancel the service they have ordered, and how likely someone is to renew the service the next year. A direct marketer can consider any or all of these actions in making a promotional decision. These various customer actions are shown in Exhibit 10.1.

A direct marketer promotes those customers most likely to fall within the darkened cell of Exhibit 10.1 and *not* promote those customers most likely

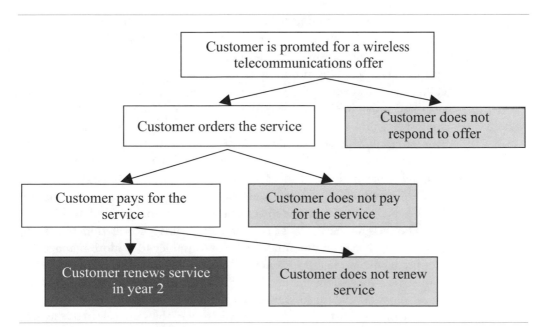

Exhibit 10.1   Possible Customer Actions to a Wireless Telecommunications Offer

to fall within the lighter shaded cells. Multiple regression models help you determine how likely a customer is to fall within each of these cells.

For many years, CareerTrack, a seminar learning company, had been using simple recency/frequency selects in identifying candidates for their catalog promotions. Using such techniques, they had been unsuccessful at increasing any response. The company decided to try regression modeling in an attempt to allow them to not only increase response rates but also reduce mail quantities. The company had extensive information on their database, including purchase data, seminar types purchased, audios/videos purchased, and dollars spent. In addition, they also enhanced their database with **SIC codes** (the Standard Industrial Classification codes assigned to business types by the U.S. government), giving them valuable information pertaining to the industries in which their customers work. CareerTrack tested the old selection method head-to-head with regression modeling and found that regression modeling yielded a higher response rate, higher average order size, and lower mail quantities. As a result, more revenue and profit were generated. CareerTrack is using the regression model as a regular part of its marketing strategy ("Regression Modeling," 1998).

Preparing the Data to Build the Multiple Regression Model

Before you can build a multiple regression model to help predict customer actions, you must first apply what was taught in Chapters 6 and 7. For example, Mega Telecom test promoted a new wireless Internet service last year to a sample of 10,000 current cellular customers and, based on the results of the promotion, has decided to roll out with this offer to the entire database. The product manager in charge of this marketing campaign, however, only wants to promote those customers on the database most likely to respond to the offer. Therefore, she asks her analyst to build a multiple regression model using the test sample to be able to rank-order prospective customers from those most likely to respond to the wireless Internet offer to those least likely to respond.

Using what he learned in Chapters 6 and 7, the analyst takes the test sample, including all customer data saved point-in-time of the promotion (see Chapter 6), and splits it into one sample for analysis and another for validation. Using the analysis portion, he first runs a correlation analysis to help reduce the set of potential predictor variables to a more manageable number, as mentioned in Chapter 7. He then more intensely analyzes and manipulates those data elements most correlated with ordering by creating ratios, cross-tabulations, longitudinal variables, and so on.

Once the final list of candidate predictor variables are selected, the next step prior to regression development is the "recoding" of these candidate variables. The variables to be considered in the model are either continuous, categorical, or discrete in form.

Continuous variables are variables that can take on any value within a range of values. Typically, the values of the variable have some meaning relative to one another. Examples include age, ratios, product paid counters, average cellular minutes per month.

Categorical variables are variables that take on only a very finite number of values and are usually of a descriptive nature. For example, the variable "car type" is of a categorical nature and on the database may take on values of 1 = Sedan, 2 = SUV, 3 = Compact, 4 = Luxury, and so on. The numerical values have no meaning relative to each other.

Discrete variables are similar to categorical variables in that they take on only a very finite and countable number of values, but in this case the values themselves have some meaning relative to one another. Examples include number of children and number of cars owned.

Suppose a univariate tabulation (see Chapter 7) of age information produced on the analysis portion of the wireless Internet service test sample is as shown in Exhibit 10.2. The response rate for all customers promoted for the wireless Internet service was 5.85%. The analyst has three options regarding how to recode the age information.

Option 1. Use the continuous age variable in its raw continuous form. One issue that must be addressed is the value to be given to the 795 people in the sample who lack age information. By ignoring them, many analysis routines, including SAS and SPSS, throw out the names. For those customers who lack age information, the analyst has several options for imputing (calculating) the missing data:

- The analyst can fill in the missing age values with the mean, median, or mode derived from customers for which age data are not missing.
- The analyst can first determine the distributional form of age based on nonmissing observations. Once determined, the analyst randomly assigns age values to individuals with missing data from the same

Exhibit 10.2 Univariate Tabulation of Age

Head of Household Age	Number	% of Sample	Number of Orders	Response Rate	Index to Total
25 and under	1,945	19.45	97	4.99	85
26–30	2,856	28.56	197	6.90	118
31–35	2,493	24.93	156	6.26	107
36–40	1,365	13.65	65	4.76	81
41 and over	546	5.46	20	3.66	63
No age info available	795	7.95	50	6.29	108
Total	10,000	100.00	585	5.85	100

distribution. The advantage of this method over the prior method is that it does not have an impact on the distributional shape of the age variable.

♦ The analyst can create a regression model predicting age based on other data elements using the subsample of names for which age is available. Once created, the analyst can "score" the individuals for which age is missing.

The other issue that must be considered when planning to use a continuous variable is its functional form. Regression models assume a linear relationship between the dependent variable and the predictor variables. For example, consider a simple linear regression model in which we are predicting "LTV" (y) as a function of only "income" (x). If a scatter diagram between "LTV" and "income" reveals a curvilinear relationship as opposed to a linear relationship, a mathematical transform (square root, logarithm, cosine, etc.) of the income data may be required to get the best fit of the model possible. Taking, for example, the square root of income may result in the appropriate relationship observed.

The Enterprise Miner, a data mining tool offered by the SAS Institute, takes the guesswork out of determining the appropriate transform for continuous data elements by automating the process. It also presents the analyst with several options for dealing with missing data. The Enterprise Miner is discussed in more detail later in this chapter.

In many direct marketing companies, transforms are not always practical to implement. A transform may take too much computer processing time to run, or a computer routine to perform the transform may not be available. If this is the case, you must realize that the model may not be as strong as it could be if nonlinear relationships in your data are present. To learn more about various transforms and their applications, read any intermediate or advanced statistics book.

Option 2. Collapse the best age categories (those with high index values well over 100) and create a "dummy" variable that takes on only one of two values: 1 = all age categories with a high index value, 0 = all other age categories.

Option 3. Collapse the age categories to three, four, or more categories and create an "x-value" variable that takes on the index value associated with each new category. The analyst collapses categories that have similar index values. For example, the analyst might decide to recode this variable into three categories as follows:

♦ Group 1: "25 and under" plus "36 and over"
♦ Group 2: "26–30"
♦ Group 3: "31–35" plus "No age info available"

Customers falling into Group 1 are assigned a value equal to 81, customers falling into Group 2 are assigned a value equal to 118, and customers falling into Group 3 are assigned a value equal to 107. For those with an in-depth knowledge of statistics, this yields similar results to setting up two dummy variables when multiple regression modeling is employed.

The Multiple Regression Model

Assuming ample time was spent identifying and analyzing powerful predictor variables, the development of the model itself is quite simple. Such models can only be determined by using a computer program.

The model is specified by a linear equation:

$$y = a + b_1 x_1 + b_2 x_2 + b_3 x_3 + \ldots$$

Where
y is the **response variable**, or what you are predicting (e.g., an order, a cancel)
$x_1, x_2, x_3, \ldots$ are the multiple predictor variables (e.g., age, income, RFM data elements)
a is a constant numerical value
$b_1, b_2, b_3, \ldots$ are the numerical coefficients (weights) associated with each of the predictor variables

The response variable is also called the *dependent* **variable** and the predictor variables the *independent* **variables**.

The final multiple regression model may have as few as 2 predictors or as many as 20 or more, depending on the data richness of the list being modeled.

As with SLR models, the coefficients associated with each predictor variable in a multiple regression model are determined such that the predictive error of the model is minimized. That is, the sum of the squared predictive errors is minimized for multiple regression models the same as it is for SLR models (see Chapter 9). Similarly, like that for SLR models, we call these multiple regression parameters, a, b_1, b_2, b_3, $\ldots$, least squares estimates.

Model Interpretation

To examine what an actual multiple regression model looks like and how to interpret such a model, assume Mega Telecom test promoted 20,000 currently active customers selected at random from the database last year for a high-speed Internet service. The sample was saved and included all data for each customer at the point-in-time of the promotion. The Mega Telecom analyst was asked by the product manager to build a multiple regression model that would help identify those most likely to order this high-speed

Internet service. The Mega Telecom analyst split the saved sample: 10,000 for analysis and 10,000 for validation. Using the analysis portion, he next created the *binary* response variable "order," which took on the two values: 0 if the customer did not order the service, and 1 if the customer ordered the service. Using techniques described in Chapter 7, he then analyzed the data and identified customer attributes that appeared to be strong predictors of ordering this particular service. Once recoded, he used SAS to generate the final multiple regression model shown in Exhibit 10.3.

Notice that some variables were coded by the analyst as binary. For example, rather than the logic counter variable taking on any value between 0 to 4 (indicating the number of the nonbasic services bought), it simply takes on two values: 1 if the person bought one or more of the four services, or 0 if they bought none of the four services. (For a discussion on how logic counter variables are created, see Chapter 7.)

Because the coefficient associated with variable X4 is less than the coefficient associated with variable X3, can we say that variable X3 is more important than variable X4? Absolutely not. The values of the coefficients depend on the scaling of the "predictor variables" relative to what you are trying to predict. Do not try to infer the importance of one variable versus another by examining the size of the coefficients.

In general, think of a multiple regression model as a set of specific criteria used to create a score for each customer that indicates their *relative* likelihood of ordering (or paying, canceling, renewing, etc.) the product of concern. Some characteristics/attributes add to a customer's score, whereas others lower the score. The way in which each variable affects a customer's overall value when scored is shown in Exhibit 10.4. The higher

Exhibit 10.3   High-Speed Internet Service Regression Model

Variable	Definition	Coefficient/Weight
Constant	A constant value	0.151767
X1	= 1, if age between 26 and 30 = 0, otherwise	 0.023618
X2	= Total # services ordered ever	0.060634
X3	= 1, if said yes to an outside questionnaire asking if use the Internet = 0, otherwise	 0.008761
X4	= Average dollars paid per month in the past 6 months	 0.003259

X5	= 1, if currently active on one or moreof the
	   following non-basic services: long
	   distance, wireless, multiple lines,
	   toll-free number
	= 0, otherwise
		
		0.086853

Exhibit 10.4 Application Scoring Rules for the High-Speed Internet Service Multiple Regression Model

Variable	Definition	Coefficient/Weight	Application Scoring Rules
Constant	A constant value	0.151767	Every customer "scored" on the regression model begins with a score equal to the constant value of 0.151767
X1	= 1, if age between 26 and 30; = 0, otherwise	0.023618	If a customer's age is between 26 and 30, his or her score is increased by 0.023618; otherwise, the score is unaffected.
X2	= Total # services ordered ever	0.060634	Each customer's score is increased by the number of services ordered ever when multiplied by 0.060634
X3	= 1, if said yes to an outside questionnaire asking if use the Internet; = 0, otherwise	0.008761	If customers say they use the Internet on the outside questionnaire, their score is increased by 0.008761; otherwise, their score is unaffected.
X4	= Average dollars paid per month in the past 6 months	0.003259	Each customer's score is increased by the average dollars paid per month in the past 6 months when multiplied by 0.003259. For customers with no dollars spent in the past 6 months, their score will be unaffected.
X5	= 1, if currently active on one or more of the following nonbasic services: long distance, wireless, multiple lines, toll-free number; = 0, otherwise	0.086853	If a customer is currently active on 1 or more of the four nonbasic services listed, their score is increased by 0.086853; otherwise, their score is unaffected.

the score, the more likely the customer is to order. Such a regression score is called a linear compensatory measurement in the field of quantitative marketing.

Exhibit 10.5 shows two currently active customers from the Mega Telecom database along with all relevant data. Assume today's date is March 1, 2001. Which customer, Smith or Jones, is more likely to order the high-speed Internet service, based on the multiple regression shown in Exhibit 10.3 and the scoring rules presented in Exhibit 10.4?

The Smith and Jones regression scores are calculated in Exhibit 10.6. Because Smith has a higher regression score than Jones, Smith is more likely

Exhibit 10.5 Customer Smith and Customer Jones Records

Customer	Age	Total # Services Ordered Ever	Monthly Dollars Paid						Outside Questionnaire —Do You Use the Internet?	Non-Basic Services Currently Active on			
			Sept 2000	Oct 2000	Nov 2000	Dec 2000	Jan 2001	Feb 2001		Long Distance	Wireless	Multiple Lines	Toll-Free Number
Smith	31	7	$102	$110	$125	$153	$120	$106	Yes	No	Yes	Yes	No
Jones	27	4	$90	$86	$99	$105	$89	$79	Yes	No	no	No	No

Exhibit 10.6 Resulting Regression Scores for Customers Smith and Jones

Variable	Smith Status	Smith Score	Jones Status	Jones Score
Constant	yes	0.151767	yes	0.151767
Age between 26 and 30?	no	0	yes	0.023618
Total # services ordered ever	7	7×0.060634 $= 0.424438$	4	4×0.060634 $= 0.242536$
Question—use Internet?	yes	0.008761	yes	0.008761
Average $ paid in past 6 months	($102 + $110 + $125 + $153 + $120 + $106)/6 = $119.33	119.33×0.003259 $= 0.388896$	($90 + $86 + $99 + $105 + $89 + $79)/6 = $91.33	91.33×0.003259 $= 0.297644$
Active on 1+ services?	yes	0.086853 1.060715	no	0 0.724326

191

to order the high-speed Internet service. Think of the score as a probability: the higher the value, the more likely the customer is to take the action modeled (in this case, order). Do not, however, mistake a multiple regression score for an *exact* probability, as it is not. Some customers may have scores greater than 1 or less than 0 when multiple regression is used, as is the case with customer Smith. As will be seen shortly, this problem is alleviated with the use of *logistic* **regression** models.

The formulas for determining the regression parameters $(a, b_1, b_2, b_3, \ldots)$ are not as simply stated as those for simple linear regression models (see Chapter 9). Therefore, no formulas for the coefficients will be given. Coefficients are determined solely by computer programs such as Excel, SAS, or SPSS.

Assumptions of the Model

Up to this point, we have made no reference to any assumptions or properties regarding multiple regression models. For those lacking a detailed knowledge of statistics, several assumptions or properties must be true in order for the model to be strong, robust, and hold up in a roll-out situation. The issues surrounding most of these properties are too complex for the novice. Because the intent of this book is not to teach readers how to become professional statisticians or modelers but rather give them a general understanding of what regression modeling is and how it is used in the field of database marketing, most of these properties will only be discussed at a fairly high level.

Multicollinearity

As you can see in Exhibit 10.3, the sign of the coefficients indicates the direction of the relationship between the predictor and the response variable. In multiple regression, if the predictors are correlated, the sign of the coefficient may change, depending on the other predictors in the model. The problem of strong relationships between the predictor variables is commonly referred to as **multicollinearity**. When predictor variables are related to each other, regression modeling can be very confusing. The coefficients of correlated predictors can change magnitude or even sign.

In addition, the error variance associated with the coefficients can become quite large. Inflated variances can be very harmful to the use of regression analysis for estimation, hypothesis testing, and forecasting and lead one to false conclusions.

When it comes to model development, many direct marketing analysts believe in the principle of parsimony. As such, most analysts try to eliminate any multicollinearity from the model. With experience, a direct marketing analyst gains much insight into how various customer attributes correlate to various customer behaviors and how those relationships differ by customer segment, offer, or product. A well-built and understood model is more stable and therefore less sensitive to changes in customer composition than a complex model not easily interpretable or understandable by the marketer or analyst.

For example, would it be wise to consider using both "household income" and "home value" as separate predictors in a multiple regression model? No, because both are measures of wealth and may be correlated with one another. Using both in the final regression model may result in multicollinearity.

To safely use both measures of wealth in a multiple regression model, you can combine them into a single measure by creating a cross-tabulation or logic counter variable (see Chapter 7). Combining correlated data elements into a single data element, as opposed to excluding one of the correlated data elements, is one way to reduce the chances of building models that exhibit multicollinearity without jeopardizing the predictive strength of the final model.

Other Properties

Because the model is built on a sample, each prediction made by the model has a certain amount of error. We assume these predictive errors have a mean of 0, constant variance, and are uncorrelated with one another. In addition, we assume these errors are independent of the predictor variables. For more information on these properties and how violations of such properties affect the multiple regression model, read any intermediate to advanced statistics book.

_____ A Note on Modeling Binary Response Data

Modeling customer behaviors such as ordering, paying, and renewing is, in essence, modeling **binary data**. That is, the response variable takes on only two values, 0 or 1. In the case of building a model predicting the likelihood of a customer ordering a particular product offer, the response variable "order" takes on two values: 0 if the customer did not order, and 1 if the customer did order the product.

When modeling binary data using multiple regression, you will observe *very* low (close to 0) R^2 values. Rest assured, this is *not* a problem. Direct marketers ignore the R^2 value as an overall indicator of how good a "customer action model" fits the data and instead use what is called the **gains chart** (see Chapter 11). Many theoretical statisticians balk at this notion. Keep your application in mind. Your goal is not so much to perfectly model orderers and nonorderers (this is impossible) but to simply give those customers who appear to be more likely to order a higher score and those who appear to be less likely to order a lower score. You promote those customers with the highest scores. If your model ranks those most likely to order higher than those least likely to order, then you have succeeded.

As you will soon see, it is difficult to develop a response model with an R^2 above 0.20. In general, most models have an R^2 value of 0.10 or lower, depending on the amount of customer data available. Simply ignore it.

Regression Diagnostics

You are now ready to learn some very important investigative techniques to help ensure the validity of the model built. In particular, you will learn how to examine the model for evidence of multicollinearity and also ensure that the variables in the final model are statistically valid.

Consider again ACME Direct. Assume that the ACME Direct product manager in charge of the music product line test promoted 10,000 customers from the database "Country Music USA." The model built by the analyst used the following variables to determine the customers most likely to order this title:

- TIME_LASTO = elapsed time measured in months since last order
- NUM_ORDERS = total number of orders ever, all product lines
- RATIO_CPD/CPR = ratio of total country music products paid ever to total country promotions sent ever
- TOTAL_DOLLPD = total dollars spent ever, all product lines

The regression output from Excel for this regression run is shown in Exhibit 10.7. Notice the low R^2 value of 0.306273019. Again, this measure should be ignored as a measure of model strength.

Examining the Model for Indications of Multicollinearity

To determine whether or not problems exist with respect to multicollinearity, examine the coefficients associated with each variable to ensure they look as expected. For example, if the relationship of the response variable to a predictor variable is a positive one, you should expect to see a positive coefficient associated with that predictor variable. If the relationship is negative, you should expect to see a negative coefficient. If anything else is observed for a particular predictor variable, multicollinearity is most likely an issue.

```
SUMMARY OUTPUT

        Regression Statistics
Multiple R              0.553419388
R Square                0.306273019
Adjusted R Square       0.277063462
Standard Error          0.410179289
Observations                 10,000
```

	Coefficients	Standard Error	t Stat	P-value
Intercept	-0.06266613	0.142680112	-0.439207182	0.661508811
TIME_LASTO	-0.020662188	0.016235476	-1.272656771	0.206245778
NUM_ORDERS	0.167054928	0.135725001	1.230833869	0.2214237
RATIO_CPD/CPR	2.361839091	0.540441502	4.37020303	3.17046E-05
TOTAL_DOLLPD	-0.004466228	0.00585551	-0.762739389	0.447508633

Exhibit 10.7   Microsoft Excel Regression Output

Examining each coefficient associated with the example model, we note the following:

- TIME_LASTO. For this variable, we expect that the longer it has been in months since a customer's last order, the lower the likelihood of that customer ordering. This represents a negative relationship. Because the coefficient is negative, there appears to be no problem.
- NUM_ORDERS. For this variable, we expect that the more orders a customer has placed, the higher the likelihood of ordering. This represents a positive relationship. Because the coefficient is positive, there appears to be no problem.
- RATIO_CPD/CPR. For this variable, we expect that the higher the ratio of country paid to country promotions, the higher the likelihood of ordering. This represents a positive relationship. Because the coefficient is positive, there appears to be no problem.
- TOTAL_DOLLPD. For this variable, we expect that the more dollars a customer has spent with ACME Direct, the higher the likelihood of ordering. This represents a positive relationship. However, we notice the coefficient is negative, indicating a possible problem with multicollinearity. Therefore, this variable must be highly correlated with another in the model.

To confirm that we have a problem with the variable dollars credited, we run a correlation analysis to determine if dollars credited is highly correlated with any of the other variables in the model. Exhibit 10.8 shows

	TIME_LASTO	NUM_ORDERS	RATIO_CPD/CPR	TOTAL_DOLLPD
TIME_LASTO	1			
NUM_ORDERS	-0.161209483	1		
RATIO_CPD/CPR	-0.163132058	0.140519834	1	
TOTAL_DOLLPD	-0.225144053	0.989429908	0.153392056	1

Exhibit 10.8   Microsoft Excel Correlation Analysis

the output of a correlation matrix produced on this data using the Analysis ToolPak feature of Excel.

On the basis of this correlation matrix, TOTAL_DOLLPD is highly correlated with NUM_ORDERS. In fact, the correlation is very close to 1 (0.989429908). Does this make sense? Yes, because the more orders customers have placed, the more money they have spent.

You have two options to rid the model of multicollinearity: delete one of the two correlated variables or combine the two correlated variables into one variable via the creation of a cross-tabulation, logic counter, or ratio. If the correlation between the two variables is quite strong, as is the case in our example, you will not lose much in terms of the predictive strength of the model by deleting one of the variables.

If you decide to exclude one of the two correlated variables, which one do you choose—TOTAL_DOLLPD or NUM_ORDERS? As a rule of thumb, remove the variable that is least correlated with the response variable or reduces R^2 the least. Because TOTAL_DOLLPD is less correlated with ordering than NUM_ORDERS, we will exclude it from the model and keep NUM_ORDERS (see Exhibit 10.9).

In addition, an experienced data analyst may have further insight into which one to delete, based on historical information. Experience goes a long way in the development of strong and robust models.

A second run of the regression model *excluding* TOTAL_DOLLPD (see Exhibit 10.10) solves the problem of multicollinearity. All coefficients now appear to be in order.

Unfortunately, not all problems of multicollinearity are as obvious as the one shown here (the direction of a coefficient has reversed). To assist you in identifying problems of multicollinearity, you can also examine

	ORDER
NUM_ORDERS	0.378895052
TOTAL_DOLLPD	0.377912201

Exhibit 10.9   Microsoft Excel Correlation Analysis

SUMMARY OUTPUT				
Regression Statistics				
Multiple R	0.549567738			
R Square	0.302024698			
Adjusted R Square	0.28021297			
Standard Error	0.40928483			
Observations	10,000			
	Coefficients	*Standard Error*	*t Stat*	*p value*
Intercept	-0.087685711	0.138555492	-0.632856264	0.528332127
TIME_LASTO	-0.015074906	0.014457397	-1.042712336	0.29970027
NUM_ORDERS	0.064453779	0.018031186	3.574572362	0.000551127
RATIO_CPD/CPR	2.345871547	0.538858262	4.35341111	3.35086E-05

Exhibit 10.10   Second Microsoft Excel Regression Run

the *variance inflation factor scores*[1] (also called the VIF scores) associated with each predictor. Although Excel does not calculate the VIF scores for the predictors, most statistical software packages such as SAS do. Exhibit 10.11 shows the SAS output for this same multiple regression model along with each predictor's VIF scores (circled). Predictors with VIF scores close to 1 imply they are *not* correlated with any other predictor in the model. Predictors with VIF scores greater than 1 suggest they *are* correlated with another predictor. The larger the VIF score, the more likely there is redundant information in the model causing multicollinearity.

When examining the SAS output shown in Exhibit 10.11, notice that the VIF scores associated with TOTAL_DOLLPD and NUM_ORDERS are both greater than 1, suggesting that they are correlated with one another.

Examining the Model for Variable Significance

Your final model may contain predictors that, although independent of one another, are not adding strength to the model. To determine which variables are not adding strength to the overall model, we conduct a hypothesis test for each coefficient to determine if it is statistically different from 0. The *p* value[2] associated with each predictor variable as shown in Exhibit 10.9 tells you whether or not the coefficient is statistically different from 0. If the *p* value is under 0.10, you can conclude that the variable is statistically

```
The SAS System

                              Analysis of Variance

                                 Sum of         Mean
              Source        DF   Squares        Square      F Value      Prob>F

              Model          4   7.05653        1.76413      10.485      0.0001
              Error      9,995   15.98347       0.16825
              C Total    9,999   23.04000

                     Root MSE      0.41018     R-square      0.3063
                     Dep Mean      0.36000     Adj R-sq      0.2771
                     C.V.        113.93869

                              Parameter Estimates

                      Parameter     Standard      T for H0:                 Variance
        Variable      Estimate      Error        Parameter=0   Prob > |T|   Inflation

        INTERCEPT     -0.062666     0.14268011    -0.439       0.6615       0.00000000
        TIME_LASTO    -0.020662     0.01623548    -1.273       0.2062       1.31631579
        NUM_ORDERS     0.167055     0.13572500     1.231       0.2214      58.72575805
        RATIO_CPD/CPR  2.361839     0.54044150     4.370       0.0001       1.04323929
        TOTAL_DOLLPD  -0.004466     0.00585551    -0.763       0.4475      60.31303895
```

Exhibit 10.11   SAS Regression Run Displaying the VIF Scores

significantly different from 0 with at least 90% probability ($1 - p$ value) and adds value to the final model. If the p value is greater than 0.10, you can conclude that the variable is not adding value to the model. Remember, the model is built on a sample, and a sample has a certain amount of error associated with it. The coefficients, although guaranteed to minimize the predictive error, have a certain level of error associated with them. As such, some may have so much error associated with them that they may be unstable. The p value helps you identify such variables.

When you examine the p values associated with each of the predictors in the model shown in Exhibit 10.10 (excluding the constant), you will notice a problem with the variable TIME_LASTO. The p value associated with this variable is almost 0.30, suggesting that it should be removed. In other words, the variance is so great with this particular coefficient that it could actually be 0. All remaining p values are well below the 0.10 threshold and should be retained.

When you examine the p values shown in Exhibit 10.10, you will notice one of the numbers shown is "3.35086E-05." The "E-05" means to move the decimal point five places to the left, adding zeros. The result of moving the decimal place five places to the left yields a value of 0.0000335086. Excel uses this notation to give more precision in numerical values containing multiple leading zeros.

SUMMARY OUTPUT				
Regression Statistics				
Multiple R	0.542328103			
R Square	0.294119772			
Adjusted R Square	0.27956554			
Standard Error	0.40946886			
Observations	10,000			
	Coefficients	*Standard Error*	*t Stat*	*P-value*
Intercept	-0.191855271	0.096048983	-1.99747321	0.048574733
NUM_ORDERS	0.067115456	0.01785761	3.758367172	0.000292177
RATIO_CPD/CPR	2.426650617	0.533500126	4.548547407	1.56322E-05

Exhibit 10.12   Third and Final Microsoft Excel Regression Run

A third run of the regression model excluding TIME_LASTO yields the model shown in Exhibit 10.12. All p values associated with the remaining variables are below the threshold of 0.10. This is the final model.

Multiple "Logistic" Regression Models

Another type of regression model you can build is a **multiple *logistic* regression** model, also known as a logit model. This type of model has two main advantages over standard multiple regression models:

1. This model was specifically designed to deal with binary response variables, resulting in a slightly better model.

2. The predicted value of a logistic model is a *true* probability that can be easily rolled into an **expected profit** calculation jointly with marketing assumptions. (This is discussed in greater detail in Chapter 11.)

Logistic regression models are the correct application for most direct marketing applications. However, with sample sizes greater than 10,000, you will see little difference between a logistic or multiple regression model in terms of their predictive strength. Logistic models are also quite computer intense to develop. In addition, your information systems department or database fulfillment shop may not have the appropriate computer routines to allow them to apply such models against your customer file.

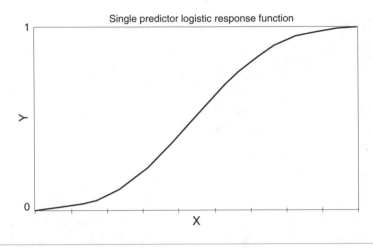

Exhibit 10.13   Logistic Response Curve

When the response variable is binary, the shape of the response function is curvilinear with the following logistic functional form:

$$y = \frac{e^{a + b_1 x_1 + b_2 x_2 + b_3 x_3 + \ldots}}{1 + e^{a + b_1 x_1 + b_2 x_2 + b_3 x_3 + \ldots}}$$

Where
y is the response variable, what you are predicting (e.g., an order, a cancel)
$x_1, x_2, x_3, \ldots$ are the multiple predictor variables (e.g., age, income, RFM data elements)
a is a constant numerical value
$b_1, b_2, b_3, \ldots$ are the numerical coefficients (weights) associated with each of the predictor variables
e represents the numerical value 2.71828.

To illustrate, a logistic model with only *one* predictor variable is shown in Exhibit 10.13. Notice that the function is bound between 0 and 1 as it yields a true probability score.

Excel does not allow the creation of logistic regression models because of the model's complexity; however, most statistical analysis software packages such as SAS or SPSS do have such features. We will not discuss this topic in more detail, but we recommend further study using an advanced statistics book.

Sample Composition

Multiple or logistic regression models can be built to predict many customer actions, not just response, as most examples so far in the chapter have considered. You may also build a payment model to help you identify those

Exhibit 10.14 Sample Specifications by Type of Model

Model Type	What Model Predicts	Sample Comprised of	How Response Action Is Coded
Response model	Predicts those most likely to respond	All customers test promoted	1 = order, 0 = all others
Payment model	Predicts those most likely to pay	All orders to test promotion	1 = pay, 0 = all nonpayers
Nonpay model	Predicts those most likely not to pay	All orders to test promotion	1 = nonpay, 0 = all payers
Net paid model	Predicts those most likely to order and pay	All customers test promoted	1 = paid order, 0 = all others
Cancel/Attrition model	Predicts those most likely to cancel a magazine subscription or club offer	All orders to test promotion	1 = cancel, 0 = all others
Nonresponse/dormancy model	Predicts those most likely to not respond or become dormant	All customers test promoted	1 = nonresponse, 0 = all others
Renewal model	Predicts those most likely to renew a magazine subscription	All paid orders to initial introductory subscription offer	1 = paid renewal, 0 = all others

on your database most likely to pay for a particular product if ordered. This is of particular interest to those offering free trials or where high return or cancel rates are of a concern. In addition, you may want to build a cancel or attrition model predicting those most likely to drop out of a club.

The only difference in the creation of these other models is the makeup of the sample and how the response variable is coded. Exhibit 10.14 shows the sample specifications required, depending on the type of model to be built.

Outside List Modeling Options

In today's competitive environment, most list owners are allowing others to model their files. Because list owners allow this option, many direct marketers can now successfully penetrate lists once deemed unprofitable.

As a list renter, you have two options available for modeling outside lists: (1) response models and (2) clone or best customer models

From a list renter's point of view, consider the use of these when you have a large outside list that you have not been able to successfully penetrate. The use of a model helps you identify your most likely candidates.

Most list owners offer both types of modeling on their files, using their own customer data as well as demographic and psychographic data at both the individual and geo-demographic level.

Response Models

These models are no different from house response models previously
discussed in this chapter. The only difference is that you are building the
model on someone else's file. You test promote a sample of prospects from
an outside list, and the list owner creates a frozen file that contains all the
customer data frozen point-in-time of your promotion. From this sample,
the list owner helps build a model on the file that predicts those prospects
most likely to respond to your promotion. You then use this model to select
more prospects from the list owner's file for a large scale rollout.

You must also pay careful attention to the universe selected for testing:

♦ Do not apply to many up-front selects when you define the list
universe for testing response models. For example, you may believe
that those under the age of 30 will not perform well, and tell the list
owner to exclude them from the test, when, in reality, it may very
well be that those people on the list under 30 years of age do perform
well if they are employed, married, and have children. A regression
model helps you spot and define these types of interactions. Let the
model do the work for you of defining your target market.

♦ If this is the first time you are trying to model a specific list, take a large
enough sample so that a certain portion of the sample can be set aside to
validate the modeling results. Validation is important when you have no
experience with a certain list and how its variables correlate with ordering your particular product. Give the analyst the opportunity to validate
the results of the new model to help ensure that you are successful.

Clone or Best Customer Models

From a list renter's point of view, a **clone model** identifies prospects on an outside
list that matches or "looks like" your best customers (as the list renter defines
them). Unlike response models, clone models do not predict a prospect's likelihood of responding to a particular offer. Rather, a clone model only tells you if
certain prospects look more like your best customers than other prospects.

The main benefit of a clone model is that you do not have to promote
a sample of prospects in advance. Therefore, you avoid testing costs and
time delays. You can build a clone model immediately, if desired.

To build a clone model, follow these steps:

1. Define a group of customers on your database you would like to
have more of (i.e., clone).

2. Pull a sample of these customers from your database and deliver it
to the list owner whose list you would like to penetrate.

3. The list owner will match these best customers to the file he or she owns that you are interested in penetrating.

4. The list owner will place a mark on each of the names that match your best customers. We will call this mark the best customer match indicator.

5. A sample will be created containing the match names and a sampling of nonmatches.

6. The list owner will build a regression model using this sample to determine which characteristics are most predictive in identifying your best customers. Note that the response variable for this model is the best customer match indicator mentioned in No. 4 above, and the predictor variables are all characteristics residing on the list owner's file.

7. Once the clone model is complete, the list owner will use the model to score all names on their database that do *not* match your file and give you those with the highest score (those most like a match to your best customers).

Building clone or best customer models has provided many large and small direct marketers with new and more successful ways to prospect for customers. Consider the case of Eximious, the Anglo American gift cataloger. Due to the lack of lists appropriate for the Anglo-centric market, prospecting for new customers was becoming an issue. The solution? Clone models. Working with the Polk Company, the Eximious file was matched up against two of Polk's databases: Response Selector, a cooperative database containing names of both catalog buyers and magazine subscribers, and Lifestyle Selector, the warranty card registration database. A clone model was built to predict those people on their two databases who most mirrored Eximious customers. As a result, Eximious was able to more successfully prospect for new customers than it had in the past ("A Better Supermodel," 1999).

Before embarking on the development of a clone model, you must first determine the definition of best customers. If you are not careful in selecting names from the database to be cloned, your model will fail when applied in rollout. In particular,

♦ Take into consideration the *media format* you will be sending the clones. For example, if you are going to send these clones a direct mail piece, do not select names from your database for cloning that were generated via television spot ads. Television names may not be responsive to direct mail.

♦ Take into consideration the *promotional offer* you will be sending the clones and define your best customers as ones that came on file in a similar fashion. For example, if you are going to send the clones a hard offer, do not select names from your database for cloning that you generated via a soft free trial offer. The composition of responders to these two types of offers are different.

♦ Last, determine if you wish to clone only certain demographic groups on your database. For example, if the future direction of your company is to create a younger customer base, you may only want to clone your best customers who are under the age of 55.

When you should consider the use of a response model or a clone model depends on your particular circumstances. Without question, you will be most successful at penetrating a new list with a response model. But there is a cost in terms of the time and budget.

You should consider the use of a clone model over a response model if

♦ You cannot wait 6 to 12 months to roll out with a particular product offer, which is required with the building of traditional response models
♦ You have time in the schedule but you do not have the budget for a list test
♦ You have time in the schedule but you do not have the budget required to test enough names for traditional response modeling

Under no circumstances should you consider the use of a clone model if either of the following two conditions is true:

1. You have a brand new promotional strategy (offer and/or source) you are about to implement

2. You wish to get into a brand new segment of customers never before tapped

If either of these conditions is true, you will not have any ideal candidates residing on your database for cloning. You are advised to only consider the use of a response model.

Another consideration to keep in mind is whether or not your transactional data clearly point out who the purchaser of a "household" is. For example, Mr. and Mrs. Jones both purchased regularly from the Williams-Sonoma catalog. At first, both received separate catalogs. Eventually, Williams-Sonoma realized they were the same "household" and began sending them only one catalog, addressed to the two of them and with one customer ID. Because Mr. and Mrs. Jones have been "householded" and share the same customer ID, it is difficult to determine who the true buyer is for any particular product. Therefore, the Joneses' record may not be an ideal candidate for cloning.

A summary of comparisons between the two outside list modeling options at your disposal is shown in Exhibit 10.15.

	Response Model	**Clone**
Advantages	• The most powerful technique for identifyingresponders from an outside list to particular promotional offers.	• No initial promotional testing is required. • No frozen test files are required. • Lead time for implementation is short.
Disadvantages	• Budget considerations due to the need to send out test promotions. • Frozen files are required. • Long lead times, because testing is required prior to model building.	• The model will not predict responders but only matches to your best customers. • Cannot be used to penetrate new segments, but only tosegments similar to those on your database. • Cannot be used to penetrate lists with new promotionaloffers, but only with offers similar to those used in thepast.

Exhibit 10.15   Summary of Comparisons—Response vs. Clone Models

Stepwise Regression Models

If you have many possible predictor variables to consider in the modeling process (response, payment, or cloning), the longer it will take you to develop the final model. Fortunately, many statistical software packages have automated the process of variable selection for you, deleting the insignificant ones based on low p values and little contribution to the overall R^2 value (see Chapter 9). Software packages such as SAS have several options to help you quickly and efficiently build the best model; Excel does not.

*All Possible Regressions.*This technique develops every possible model that can be formed, given the variables. It selects the best models based on R^2 values. Although not perfect, it can help you reduce your input predictor variables to a smaller, more manageable set.

Forward Selection. This technique first identifies the single most important predictor variable in terms of explaining the variation in the y data. The next variable to enter into the model is the one that, simply speaking, contributes the most to the R^2 value. This process continues until no further significant contribution to the R^2 value occurs. As new variables enter, others are checked to determine the current significance of their contribution.

Backward Elimination. This technique begins with every variable in the model and, one by one, backs out the weakest, least significant variables until only the strongest variables remain.

   It should be pointed out that the forward selection and backward elimination methods listed above are also called **stepwise regression** routines because they "step in" or "step out" candidate variables from the final model.

You can use any of these options, whether you are building a multiple regression model or a logistic model. However, a stepwise logistic model takes considerably more computer and elapsed time to run, perhaps several hours, depending on the size of the sample and number of possible predictor variables.

Also keep in mind that none of these methods check for multicollinearity. This must be checked manually. We do not recommend that you let any of these methods blindly develop the final model for you. Use these regression techniques only as a means to reduce your list of predictors to a more manageable, smaller set.

Neural Networks

Neural networks are often defined as a computer application that attempts to mimic the neurophysiology of the human brain by learning from examples. More specifically, it is a set of flexible nonlinear mathematical models that are interconnected in a nonlinear dynamic system. Patterns in the data are presented to the network via an input layer, which communicates to various hidden layers where the actual processing is done via a system of weighted connections. The hidden layers then link to an output layer where the answer is revealed.

Credit fraud detection is a common application of neural networks because of the learning aspect of neural networks. The final weights of the neural network are determined by learning the data. That is, the neural network learns the patterns of spending that indicate fraud. This is how it works: When a neural network is initially presented with a pattern in the data, it makes a "guess" as to what it might be. It then sees how far its answer was from the actual pattern and makes an appropriate adjustment to its weights. The process iteratively continues until the data are learned.

Once a neural network is "trained" to a satisfactory level, it can be used as an analytical tool on other data. It is also possible to overtrain a neural network, which means that the network has been trained exactly to respond to only the input data provided for training.

Neural networks are not used more within the direct marketing industry for three reasons:

1. Data preparation for neural networks is much more complex and time consuming than that required for regression analysis.

2. The results of neural networks are very difficult, if not impossible, to interpret by the analyst or marketer—unlike the results of regression analyses.

3. Neural networks do not consistently outperform traditional regression analyses.

Data Mining, Tools, and Software

We briefly mentioned data mining in Chapter 7 in the discussion of the analysis and manipulation of customer data. What is data mining? Data mining is the iterative process of identifying previously unknown relationships and patterns in data, in particular in customer databases, to solve a business problem. It is really what we have been discussing throughout the latter half of this book.

You mine your customer data to determine those characteristics that most separate out responders from nonresponders, payers from nonpayers, attritors from nonattritors, and so on. You do so using the lessons learned not only in this chapter but also in Chapters 7, 8, and 9.

Data mining has its roots in several academic disciplines: traditional statistics, computer science, machine learning, and artificial intelligence. Data mining has been employed for decades to predict outcomes based on past events. One of the first commercial applications of data mining was to score loan applications by banks as early as the 1960s. It has only recently been adopted by the general business public as a standard practice for turning vast amounts of corporate data into actionable information and knowledge. The recent adoption of data mining by the mainstream is due largely to the acceptance and availability of corporate data warehouses and the exponential improvements in computer resources, including faster processing and the ability to score large amounts of data easily.

Data mining is, above all else, a process that focuses on solving strategic business problems by employing best practices.

So the question now becomes, what is a data mining tool? Data mining tools can be viewed as the computer-automated analysis of customer data. You can choose from somewhere between 50 to 75 different data mining software packages. Examples include the Enterprise Miner by SAS, Model 1 by Group 1, KnowledgeSEEKER by Angoss, and MarketMiner. Each one has different options, and some are built for specific applications. For example, some have built-in reporting options, others do not. Some offer neural network models, others do not. And as a result, prices vary greatly. For a listing of such tools, visit the *Software* magazine Web site at www.softwaremag.com and search the archives for knowledge decision tools. Most companies are listed on the Web.

But all these tools have one thing in common: They are statistically based and therefore should be operated by someone familiar with the applications such as a data analyst or trained statistician. Data mining tools are not a magic box into which raw customer data can be fed and out comes the solution. Nothing could be further from the truth. They require a detailed knowledge of data analysis.

What a data mining tool helps you do is more efficiently and, depending on the tool, more effectively prepare the data, build segmentation trees, perform a **multivariate analysis,** and create many types of models, including neural networks.

Before deciding on a specific software package, you are well advised to have your analyst test those you think will best meet your corporate needs. Most data mining software companies will give you a free trial period during which you can test the product for your applications. The single most important feature you should look for in any data mining package is flexibility to tailor the software to your needs. Some data mining software packages on the market today are quite restrictive in terms of how you operate them. As a result, they tie the data analyst's hands from being creative in the analysis process.

What do these tools look like? Most are built with a graphical user interface (GUI) and are point-and-click operated.

For example, the SAS Enterprise Miner is an integrated product that provides an end-to-end business solution for data mining. A GUI interface provides a user-friendly front end to the mining process. The user builds a process flow diagram that can be modified or saved. It contains a collection of sophisticated analysis tools:

- ♦ Sampling: These tools include data set selection and validation sample creation via various sampling techniques.
- ♦ Exploring: These tools allow the user to view data distributions in graphical formats.
- ♦ Modifying data: These tools include outlier detection, variable transformation, and data imputation (filling in missing data values).
- ♦ Modeling: These tools include variable selection, clustering, trees, linear and logistic regression, and neural networks.
- ♦ Assessing models: These tools include model comparison reports and scoring of **validation sample/data sets** in preparation for gains (or lift) chart creation (to be discussed in Chapter 11).
- ♦ Building utility: These tools allow users to build custom tools by incorporating their own code and procedures into the data mining process, an important feature for any data mining tool.

Each of the Enterprise Miner's processes described above is driven by what SAS calls a node. Think of a node as nothing more than a module containing programming and processing code hidden behind the scenes. You build the process flow by adding and connecting nodes. Although many of the nodes have default settings for generating code in the background, analysts are encouraged to open each node and modify the settings to be appropriate for the analysis at hand. Exhibit 10.16 displays a screen print showing an example process flow diagram built within the Enterprise Miner. In this process diagram, the sample is first defined and is then fed into a node, which splits the sample into two: one for analysis and the other

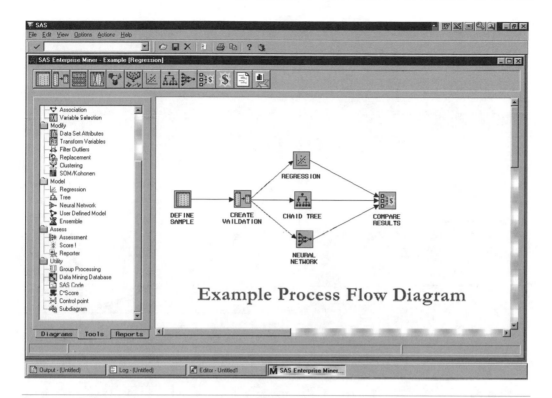

Exhibit 10.16   Enterprise Miner Process Flow Diagram

for validation. Next, the analysis sample is fed into the regression node, tree node, and neural network node. Last, the results of each modeling technique are fed into the assessment node for comparison via validation lift charts. No programming code is required. All code is built behind the scenes upon the execution of this process flow.

On the basis of the results of the lift chart comparisons (see Exhibit 10.17), the analyst can go within, for example, the regression node and fine-tune the options available. Once fine-tuned, the analyst then reexecutes the process flow.

Data mining tools also offer graphical capabilities. For example, Exhibit 10.18 shows the distribution of the variable "gender." Two- and three-dimensional views can also be created by the Enterprise Miner showing how the orders distribute for each category of the predictor variable.

The MarketMiner is also built with a GUI and is point-and-click operated. With the MarketMiner, you do not build a process flow diagram, as in the Enterprise Miner, but rather select and save the various analysis steps you desire in a project folder.

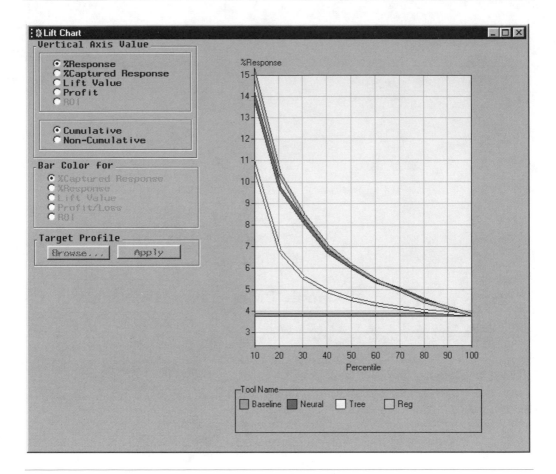

Exhibit 10.17   Enterprise Miner Lift Chart Comparisons

Begin by selecting the source of the data via the "Data" tab, as shown in the following screen print (Exhibit 10.19).

Once the data source is selected, click on the "Transforms" tab as shown in Exhibit 10.20. In this area of MarketMiner, you create the holdout sample for validation or training. In addition, this is where you perform the recoding of your data prior to running any models.

Next, select the various analysis techniques you wish to employ by clicking on the "Mining Agendas" tab as shown in Exhibit 10.21. In this area, you have several options, including logistic regression analysis, tree segmentations, and even cluster analysis as discussed in Chapter 8.

You can learn more about the MarketMiner software package at its company web site, www.marketminer.com.

Remember, data mining tools do not provide a quick analytical solution. But they do have the capability, if used properly, to help analysts be more efficient and effective in their role by providing a suite of analytical tools at their ready disposal.

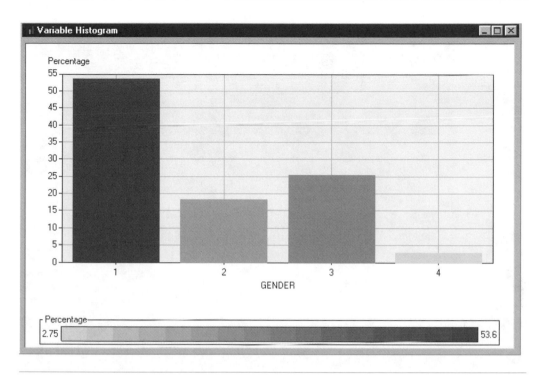

Exhibit 10.18   Enterprise Miner Graphing Example

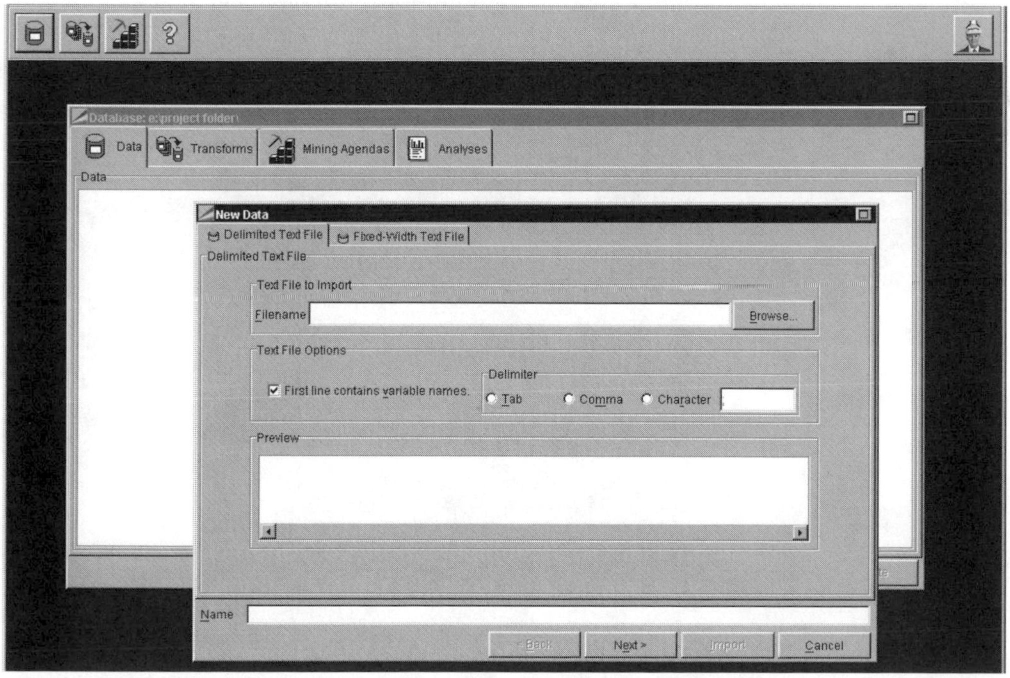

Exhibit 10.19   Defining the Analysis Data Set in MarketMiner

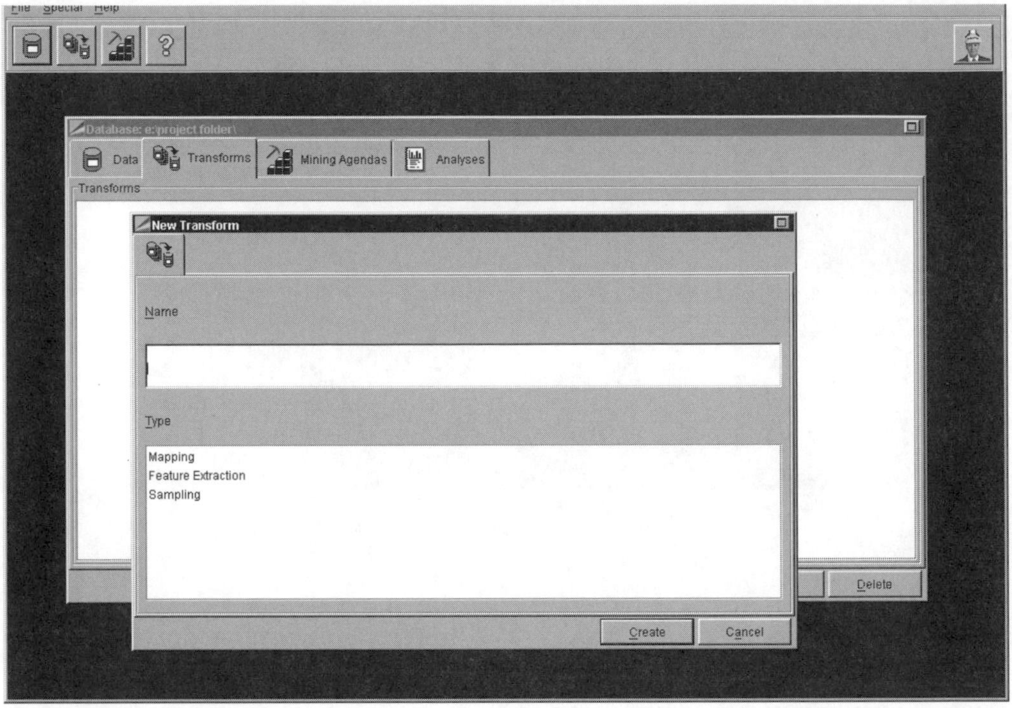

Exhibit 10.20   Performing Subsampling and Recoding Techniques in MarketMiner

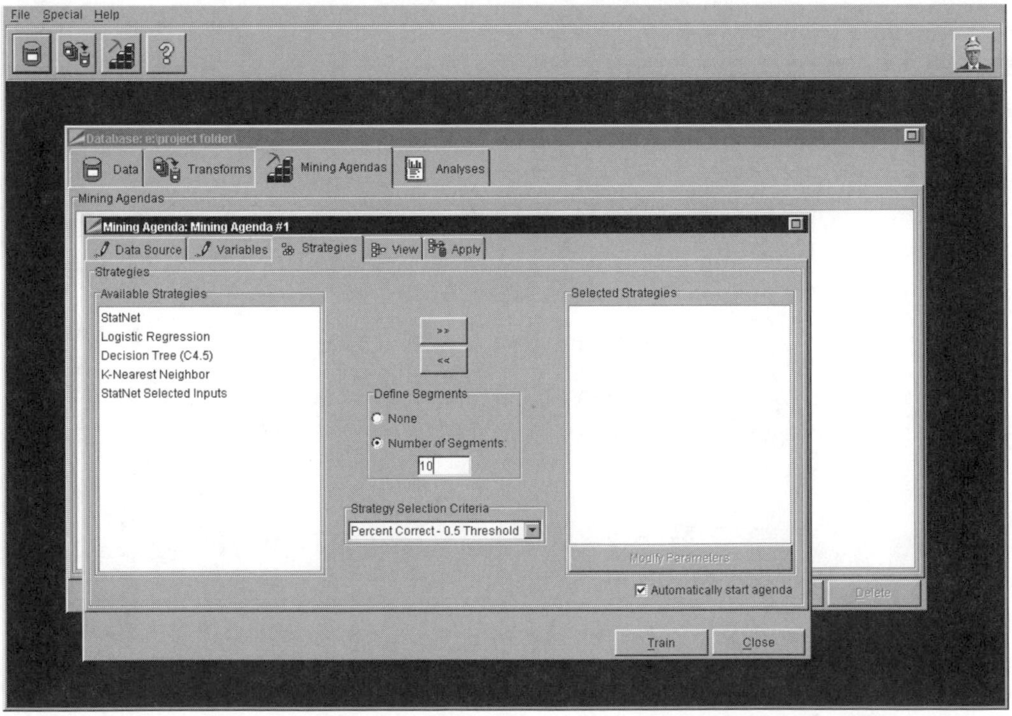

Exhibit 10.21   Selecting the Analysis Techniques to Employ in MarketMiner

Ensuring That Your Model Holds Up in Rollout

The success or failure of a model has nothing to do with whether it is built on an internal or external file or if it was built to predict response or payment. It has more to do with following certain rules and guidelines of model building, which, if not adhered to, you will fail, regardless of the model type. It is that simple.

You can use six guidelines, some of which we have already discussed, to ensure stability when building any model. We call these guidelines Modeling with MUSCLE. Adhering to the MUSCLE guidelines will guarantee your models to be robust and hold up when applied in rollout.

Materials Treatment Consistency Between Test and Rollout

If you drastically change your offer or creative approach between test and rollout, the responders identified by your model will no longer be valid in rollout. For example, a model built to predict which customers are most likely to order a product via a soft risk-free offer will differ from a model built for the same product but with a hard offer. The model built with the soft offer will incorporate some variables that identify marginally performing names that in all probability will not be attracted to a hard offer. Using this model to select names to promote with a hard offer is therefore not advised. The model will be selecting the wrong types of names to be promoted with a hard offer.

Changes in creative approach can also cause a subtle shift in the composition of responders. When you build a response model, you are not only modeling responders to your *product* but also the *product offer* (price, terms, etc.).

Universe Application

When you build a response model, you are building it on a sample taken from a particular universe of customers. Therefore, your forecast based on this response model will only be valid when applied to the same universe of customers the model was built on. For example, you cannot build a model on an entire universe of customers, apply the model to only those customers within that universe who are over the age of 30, and expect the same forecasted gains. The model will not hold up as originally forecasted.

To guarantee that your universe definitions are consistent between test and rollout, always check to ensure that the customers your programmer or list shop is pulling meet your specifications. To verify consistency between the names defined at test and at rollout, compare the distribution of regression model scores. For example, if 10% of the test names the model was built on have a score above 0.2576, you should expect close to the same percentage of names scoring above 0.2576 at rollout. If not, you probably have definitional inconsistencies.

In addition, be aware that your outside list universes may change between test and rollout without your knowledge. This is caused by changes in the way list owners build their file. If the names on a list you regularly rent were obtained by the list owner in a different way this month versus last month (e.g., a new offer), you can expect the composition of these names to change, resulting in a difference in response to your promotions. Because you have no say in how list owners obtain their customers via the "offer," the best you can do is to stay informed regarding any changes in the list owners' promotional strategies. If you notice a major change in a list owner's offer, you may want to consider rebuilding a new response model or, at the very least, adjusting your forecast. This also applies to compiled lists.

Split the Sample for Validation

Before performing your analysis, a portion of the sample should be set aside and used to validate the findings, as previously discussed in Chapter 6.

Correlation Analysis

When you build a regression model, each predictor variable used in the model must be independent of one another, as previously discussed in this chapter.

Lift and Freeze Customer Attributes at Point-in-Time of the Promotion

For an analysis of past promotional behavior to be valid, the customer characteristics residing on the sample must reflect the customers' status at the time they were promoted, as previously discussed in Chapter 6.

Examine the p Values

All variables used in the final regression model must be significant, as previously discussed in this chapter.

Strict adherence to these guidelines will help increase the odds that your model will hold up as forecasted in rollout. Of course, this assumes that occurrences outside your control do not affect your ability to achieve the forecasted gains. What do we mean by that? Consider the following example: Your final response model identified Florida residents as a prime target area, and as such had a high positive coefficient/weight associated with this region. A devastating hurricane in Florida prior to delivery of the promotion will cause your model to partially fail in rollout. These Florida names will no longer perform as expected. Luckily, these exceptions are far and few between.

The bottom line is, if your model does not hold up as forecasted, odds are that you did something wrong. Either the model built used unstable predictors with high p values, the universe changed between test and rollout, some of the predictor variables were highly correlated with one another, the characteristics upon which the model was based did not reflect the customer's status at the time of the promotion, or you lacked a validation sample upon which to check your model.

Chapter Summary

Multiple regression is a more sophisticated technique that database marketers use to predict customer response. In addition to predicting customer response to an order, multiple regression modeling can also be used to predict other customer behavior such as payment, returning a product, or renewing a subscription. Database marketers have to apply multiple regression modeling techniques in a specific way to optimize the results and avoid errors. Preparation of the data prior to analysis is an important step. Variables must be in a proper form for the regression analysis to yield meaningful results. Often variables have to be recoded for the analysis. In addition, certain assumptions have to be met about the data. For example, strong relationships between predictor variables (multicollinearity) may lead to an unstable model. Analysts attempt to eliminate multicollinearity from the model to increase stability. The statistical significance of the model also has to be examined. The significance reflects the degree of confidence that a manager can place in the ability of the model to predict behavior. Modeling on external files is also discussed. This allows a marketer to predict the response of a list of prospects. This chapter also explores other regression modeling methods, neural nets, and data mining programs. For experienced analysts, these techniques can provide additional ways to examine the data to help develop the most stable and effective predictive model. The chapter concludes with six guidelines (MUSCLE) for model development to ensure that the model holds up in rollout.

Review Questions

1. What types of customer behavior can be predicted with multiple regression modeling?
2. Explain how data are prepared prior to multiple regression analysis.

3. How is multicollinearity detected and eliminated from a regression model?

4. Discuss how variable significance is interpreted in regression output.

5. Discuss how data mining tools can help the model building process. What are the possible problems with using these tools?

6. If you are building a payment model predicting which customers are most likely to pay for a product, describe the sample composition.

7. What are the MUSCLE guidelines attempting to achieve? Summarize the key issues of the guidelines.

Notes

1. How VIF scores are calculated is not discussed in this book. It is covered in most intermediate or advanced statistics books.
2. The derivation of the p value and its statistical properties are not discussed but can be found in any intermediate statistics book.

11

Gains Charts and Expected Profit Calculations

With the first Inside Source response model built, Keri Lee was concerned with how well the model would work in rollout. Would it predict responders, as it suggests?

To answer Keri's question, her analyst created what is called a gains chart (or lift chart) using the validation sample. She was told by her analyst that such a gains chart will yield a simulation of what she can most likely expect to occur in rollout regarding the model's predictive strength. Once the predictive strength of the model was confirmed, Keri was ready to select the most profitable names for promotion.

Her goal for the overall campaign was to generate at least 5% profit after overhead. Given such a goal, she determined that she must receive at least a 2.5% response rate. Using the results of the validation gains chart (with predictions), she selected all names meeting her criteria.

It has now been 12 weeks since the promotional mailing occurred. The mailing was slightly under forecast. Keri was anxious to reconcile the forecasted gains to determine if the model was the cause. Unfortunately, Keri forgot to promote a sample of names not meeting her criteria. As a result, Keri will not be able to determine if the reason the mailing is under forecast is due to the regression model not holding up as forecasted or due to the change in promotional format.

As mentioned in Chapter 10, regression models can be built to assist the direct marketer in predicting which customers on a database are most likely to order, pay, renew, and so on for a particular product offering. Once the final regression model is built for the specified marketing campaign, the next step is the actual application of the model to determine which names to promote and which names not to promote from the entire database for an upcoming marketing campaign.

You, as a direct marketer, have several options for selecting names via regression models, some of which are easier to implement than others, depending on the number of models being applied and the flexibility of your computer systems. This book considers two applications:

1. Selecting names based on a single regression "response" gains chart

2. Selecting names based on "expected profit" calculations, which incorporates multiple regression models and marketing cost and profit figures

This chapter reviews the steps required to implement both methods, with detailed examples of the applications in the field of direct marketing, including the development of the marketing forecast.

The Response Gains Chart

After building a single regression model to help predict the customers most likely to respond to a particular product offer, you are ready to create an analysis and validation response gains chart to determine (a) model stability and (b) the most profitable customers on the database to promote.

An *incremental* response gains chart will provide you with a ranking of customers from those most likely to respond to those least likely to respond. On the basis of your marketing cost and profit figures for the product promotion under consideration, determine how many names you can promote.

To develop an incremental response gains chart on the *analysis* portion of the sample, follow these steps:

1. Score the analysis sample using the regression model. This scoring process is done in the same manner as the scoring example in Chapter 10 (see Exhibit 10.5). That is, each name in the analysis sample is passed through the model and a single score assigned to each name, indicating their overall relative likelihood of ordering.

2. Once names are scored, rank the names from highest scoring to lowest scoring.

3. Cut the ranked scores into 10 equal "buckets," each representing 10% of the sample. For example, Bucket 1 will contain the top scoring 10% of your sample, Bucket 2 will contain the next highest scoring 10% of your sample, and so on. NOTE: In some cases, you may have tied scores at a bucket cutoff level. If this occurs, move your cutpoint for that bucket up (or down) until the score changes. As a result, some buckets may have slightly more (or less) than the desired 10%.

4. For each bucket, calculate the order rate and the gain. The gain is simply the index value minus 100.

To develop an incremental gains chart on the *validation* portion of the sample, follow these steps:

1. Score the validation (or holdout) sample using the regression model.

2. Once names are scored, rank the names from highest scoring to lowest scoring.

3. Define the 10 buckets as determined on the analysis sample. For example, Bucket 1 on the analysis sample was defined as names having a score greater than or equal to 0.2139. Therefore, the names in Bucket 1 are defined as those names having a score greater than or equal to 0.2139 also (even if that represents more or less than 10% of the validation sample).

4. For each bucket, calculate the order rate and the gain.

ACME Direct test promoted a new product to 20,000 names from the customer segment "5+ paid orders in the past 24 months" (see Exhibit 11.1).

The sample was split 10,000 for analysis and 10,000 for validation. At the request of the product manager, the analyst built a regression model (using the analysis sample only) predicting those customers who were most

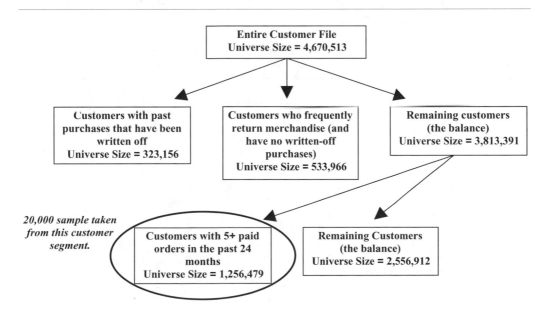

Exhibit 11.1 Segment Test Promoted a New Product Offering by ACME Direct

likely to order the product of concern. Once the model was complete, the analyst scored both the analysis and validation samples with the final regression model, ranked the names from highest scoring to lowest scoring, and developed the incremental response gains charts (see Exhibit 11.2) following the steps previously outlined.

Tie scores must have been present, because many of the 10 buckets produced on the analysis sample do not contain exactly 10% of the names.

The gain values displayed in the incremental gains charts are merely a function of the index values. They are calculated as the index to total for each bucket minus 100. Like the index values displayed for univariate tabulations (see Chapter 7), they allow you to more easily view how much better or worse each group or bucket of names performed when compared to the total and in relation to one another.

For the validation sample, the first bucket (those with a score greater than or equal to 0.7546) has a response rate 76% higher than the entire sample. In other words, this regression model has identified roughly 10% of this universe that will respond at a rate 76% higher than the response rate of the entire segment (7.48% vs. 4.25%).

Also notice that both the analysis and validation incremental gains charts have perfect monotonically (perfectly smooth) decreasing response rates when viewed from top to bottom. This is one sign of a good model.

If the incremental gains chart produced on the analysis sample reveals close to monotonically decreasing gains but it does not for the validation sample, it is an indication of a poor model. We advise you to examine the model for weak predictors with high p values or problems with multicollinearity (see Chapter 10).

Exhibit 11.2   Incremental Response Gains Charts Built on the Analysis and Validation Samples

		Incremental Gains on Analysis				Incremental Gains on Validation			
Bucket	Score Level	Sample Percent	Sample Count	Response Rate	Gain Over Total	Sample Percent	Sample Count	Response Rate	Gain Over Total
I	GE 0.7546	9.98	998	7.69	81	10.00	1,000	7.48	76
2	0.6532–0.7545	10.02	1,002	6.59	55	10.00	1,000	6.38	50
3	0.5589–0.6531	10.00	1,000	5.61	32	9.94	994	5.53	30
4	0.5013–0.5588	10.05	1,005	5.19	22	10.06	1,006	5.14	21
5	0.4429–0.5012	9.95	995	4.76	12	9.95	995	4.72	11
6	0.4013–0.4428	9.96	996	4.34	2	10.05	1,005	4.42	4
7	0.3521–04012	10.04	1,004	3.02	−29	10.04	1,004	3.19	−25
8	0.2782–0.3520	10.00	1,000	2.30	−46	9.96	996	2.38	−44
9	0.1891–0.2781	10.00	1,000	1.87	−56	9.98	998	2.00	−53
10	LE 0.1890	10.00	1,000	1.15	−73	10.02	1,002	1.28	−70
Total		100.00	10,000	4.25	0	100.00	10,000	4.25	0

If the incremental gains charts produced on both the analysis and validation samples are not close to monotonically decreasing and are very choppy, it may indicate that the model was not properly coded by your programmer, and therefore, the samples were not properly scored.

As mentioned in Chapter 6, the purpose of a validation sample is to allow the analyst to confirm the analysis results. Remember that a sample is just that, a sample, and as such, a model built on any sample will have error associated with it. How much error your final model may have depends on how careful you were in the exclusion of insignificant or correlated variables. Assessing the model on the validation sample compared to the analysis sample allows you to gauge the amount of error associated with your model. If much error is present, we say the model was "overfit."

How can we tell if the model built reveals an overfitting situation? If the projected gains for the top few buckets are similar between the analysis and validation samples, you have built a stable model. If this is the case, it implies you built little error into the model and it validates nicely on the holdout or validation sample. If the gains are significantly lower for the validation sample when compared to the analysis sample for the top few buckets, then you have a weak model that will not hold up in rollout.

For the gains shown in Exhibit 11.2, the top bucket in the analysis segment responded at a rate 81% higher than the entire sample, whereas the same bucket for the validation sample yielded a response rate 76% higher than the entire sample. This is a 6% ($[81-76]/81 = 6\%$) falloff in gains. Anything greater than a 10% falloff in the top few buckets is cause for concern. A greater than 10% falloff indicates a potential problem with your regression model, and in such cases, we strongly advise you to carefully review your regression model for potential problems (multicollinearity, weak predictors, etc.).

The only purpose of the incremental gains chart on the analysis sample is to check for falloff in gains when compared to the same on the validation sample. Once you are satisfied that the falloff in gains from analysis to validation is minimal and acceptable, you will base all marketing decisions on the incremental response gains chart produced on the validation sample only. The validation sample provides you with a more stable indicator of what you can expect the model to yield in a rollout situation.

On the basis of the validation gains chart, what percentage of the names can the product manager profitably promote, given the fact that she needs at least a 2.97% response rate to break even? According to the validation gains chart, it appears that by promoting all customers with a regression score above 0.3521 (the top seven buckets), the breakeven criteria will be met. The product manager will not promote the last three buckets of names, because the projected response rates for each are below the required breakeven response rate level.

Now that the product manager knows which buckets she will promote, she needs to determine the response rate for these seven buckets combined. To determine this, she will have to create a cumulative gains chart on the validation sample. Cumulative figures tell the associated number of names, the response rate, and the gain for all names falling into a given bucket *and all buckets above it*. These figures are determined from the incremental gains chart.

It is easy to turn any incremental gains chart into a cumulative gains chart using Excel. The cumulative gains chart shown in Exhibit 11.3 was created in Excel using the incremental gains chart figures created on the validation sample shown in Exhibit 11.2.

For example, the cumulative "Sample Count" for Bucket 2 represents the incremental "Sample Count" for Buckets 1 and 2 combined (1,000 + 1,000). The cumulative "Response Rate" for Bucket 2 represents the incremental "Response Rate" for Buckets 1 and 2 combined: $[(1,000 \times 0.0748) + (1,000 \times 0.0638)]/2,000$. The cumulative "Gain" for Bucket 2 is calculated as $[(6.93/4.25) \times 100] - 100$. This information tells the product manager what she can expect if she promotes the top two buckets. Similarly, the cumulative figures for Bucket 3 represent the total names falling into Buckets 1, 2, and 3, the combined response rate for Buckets 1, 2, and 3, and the gains associated with the combined response rate for Buckets 1, 2, and 3. This information tells the product manager what she can expect if she promotes the top three buckets.

The product manager instructs her programmer to score all 1,256,479 customers falling into the "5+ paid orders in the past 24 months" segment (see Exhibit 11.1) using the regression model built and to transmit only those

Exhibit 11.3 Cumulative Gains on Validation

Bucket	Score Level	Incremental Gains on Validation				Cumulative Gains on Validation			
		Sample Percent	Sample Count	Response Rate (%)	Gain Over Total	Sample Percent	Sample Count	Response Rate (%)	Gain Over Total
1	GE 0.7546	10.00	1,000	7.48	76	10.00	1,000	7.48	76
2	0.6532–0.7545	10.00	1,000	6.38	50	20.00	2,000	6.93	63
3	0.5589–0.6531	9.94	994	5.53	30	29.94	2,994	6.46	52
4	0.5013–0.5588	10.06	1,006	5.14	21	40.00	4,000	6.13	44
5	0.4429–0.5012	9.95	995	4.72	11	49.95	4,995	5.85	38
6	0.4013–0.4428	10.05	1,005	4.42	4	60.00	6,000	5.61	32
7	0.3521–04012	10.04	1,004	3.19	−25	70.04	7,004	5.26	24
8	0.2782–0.3520	9.96	996	2.38	−44	80.00	8,000	4.90	15
9	0.1891–0.2781	9.98	998	2.00	−53	89.98	8,998	4.58	8
10	LE 0.1890	10.02	1,002	1.28	−70	100.00	10,000	4.25	0
Total		100.00	10,000	4.25	0	100.00	10,000	4.25	0

names with a score greater than or equal to 0.3521 to the letter shop for pro-motion. How many names will the programmer be expected to transmit?

If the sample the regression equation was built on is truly a random and representative sample of all names falling into the "5+ paid orders in the past 24 months" segment, the programmer should be expected to transmit exactly 70.04% of this universe, or 880,038 names. If the programmer transmits anything significantly higher or lower than this figure, a problem exists such as

+ The database was not properly scored on the regression model, or
+ A major shift in the composition of the universe being regressed must have occurred since the time of the test promotion.

If 880,038 names are transmitted and thus promoted, how many orders should the product manager expect to receive from this campaign? She should expect to receive 46,290 orders (880,038 × 0.0526).

When creating a gains chart, there is nothing magical about 10 buckets. You can have as many or as few buckets as you wish; however, keep in mind that you do not want too few names falling into any one bucket or your estimated response rates for each bucket will have a high error associated with them. In addition, if your final regression model has few variables, you may not have the spread in scores to create 10 buckets and might need to produce your gains chart with fewer buckets. This is typically a problem when regressing "data poor" lists.

Options When Lacking Validation Samples

The importance of a validation sample cannot be stressed enough, espe-cially when an analyst has limited experience in modeling a particular product, list, or offer. If your budget does not allow for test samples large enough to be split into one for analysis and another for validation, two options are available to you.

Historical Gains Falloff Chart

If you have implemented response models in the past and can acquire some historical figures regarding forecasted and actual gains from these past campaigns, you can develop what is called a historical gains falloff chart. These are created by comparing, for several past campaigns, actual to fore-casted gains and determining the falloff observed. Once determined, you can apply this adjustment to future gains charts prior to rollout to ensure that the best possible decision regarding who to promote is made.

For example, last year the product manager at a small newsletter publishing house with two finance titles built a response model to determine which inactive customers she would promote for *Hot Stock Tips*. Unfortunately, not enough names were tested for the creation of a validation sample. Therefore, the decision to determine who to promote was based on the same sample the model was built on. The product manager, on the basis of an analysis of profit and cost figures, determined she could only promote the top 30% (top three buckets) of the incremental gains chart. For these top three buckets, the cumulative gains chart revealed a gain of 75% in response over promoting everyone. In rollout, she received a gain of only 65%. This was a falloff in gains of 13%. The product manager's boss was not happy. In all likelihood, if the product manager had had a validation sample available, the gain based on the validation sample would have been closer to what she actually obtained.

Next year, the product manager built a response model to determine which inactive customers she would promote for the other title, *The Mutual Fund Report*. Again, she lacked a large enough test sample for the creation of a validation sample. Therefore, the decision to determine who to promote was based on the same sample the model was built on. The product manager, on the basis of an analysis of profit and cost figures associated with this title, determined she could only promote the top 30% (top three buckets) of the incremental gains chart. For these top three buckets, the cumulative gains chart revealed a gain of 104% in response over promoting everyone. Is this what she used as her forecasted gain? Absolutely not. She took advantage of her experience from last year's campaign and decided to reduce the forecasted gain by 13% (the same loss in gain realized when promoting the same percentage of the file for *Hot Stock Tips* last year). Instead, the product manager will only forecast a gain of 90.5% (87% of the analysis gain). This is basically how it works. When you lack samples large enough for the creation of a validation sample, you will adjust your gain based on historical information.

Ideally, this product manager will want to determine the historical loss in gains observed for all buckets, not just for Bucket 3 of a cumulative gains chart. And she will do so for several past campaigns. This way, if the product manager decides to promote, for example, the top six buckets for her next campaign, she will know how much to adjust the gains to ensure a more accurate forecast. In other words, she will want to construct a historical gains falloff chart. Exhibit 11.4 shows forecasted cumulative gains and actual cumulative gains received for two different book titles promoted last year by a small direct marketer of children's books. In both cases, the forecasted gains were based on the same sample that the model was built on.

Exhibit 11.4   Assessment of Forecasted Versus Actual Gains

Bucket	Score (%)	Book Title X			Book Title Y			Average
		Fcst.	Actl.	Falloff (%)	Fcst.	Actl.	Falloff (%)	Falloff (%)
1	10	125	106	−15.00	101	87	−14.00	−14.50
2	20	101	89	−12.00	90	78	−13.00	−12.50
3	30	90	82	−9.00	84	76	−10.00	−9.50
4	40	67	62	−8.00	74	67	−9.00	−8.50
5	50	42	40	−5.00	55	51	−7.00	−6.00
6	60	30	29	−4.00	40	38	−5.00	−4.50
7	70	22	22	−2.00	32	31	−3.00	−2.50
8	80	14	14	−1.00	20	20	−1.10	−1.05
9	90	5	5	0.00	10	10	−1.00	−0.50
10	100	0	0	—	0	0	—	—

Using the calculated falloff in cumulative gains observed from forecast to actual for both products, an average was determined. Using this average falloff in cumulative gains, the product manager is now in a position to know exactly how to adjust each bucket of a cumulative gains chart prior to finalizing future marketing forecasts.

This technique is by no means perfect, but it does give valuable information to help small direct marketers make better promotional decisions and build more stable forecasts. Falloff in gains is typically a function of an analyst's experience and that experience in relation to the product, list, and offer being promoted. A more seasoned analyst typically builds models with less falloff than a new analyst.

Bootstrapping

Bootstrapping or bagging is another method that can be employed when samples are too small to be split into one for analysis and another for validation. It is a bit more complex to implement than the gains falloff chart but will yield forecasted gains much closer to actual.

To bootstrap, many subsamples are taken from the main test sample and a regression model built on each. For example, a major entertainment company test promoted a new music club offer to 10,000 names. Rather than build the response model on all 10,000 names, they will instead build many regressions on subsamples of this main sample. They will randomly take 100 subsamples from the main sample of size 1,000 each. For each of these 100 samples, they will build a regression model. Obviously, they will do so using a more automated technique such as the stepwise routine discussed in Chapter 10.

Once all models are built, they will examine them and determine which variables consistently entered the models. For the final model, they will choose the variables that consistently entered each model some percentage (e.g., 75%) of the time. By employing this technique, they have avoided the use of any variable that may have been unstable in rollout.

In fact, many direct marketers are closely examining this technique as a replacement for the current analysis and validation methodology. The belief is that the result of a bootstrapped model is a more stable and robust model than a model built on analysis samples and validated on holdout samples.

For more information on bootstrapping, read the paper "On Bagging and Nonlinear Estimation" (May 1999) by Jerome H. Friedman, Stanford University, and Peter Hall, Australian National University (www-stat.stanford.edu/~jhf).

Expected Profit Calculations

In business decisions, you may not only want to consider the likelihood of an event occurring but also consider the costs and profit figures associated with each of the events. Considering both enables you to base your marketing decisions on the likely payoff.

For example, you are promoting a magazine subscription offer for which the cancel rate is high. In determining who to promote, you build both a response model and a payment model to help you select not only customers most likely to order but customers most likely to order *and pay*. As previously discussed, this is a case in which you will not be able to use a standard response gains chart. This is where the calculation of expected profit comes into play. To determine the expected profit or loss for a particular business scenario, multiply the probabilities associated with each possible outcome by their respective *net* costs or profit values and then sum.

The expected monetary value calculation (EMV) is written as

$$EMV = P(O_1)M_1 + P(O_2)M_2 + P(O_3)M_3 + \ldots + P(O_n)M_n$$

Where

$P(O_1), P(O_2), P(O_3), \ldots P(O_n)$ = the probabilities associated with each of the n possible outcomes of the business scenario and the sum of these probabilities must equal 1

$M_1, M_2, M_3, \ldots M_n$ = the net monetary values (costs or profit values) associated with each of the n possible outcomes of the business scenario

The easiest way to understand EMV is to review a lottery example. Assume you are considering the purchase of a lottery ticket in which the probability of winning the $1 million jackpot is 1 in 10 million. If the lottery ticket costs $1 to purchase, what is the expected monetary value or expected profit/loss for this scenario (purchasing of a lottery ticket)?

First, list the various outcomes $(O_1, O_2, O_3, \ldots O_n)$ of this scenario. In this case, there are only two $(n = 2)$:

Possible Outcomes

O_1 = You win the lottery
O_2 = You don't win

Next, determine the probabilities $P(O_1)$ and $P(O_2)$ associated with each of the two outcomes:

Possible Outcomes	*Probability*
O_1 = You win the lottery	$P(O_1) = 1/10,000,000 = 0.0000001$
O_2 = You don't win	$P(O_2) = 9,999,999/10,000,000 = 0.9999999$

Now, determine the associated net monetary values M_1 and M_2 for each of the two outcomes:

Possible Outcomes	*Probability*	*Monetary Value*
O_1 = You win the lottery	$P(O_1) = 1/10,000,000$ $= 0.0000001$	$M_1 = \$999,999$
O_2 = You don't win	$P(O_2) = 9,999,999/$ $10,000,000 = 0.9999999$	$M_2 = -\$1$

Note: The net monetary value associated with winning the lottery is calculated by taking the winnings of $1,000,000 and subtracting the $1 cost of the ticket. The net value is $999,999.

Finally, calculate the EMV as

$$\begin{aligned}
\text{EMV} &= P(O_1)M_1 + P(O_2)M_2 \\
&\quad \text{(probability you win)(value if you win)} + \text{(probability} \\
&\quad \text{you don't win)(value if you don't win)} \\
&= (0.0000001)(\$999,999) + (0.9999999)(-\$1) \\
&= \$0.0999999 - \$0.9999999 \\
&= -\$0.90
\end{aligned}$$

In other words, if you play this particular lottery game, your expected payout is a loss of $0.90. Keep in mind that this is an average value, meaning that if you play this particular game over and over again, your average payout per play is a loss of $0.90.

To implement EMV calculations into your direct marketing campaigns, the regression models built predicting a customer's likelihood of ordering, paying, renewing, and so on must be of the logistic form. As you recall from Chapter 10, a logistic regression model yields a probability associated with the action being modeled. A standard multiple regression model will *not* give you a probability. It should be noted, however, that there are ways to convert a multiple regression score into a probability based on gains chart information; however, this will not be covered in this book.

For the remainder of this section, assume that all regression models are of the logistic variety, meaning the scores assigned to each name (when passed through the model) are a probability bound between 0 and 1, thereby allowing use of the EMV formula.

A review of the important customer actions you wish to consider in the EMV formula is first required. Suppose you are interested in determining who to promote and not promote for a new product offer by assessing the probabilities and costs associated with a customer, taking each path shown in Exhibit 11.5.

To calculate the EMV for each customer, we must first write out the possible customer paths or outcomes:

- Order and pay
- Order and not pay
- Not order

Next, determine the probability of each path or outcome:

Outcome	Probability of Outcome
Order and pay	(Probability of ordering and paying) = (Probability of ordering) × (Probability of paying)
Order and not pay	(Probability of ordering and not paying) = (Probability of ordering) × (Probability of not paying)
Not order	(Probability of not ordering)

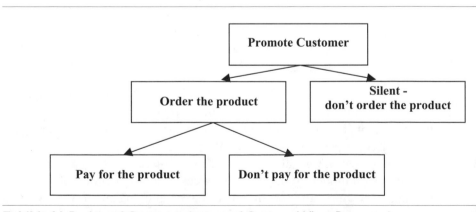

Exhibit 11.5 List of Customer Actions of Concern When Promoted

Note: The derivation for the probability formulas listed above will not be discussed here. For this application, it is only necessary for you to realize that the probability of "Event A and Event B both occurring" is equal to the probability of "Event A occurring" multiplied by the probability of "Event B occurring." These rules follow the basic rules of probability and can be found in any intermediate level statistics book.

As you can see, we will need to build two logistic regression models in order to determine these probabilities: one predicting the probability of ordering and another predicting the probability of paying. To determine the probability that a customer will not order, you take 1 minus the probability that a customer will order. To determine the probability that a customer will pay, you take 1 minus the probability that a customer will not pay.

Now determine the cost and profit figures associated with each of these three paths or outcomes.

Outcome	Monetary Value of Outcome
Order and pay	= Cost of the promotion piece + net value of a paid product (including average billing costs)
Order and not pay	= Cost of the promotion piece + cost of an unpaid order (including average billing costs)
Not Order	= Cost of the promotion piece

To determine most of these costs, your marketing finance department should be able to assist you. The cost of an unpaid order for a magazine subscription will include the cost of the copies already sent before stopping the subscription (called grace copies). Typically, two to three grace copies are sent. Regarding the sale of merchandise, the cost of an unpaid order includes costs associated with returns and kept merchandise (if applicable). When determining the cost of a return, keep in mind that a certain portion of the returned merchandise may be refurbishable and a certain portion not refurbishable.

Determining billing costs (if applicable) are fairly straightforward. For a paid order, use the average number of bills sent to get payment, multiplied by the average cost per bill. For an unpaid order, use the cost of the entire billing series for nonpayers and the average billing costs expended for those who return merchandise.

Calculate the EMV by multiplying the probabilities associated with each of the three actions previously listed by their respective cost and profit values:

$$EMV = [(\text{Probability of ordering}) \times (\text{Probability of paying})$$
$$\times (\text{Value of a paid order})] + [(\text{Probability of ordering})$$
$$\times (\text{Probability of not paying}) \times (\text{Value of an unpaid order})]$$
$$+ [(\text{Probability of not ordering}) \times (\text{Value of a nonorder})]$$

Assume the following marketing costs and profit values associated with an upcoming promotional campaign:

Promotional cost per piece mailed: $0.87

Net value of a paid order (including average billing costs): $13.56

Cost of an unpaid order (including average billing costs): $6.56

Also assume the following probabilities of ordering and paying for two customers (Mr. Jones and Ms. Smith), scored on two logistic regression models:

Customer	Probability of Ordering	Probability of Not Paying
Mr. Jones	28%	5%
Ms. Smith	34%	18%

Which customer is more profitable if promoted for this particular product?

$$\text{EMV (Mr. Jones)} = [(0.28) \times (1 - 0.05) \times (\$13.56 - \$0.87)]$$
$$+ [(0.28) \times (0.05) \times (-\$6.56 - \$0.87)]$$
$$+ [(1 - 0.28) \times (-\$0.87)]$$
$$= \$3.38 - \$0.10 - \$0.63$$
$$= \$2.65$$

$$\text{EMV (Ms. Smith)} = [(0.34) \times (1 - 0.18) \times (\$13.56 - \$0.87)]$$
$$+ [(0.34) \times (0.18) \times (-\$6.56 - \$0.87)] + [(1 - 0.34) \times (-\$0.87)]$$
$$= \$3.54 - \$0.45 - \$0.57$$
$$= \$2.52$$

Although more likely to order (34% vs. 28%), Ms. Smith is less likely to pay (82% vs. 95%), resulting in an expected profit value less than that of Mr. Jones. Therefore, it is more profitable to promote Mr. Jones than Ms. Smith. If the promotion decision was based on a single regression response gains chart, Ms. Smith would have been erroneously promoted.

We used a very simple EMV exercise to present this topic so it would be easy to understand. In reality, these EMV models are much more complex. In the publishing industry, for example, the EMV formula may include 2-year values and consider the likelihood of renewing. For continuity clubs, the EMV formula may include the likelihood of future shipments being accepted and paid for by the customer.

Once you have calculated the expected profit values for each name in your customer segment, rank the names based on their EMV score from highest to lowest scoring, just like that for a response gains chart. Once done, a promotional decision will be made.

Determining who to promote and not promote will be based on the EMV scores themselves. If the goal of your particular promotion is to break even, then you will select any name with an EMV score greater than or equal to $0.00.

Implementing EMV is also very useful when you have multiple offers and need to decide what offer to send a customer. For example, to determine which of two product promotions to send to each customer on the database, you need to develop two models: one predicting a customer's likelihood of ordering Product 1 and another predicting a customer's likelihood of ordering Product 2. Then score each customer on both equations and calculate their respective EMV scores. Promote each customer with the product for which they have the highest EMV.

Reconciling Gains

The model had been applied and the highest scoring names selected to be promoted. When the marketing campaign results are final and all orders have been received, the next step is to determine how well the model held up in rollout. That is, if you expected a 20% gain in response over promoting everyone, did you achieve that gain in rollout?

To reconcile the selection gains, a sample of names not meeting your criteria must be promoted. This is called a fails sample. For example, you promoted the top 50% of the names in your gains chart or the top five buckets. You received a 4% response rate. Unless you promoted a sampling of the bottom five buckets (the "fails"), you will have no way to determine the actual gain received in rollout over mailing everyone.

You do not need to promote a large fails sample; 5,000 or 10,000 names will suffice. Of course, the larger the fails sample, the better the estimate will be regarding how these fails would have actually performed in rollout had they all been promoted.

The importance of taking a fails sample when employing any selection criteria (manual selects or regressed) cannot be stressed enough. Without such a sample, you will not know if you were successful in defining your target market. In addition, if the results of a campaign were underforecast, you will not be able to isolate the problem (e.g., was it underforecast due to the regression gain or the new creative/format gain not holding up?).

For example, a cataloger test promotes a new children's toy catalog featuring toys from around the world and receives a response rate of 2.54%. Due to the success of this unique children's catalog, the analyst was asked by the product manager to build a response model to assist her in determining who to promote and not promote in rollout. On the basis of the incremental gains chart produced on the validation sample, the product

Exhibit 11.6 Actual Campaign Results

	Campaign Order Intake Report		
Source	# Promoted	Orders	Response Rate
Primary Universe:			
Top Scoring 40%	1,740,858	66,153	3.80%
Fails Sample	10,000	177	1.77%

manager decides to promote the highest scoring 40%, or top four buckets, of her primary customer segment. In addition, the product manager test promoted a sampling of 10,000 fail names (names falling into the bottom six buckets of her gains chart).

Assume the forecasted gain in response for these names (based on the cumulative gains chart) was +49%. Also assume that her primary customer segment was comprised of 4,352,145 names in total. Exhibit 11.6 is a report generated by this cataloger's fulfillment shop showing the rollout results of this campaign 8 weeks after the mail date. Did the cataloger receive the forecasted gain of +49%?

The easiest way to determine if forecasted gains were obtained is through the creation of a **reconciliation** table, as shown in Exhibit 11.7. This table lists all known information regarding the pass (promoted) and fail (not-promoted) names for the universe being reconciled.

Because you did not promote all 4,352,145 names, you will estimate the response rate of the total universe by weighing together the actual pass response rate and the fails sample response rate. The weights used are equal to what the pass and fail names represent out of the total universe. In our example, the pass names represented 40% and the fails (in total) represented 60%.

Calculate the estimated response rate of the total universe as a weighted average of the pass and fail response rates:

$$\text{Total Universe Response Rate} = (3.80\% \times 0.40) + (1.77\% \times 0.60)$$
$$= 1.52 + 1.06$$
$$= 2.58$$

Exhibit 11.7 Reconciliation Table

	List Size	Percentage	Response Rate (%)	Gain
Pass Names	1,740,858	40%	3.80%	?
Fail Names	2,611,287	60%	1.77%*	
Total Universe	4,352,145	100%	?	

*Based on a sample of 10,000 names promoted.

Now, given our estimated total response rate, we can calculate the gain achieved via the regression selection:

$$\text{Estimated Gain in Response} = [(3.80/2.58) \times 100)] - 100$$
$$= + 47.3\%$$

Actual was very close to forecast. In fact, we were only off by 3.4%— $(49 - 47.3)/49$—in forecasted gain.

Had the gains been off significantly (e.g., greater than 10%), we advise you to closely examine the regression model to determine which variable(s) did not perform as expected.

Chapter Summary

A response gains chart is used to determine who to promote and not promote for an upcoming offer. A response gains chart reveals those customers most likely to order by ranking them based on their regression scores. Those with the highest regression score are the most likely to respond, and those with the lowest regression score are the least likely to respond. In addition, the gains chart is used to determine the stability of a regression response model. Gains on the analysis and validation samples are compared to assess model stability. If a major falloff in gains is observed between the analysis and validation samples, model stability is in question. In addition to response gains charts, names can also be ranked on expected profit values. Such values are a function of not only customers' likelihood to order but also their likelihood to pay and marketing cost and profit figures.

Review Questions

1. What are the steps used to create an incremental gains chart on the analysis sample?

2. What are the steps used to create an incremental gains chart on the validation sample?

3. Why is it important to base the promotional decision on the gains chart produced on the validation sample rather than the analysis sample?

4. What options are available for forecasting gain based on a response model when lacking a validation sample?

5. What is the benefit of basing the promotional decision on expected profit as opposed to a simple response gains chart?

6. Why is it important to promote a sample of names not meeting the selection criteria when rolling out with a new selection criteria?

12

Strategic
Reporting and Analysis

Due to the cutting edge analysis techniques brought forth by Keri Lee at Inside Source over the past 2 years, their subscriber base has grown by more than 25%. As a result, Keri was promoted to corporate vice president.

In her new role, no longer having an opportunity to oversee the day-to-day operations of the marketing team, Keri decided to request some key strategic reports to help her keep an eye on the health of the business. In particular, she wanted to see monthly counts of active subscribers and their key demographics. She also asked that LTV analyses for the various sources of new-to-file customers be performed on a semiregular basis. In addition, she was also eager to assess the long-term value to the corporation of implementing a new retention program tested 2 years ago.

Realizing the workload implications of such requests, she created a new division whose sole responsibility was to create such key strategic reporting and analyses. She realized that this would not be a small undertaking and would require the dedicated efforts of a team. Because no database is 100% clean, inconsistencies in monthly counts would undoubtedly result and investigation would be required. In addition, she also realized that to properly calculate customer LTV, time would be required to obtain and then link each customer to actual cost and revenue figures associated with the various promotions.

Key to the establishment of proper strategy for any database marketer is the tracking of customer counts, activity, demographics, and value over time. Without such analyses, a database marketer will be unable to make the best long-term decisions regarding name sourcing, offers, or treatments. Unfortunately, most direct marketers do not know how to properly assess customer information over time or determine customer value. This is mostly due to a lack of understanding by the direct marketer of the issues involved in the proper implementation of such strategic reporting and analysis. In fact, according to the 2001 *Direct* magazine annual database survey, only 27% of b-to-b direct marketers and 56% of consumer direct marketers calculate LTV of their customers. With respect to the catalog industry (both b-to-b and consumer), only 23% calculate the LTV of their customers, based on the 1999 DMA State of the Catalog Industry Report.

Undertaking the development of strategic reporting and analysis is by no means a small task. Dedicated and properly trained resources must be put in place to ensure success. This is especially true for direct marketers with complex business models. For example, a direct marketer offering only a single magazine title such as *Aficionado* will have an easier time of properly tracking customers over time than companies like Time-Life, Rodale Press, or The Reader's Digest Association, in which each has multiple product lines and divisions offering an array of products. In fact, the *Aficionado* database may be leveraged more for advertisers' communications to its readers than the offers from the publisher. Strategic reports would reflect subscriber counts by demographic groups.

In this chapter we discuss how to set up and establish some key strategic reports and analyses for your business. In particular, we discuss

- ♦ How to set up key "active customer" counts to help you monitor your customer base
- ♦ How to calculate various statistics to assist you in monitoring the health of your business
- ♦ How to establish LTV profiles to help you better understand the worth of certain marketing programs or sources of names
- ♦ How to calculate customer LTV

In addition, we also discuss

- ♦ How to set up impact studies so you can properly assess the impact of new product lines or profit centers on already established business units
- ♦ How to monitor promotional intensity within your company
- ♦ The importance of key coding names to ensure analyses discussed in this chapter can be properly conducted

Key Active Customer Counts

We begin our discussion of strategic reporting with the creation of a key active customer counts report. Such a report allows you to properly monitor your core customer base over time. These types of reports show the number of active customers by each major product line, magazine title, service offered, key demographic group, or source of customer. They prove valuable for monitoring your core customer base, allowing you to observe trends over time.

In the case of a magazine publisher of two niche magazine titles, the key customer counts they want to create and track over time are the

- Number of customers receiving own copy on Title A
- Number of customers receiving own copy on Title B
- Number of active donors of Title A (those giving the magazine as a gift)
- Number of active donors of Title B (those giving the magazine as a gift)
- Number of active recipients of Title A (those receiving the magazine from a donor)
- Number of active recipients of Title B (those receiving the magazine from a donor)
- Number of customers receiving own and active donor of Title A
- Number of customers receiving own and active donor of Title B

Each category can then be broken down further by key demographics to assist in monitoring, for example, readership age.

For a direct marketer such as Rodale Press, which offers one-shot products, they need to decide what constitutes an active customer. Defining active customers is not as straightforward for these direct marketers as it is for a magazine publisher.

Consider a direct marketer offering one-shot books and videos. Such a direct marketer may decide to define an active customer as anyone who has made any payment (greater than or equal to $0.01) within a certain amount of time for the product line of concern (e.g., within 24 months). For this example, the key segments to track include

- Active within the past 24 months on the books product line
- Active within the past 24 months on the video product line

The direct marketer may also want to assess the counts from a corporate point of view. For example, active from a corporate point of view may mean any payment on any product line within the past 24 months. Or they may decide it to mean activity of any kind (payment, order, address change, etc.) initiated by the customer. Either way, this is a decision the direct marketer must make.

For continuity or club direct marketers, active customers may be defined as "still in club" or "paid shipment made within a certain amount of time."

Key active customer counts should be generated as often as needed. They can be generated weekly, monthly, or quarterly, depending on the promotional activity of the company. Companies that promote customers weekly want more frequent count reports than those that promote customers monthly or quarterly.

In addition, companies with very large databases in the millions may find it beneficial to run such counts on a sample of the customer file. For example, a company may elect to pull a 10% sample of the customer database each month to generate the monthly active customer counts and any other counts requests (ad hoc or standard). The savings in computer processing time may be substantial, with differences ranging in the hours.

List Vitality Customer Statistics

In addition to simply monitoring counts of key active customers, important statistics can be created for these groups, allowing you to monitor the vitality of your customer base. The key statistics include

- ◆ Percentage new-to-file
- ◆ Conversion rates to other titles, product lines, or services
- ◆ Retention or renewal rates
- ◆ Reactivation rates of nonactive customers

These statistics will allow you to more easily determine the success, at a corporate level, of various marketing strategies. This is done by breaking down the number of active customers (however they are defined) as shown in Exhibit 12.1.

View these counts weekly, monthly, or quarterly, depending on the promotional activity of your company.

Key List Segment Counts and Statistics

New-to-file, conversion, retention, and reactivation statistics can also be generated for each product line's core customer segments. Suppose the book product line segmentation scheme for a direct marketer of books and videos is as shown in Exhibit 12.2.

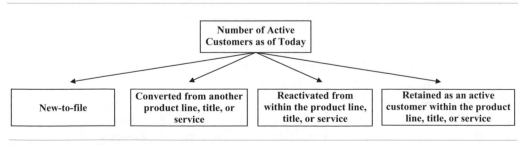

Exhibit 12.1   Key Active Customer Statistics

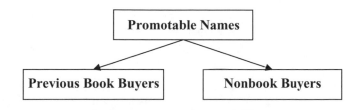

Exhibit 12.2   Book Product Line Segmentation Scheme

To better monitor the health of the book product line, the book product line manager views new-to-file, conversion, retention, and reactivation statistics by each major segment as follows:

- Number of all promotable names on the database
  - Number of previous book buyers
    - Number of customers with book activity within the past 24 months
      - Percentage new-to-file
      - Percentage retained
      - Percentage reactivated
      - Percentage converted
    - Number of customers with book activity greater than 24 months
  - Number of nonbook buyers

The video product line manager creates the same set of statistics but from his product line's perspective/segmentation scheme.

Again, you should view these statistics weekly, monthly, or quarterly, depending on the promotional activity of your company.

Calculating LTV

Calculating LTV of a customer or a group of customers can be a very powerful tool for any direct marketing division. Doing so will allow a direct marketer to

- Assess the long-term results of various marketing programs, name sources, treatments, or strategies
- Effectively conduct what-if analyses to assist in determining the likely long-term benefits to be derived prior to test or rollout of a new program, source, or treatment
- Segment the customer file

To be successful, the information must be given in a meaningful way with appropriate directions about its use. When properly presented, this information will not only allow product managers to better manage their individual product line but also take into account the corporate impact of their decisions.

The value of a group of names has been observed to reverse in comparison to other groups when the contribution of those names to the corporation was examined over a longer period of time. LTV calculations allow you to look at exactly this—the effectiveness of a campaign, treatment, or strategy not only with respect to the initial results but also its impact across all product lines over time, thus allowing better decision making.

Examples of how LTV calculations can assist you include

- Determination of which outside lists generate the most cost-effective customers over the long run by division or for the company as a whole
- Evaluation of a particular resuscitation or customer reactivation effort's payout over time
- Understanding of various name acquisition programs (co-op mailings, card decks, banner ad placements, etc.) and how they compare in terms of the customers' value over time
- In subscription rate base management, identification of the most cost-effective rate base from an overall company perspective via what-if analysis
- Assistance in prioritizing opportunities for strategic alliances with other companies through coendorsements and so on
- Evaluation of which product lines or products are more beneficial to the corporation as the front door to the company

LTV Methodologies

There are three basic ways to calculate the LTV of a customer or group of customers. Some are less complicated to implement than others. It depends on the ease of obtaining and then linking accurate and complete cost and revenue information associated with each promotion and purchase for the time period under consideration. For example, when we compare various outside list sources of names or categories of names for a given fiscal year, there are three possible ways to view the customer information to access their long-term value to the corporation:

1. Display key information regarding purchase and promotion activity (also called LTV profiles)

2. LTV calculations based on *average* cost and revenue figures and *aggregate* promotion and purchase data

3. LTV calculations based on *actual* cost and revenue figures and *actual* promotion and purchase data

The details of each method and examples follow.

LTV Profiles

LTV profiles allow you to gain valuable information about long-term behavioral differences for various groups of names or the treatments thereof. LTV profiles give you, for example, a very clear picture of why one source of names may be more profitable than another. For a magazine publisher, such reports can reveal which source of names become better donors, which group of names renew their subscriptions the next year at a higher rate, and which group of names are more likely to purchase cross-sell products. In this respect, LTV *profiles* are preferred over *actual* LTV calculations. They tell you which group is the most profitable in the long term and why.

For direct marketers with a complex business model, this may be the only or preferred method of assessing customer value over time. It may not be feasible to obtain accurate cost and revenue figures across the multiple promotions, products, and services.

Exhibit 12.3 is a sample LTV profile as previously described for a new source of names for a cataloger of home decorating products. The fields were chosen such that simple estimates of LTVs could be calculated by the product manager if desired. Additional information could be added to this report such as age and income information. What you display will depend on your needs.

By developing these reports across various sources, comparisons can be made to determine which are the best from a corporate point of view. Such reports will help highlight sources in which, although the initial order rate was quite high, there is a lower long-term value when compared to other sources.

Exhibit 12.4 is a 2-year LTV profile comparison report for each major source of new names for a b-to-b direct marketer of custom-imprinted products, business forms, and motivational prints. Product managers in

Exhibit 12.3 1-Year LTV Profile

1-Year LTV Profile as of 12/1/00

Source:	New Outside List 1
Catalog Mail Date:	12/1/99
Promotion Plan Specifics:	PLAN 12345

Corporate Statistics	Value
Average total $ spent	$67.34
Average number of paid products	4.28
Average number of returned products	0.29
Average number of catalogs sent	2.80
Average number of repeat purchases	1.76

Exhibit 12.4   2-Year LTV Profile Comparison Report

2-Year LTV Profile Comparison Report By Source Category

Profile of new-to-file customers coming on file via a custom
imprinted products catalog offer between 1/1/98 and 6/1/98

	Outside List Program	Business Co-op Mailers	E-mail Solicitations
Custom Imprinted Products:			
Percentage active	35	23	18
Total number of orders	4.3	3.2	1.6
Business Forms:			
Percentage converted	14	19	11
Total number of orders	1.4	1.3	0.9
Motivational Prints:			
Percentage converted	20	21	14
Total number of orders	2.5	2.6	2.0

charge of the custom-imprinted products catalog need to assess the value of various sources of new names not just for their product line but corporatewide. This is done by developing an LTV profile that includes key statistics on the other product lines.

Again, quick calculations could be made for each major source to assist the product managers in determining where to focus their attention. Additional variables could also be displayed in this report depending on the needs.

To properly assess the 2-year value of new-to-file customers by source as displayed in Exhibit 12.4, you must not purge names from the database that became inactive during the evaluation period. Otherwise, the statistics will be inflated, because they will only be based on "actives." If purging of inactive customers is a regular maintenance routine at your company, you can avoid the problems this will cause by the creation of a "perpetual" file that contains and tracks a large sample of all names residing on the database. This allows you to go back in time to conduct such strategic analyses.

Exhibit 12.5 shows the results of an expensive retention offer made by a cellular telecommunications company to their customers. In this example, the cellular telecommunications company gave free voice mail to their current customers for the life of their contract in hopes of increasing billable air-time usage and retention rates. The value of this promotion will be determined by comparing, after 1 year, phone usage for those customers given the free voice mail versus a holdout sample of customers not given free voice mail. An LTV profile was developed for assessing the value of this offer. Statistics were generated for key variables.

On examination of this report, we notice that the free voice mail has certainly increased air-time usage and revenue. But is it enough to offset the yearly cost of managing voice mail for each customer? To determine

Exhibit 12.5   1-Year LTV Profile Comparison Report

One-Year LTV Profile Comparisons Report By Offer

Profile of customers receiving and not receiving the free voice mail option one year later

One-Year Statistics	Received Free Voice Mail	Did Not Receive Free Voice Mail
Total Air Time in Minutes	1,740	1,140
Percentage renewed contract		
at end of 1-year period	89	82
Total dollars paid	$474.72	$414.60
Total number of calls placed	468	312

this, the product manager can perform some simple calculations by weighing all costs against revenues.

The product manager may also want to display in Exhibit 12.5 such statistics as the conversion rate to other add-on options (e.g., call waiting, caller ID) or the percentage of customers ordering new phones for their spouse or children.

Actual and Aggregate LTV Calculations

You have two options when you calculate LTV values associated with customers or groups of customers: you can base the calculations on *actual* or on *average* cost and revenue figures.

Actual Cost and Revenue Figures. Although this method provides the most relevant analysis for precision decision making, it is often a tedious and difficult method for organizations not currently set up to directly link the revenues and costs to each promotion. In addition, the more complex the business model, the more difficult this type of calculation is.

Average Cost and Revenue Figures. This method is easier to apply than using actual cost and revenue figures because aggregate cost and revenue figures can be used. This is a preferred method by direct marketers when they have complex business models or when they cannot link revenues and costs to each promotion.

As previously mentioned, obtaining and linking actual cost and revenue figures to each promotion in order to calculate an actual LTV can be quite tedious and difficult. This is especially true for direct marketers who have a complex business model with multiple product lines and divisions. In these instances, calculating and applying average cost and revenue figures to actual or aggregate promotional and purchase data by product line or division will be much easier to implement. For example, when comparing the 2-year value of one source of new names versus another source during fiscal 1999, direct marketers can use average cost and revenue figures by product line or division for the combined fiscal 1999–2000 periods in the LTV calculations.

The basic components of the LTV calculation, whether using actual or aggregate data, include

- ◆ Total revenues
- ◆ Total costs
- ◆ Adjustment for the **net present value (NPV)** of future profits

LTV is simply the sum of all revenues derived by the customer, less costs expended, for a set time period when adjusted for the NPV of future profits.

To determine how to adjust future profits for the present, you must first calculate the **discount rate**.

Calculating the Discount Rate and NPV

Future profits will not be worth as much in today's money. For example, $1.00 in the future will buy less than $1.00 today. Because of this fact, when you determine the future value of customers, you must adjust the profit value calculated to reflect its true value in today's money. To determine the value of $1.00 next year as of today, you must apply what is called a discount rate. Not doing so can result in making incorrect decisions.

The formula for calculating the discount rate is

$$\text{Discount Rate} = [1 + (m \times \text{market lending rate})]^y$$

Where
y is an exponent that represents the number of years from the present
m is a multiplier representing the risk associated with the business venture (most companies double the current market lending rate)

Once determined, you will calculate the discounted future profit, also known as NPV, as follows:

$$\text{NPV} = \text{Profits/discount rate}$$

LTV calculations are often represented in a table that provides a modified income statement. Exhibit 12.6 shows the LTV calculations for a book club direct marketer who sent a special offer to a group of 10,000 currently active members drawn randomly from the database. The market lending rate was 10% and the risk multiplier was 2.

Exhibit 12.6 LTV

	Year 1	Year 2	Year 3	Year 4
Customers	10,000	5,000	3,000	2,250
Retention rate (%)	50	60	75	80
Revenue	$150,000	$60,000	$27,000	$13,500
Costs	$75,000	$30,000	$13,500	$6,750
Profit	$75,000	$30,000	$13,500	$6,750
Discount rate	1.0	1.2	1.44	1.77
NPV profit	$75,000	$25,000	$9,375	$3.750
Cumulative NPV Profit/LTV	$75,000	$100,000	$109,375	$113,125

The discount rate and NPV for Year 1 were determined as follows:

$$\text{Discount rate in Year 1} = [1 + (2 \times 0.10)]^0$$
$$= (1.20)^0$$
$$= 1.00(\textit{any figure raised to}$$
$$\textit{the zero power is 1})$$

$$\text{NPV for Year 1} = \$75,000/1.00$$
$$= \$75,000$$

The discount rate and NPV for Year 2 were determined as follows:

$$\text{Discount rate in Year 2} = [1 + (2 \times 0.10)]^1$$
$$= (1.20)^1$$
$$= 1.20$$

$$\text{NPV for Year 2} = \$30,000/1.20$$
$$= \$25,000$$

The discount rate and NPV for Year 3 were determined as follows:

$$\text{Discount rate in Year 3} = [1 + (2 \times 0.10)]^2$$
$$= (1.20)^2$$
$$= 1.44$$

$$\text{NPV for Year 3} = \$13,500/1.44$$
$$= \$9,375$$

The discount rate and NPV for year 4 were similarly derived.

Using the information provided in Exhibit 12.6, you can also derive average LTV per customer. To determine the average LTV of a customer after 4 years, you divide the cumulative NPV by the number of customers at the beginning of the evaluation period:

$$\text{Average 4-year LTV} = \$113,125/10,000$$
$$= \$11.31$$

Consider a small cataloger of imported children's toys from around the world. In 1998, they decide to track all new customers for 3 years. They do not purge any customers coming on file during this time period, regardless of inactivity. At the end of this 3-year evaluation period, they will calculate each customer's average LTV. To do so, they will need to

- Calculate total dollars spent and the average number of catalogs sent per year for these customers; they will derive these fields from the database
- Estimate revenue as a percentage of sales
- Determine the average catalog costs per year

The LTV calculations are shown in Exhibit 12.7 with all necessary formulas displayed. We see that a new-to-file customer after 3 years is worth $42.46 on average.

In an effort to increase the retention rates, this cataloger is considering sending a free surprise toy to all customers with their first order and again every year afterward on their 12-month anniversary. On the basis of a similar test last year, the cataloger determined, via key coding, that retention increased by 3% and sales increased by 4%. Assuming this same increase in retention and sales holds true for future years, this cataloger will perform a what-if LTV analysis. Doing so will allow them to assess

Exhibit 12.7   LTV Report for Toy Cataloger

	Year 1-1998	Year 2-1999	Year 3-2000
Customer Figures:			
Customers (A)	20,000	8,000	5,000
Retention Rate (B)	40%	62.50%	75%
Revenue Figures:			
Total $ Spent (C)	$1,600,000	$720,000	$525,000
Average $ Spent (D = C/A)	$80	$90	$105
Revenue as % of Sales (E)	40%	40%	40%
Total Net Revenue (F = C × E)	$640,000	$288,000	$210,000
Mailing Cost Figures:			
Average # Catalogs Sent (G)	4.6	4.7	4.5
Cost Per Catalog (H)	$1.25	$1.29	$1.36
Total Mailing Costs (I = A × G × H)	$115,000	$48,504	$30,600
Profit Figures:			
Net Profit (J = F − I)	$525,000	$239,496	$179,400
Discount Rate (K)	1	1.2	1.44
NPV Profit (L = J/K)	$525,000	$199,580	$124,583
Cumulative NPV Profit (M)	$525,000	$724,580	$849,163
Average Customer LTV (N = M/20,000)	$26.25	$36.23	$42.46

the long-term value of implementing such a program, ensuring that they make the correct decision. The LTV table for this what-if analysis is shown in Exhibit 12.8.

By comparing the 1-year average LTV of names receiving the special treatment to the 1-year average LTV from Exhibit 12.7, it is obvious that this new strategy does not pay out. However, when it is assessed over time, we notice that breakeven occurs at Year 3. As a result, the cataloger has a decision to make: Is a 3-year breakeven a viable option?

Sample Types Used in LTV Calculations

Numerical calculations in LTV reports will differ, depending on the type of customer data/sample you are examining. There are two types of customer samples typically analyzed:

1. New-to-file names
2. Current customers (e.g., when analyzing the effect of a resuscitation effort on a group of current customers)

Exhibit 12.8 What-If LTV Report for Toy Cataloger

	Year 1	Year 2	Year 3
Customer Figures:			
Customers (A)	20,000	8,240	5,307
Retention Rate (B)	41.20%	64.40%	77.30%
Revenue Figures:			
Total $ Spent (C)	$1,664,000	$771,264	$579,524
Average $ Spent (D = C/A)	$83.20	$93.60	$109.20
Revenue as % of Sales (E)	40%	40%	40%
Total Net Revenue (F = C × F)	$665,600	$308,506	$231,810
Mailing Cost Figures:			
Average # Catalogues Sent (G)	4.6	4.7	4.5
Cost Per Catalogue (H)	$1.25	$1.29	$1.36
Total Mailing Costs (I = A × G × H)	$115,000	$49,959	$32,479
Gift Cost Figures:			
Cost of Free Toy (J)	$1.75	$1.75	$1.75
Total Gift Cost (K = J × A)	$35,000	$14,420	$9,287
Profit Figures:			
Net Profit (L = F − I − K)	$515,600	$244,126	$190,044
Discount Rate (M)	1	1.2	1.44
NPV Profit (N = L/M)	$515,600	$203,439	$131,975
Cumulative NPV Profit (O)	$515,600	$719,039	$851,013
Average Customer LTV (P = O/20,000)	$25.78	$35.95	$42.55

For example, to calculate total motivational print orders (see Exhibit 12.4) after a 2-year period for new-to-file customers, the reports will simply pick up the value of that summary field on the marketing database. However, this is not the case for LTV profiles involving current customers. In the case of our telecommunication example (Exhibit 12.5) and determining "Total Air Time in Minutes" after 1 year, the report will subtract the value of the summary field when the customer was first given the free voice mail option from the same data field 1 year later. For this example, a frozen file is required, reflecting what the customer looked like at the time of the test promotion. (Chapter 6 contains additional information on frozen files.)

Forecasting LTV

In addition to calculating the historical LTV of customers or groups of customers, you can also forecast LTV. This is done via regression modeling. For example, you can build a model to predict the value of customers after 2 years on file, based on the customers' actions during their first few months on file. The model can additionally incorporate any demographic, psychographic, and census-level data that might be available.

With these models, a direct marketer can rank customers shortly after they come on file from those most likely to become good customers to those less likely to become good customers. On the basis of this knowledge, the direct marketer is in a strong position to implement appropriate strategies to deal with likely strong and weak customers.

Impact Studies

If you are a direct marketer considering the addition of a new multiple product line, you must be prepared to properly gauge the impact of this addition on your current product lines. You do this by establishing an impact study, which allows you to compare the value of the new product line with the costs of the potential cannibalization of customers from your current product lines. In all likelihood, the new product line will have a negative impact on the rest of the business. The question is, How much? It depends on your customers and how much competition there will be between the new product line and your current product lines. For example, direct marketers currently selling one-shot do-it-yourself books will in all likelihood see a large impact to this business unit if they decide to launch a new do-it-yourself book club. You can gauge how much by establishing an impact study during the test phase. However, if these same direct marketers are looking to launch a new catalog of collectable plates and they do not currently sell plates or collectable items of any type, the impact may be minimal.

The steps involved in establishing an impact study to determine the effect on the one-shot business of starting a do-it-yourself book club are as follows:

1. Select a large sample of names

2. Split the sample 50/50—half of which will be key coded to receive the new do-it-yourself book club offer and half will be key coded *not* to receive the new do-it-yourself book club offer

3. Promote only those names key coded as such with the new do-it-yourself book club offer

4. At a later time, promote both groups with a one-shot do-it-yourself book offer

After a certain amount of time has elapsed, you can determine the impact of the new do-it-yourself book club on the one-shot do-it-yourself book business by examining the one-shot response rates for each group. Is the one-shot response rate lower for those names promoted with the club offer, or is it the same? To assess the long-term implication of rolling out with such a club, you can even prepare a 1- or 2-year LTV profile or calculation.

Monitoring Promotional Intensity

If direct marketers begin to experience significant reductions in response rates, they may want to monitor promotional intensity. In other words, the direct marketers may be mailing too many promotions, which results in list fatigue. To establish a test of this hypothesis, execute the following steps:

1. Select a random sample of active customers for the product line or division of concern

2. Split the sample into two equal samples

3. Key code one group to receive promotions as usual

4. Key code the other group to receive fewer promotions

You need to decide on the definition of "fewer promotions." You may want to test a few variations of fewer promotions in an attempt to gauge intensity more accurately.

After a set period of time, for example 1 year, examine responses to promotions for each group and determine if those receiving fewer promotions eventually yield higher response rates to promotions they did receive. Did the rebound in response rates cover the lost revenue from fewer promotions? Did you receive fewer customer complaints for this group? On the basis of the answers to these questions, a marketing plan may be built to combat these issues.

Through proper strategic reporting and analysis, the health of any direct marketing firm can be monitored and proactively managed.

Chapter Summary

Many types of reports are key to the establishment of proper marketing strategy. In this chapter, we discuss key active customer counts, which monitor the size of important universes of customers, and list vitality customer statistics, which allow a marketer to monitor the vitality of the customer base. Calculating customer LTV is also a very important marketing tool but also one of the most complex to implement. Several LTV methodologies are discussed, some of which are easier to implement than others. In addition, we discuss ways to assess the impact of new product lines on existing product lines and how to monitor promotional intensity.

Review Questions

1. What measures are used to monitor the vitality of the customer base?

2. What is the advantage of producing LTV profiles over actual LTV calculations?

3. Why would a direct marketer calculate LTV based on average cost and revenue figures as opposed to actual cost and revenue figures?

4. What is NPV and why is it important when calculating LTV?

5. Discuss the steps involved in establishing an impact study.

6. Discuss the steps involved in successfully monitoring promotional intensity.

13

Assessing
Marketing Test Results

At a recent off-site marketing planning meeting, Keri Lee noticed that several mistakes had been made regarding promotional format changes. She was concerned that the product managers were not properly assessing the test results with statistical rigor and were therefore making incorrect decisions. New formats, thought to be winners on the basis of test results, were not yielding the lift in rollout response as expected.

As a result, she hired a consulting firm to hold a training session on proper test design and evaluation for all Inside Source product managers.

Keri, who also attended the full-day training session, was surprised at the issues that must be considered when reading test results. She did not realize the thought process required in choosing the right significance level. Keri had thought that reading all test results with 90% confidence was appropriate. In addition, she did not realize that there is more than one way to assess test results.

Once the session was over, Keri had her product managers go back and reassess all of last year's test results. The results were astounding. Two thirds of those tests thought to be winners prior to the training session were either not winners or were on the fence and required retesting.

The measures of concern when conducting a marketing test are the percentage responding, the percentage paying, or the mean dollars spent. Depending on what these values are, in conjunction with the marketing cost and revenue figures, you will make a business decision about whether or not to roll out with a particular new product, offer, or promotion.

Being confident in the sample estimates is critical to making correct marketing decisions. Unfortunately, regardless of how good your sample is or how little things change from test to rollout, with almost 100% certainty you will never receive the exact result in rollout that you did in test.

The problem is an "error" associated with sample measures. For example, if the test reveals a 2.50% response rate to a particular offer, you will not receive that response rate in rollout even if the sample was large and properly drawn. It has to do with the concept of a sample. Sample measures such as a mean or proportion have a certain level of associated error variance. The higher the error variance associated with the sample measures, the more likely your test results will be off from what you can expect in rollout. This does not mean, however, that you cannot make accurate marketing decisions based on sample estimates.

In this chapter we discuss the two methods available for assessing marketing test results with confidence:

1. **Confidence Interval Calculation**: Allows a direct marketer to determine a range in which the true measure of concern (e.g., response rate, payment rate) can be expected to lie in a rollout situation. The direct marketer can run various profit calculations using the upper and lower bounds of the interval to determine a best and worst case profit scenario for the rollout

2. **Hypothesis Test for Significance**: Allows a direct marketer to form a hypothesis about the measure of concern (e.g., response rate, payment rate), followed by a test of that hypothesis. For example, you might be interested in determining at what exact level of confidence you can make the statement "The response rate of the new direct mail format test has beaten that of the control format." With a hypothesis test, you can determine the answer to such questions.

Confidence Interval Calculations

We discuss in this section four different types of confidence intervals to help you assess marketing test results. In particular, you will learn how to construct confidence intervals around

- Sample averages or means
- Sample proportions
- Difference between two sample averages
- Difference between two sample proportions

In addition, you will learn how to interpret these confidence intervals, enabling you to make the best marketing decision possible.

Confidence Interval Estimation
for a Sample Mean

This formula is used when interest revolves around determining the accuracy of a single sample mean. For example, you are about to launch a new catalog, and on the basis of the results of the test, you want to determine a range in which the true average dollars spent per customer order are likely to fall in a full-scale rollout. This is done by constructing a confidence interval around the sample average. On the basis of the lower bound (worst case scenario) and upper bound (best case scenario), you can determine various profit calculations for determining the rollout potential of the catalog.

To calculate a confidence interval around a mean, the following information is required:

- The sample mean $\bar{x}$ obtained from the test data.
  This is the measure upon which you will base your marketing decision (i.e., mean dollars spent per catalog order, mean number of products bought per Web site visit).
- The standard deviation S associated with the test data.
  Many software packages, including SAS and Excel, can automatically calculate this value for you. (This formula can be found in any elementary statistics book.)
- The sample size n of the test.
  This is the number of observations used to calculate the mean. To construct this interval, the sample size must be greater than or equal to 30.
- The desired error rate α% and confidence level $(1 - \alpha)$%
  A confidence interval constructed around the sample mean will guarantee, with your specified level of confidence, that the true mean will fall within its bounds. We recommend that all confidence intervals be constructed with a 90% or better confidence level (or an error rate α of 10% or less). Employing lower levels of confidence drastically increases the risk of obtaining misleading results, which could lead to incorrect and costly decisions. For example, with an 85% confidence interval, there is a 15% chance (error rate α) that the true mean you can expect in a rollout situation will not be contained in the constructed interval.

Once all this information is known, construct the confidence interval around the mean by adding and subtracting from the mean a multiple of your standard deviation associated with the sample mean as follows:

$$\bar{x} \pm (z)(S_{\bar{x}})$$

Where

$\bar{x}$ is the sample mean or average

$S_{\bar{x}}$ is the standard deviation associated with the sample mean and is equal to $S/\sqrt{n}$

z is the multiplier and is equal to 1.645, 1.96 and 2.575 for 90%, 95%, and 99% confidence levels, respectively (z values associated with other confidence levels can be found in Exhibit 13.1).

Because the intent of this book is not to teach statistics but merely show the various applications, we will not discuss the derivation for this formula. For those readers with a statistics background, the derivation of all confidence interval formulas is based on the Central Limit Theorem. (You can find further information on this topic in any elementary statistics book.)

Let's go back to direct marketer ACME Direct. Assume the product manager at ACME Direct has conducted a new catalog test and estimated that the average expenditure or sample mean per order is $34.51, with a sample standard deviation of $6.81 based on 187 orders. In preparation for a marketing assumptions meeting with her director, the product manager created a confidence interval around this sample mean in order to calculate various profit scenarios based on the lower bound and the upper bound. She wants to be 99% certain that the range she calculates will contain the true population mean she expects in a rollout situation.

In this example,

$$\bar{x} = \$34.51$$
$$S_{\bar{x}} = \frac{S}{\sqrt{n}}$$
$$= \frac{\$6.81}{\sqrt{187}}$$
$$= \$0.50$$
$$z = 2.575 \text{ for a 99\% confidence level}$$

Plugging all known data into the formula yields the following confidence interval:

$$\bar{x} \pm (z)(S_{\bar{x}})$$
$$= \$34.51 \pm (2.575)(\$0.50)$$
$$= \$34.51 \pm \$1.28$$
$$= \$33.23 \text{ to } \$35.79, \text{ or } (\$33.23, \$35.79)$$

The product manager has determined, with 99% confidence, that the true mean expenditures per catalog order in rollout will fall in the range

Exhibit 13.1 Z Values and Confidence Levels Required for Confidence Intervals, Hypothesis Tests, and Sample Sizes

Z Values and Confidence Levels for Conducting Confidence Intervals, Two-Tailed Hypothesis Tests, and Sample Size Calculations		Z Values and Confidence Levels for Conducting Right- or Left-Tailed Hypothesis Tests Only	
Confidence Level (%)	Z Values	Confidence Level (%)	Z Values
80.0	1.280	80.0	0.840
80.5	1.300	80.5	0.860
81.0	1.310	81.0	0.880
81.5	1.330	81.5	0.900
82.0	1.340	82.0	0.920
82.5	1.360	82.5	0.930
83.0	1.370	83.0	0.950
83.5	1.390	83.5	0.970
84.0	1.410	84.0	0.990
84.5	1.420	84.5	1.020
85.0	1.440	85.0	1.040
85.5	1.460	85.5	1.060
86.0	1.480	86.0	1.080
86.5	1.490	86.5	1.100
87.0	1.510	87.0	1.130
87.5	1.530	87.5	1.150
88.0	1.560	88.0	1.180
88.5	1.580	88.5	1.200
89.0	1.600	89.0	1.230
89.5	1.620	89.5	1.250
90.0	1.645	90.0	1.280
90.5	1.670	90.5	1.310
91.0	1.700	91.0	1.340
91.5	1.720	91.5	1.370
92.0	1.750	92.0	1.410
92.5	1.780	92.5	1.440
93.0	1.810	93.0	1.480
93.5	1.850	93.5	1.510
94.0	1.880	94.0	1.560
94.5	1.920	94.5	1.600
95.0	1.960	95.0	1.645
95.5	2.010	95.5	1.700
96.0	2.060	96.0	1.750
96.5	2.110	96.5	1.810
97.0	2.170	97.0	1.880
97.5	2.240	97.5	1.960
98.0	2.330	98.0	2.060
98.5	2.430	98.5	2.170
99.0	2.575	99.0	2.330
99.5	2.810	99.5	2.575

($33.23, $35.79). She can now calculate worst and best case profit scenarios by incorporating marketing costs and revenue figures in preparation for her assumptions review meeting. We will address shortly how the product manager determined that a 99% confidence level as opposed to a 90% or 95% confidence level was most appropriate.

Confidence Interval Estimation for a Sample Proportion

You will use this formula when you want to determine the accuracy of a single sample proportion. A confidence interval around a single response rate is primarily used to assess new list tests in terms of their potential as "new name" generators or to assess new products in terms of their potential for a large-scale rollout. A product manager will use the formula to place bounds around the results of a new list or product test. On the basis of the lower bound, the product manager can determine the risk associated with rolling out with the new list or new product in larger quantities.

To calculate a confidence interval around a sample proportion, you need the following information:

♦ The sample proportion $\hat{p}$ obtained from the test data
This is the measure upon which you base your marketing decision (e.g., percentage responders, payment rate, percentage telemarketing hits).

♦ The sample size n of the test
This is the number of observations used to calculate your proportion. To construct this interval, the sample size, when multiplied by the sample proportion and by 1 minus the sample proportion, must be greater than or equal to 5. That is, $n\hat{p}$ and $n(1 - \hat{p})$ must both be greater than or equal to 5.

♦ The desired error rate α% and confidence level $(1 - \alpha)$%
A confidence interval constructed around the sample proportion will guarantee, with your specified level of confidence, that the true population proportion will fall within its bounds. We recommend that all confidence intervals be constructed with a 90% or better confidence level (or an error rate a of 10% or less). Employing lower levels of confidence drastically increases the risk of obtaining misleading results, which could lead to incorrect and costly decisions. For example, with an 85% confidence interval, there is a 15% chance (error rate a) that the true population proportion you can expect in a rollout situation will not be contained in the constructed interval.

Once all this information is known, construct the confidence interval around the sample proportion by adding and subtracting from the proportion a multiple of your standard deviation associated with the sample proportion as follows:

$$\hat{p} \pm (z)(S_{\hat{p}})$$

Where

$S_{\hat{p}}$ is the standard deviation associated with the sample proportion and is equal to $\sqrt{\hat{p}\,(1-\hat{p}\,)/n}$.

z is the multiplier and is equal to 1.645, 1.96, and 2.575 for 90%, 95%, and 99% confidence levels, respectively (z values associated with other confidence levels can be found in Exhibit 13.1).

For example, assume that the marketing director at ACME Direct tested a new prospect list to 10,000 names. The results for this new list test yielded an order rate of 3.42%. To assess the potential for this new prospect list in rollout, he decides to construct a confidence interval. In particular, he wishes to calculate an interval around this sample response rate such that he can be 95% confident that the true response rate of this list to expect in rollout will fall within the interval bounds. Constructing such an interval allows him to calculate the true potential of this new list as a new name generator based on the lower and upper bounds.

In this example,

$$\hat{p} = .0342$$

$$S_{\hat{p}} = \sqrt{\frac{\hat{p}\,(1 - \hat{p}\,)}{n}}$$

$$= \sqrt{\left(\frac{(.0342)(1 - .0342)}{10,000}\right)}$$

$$= .001817$$

$$z = 1.96 \text{ for a 95\% confidence level}$$

Plugging all known data into the formula yields the following confidence interval:

$$\hat{p} \pm (z)(S_{\hat{p}})$$

$$= .0342 \pm (1.96)(.001817)$$

$$= .0342 \pm .00365$$

$$= .03064 \text{ to } .03776, \text{ or } (3.06\%, 3.78\%)$$

The marketing director can be 95% confident, should he decide to roll out with the new list, that the response rate will not be less than 3.06%. He can use the lower bound to determine the worst case scenario in terms of profitability. Upon examination of this profit scenario, he will make his decision. We will address shortly how the marketing director determined that a 95% confidence level as opposed to a 90% or 99% confidence level was most appropriate.

Confidence Interval Estimation for the Difference Between Two Sample Means

Interest often revolves around the difference between two sample means. For example, of concern might be the difference in average customer service satisfaction scores for a control group of customers versus a group of customers who were part of a special customer servicing test.

To calculate a confidence interval around the difference between two sample means, the following information is required:

- The means obtained from both samples' test results ($\overline{x}_1$ and $\overline{x}_2$)
  These are the measure of comparative interest (i.e., difference in rating scores between control and test groups, the difference in mean web site expenditures for the old vs the new web sites, etc.).
- The standard deviation associated with both samples' test results (S_1 and S_2)
  Many software packages, including Excel, can automatically calculate these values. (This formula can be found in any elementary statistics book.)
- The size of both samples (n_1 and n_2)
  These are the number of observations that went into calculating each of the means. To calculate this interval, both sample sizes n_1 and n_2 must be greater than or equal to 30 in size.
- The desired error rate α% and confidence level $(1 - \alpha)$%
  A confidence interval constructed around the difference between two sample means will guarantee, with your specified level of confidence, that the true difference in means will fall within its bounds. We recommend that all confidence intervals be constructed with a 90% or better confidence level (or an error rate a of 10% or less). Employing lower levels of confidence drastically increases the risk of obtaining misleading results, which could lead to incorrect and costly decisions. For example, with an 85% confidence interval, there is a 15% chance (error rate a) that the true difference in means will be outside the constructed interval.

Once all the information is known, construct the confidence interval around the difference between two means by adding and subtracting from the difference in means a multiple of the standard deviation associated with the difference as follows:

$$(\overline{x}_1 - \overline{x}_2) \pm (z)(S_{\overline{x}_1 - \overline{x}_2})$$

Where

$S_{\overline{x}_1 - \overline{x}_2}$ is the standard deviation associated with the difference in sample means and is equal to $\sqrt{((S_1^2/n_1) + (S_2^2/n_2))}$.

z is the multiplier and is equal to 1.645, 1.96, and 2.575 for 90%, 95%, and 99% confidence levels, respectively (z values associated with other confidence levels can be found in Exhibit 13.1).

For example, assume the marketing director in charge of Internet sales at ACME Direct has developed a new Web site geared to generate more multiple orders by displaying similar products via pop-up ads when the first item goes into a customer's shopping cart. During the month of November, half of the customers who placed an item into their shopping cart received the pop-up ads and the other half did not. The results of the test and control panels are shown in Exhibit 13.2.

The marketing director must determine the true value of pop-up ads in preparation for his monthly status report. To do so, he has decided to develop a confidence interval for the mean difference between customer expenditures with and without the pop-up ads. He has chosen an α level of 10% (the error rate). He will recommend that ACME Direct switch to the new Web site as long as the worst case scenario (the lower bound of the confidence interval) is not less than 0. A lower bound less than 0, in this case, would suggest that the new Web site may actually perform worse than the control Web site in rollout (with 90% confidence).

In this example,

$\overline{x}_1 = \$35.55$ (the mean for the new Web site)

$\overline{x}_2 = \$34.96$ (the mean for the control web site)

Exhibit 13.2 Web Site Test Results

	Number of Customers Who Ordered	Total Dollars Spent	Average Dollars Spent
Control Web site	243	$8,495.28	$34.96
New Web site with pop-up ads	239	$8,496.45	$35.55

Where $S_{control} = 2.06$ and $S_{test} = 2.09$

$$S_{\bar{x}_1 - \bar{x}_2} = \sqrt{\left(\frac{S_1^2}{n_1}\right) + \left(\frac{S_2^2}{n_2}\right)}$$

$$= \sqrt{\left(\frac{2.09^2}{239}\right) + \left(\frac{2.06^2}{243}\right)}$$

$$= \sqrt{\left(\frac{4.37}{239}\right) + \left(\frac{4.24}{243}\right)}$$

$$= \sqrt{.018277 + .0177463}$$

$$= \sqrt{.035740}$$

$$= .18905$$

$$z = 1.645 \text{ for a } 90\% \text{ confidence level}$$

Plugging all known data into the formula provided yields the following confidence interval:

$$(\bar{x}_1 - \bar{x}_2) \pm (z)(S_{\bar{x}_1 - \bar{x}_2})$$

$$= (\$35.55 - \$34.96) \pm (1.645)(.18905)$$

$$= \$0.59 \pm \$0.31$$

$$= \$0.28 \text{ to } \$0.90, \text{ or } (\$0.28, \$0.90)$$

With 90% confidence, the new Web site can be expected to outperform the old Web site in rollout by anywhere between $0.28 and $0.90 per order placed. Because the worst case scenario reveals the new Web site as outperforming the control by an amount greater than $0.00 ($0.28 to be exact), she will recommend that ACME Direct use the pop-up ads. How the marketing director determined that a 90% confidence level as opposed to a 95% or 99% confidence level was most appropriate will be addressed shortly.

Using the same formula, the marketing director could have substituted the mean, variance, and sample size associated with the new Web site for $\bar{x}_2$, S_2, and n_2 and the mean, variance, and sample size associated with the control Web site for $\bar{x}_1$, S_1, and n_1. The resulting confidence interval $(-\$0.90, -\$0.28)$ would reveal how much *worse* the control Web site performed compared to the new Web site. The conclusion remains the same.

Confidence Interval Estimation for the Difference Between Two Sample Proportions

Interest also often revolves around the difference between two sample proportions or response rates. For example, the measure of concern might be the difference in response rates for the format with a "premium for order" versus the same format without a "premium for order."

To calculate a confidence interval around the difference between two sample proportions, the following information is required:

♦ The proportions obtained from both samples' test results ($\hat{p}_1$ and $\hat{p}_2$)
These are the measures of comparative interest (i.e., difference in the response rates for a new format test vs. the control format).

♦ The size of both samples (n_1 and n_2)
These are the number of observations used in calculating each of the sample proportions. To calculate this interval, both sample sizes, when multiplied by their respective sample proportions and by 1 minus their respective sample proportions, must all be greater than or equal to 5. That is, must all be greater than or equal to 5.

♦ The desired error rate $\alpha\%$ and confidence level $(1 - \alpha)\%$
A confidence interval constructed around the difference between two sample proportions will guarantee, with your specified level of confidence, that the true difference will fall within its bounds. We recommend that all confidence intervals be constructed with a 90% or better confidence level (or an error rate a of 10% or less). Employing lower levels of confidence drastically increases the risk of obtaining misleading results, which could lead to incorrect and costly decisions. For example, with an 85% confidence interval, there is a 15% chance (error rate a) that the true difference you can expect in a rollout situation will not be contained in the constructed interval.

Once all information is known, construct the confidence interval around the difference between two proportions by adding and subtracting from the difference in proportions a multiple of the standard deviation associated with the difference as follows:

$$(\hat{p}_1 - \hat{p}_2) \pm (z)(S_{\hat{p}_1 - \hat{p}_2})$$

Where
$S_{\hat{p}_1 - \hat{p}_2}$ is the standard deviation associated with the difference in proportions and is equal to $\sqrt{(\hat{p}_1(1-\hat{p}_1)/n_1) + (\hat{p}_2(1-\hat{p}_2)/n_2)}$.
z is the multiplier and is equal to 1.645, 1.96, and 2.575 for 90%, 95%, and 99% confidence levels, respectively (z values associated with other confidence levels can be found in Exhibit 13.1).

For example, assume that the senior product manager at ACME Direct has conducted a new direct mail format test. The results of this new format test and the current control format are shown in Exhibit 13.3.

The senior product manager determined that the new and more expensive format test must yield an additional two orders per 1,000 names promoted in order to cover the incremental costs. In other words, it must outperform the control format by at least 0.20% (two tenths of 1 percentage point). To properly assess the value of the new format test, the senior product manager will construct a 95% confidence interval around the difference in response rates between the test and control formats to more accurately examine the true difference, taking into account any error in her test estimates. If the lower bound (worst case scenario) of the confidence interval is greater than 0.20%, she will feel confident in switching to the new format.

In this example,

$$\hat{p}_1 = .0416 (\textit{the response rate for the new format})$$

$$\hat{p}_2 = .0349 (\textit{the response rate for the control format})$$

$$S_{\hat{p}_1 - \hat{p}_2} = \sqrt{\left[\frac{\hat{p}_1 (1 - \hat{p}_1)}{n_1}\right] + \left[\frac{\hat{p}_2 (1 - \hat{p}_2)}{n_2}\right]}$$

$$= \sqrt{\left[\frac{.0416(1 - .0416)}{10,002}\right] + \left[\frac{.0349(1 - .0349)}{9,978}\right]}$$

$$= \sqrt{.0000040 + .0000034}$$

$$= .0027$$

$$z = 1.96 \text{ for a 95\% confidence level}$$

Plugging all known data into the formula provided yields the following confidence interval:

$$(\hat{p}_1 - \hat{p}_2) \pm (z)(S_{\hat{p}_1 - \hat{p}_2})$$

$$= (.0416 - .0349) \pm (1.96)(.0027)$$

$$= .0067 \pm .0053$$

$$= .0014 \text{ to } .0120, \text{ or } (.0014, .0120)$$

With 95% confidence, the new format test is guaranteed to outperform the current format by anywhere from 0.14% to 1.20%. Because the lower bound of this difference is less than the minimum required difference of

Exhibit 13.3 Direct Mail Format Test Results

	Number of Customers Mailed	Number of Customers Who Ordered	Response Rate (%)
Control format	9,978	348	3.49
New format test	10,002	416	4.16

0.20%, the senior product manager should proceed cautiously before changing to the new format. In other words, the new format in rollout may *not* meet the minimum difference required to cover the incremental costs. She, however, can feel confident that the new format has at least beaten the control, because the lower bound is greater than 0.

Using the same formula, the senior product manager could have substituted the response rate and sample size associated with the new format test for $\hat{p}_2$ and n_2 and the response rate and sample size associated with the control format for $\hat{p}_1$ and n_1. The resulting confidence interval $(-0.0120, -0.0014)$ would reveal how much worse the control format performed compared to the new format. The conclusion remains the same.

Had the senior product manager constructed a 90% confidence interval, the calculations of the confidence interval would remain the same, with the exception of using $z = 1.645$ (which corresponds to a 90% confidence level).

$$(\hat{p}_1 - \hat{p}_2) \pm (z)(S_{\hat{p}_1 - \hat{p}_2})$$

$$= .0067 \pm (1.645)(.0027)$$

$$= .0067 \pm .0044$$

$$= 0.0023 \text{ to } 0.0111, \text{ or } (0.0023, 0.0111)$$

Notice how the decrease in the confidence level associated with the difference between these two sample response rates has caused the interval to lessen in width. In general, if you want to be *less* confident that the constructed interval will contain the true estimate expected in rollout, the confidence interval will lessen in width. If you want to be *more* confident that the constructed interval will contain the true estimate expected in rollout, the confidence interval will widen.

In the case of a 90% confidence interval, the lower bound exceeds the required minimum difference (0.20%) required to cover the incremental costs. On the basis of this confidence interval, the senior product manager can feel confident that the new format test will outperform the control by the required minimum difference of 0.20%.

Should she base her decision on the results of the 95% or 90% confidence interval? She will come to two different conclusions, depending upon her choice. With the 95% confidence interval, she will conclude that the new format has *not* beaten the control format by an acceptable level. With the 90% confidence interval, she will conclude that the new format test is a winner.

Setting the Confidence Level

At what percentage should you set the confidence level of your interval? To answer this question, ask yourself, How much risk am I willing to take in making an incorrect decision of assuming that, for example, the true response rate I can expect in rollout falls within the constructed interval, when in reality it falls outside the interval?

Single Sample Measures

When you construct a confidence interval around a single test estimate to gauge a new list's or new product's potential, you need to determine which of the following situations best fits your testing circumstances:

- If the costs associated with a new list or new product are significantly higher compared to the lists or products currently being promoted, there is a major risk associated with rolling out with the new list or product, if in reality it ends up performing poorly. Set your confidence level high (95% or 99%) to minimize the chance of concluding that the list or product test has met your requirements, when in reality it does not.
- If the costs associated with a new list or new product are similar to other lists or products currently being promoted, there is certainly less risk associated with rolling out when in reality it ends up performing poorly. Set your confidence level at industry standard levels (90% or 95%), because the risk in making an incorrect decision is not as high, relatively speaking, as in the first scenario.
- If the costs associated with a new list or new product are lower in comparison to other lists or products currently being promoted, there is also less risk associated with rolling out with the new list or product if, in reality, it ends up performing poorly. Set your confidence level at industry standard levels (90% or 95%), because, relatively speaking, the risk in making an incorrect decision is not as high as in the first or second scenario.

Consider the example previously mentioned in which the marketing director conducted a new list test to 10,000 names and received a 3.42% response rate. Assume this new prospect list costs only slightly more (+ $10 per 1,000 names rented) than most other prospect lists promoted by ACME Direct. What would be an appropriate confidence level to use when assessing the response range this list may produce in rollout? In this case, because the cost is only slightly more expensive than the others, 95% seems appropriate.

Difference Between Two Sample Measures

To best understand the process of determining the confidence level to use when interest revolves around the difference between two test results, consider the data presented in Exhibit 13.3. In that example, the senior product manager was faced with not knowing whether or not to use a 90% or 95% confidence level.

Her decision will be based on the amount of risk she is willing to take:

- If the costs associated with the new format are significantly higher than the costs associated with the control format, there is a major risk in changing to a new format, if in reality it ends up performing worse or the same as the control format. In this case, if the new format's results are no better or worse than the control format, erroneously changing to the new format will yield an increase in promotional costs with a 0 to negative change in the overall response rate. She must set the confidence level high (95% or 99%) to minimize the chance of concluding that the test format has outperformed the control format, when in reality it did not. The degree of the risk depends on how much higher the costs are for the new format test compared to the control format.

- If the costs associated with both promotional formats are similar, there is certainly less risk if she decides to change to the new format, when in reality it performs worse than the control format. In this case, if the new format's results are worse than the control format, erroneously changing to the new format will yield a negative change in the overall response rate but leave promotional costs unchanged (unlike the first scenario). As a result, she can keep the confidence level at industry standard levels (90% or 95%), because the risk in making an incorrect decision is not as high, relatively speaking, as in the first scenario.

- If the costs associated with the new format are lower than the costs associated with the control format, there is also less risk if she decides to change to the new format, when in reality it ends up performing worse than the control format. In this case, erroneously changing to a new format will yield a negative change in the overall response rate, but this time, promotional costs will decline, offsetting this fact. She can keep the confidence level at industry standard levels (90% or 95%), because, relatively speaking, the risk in making an incorrect decision is not as high as in the first or second scenario. The degree of risk depends on how much lower the costs are for the new format test compared to the control format.

On the basis of this information, and assuming the test format is only moderately more expensive than the control format, a 95% confidence interval seems appropriate: (0.0014, 0.0120). Because this interval reveals that the difference can be as low as 0.14%, which is lower than the required minimum to break even (0.20%), the senior product manager is advised not to change to the new format. Or should she?

Making a Business Decision
Based on the Confidence Interval

Once the confidence level has been determined and the confidence interval calculated, the interpretation of the interval is not clear cut. Business experience and knowledge play a major role in the final decision. A confidence interval will *not* provide you with a definitive answer to a business question, but it will provide you with valid best and worst case scenarios to consider.

Single Sample Measures

Confidence intervals around single point estimates such as the sample mean or response rate provide you with true estimates of the upside and downside potential of your business decisions. For example, your list test reveals a response rate of 2.50% with a resulting 95% confidence interval of (2.00%, 3.00%). With 95% confidence, you know that the lowest this response rate can be in rollout is 2.00% and the highest is 3.00%. As a precautionary measure and before making a decision based on the lower and upper bounds of this confidence interval, we advise you to calculate a slightly less aggressive confidence interval (90% in this case) and see what it is telling you. If, when you examine the lower and upper bounds of both intervals, they are telling you that the same action should be taken (i.e., roll out or not roll out with the new list), the answer is easy. If you see conflicting information, you need further analysis. In particular,

- First, determine how close your go/no-go response rate level for outside lists is to the lower and upper bounds of both intervals constructed.
- Next, consider the true upside and downside potential of a business decision by performing profit calculations using the upper and lower bounds of both confidence intervals. What are the worst and best case profit scenarios telling you?

By running through these steps, you will have adequate information upon which to base your marketing decision.

Reconsider the example previously mentioned in which the marketing director conducted a new list test to 10,000 names and received a 3.42% response rate. He determined that a 95% confidence level was appropriate. The resulting 95% confidence interval was determined to be (3.06%, 3.78%). Calculating a slightly less aggressive confidence interval (90% in this case), as suggested above, would yield the interval (3.12%, 3.72%). Assuming the minimum response rate that must be achieved for any outside list is a breakeven response rate of 3.00%, should the marketing director roll out with this list to larger quantities? Absolutely. Both the 90% and 95% confidence intervals guarantee that the minimum response that can be expected in rollout is well above the breakeven response rate level. What if the breakeven determined was instead 3.10%? In this case, the lower bound meets the requirement when examining the 90% confidence interval but not for the 95% confidence interval. If this prospect list is large and ACME Direct is in need of new names, the marketing director should roll out to larger quantities. The upside potential in response based on either interval far exceeds the small downside potential based on the 95% confidence interval. What if the breakeven determined was instead 3.30%? You would not be advised to roll out with this new list. Neither interval constructed can guarantee that ACME Direct will be even close to meeting this minimum requirement. However, because the point estimate (3.42%) is above the breakeven level, ACME Direct may consider a retest to a larger quantity (say, 50,000) if the list is quite large and they are in serious need of new names. Doing so will yield a better test estimate with less error.

Difference Between Two Sample Measures

When comparing two tests and examining the difference in their sample means or response rates, you must closely examine the true upside and downside potential of your business decisions. Again, as was the case before, decide if a slightly less aggressive confidence interval reveals that a different action should be taken. If the two confidence intervals are telling you that the same action should be taken, the answer is easy. If conflicting information is found, you need further analysis. In particular,

- First, determine how close the "difference" you are interested in is to the lower and upper bounds of both intervals. That is, examine the upside and downside potential of your business decision.
- Next, consider the true upside and downside potential of a business decision by performing profit calculations using the upper and lower bounds of both confidence intervals. What are the worst and best case profit scenarios telling you?

On the basis of the data presented in Exhibit 13.3, the senior product manger was faced with a major problem: The 95% confidence interval suggested that she maintain the current control format, but the 90% confidence interval suggested she should change to the new format. She needs to closely examine the bounds of both confidence intervals in terms of what they are telling her. What does she know?

- The lower bound of the 95% confidence interval (0.0014) is less than but very close to the required minimum of 0.0020.
- The lower bound of a less aggressive 90% confidence interval (0.0023) is above the required minimum of 0.0020.
- The new format has definitely beaten the control, because the difference in response rates is guaranteed to be greater than 0, based on both the 90% and 95% confidence intervals (the lower bounds of both exceed 0).
- The upside potential for the true difference can actually exceed 1%, based on both confidence intervals.
- The upside potential (greater than a 1% difference in response) far exceeds that of the downside potential (only a 0.14% difference in response) for both confidence intervals, given the required minimum response of 0.20%.

Given this information, we recommend that the senior product manager switch to the new format and back test[1] the old format to a sample of names. Doing so will allow her to determine if in fact she made the correct decision.

However, had the required difference in response rates been greater than 0.20% (e.g., 0.50%), the senior product manager would be well advised not to change to the new format. In this case, she would find a much greater downside potential and far less upside potential in changing to the new format.

Used properly, confidence intervals can greatly assist you in the analysis of your test results and enable you to make the best possible business decision.

Hypothesis Tests for Significance

The other approach to assessing your marketing test results is by employing hypothesis tests for significance. For example, if you are merely interested in determining if the new format test has a response rate significantly greater than the response rate of the control format, without regard to the degree of difference (as is given with confidence intervals), a hypothesis test for significance is in order.

In this section we discuss the two hypothesis tests most commonly used in the field of direct marketing: (1) test for the difference between two sample means, and (2) test for the difference between two sample proportions

Before going into the details of each type of hypothesis test, we must first discuss a few facts and rules regarding hypothesis tests for significance as well as the proper form of the hypothesis test.

Establishing the Hypothesis

You conduct a new format test and are interested in assessing how it compares to the control test. In particular, you are interested in determining if the response rate of the new format is significantly greater than the control format.

You must first turn this statement into a formal hypothesis for testing as follows:

H_0: The response rate of the new format is equal to the response rate of the control format

versus

H_1: The response rate of the new format is greater than the response rate of the control format,

Where H_0 is called the null hypothesis and is assumed to be true until proven otherwise. H_1 is called the alternative hypothesis and is to be determined if true, based on the sample results. The null hypothesis *always* states that the two measures (means or proportions) are equal (as above).

On the basis of the sample results and the amount of error variance associated with each test panel, you either accept the null hypothesis as true or reject the null hypothesis and accept the alternative hypothesis as true. Keep in mind that the alternative hypothesis is typically what you are wanting to prove true by way of rejecting the null hypothesis.

Setting the Error Rate of the Hypothesis Test

The error associated with rejecting a *true* null hypothesis is called the *Type I error* and is denoted by the Greek letter alpha (α). In other words, you have rejected the null hypothesis and accepted the alternative hypothesis as true, when in fact it is not. This is the same α error associated with confidence intervals: *assuming the true measure falls within the bounds of the confidence interval, when in fact it does not.*

From a direct marketer's perspective, this is the most critical type of error to make. It can cost the enterprise significantly in terms of lost revenue. For example, the product manager changes to the new and more expensive format, thinking it has beaten the control, when in fact it was no different from the control in terms of response rate. Luckily, as you will soon see, you can control for the amount of Type I error you are willing to accept in making your conclusion as to whether or not H_0 or H_1 is true.

The second error made in conducting hypothesis tests is called the *Type II error*. This error occurs when you accept the null hypothesis as true, when in fact it is not. This error is one of lost opportunity. For example, the product manager should have changed to the new test format and *not* assumed it was the same as the control.

Because the error of most concern to direct marketers is a Type I error, it will be our focus. We are not implying that a Type II error is unimportant. If you wish to learn more about a Type II error and how it relates to the Type I error, read any intermediate applied statistics book.

The degree of Type I error you are willing to accept will depend on the consequences to your organization in making a wrong decision. In general, we recommend that all hypothesis testing be conducted with a Type I error rate of 10% or less. Allowing a Type I error rate greater than 10% drastically increases the risk of falsely rejecting the null hypothesis beyond a tolerable level.

The value obtained from taking 1 minus the Type I error rate $(1 - \alpha)$ is called the *confidence level* of the test. Therefore, if you are conducting a hypothesis test with a maximum Type I error rate of 5%, the confidence level of your test decision is said to be 95% ($1-0.05 = 0.95$ or 95%).

Establishing the Direction of the Hypothesis Test

When you conduct hypothesis tests, your alternative hypothesis can assume one of three forms, as shown in Exhibit 13.4.

We call Form 1 of the hypothesis a left-tailed test, Form 2 a right-tailed test, and Form 3 a two-tailed test. (For those with a statistical background, the tails refer to the tails of a normal distribution.)

When you conduct a new format, offer, or price test, you are generally concerned with assessing if it did the same, worse, or better than the control; therefore, we only concern ourselves with the application of two-tailed tests. We give decision rules for both types of hypothesis tests; however, our examples are based on hypothesis tests of the two-tailed variety only.

Hypothesis Test for the Difference Between Two Sample Means

We are now ready to discuss the two types of hypothesis tests. When you conduct hypothesis tests about the difference in means, your interest typically lies in testing the null hypothesis "the two means are equal" versus the

Exhibit 13.4   Forms of the Hypothesis

Form 1 of Hypothesis	Form 2 of Hypothesis	Form 3 of Hypothesis
H_0: The control format response rate *equals* the test format response rate	H_0: The control format response rate *equals* the test format response rate	H_0: The control format response rate *equals* the test format response rate
vs.	vs.	vs.
H_1: The control format response rate is *less than* the test format response rate	H_1: The control format response rate is *greater than* the test format response rate	H_1: The control format response rate is *not equal to* the test format response rate

alternative hypothesis, "the two means are not equal." This is identical to testing the null hypothesis "the difference d between the two means is equal to 0" versus the alternative hypothesis "the difference between the two means d is not equal to 0."

To conduct a hypothesis test on the difference between two sample means, you need the following information:

- The means obtained from both samples' test results ($\overline{x}_1$ and $\overline{x}_2$)

   These are the measures of comparative interest (i.e., the difference in rating scores between control and test groups, the difference in mean Web site expenditures for the old vs. the new Web sites, etc.).

- The standard deviation associated with both samples' test results (S_1 and S_2)

   Many software packages, including Excel, can automatically calculate these values. (See any elementary statistics book for this formula.)

- The size of both samples (n_1 and n_2)

   These are the number of observations that go into calculating each of the means. To perform this test, both sample sizes n_1 and n_2 must be greater than or equal to 30 in size.

- The difference d of interest

   Most often, you are interested in testing the null hypothesis that the two means are the same. This is the same as testing the difference between the two means is zero (i.e., $d = 0$).

- The desired error rate $\alpha\%$ and confidence level $(1 - \alpha)\%$

   The confidence level of your test should be set at 90% or greater (or with an error rate of 10% or less). Conducting your test at lower levels of confidence drastically increases the risk of making a wrong decision based on the test. For example, with an 85% confidence level, there is a 15% chance (Type I error rate α) that you will conclude the two sample means statistically differ from one another, when in fact they do not.

Once all this information is known, set up the hypothesis by choosing one of the following formats:

Left-tailed test H_0: The true mean of Panel 1 minus the true mean of Panel 2 $= d$

versus

H_1: The true mean of Panel 1 minus the true mean of Panel 2 $< d$

Right-tailed test H_0: The true mean of Panel 1 minus the true mean of Panel 2 $= d$

versus

H_1: The true mean of Panel 1 minus the true mean of Panel 2 $> d$

Two-tailed test H_0: The true mean of Panel 1 minus the true mean of Panel 2 $= d$

versus

H_1: The true mean of Panel 1 minus the true mean of Panel 2 $\neq d$

Once the format is determined, calculate the value of the test statistic (TS) that you will use to make your decision to either accept or reject the null hypothesis:

$$TS = \frac{[(\bar{x}_1 - \bar{x}_2) - d]}{(S_{\bar{x}_1 - \bar{x}_2})}$$

Where
$S_{\bar{x}_1 - \bar{x}_2}$ is the standard deviation associated with the difference in sample means and is equal to $\sqrt{(S_1^2/n_1) + (S_2^2/n_2)}$

Finally, make your decision about the acceptance or rejection of the null hypothesis based on the following rules:

- For *left-tailed tests*, if the value of the TS is less than $-z$, reject the null hypothesis in favor of the alternative hypothesis (where z is equal to 1.28, 1.645, and 2.33 for 90%, 95%, and 99% confidence levels, respectively; z values associated with other confidence levels can be found in Exhibit 13.1).
- For *right-tailed tests*, if the value of the TS is greater than z, reject the null hypothesis in favor of the alternative hypothesis (where z is equal to 1.28, 1.645, and 2.33 for 90%, 95%, and 99% confidence levels, respectively; z values associated with other confidence levels can be found in Exhibit 13.1).

♦ For *two-tailed tests*, if the absolute value of the TS is greater than z, reject the null hypothesis H_0 in favor of the alternative hypothesis H_1 (where z is equal to 1.645, 1.96, and 2.575 for 90%, 95%, and 99% confidence levels, respectively; z values associated with other confidence levels can be found in Exhibit 13.1).

Because the intent of this book is not to teach statistics but merely to show the various applications, we will not discuss the derivation for this formula. For those with a statistics background, the derivation of all hypothesis tests for significance is based on the Central Limit Theorem. You can find more information in any elementary statistics book.

On the basis of the data presented in Exhibit 13.2, assume that the marketing director in charge of Internet sales at ACME Direct has developed a new Web site geared to generate more multiple orders by displaying similar products via pop-up ads when the first item goes into a customer's shopping cart. During the month of November, half of the customers who placed an item into their shopping cart received the pop-up ads and the other half did not.

The marketing director decided to test the null hypothesis that the mean dollars spent via the new and control Web sites are equal versus the alternative that they are not equal, with no higher than a 0.05 Type I error rate (the α level).

He will set up the null and alternative hypotheses as follows:

H_0: The true mean expenditures associated with the new Web site minus that of the control Web site = $0.00

versus

H_1: The true mean expenditures associated with the new Web site minus that of the control Web site $\neq$ $0.00

In this example,

$$\bar{x}_1 = \$35.55 \text{(the mean for the new web site.)}$$

$$\bar{x}_2 = \$34.96 \text{(the mean for the new web site.)}$$

$$
\begin{aligned}
S_{\bar{x}_1 - \bar{x}_2} &= \sqrt{\left(\frac{S_1^2}{n_1}\right) + \left(\frac{S_2^2}{n_2}\right)} \\
&= \sqrt{\left(\frac{2.09^2}{239}\right) + \left(\frac{2.06^2}{243}\right)} \\
&= \sqrt{\left(\frac{4.37}{239}\right) + \left(\frac{4.24}{243}\right)}
\end{aligned}
$$

$$= \sqrt{.018277 + .0174663}$$

$$= \sqrt{.035740}$$

$$= .18905$$

$z = 1.96$ for a two-tailed test at a 95% confidence level

Plugging all known data into the formula provided yields the following TS calculation:

$$TS = \frac{[(\bar{x}_1 - \bar{x}_2) - d]}{S_{\bar{x}_1 - \bar{x}_2}}$$

$$= \frac{[(35.55 - 3.96) - 0]}{(.18905)}$$

$$= \frac{.059}{.18905}$$

$$= 3.12$$

The decision rule is to reject the null hypothesis if the absolute value of the TS is greater than $z = 1.96$. The absolute value of the TS is 3.12, and it is greater than 1.96; therefore, the marketing director will reject the null hypothesis and conclude that the average dollars spent via the new Web site are significantly different from the average dollars spent via the old Web site with 95% confidence. And on the basis of the direction of the difference (since $\bar{x}_1 - \bar{x}_2 > 0$), he will conclude that the new Web site has beaten the control in terms of average dollars spent.

The marketing director can now state, with 95% confidence, that the new Web site containing pop-up ads outperforms the old Web site in terms of revenue generation. With 95% confidence, there is only a 5% chance (Type I α error) that he has reached the wrong conclusion.

If the marketing director wants to be 99% confident in his results of the test, he will reject the null hypothesis if the absolute value of the TS is greater than $z = 2.575$. Because the absolute value of the TS is 3.12 and it is greater than 2.33, he will again reject the null hypothesis and conclude that the new Web site outperformed the old in terms of revenue generation with 99% confidence. On the basis of the results of this test, the marketing director can feel even more confident in his decision to reject the null hypothesis, because the odds of making a wrong decision in this case is only 1% (Type I α error rate).

How much better or worse the new Web site is expected to do compared to the control Web site cannot be answered with a hypothesis test. To assess this question, the marketing director will develop a confidence interval. A hypothesis test alone will give him a yes/no answer to a particular question (the hypothesis) only. For example, was there any difference in the average dollars spent between the control and test Web sites?

Hypothesis Test for the
Difference Between Two Sample Proportions

The hypothesis test for the difference between two proportions is similar to the test for the difference between two means.

To conduct a hypothesis test on the difference between two sample proportions, you need the following information:

- The proportions obtained from both samples' test results ($\hat{p}_1$ and $\hat{p}_2$)
  These are the measures of comparative interest (i.e., the difference in the response rates for a new format test vs. the control format).

- The size of both samples (n_1 and n_2)
  These are the number of observations used in calculating each of the sample proportions. To perform this test, both sample sizes, when multiplied by their respective sample proportions and by 1 minus their respective sample proportions, must all be greater than or equal to 5. That is, $n_1\hat{p}_1$, $n_2\hat{p}_2$, $n_1(1 - \hat{p}_1)$ and $n_2(1 - \hat{p}_2)$ must all be greater than or equal to 5.

- The difference d of interest
  Most often, you are interested in testing the null hypothesis that the two proportions are the same. This is the same as testing that the difference between the two proportions is 0 (i.e., $d = 0$).

- The desired error rate $\alpha\%$ and confidence level $(1 - \alpha)\%$
  The confidence level of your test should be set at 90% or greater (or with an error rate of 10% or less). Conducting your test at lower levels of confidence drastically increases the risk of making an incorrect decision based on the test. For example, with an 85% confidence level, there is a 15% chance (Type I error rate α) that you will conclude that the two sample proportions statistically differ from one another, when in fact they do not.

Once all the information is known, set up the hypothesis by choosing one of the following formats:

Left-tailed test H_0: The true response rate of Panel 1 minus the true response rate of Panel 2 = d

versus

H_1: The true response rate of Panel 1 minus the true response rate of Panel 2 < d

Right-tailed test H_0: The true response rate of Panel 1 minus the true response rate of Panel 2 = d

versus

H_1:   The true response rate of Panel 1 minus the true response rate of Panel 2 $> d$

Two-tailed test H_0:   The true response rate of Panel 1 minus the true response rate of Panel 2 $= d$

versus

H_1:   The true response rate of Panel 1 minus the true response rate of Panel 2 $\neq d$

Once the format is determined, calculate the value of the following TS, which you will use to make your decision to either accept or reject the null hypothesis:

$$\text{TS} = \frac{[(\hat{p}_1 - \hat{p}_2) - d]}{(S_{\hat{p}1 - \hat{p}2})}$$

Where
$S_{\hat{p}1 - \hat{p}2}$ is the standard deviation associated with the difference in proportions and is equal to

$$= \sqrt{[(\bar{p})(1 - \bar{p})]\left[\left(\frac{1}{n_1}\right) + \left(\frac{1}{n_2}\right)\right]}$$

and

$$\bar{p} = \frac{[(\hat{p}_1)(n_1) + (\hat{p}_2)(n_2)]}{(n_1 + n_2)} \text{ is called the averaged proportion}$$

Finally, you will make your decision regarding the acceptance or rejection of the null hypothesis based on the following rules:

♦ For *left-tailed tests*, if the value of the TS is less than $-z$, reject the null hypothesis in favor of the alternative hypothesis (where z is equal to 1.28, 1.645, and 2.33 for 90%, 95%, and 99% confidence levels, respectively; z values associated with other confidence levels can be found in Exhibit 13.1).
♦ For *right-tailed tests*, if the value of the TS is greater than z, reject the null hypothesis in favor of the alternative hypothesis (where z is equal to 1.28, 1.645, and 2.33 for 90%, 95%, and 99% confidence levels, respectively; z values associated with other confidence levels can be found in Exhibit 13.1).
♦ For *two-tailed tests*, if the absolute value of the TS is greater than z, reject the null hypothesis H_0 in favor of the alternative hypothesis H_1

(where z is equal to 1.645, 1.96, and 2.575 for 90%, 95%, and 99% confidence levels, respectively; z values associated with other confidence levels can be found in Exhibit 13.1).

On the basis of the data presented in Exhibit 13.3, assume that the senior product manager at ACME Direct has conducted a new direct mail format test. She wants to determine if the difference in response rates between the new format and the control format is statistically significantly different from 0 with 95% confidence. In other words, can she say one or the other formats has won with 95% certainty?

She will set up the null and alternative hypotheses as follows:

H$_0$:   The true response rate of the new format minus the true response rate of the control format = 0.00%

versus

II$_1$:   The true response rate of the new format minus the true response rate of the control format ≠ 0.00%

In this example,

$\hat{p}_1$ = .0416(the response rate for the new format)

$\hat{p}_2$ = .0349 (the response rate for the control format)

$$p = \frac{[(\hat{p}_1)(n_1) + (\hat{p}_2)(n_2)]}{(n_1 + n_2)}$$

$$= \frac{[(.0416)(10,002) + (.0349)(9,978)]}{(10,002 + 9,978)}$$

$$= \frac{(416.0832 + 348.2322)}{19,980}$$

$$= \frac{764.3154}{19,980}$$

$$= .038254$$

$$S_{\hat{p}_1 - \hat{p}_2} = \sqrt{[(\bar{p})(1-\bar{p})]\left[\left(\frac{1}{n_1}\right) + \left(\frac{1}{n_2}\right)\right]}$$

$$= [(.038354)(1 - .038254)]\left[\left(\frac{1}{10,002}\right) + \left(\frac{1}{9,978}\right)\right]$$

$$= \sqrt{[(.038254)(.961746)][(.0000999) + (.0001002)}$$

$$= \sqrt{(.0367906)(.0002001)}$$

$$= \sqrt{.0000073}$$

$$= .0027$$

$z = 1.96$ for a two-tailed test at a 95% confidence level

Plugging all known data into the formula provided yields the following TS calculation:

$$TS = \frac{[(\hat{p}_1 - \hat{p}_2) - d]}{(S_{\hat{p}_1 - \hat{p}_2})}$$

$$= \frac{[(.0416 - .0349) - 0]}{.0027}$$

$$= \frac{.0067}{.0027}$$

$$= 2.48$$

The decision rule is to reject the null hypothesis if the absolute value of the TS is greater than $z = 1.96$. The absolute value of the TS is 2.48, which is greater than 1.96. Therefore, the senior product manager will reject the null hypothesis and conclude that the two response rates are, in fact, different with 95% confidence. And on the basis of the direction of the difference ($\hat{p}_1 - \hat{p}_2 > 0$), the senior product manager will conclude that the new format has beaten the control in terms of response.

If the senior product manager wants to assess the degree to which the control and test formats differ in terms of their response rates, she will need to construct a confidence interval. A hypothesis test alone will give her a yes/no answer to a particular question (the hypothesis) only. For example, are the response rates of the new and the control formats the same?

If the senior product manager wants to be 99% confident (as opposed to 95%) in her results of the hypothesis test for significance, she will reject the null hypothesis if the absolute value of the TS is greater than $z = 2.575$. Because the absolute value of the TS is 2.48 and it is *not* greater than 2.575, she will be unable to reject the null hypothesis and will conclude that the test format is *not* different from the control format in terms of response.

Should the senior product manager base her decision on the results of the hypothesis test at the 95% or 99% level of confidence? She will come to two totally different conclusions, depending on her choice. At the 95% level, she will conclude that the test format has beaten the control. At the 99% confidence level, she will conclude that the test format has *not* beaten the control.

Setting the Confidence Level of Hypothesis Tests for Significance

At what percentage should you set the confidence level of your hypothesis test of significance? To answer this question, as was the case for confidence intervals, you must ask yourself, How much risk am I willing to take in concluding that the two means or response rates are different, when in reality they are *not* different?

To answer this question, follow the same rules for confidence intervals.

Making a Business Decision Based on Hypothesis Tests for Significance

Once the confidence level has been determined and the hypothesis test conducted, interpretation of the results (like that for confidence intervals) is not black and white. Although it is true that the outcome of a hypothesis test is an answer to a yes/no question, you must weigh the risk associated with these answers.

Decide if a slightly less aggressive confidence level reveals a different conclusion:

- ♦ If both hypothesis tests are telling you the same action be taken, the answer is easy.
- ♦ If running a slightly less aggressive hypothesis test reveals conflicting conclusions be drawn, assess the degree to which the control and test formats differ in terms of their response rates by constructing a confidence interval.

By following these steps, you will have adequate information upon which to base your marketing decision.

P Value of the Hypothesis Test for Significance

When conducting hypothesis tests for significance, typically analysts will *not* preset a confidence level (or Type I error rate) by which to draw their conclusions. Rather, they will determine the *p* value associated with the hypothesis test for significance.

The *p* value tells you the lowest Type I error rate for which you can conduct the hypothesis test for significance and still be able to reject the null hypothesis in favor of the alternative hypothesis.

To determine this value, use Exhibit 13.1 backwards. Rather than find the *z* value associated with a specific confidence level, find the confidence level associated with a *z* value equal to your calculated TS value. To determine the *p* value, subtract that value from 100%.

On the basis of the data presented in Exhibit 13.3, the TS value was calculated as 2.48. The corresponding confidence level (for a two-tailed hypothesis test) associated with a z value equal to 2.48 found in Exhibit 13.1 is approximately 98.5%. Therefore, the resulting *p* value of the test is $1.00 - 0.985 = 0.015$.

The value 0.015 in this example is the lowest Type I error rate at which analysts can conduct the hypothesis test and still be able to reject the null hypothesis and conclude that the new format has beaten the control format. If analysts try to conduct this hypothesis test for significance with any Type I error rate lower than 0.015, say 0.01, they will *not* be able to reject the null hypothesis. As you can see, the *p* value associated with a hypothesis test for significance is somewhat more revealing than merely conducting the hypothesis test with a single fixed Type I error rate.

Conducting Hypothesis Tests for Significance Using Confidence Intervals

It is now evident that confidence intervals and hypothesis tests are very much related to one another. The results of a confidence interval can be used to conduct a two-tailed hypothesis test.

On the basis of the data presented in Exhibit 13.3, the 95% confidence interval constructed for the difference in response rates for the control and test formats is (0.0014, 0.0120).

Using this example, you can test the following two-tailed hypothesis with the same confidence level:

H_0:   The true response rate of the new format minus the true response rate of the control format $= d$

versus

H_1:   The true response rate of the new format minus the true response rate of the control format $\neq d$

If the value of *d* is contained in the confidence interval, accept the null hypothesis as true. If the value of *d* is not contained in the confidence interval, reject the null hypothesis and accept the alternative hypothesis as true.

Confidence intervals *can* be used to conduct a hypothesis test of the *two*-tailed variety only. Confidence intervals *cannot* be used to test *one*-tailed hypothesis tests.

Gross Versus Net

When your marketing tests have payment implications, you want to examine net response rather than gross. This includes

- Pricing tests
- Soft versus hard offer tests
- Billing tests

You can further analyze these tests for significant payment differences, but keep in mind that if your sample sizes are not large enough, you will never be able to significantly detect any meaningful difference from a marketing perspective. To detect a certain decrease or increase in payment rates as significant, plan those tests accordingly, using the rules outlined in Chapter 14.

Multiple Comparisons

Occasionally, a direct marketer may wish to simultaneously state the results of *several* hypothesis tests with an overall level of confidence.

Consider the following test series:

- Control package
- As control, but price is $1.00 lower
- As control, but with a premium for order

The marketing director wishes to compare the response rate of the control package to both test panels via hypothesis tests for significance and state the results of both comparisons with an overall 95% level of confidence.

For the marketing director to be able to state the results of both comparisons as a family of comparisons with an overall 95% confidence level, he will have to test each comparison at a confidence level *higher* than 95%. To determine the confidence level for each comparison, ensuring that an overall 95% confidence level is maintained, he will perform the following steps:

1. Calculate the overall Type I error rate desired by taking 100% minus the overall confidence level desired.

2. Divide the number obtained in Step 1 by the number of comparisons to be made.

3. Subtract the number obtained in Step 2 from 100%.

In this example, the marketing director desires to make a single statement about two comparisons with an overall 95% confidence level. To determine the confidence level at which each of the two comparisons must be tested, he calculates as follows:

1. $100\% - 95\% = 5\%$

2. $5\% \div 2 = 2.5\%$

3. $100\% - 2.5\% = 97.5\%$

Therefore, the marketing director will perform each hypothesis test for significance with a 97.5% confidence level. Doing so will allow him to state the results of both hypothesis tests simultaneously or as a family of comparisons with 95% confidence.

Assume (a) the "lower price" test panel was found to have a significantly higher response rate compared to the control package, based on the results of a hypothesis test conducted at a 97.5% confidence level, and (b) the "premium" test panel was also found to have a significantly higher response rate compared to the control package, based on the results of a hypothesis test conducted at a 97.5% confidence level.

Given the above, the marketing director can now say any of the following three statements:

1. With 97.5% confidence, the lower price test has beaten the control package.

2. With 97.5% confidence, the premium test has beaten the control package.

3. With 95% confidence, both the lower price test *and* the premium test have beaten the control.

Typically, this technique is only considered when the tests being compared are related in some manner and several simultaneous package changes are being considered on the basis of the results of a test series.

Calculating Breakeven

Throughout this book, we mention **breakeven** response rate levels. The two most common types of breakeven calculations conducted by marketing managers are

1. The response required for a new list or product in order to break even and

2. The increase in response required for a new and more expensive format or creative test versus the control in order to break even

Response Rate Required to Break Even

The breakeven response rate for a new list or product test is the lowest response rate you can tolerate and not lose any money. It is easily calculated by the following formula:

$$\text{Breakeven} = \frac{(\text{promotion cost per piece})}{(\text{profit per response prior promotion})}$$

Assume you sell collector plates via direct mail. The average profit per order before promotion costs is $55.00. You promote all prospect lists with the same control format at a cost of $500.00 per 1,000 names promoted, not including list rental costs. You are considering the test of a new and quite expensive prospect list that will cost $150.00 per 1,000 names rented. What is the minimum response rate you must achieve on this list test in order to break even and not lose any money?

In this example, the promotion cost per piece mailed will be $0.65, which is calculated as ($500.00 + $150.00)/ 1,000.

$$\text{Breakeven} = \frac{\$0.65}{\$55.00}$$
$$= 1.18\%$$

Therefore, in order for this list not to lose money, a response rate of at least 1.18% must be achieved.

Increase in Response Rate Required to Break Even

When you want to assess the response rate you must obtain on a new and more expensive format test in order to generate at least the same profit as the control format, you use the following formula:

Breakeven = control response rate

$$+ \left[\frac{(\text{test-control promotion cost per piece})}{(\text{profit per response prior promotion})} \right]$$

Assume you sell diet pills by mail to your house file. Your control format costs $500.00 per 1,000 names mailed and generates a 5.00% response rate. You are testing the addition of sample diet pills to your control package. This new package will cost $700.00 per 1,000 names mailed. If the profit before promotion per order is $20.00, then what response rate must you achieve on the test in order to ensure no loss in revenue versus the control format?

$$\text{Breakeven} = 0.05 + \left[\frac{(\$0.70 - \$0.50)}{\$20.00} \right]$$

$$= 0.05 + \left(\frac{\$0.20}{\$20.00} \right)$$

$$= .05 + 0.01$$

$$= 0.06 \text{ or } 6.00\%$$

You must obtain at least a 6.00% response rate on the new test in order to guarantee no loss in revenue versus the control. In other words, you must observe at least a 1 percentage point (6.00%-5.00%) difference in response (or an additional 10 orders per 1,000 names mailed) versus the control in order to break even on this test.

Facts Regarding Confidence
Intervals and Hypothesis Test Results

Regardless of the amount of time you spend planning a test, the results of a confidence interval of a hypothesis test of significance are only valid if nothing outside your control occurs from the time of the test to rollout that may somehow affect your test universe. Various scenarios that could negatively impact either (a) the likelihood that the true mean or response rate obtained in rollout will fall within the bounds of your confidence interval or (b) the likelihood that the correct decision was made with respect to a hypothesis test of significance include

- The timing of the test versus rollout (e.g., the test was conducted in May with a rollout the following January)
- A major competitor emerged on the market after the test and before rollout
- For direct mail marketers, competition (of any kind) in the mailbox during the test versus rollout
- For telemarketers, a change (of any kind) in the amount of telemarketing calls being placed during the test versus rollout
- Bad press regarding direct marketing or telemarketing practices during rollout not seen during the test
- A major natural disaster in a specific region of the country during rollout not seen during the test
- Innocent and minor changes in the promotional package or offer prior to rollout

If any of these scenarios occurred after the original test upon which you are basing your rollout decision, proceed with caution.

Marketing Test Analysis Software

With Excel, you can perform confidence interval calculations on sample means using the CONFIDENCE function. In addition, you can perform hypothesis tests for the difference between two sample means using Excel's Analysis ToolPak feature. However, Excel does not perform these calculations for sample proportions.

Drake Direct, a database marketing consulting firm, offers a software package that allows direct marketers to plan and analyze their marketing test by performing hypothesis tests, confidence intervals, and **sample size estimation** (see Chapter 14) as shown in Exhibit 13.5. The Plan-alyzer© is a point-and-click software package and is compatible with Windows 95 and above. Free of charge, The Plan-alyzer can be downloaded from the Drake Direct Web site at www.DrakeDirect.com.

Chapter Summary

Properly assessing marketing tests is critical to making correct marketing decisions. Unfortunately, many direct marketers do not know how to properly analyze marketing tests. Decisions are often made regarding new formats or copy approaches based simply on comparing the response rate

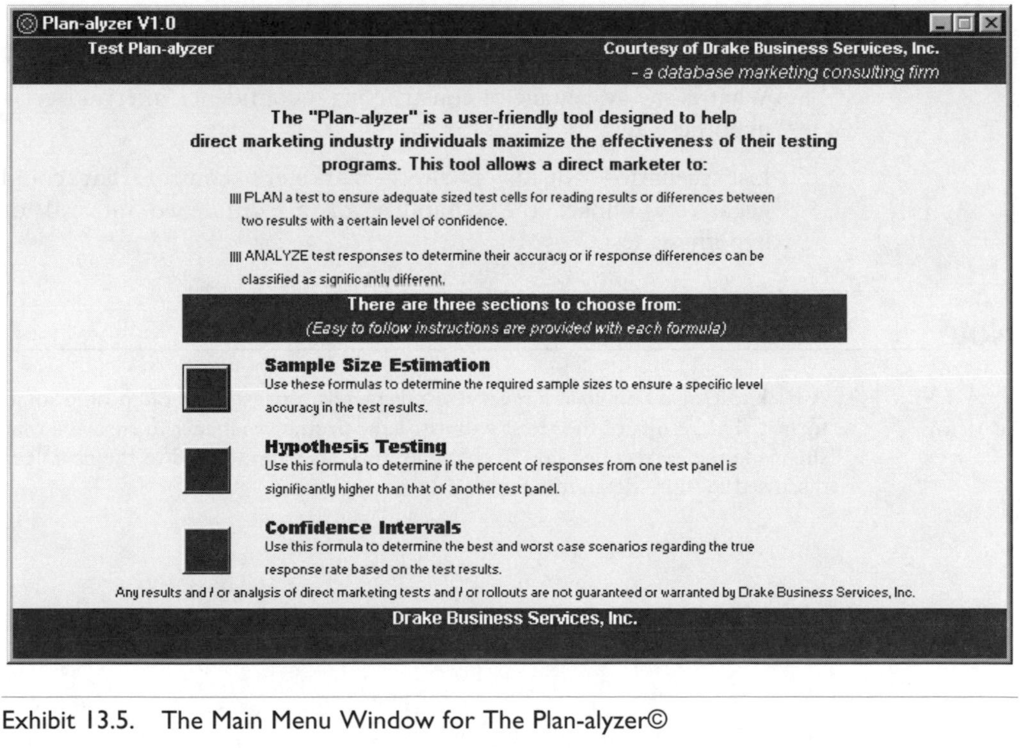

Exhibit 13.5.   The Main Menu Window for The Plan-alyzer©

of one panel to another without regard to the sampling error associated with those response rates. Many tools are revealed in this chapter to help the marketer assess such tests with confidence, taking into account this sampling error. Confidence intervals allow a direct marketer to determine a range in which the true response rate can be expected to lie in a rollout. Hypothesis tests for significance allow a direct marketer to determine with confidence if a new test panel has beaten the control panel. In addition, this chapter discusses in detail the steps required to properly interpret the results of both confidence intervals and hypothesis tests. Rules are also given for choosing the proper confidence level.

Review Questions

1. Interpret the error rate associated with confidence intervals.

2. Interpret the error rate associated with hypothesis tests.

3. What are the steps involved in determining the appropriate confidence level to use when constructing a confidence interval around a single sample response rate?

4. What are the steps involved in determining the appropriate confidence level to use when constructing a confidence interval around the difference between two sample response rates?

5. Discuss how you can use the results of a confidence interval for conducting a two-tailed hypothesis test.

6. What is the advantage of constructing a confidence interval over a hypothesis test?

7. List scenarios outside a direct marketer's control that could negatively impact the reliability of a confidence interval or hypothesis test.

Note

1. A back test, also known as a reverse test, is merely a retest of an old promotional format. The results of the retest will assist the product manager in ensuring that she made the correct decision in changing formats from the old to the new. It is discussed in more detail in Chapter 14.

14

Planning and Designing Marketing Tests

At the training session, Keri Lee and her team were also taught how to set up an appropriate test design. In particular, she did not realize the importance of reverse testing package element changes or how to properly test for package element interactions such as price and premium.

Once they learned how to establish the test design, Keri and her team were taught how to determine appropriate sample sizes for each panel. As it turns out, Keri and her team were testing too few names. Fortunately, they learned how to assess tests with confidence even if budget constraints do not allow them to test an appropriate number of names.

Keri was very happy with the new testing guidelines learned at the training session and felt that her product managers were now well equipped to make solid decisions regarding their test programs.

Testing is the foundation upon which one builds and grows a direct marketing firm. With a database, similar names can be easily selected for certain treatments and comparisons of the customer's reaction to those treatments can be made. On the basis of testing, the marketer can make an informed decision. However, success depends on establishing the correct test panels and ensuring that enough names within each panel are tested.

Before you implement a marketing test program, you need proper planning to ensure that the results will be readable, reliable, and projectable. Without proper test planning, you will be left in a situation where you cannot confidently act upon the results of your tests.

In this chapter, we discuss how to properly plan the test panels, how to determine the appropriate sample sizes for your test panels to ensure the results are meaningful from a marketing perspective, and what options are available to smaller direct marketers that lack a sizable test budget.

Marketing Test Design Considerations

When preparing to test new formats, copy approaches, prices, or offers to your house or outside list names, you must follow several rules:

Rule 1: For Mailers, Include the Control Package in the Test Plan

Marketing tests (format, price, offer, etc.) are typically conducted simultaneously with a major marketing campaign (often referred to as the bulk mailing). To determine test winners, the response rate of each test panel is compared against that of the control package (the package currently being used in the bulk mailing).

One thing you must keep in mind is that the letter shop will output and deliver to the post office the names associated with the test panel and the control package in two separate streams. In other words, the promotional pieces associated with the test mailing will be delivered to the post office in one batch and the promotional pieces associated with the bulk mailing in a separate batch. Because in all likelihood the quantity of names associated with the test mailing will be significantly less than that of the bulk mailing, you will receive different handling by the post office. The larger the quantity, the finer the sort and less expensive the postage. Larger quantities are usually dropped at BMCs (bulk mail centers) directly. Smaller quantities are handled piece by piece at the local level. Therefore, names in the test mailing will be processed much more slowly than names in the bulk mailing. As a result, response will be affected. This is especially true if the promotional materials are time sensitive (e.g., reply-by dates, etc.).

Therefore, to ensure that you properly read the test panel results against the control bulk package, you must include a control panel within the test mailing. You cannot reliably determine test winners by comparing the response rates for the various test panels against the response rate for the control package from the bulk mailing.

There is absolutely no cost to you in doing this. You are simply moving a sampling of names to receive the control package from the bulk mailing to the test mailing.

Rule 2: Reverse Test Package Changes

When rolling out with a new format or creative concept, direct marketers often fail to **reverse test** the old control format. Reverse testing (also called back testing) these promotional changes provides a marketer with valuable information regarding the performance of the new test package in rollout.

When a marketing campaign is underforecast, a reverse test will help you determine if the fault or problem lies with the list or the new concept, allowing you to take proper corrective action prior to the next campaign. Without reverse tests, you cannot possibly know the corrective action to take in such a situation.

ACME Direct plans to make two changes to the control package for their next major marketing campaign. In particular, ACME Direct will add a scratch-off card action device and a mini radio premium to the control package. Within this major marketing campaign, ACME Direct will conduct reverse tests of these changes to the control package by including the following three test panels:

1. 10,000 names to receive the old control package

2. 10,000 names to receive the old control package with the scratch-off card action device

3. 10,000 names to receive the old control package with the mini radio premium

These three additional test panels within the major marketing campaign will allow ACME Direct to assess the value of each change in a rollout. If the campaign comes in under forecast (or over forecast), ACME Direct will be able to determine if it was due to either or both of the new elements not yielding the forecasted lift in response.

Rule 3: Test One Change at a Time

When applicable, test various changes to the control package one at a time. For example, if you plan to test a new format and a new copy approach to the control package, do not test them simultaneously. Test each change separately. You will gain much more information from two separate test results than if they were combined into one test panel.

In the ACME Direct example, it may be that the copy change increases response while the new format decreases response. This will not be apparent if tested simultaneously.

Consider the test series results shown in Exhibit 14.1.

Exhibit 14.1 Example Test Series Results

Test Panel	Response Rate (%)	Index to Control
Control package	3.50	100
As control with new format and copy change	3.47	99
As control with new format	3.15	90
As control with copy change	3.79	108

Examining the test panel where the new format and copy were changed simultaneously, you find no difference in response versus the control package (3.47% vs. 3.50%). On the basis of this result, you would discard both as an option and try again. However, when you examine the test results of each element tested separately, notice that the new copy approach was a winner. Without these separate element test panels, this would not be evident.

Remember, testing is the foundation upon which you will grow your company. Test wisely.

Rule 4: Test for Only Meaningful Package Element Interactions

Generally, it is unnecessary to test every possible package element combination in your test plan. For example, the product manager at ACME Direct may be interested in testing the following changes to the control package:

- Price increase
- Addition of a premium
- Addition of an action device
- New format

Testing every possible combination of price, premium, format, and action device yields a total of 16 test panels. Testing all 16 panels is called a **full factorial test design**.

The only reason a marketer would test a full factorial test design would be if it was believed that interactions will occur between all four elements with respect to response. In this example, the only possible interaction to be concerned with would be between price and premium. In other words, if testing a higher price, perhaps the minus in response (due solely to pricing) would be less for the package with a premium versus the package without the premium.

Note that other interactions may also be possible, but you would need to know more details about the other panels to make a proper judgment call. For example, if the action device is a scratch-off card in which everyone gets a $1 discount, it too may interact with price.

Assuming ACME Direct is only interested in assessing a possible interaction between price and premium, the test series would appear as shown in Exhibit 14.2.

On the basis of this test series, how will ACME Direct determine if the addition of a premium to the control package offset any or all of the negative effect that a price increase might have on response? ACME Direct will determine this by examining the index in response for Test Panels 1 and 2 versus the index in response for Test Panels 3 and 6.

Exhibit 14.2   Example Test Series

Test Panel	Description
1	Control test package
2	Price test package—as control package with $2 price increase
3	Premium test package—as control but with premium for order added
4	Format test package—as control but with a new format
5	Action device test package—as control but with an action device added
6	Price and premium test package—as test panel #3 with $2 price increase

One drawback to not testing every possible element combination is that you are left with forecasting issues in rollout. For example, considering the test series shown in Exhibit 14.2, what would happen if ACME Direct decides to roll out with the addition of both the premium and action device to the control package for their next major marketing campaign? How will they forecast the lift in response they expect in rollout, given that they did not test this combination? To determine this, most major direct marketers simply add all individual element pluses and minuses and take a certain percentage of them for the final response forecast. The percentage taken is typically derived from historical information or experience. It will vary from direct marketer to direct marketer and be based on the number and types of elements being added together. In other words, if the addition of the premium gave you a +25% in response versus the control and the addition of the action device gave you a +10% in response versus the control, do not expect to get a +35% in response if you incorporate both things in the new package simultaneously. You will get something less than that. They will not be additive.

Rule 5: Define the Universe for Testing Carefully

Careful consideration must be given to the names selected for testing. Major marketing elements are typically tested to the core or primary customer segment as a whole. They should not be tested to selects within the core or primary customer segment—a mistake often made by small direct marketers. Why is this an issue? Because you want consistency in test results. You want to bridge test results from one test series to another. If the same definition of names are not tested over time, you cannot accurately forecast lift for future campaigns based on past test results. For example, you want to use the action device tested last year for this year's campaign. Unfortunately, the names tested last year differ significantly from those you will be promoting this year. You cannot accurately forecast the lift in response for one customer group based on test results to a completely different customer group.

If you are testing a custom format designed for a unique customer segment, you must also include within your test plan a test of the same unique customer segment to receive the control format. For example, in the case of testing a new format designed specifically for converting nonbuyers, you will of course be testing it to the segment of nonbuyers and not your core customer segment. To gauge the success of this new nonbuyer format, you must make sure you have a panel within your test plan of nonbuyers receiving the standard control package. You will not be able to compare the results of this custom format sent to the nonbuyers to the control package sent to the core customer segment. Similar to comparing apples to oranges, this will yield misleading results.

Outside List Test Design Considerations

Regarding outside list testing, you may be well advised to test for interactions between lists and the package elements (format, price, offer, etc.). In other words, certain lists, depending on how they are sourced, may react differently to different package elements. For example, a list sourced via a sweepstakes promotion will in all likelihood respond better to a sweepstakes promotion than a nonsweepstakes promotion. A list sourced via a soft free trial offer will in all likelihood respond better to a similar offer than to a hard cash-with-order offer. If you do not see any reason to test for list by package element interactions, don't. Use your experience to guide you in setting up the test.

For example, if you are testing five lists, two formats, and two offers, a full factorial test design will require that you test 20 different combinations of list, format, and offer. If you have a fixed testing budget, you may not be able to test enough names within each cell to get meaningful results. In other words, the confidence intervals constructed around the response rate associated with each cell may be so wide that you cannot make a decision (see Chapter 13). If this is the case, we advise you to reduce the number of test cells, keeping only those interactions that make the most sense. Knowledgeable list brokers should be able to help you. On the basis of their experience, list brokers should know what types of offers work best for which lists. Take advantage of their expertise.

For example, ACME Direct is going to test five lists, two formats, and two offers, all within a budget of 25,000 total names. A full factorial design will yield 20 test cells with 1,250 names per cell, as shown in Exhibit 14.3.

With 1,250 names per cell, the test results will have so much error variance associated with them that they will be difficult to interpret. Exhibit 14.4 shows the 95% confidence bounds around various response rates based on sample sizes of 1,250 names. As you will notice, the widths of each interval are so wide that you cannot make a sound decision.

Another issue arises regarding this test design for the "offer" test panels. Typically, for offer tests, the payment rates are also of interest. For such

Exhibit 14.3 Full Factorial Test Design

List	Format 1		Format 2	
	Offer 1	Offer 2	Offer 1	Offer 2
List A	1,250	1,250	1,250	1,250
List B	1,250	1,250	1,250	1,250
List C	1,250	1,250	1,250	1,250
List D	1,250	1,250	1,250	1,250
List E	1,250	1,250	1,250	1,250

Exhibit 14.4 Example 95% Confidence Bounds Based on 1,250 Names

Response Rates of Test on 1,250 Names (%)	95% Confidence Bounds Around the Test Response Rate (%)
1.5	0.83 to 2.17
2.0	1.22 to 2.78
3.0	2.05 to 3.95
4.0	2.91 to 5.09
5.0	3.79 to 6.21
6.0	4.68 to 7.32

small sample sizes, few orders will fall into each cell, implying an even larger variance associated with the payment rates.

If increasing the sample sizes of the test cells is not an option, ACME Direct needs to eliminate any cells that are not necessary. For example, if there is no reason to believe that "list by package element" interactions exist, ACME Direct will not test a full factorial design. Instead, they will test the format on one list only and the offer on one list only. This allows them to test more names per cell and increase the precision of each cell's response rate while staying within their testing budget (see Exhibit 14.5).

If ACME Direct sees no reason to believe there will be an interaction between format and offer, they can further reduce the number of test cells by one more, as shown in Exhibit 14.6.

Exhibit 14.5 Reduced Factorial Test Design

List	Format 1		Format 2	
	Offer 1	Offer 2	Offer 1	Offer 2
List A	3,125	3,125	3,125	3,125
List B	3,125			
List C	3,125			
List D	3,125			
List E	3,125			

Exhibit 14.6   Further Reduced Factorial Test Design

	Format 1		Format 2	
List	Offer 1	Offer 2	Offer 1	Offer 2
List A	3,571	3,571	3,571	
List B	3,571			
List C	3,571			
List D	3,571			
List E	3,571			

On the basis of the final test design shown in Exhibit 14.6, how will ACME Direct determine the winning format? They will compare "Format 1 & Offer 1" versus "Format 2 & Offer 1" on List A.

How will ACME Direct determine the winning offer? They will compare "Offer 1 & Format 1" versus "Offer 2 & Format 1" on List A.

How will ACME Direct forecast the response rate for List C if promoted with Format 1 and Offer 2? They will determine the lift in response observed for List A when given "Format 1 & Offer 2" versus "Format 1 & Offer 1." Once determined, they will use it to index up the response rate obtained for List C (which was based on "Format 1 & Offer 1").

Sample Size Considerations

With the test panels determined, the next most important part of the planning process is to determine the appropriate sample sizes for each. Without adequate sample sizes, the time and money spent creating and developing your marketing tests will be wasted. This is true whether you are planning direct mail format or telemarketing script tests.

You have spent the time and money to create and develop new test panels, so why risk misinterpreting the results of the tests by testing fewer names to save a few dollars? Without proper sample sizes, your test results will have variance so great that the results will be unreliable. As such, odds will be that the test results will not resemble what you can expect if you decide to roll out with the new test promotion to a larger audience. In other words, the range in which the actual test result could lie (your confidence interval) will be so wide that it will be virtually meaningless and therefore difficult to make a decision with any certainty, as was seen in Exhibit 14.4.

It is important to understand the ramifications of promoting too few names. Small sample sizes can result in two possible scenarios that could negatively impact your company:

1. You misread the test result and believe the new test panel has beaten your current control package, when in fact it will do worse.

2. You believe your current control package has beaten the new test panel, which was in fact a winner.

Both situations can negatively affect the long-term profit of your company. Weigh the savings of promoting fewer names against the costs of lost revenue or lost opportunity caused by misreading test panel results. With true assessment of the costs and savings, you will undoubtedly conclude that it is a wiser business decision to test more names. If your testing budget does not allow you to test more names, cut back on test panels, not the number of names tested per panel.

We next discuss three applications for sample size determination. In particular, we show you how to determine the appropriate sample sizes when interest revolves around the accuracy of a single sample mean, a single sample proportion, and the difference between two sample proportions.

Sample Size Determination for a Sample Mean

When interest revolves around ensuring that a sample mean will be within a certain range of the true population mean, you will employ the formula provided in this section to determine the required sample size. For example, you are interested in closely approximating the mean dollars spent per customer order for a new catalog promotion based on a test.

If interest revolves around determining the required sample size when concerned with the reliability of a sample mean, you need the following information:

- The maximum allowable error variance E
  This measure represents the maximum allowable error you are willing to accept in your sample estimate. For example, you desire the sample mean to be within $\pm\$1.50$ of the true population mean. In this example, $1.50 is the allowable error variance.
- An estimate of the sample standard deviation S
  On the basis of past data, you need to estimate the average deviation around the sample mean you believe will be observed in your sample. If in doubt, it is best to err on the high side.
- The desired error rate $\alpha\%$ and confidence level $(1 - \alpha)\%$
  If, for example, your sample yields a mean estimate of $81.50 with an allowable error variance set at $1.50, a 95% confidence level will guarantee that the interval $80.00 –$83.00 will include the true population mean with 95% probability. We recommend that all sample size calculations be performed at a 90% or better confidence

level. Employing lower levels of confidence drastically increases the risk (error rate α) of obtaining misleading results, which could lead to incorrect and costly decisions.

Once you have all this information, the required sample size is calculated as

$$n = \frac{[(z^2)(S^2)]}{E^2}$$

Where

S is the estimated standard deviation associated with the sample measure

E is the maximum error you are willing to accept

z is equal to 1.645, 1.96, and 2.575 for 90%, 95%, and 99% confidence levels, respectively (z values associated with other confidence levels can be found in Exhibit 13.1).

Sample size formulas are derived from the same formulas for confidence intervals.

Note that if the actual sample standard deviation achieved is greater than estimated, the error variance around the test estimate will be greater than what was specified as the maximum allowable error variance. On the other hand, if the actual sample standard deviation achieved is less than estimated, the error variance around the test estimate will be less than what was specified. If in doubt about your estimate of the sample standard deviation, it is best to err on the high side. This will safeguard against the resulting variance being greater than your desired maximum allowable variance.

To illustrate further, the market research director at ACME Direct is prepared to survey a sample of active customers on the database in an attempt to estimate their true annual direct marketing expenditures from all sources (catalog, Internet, direct mail, telemarketing, infomercials, etc.) and all companies. An accurate estimate is required. In fact, he wants the estimate of annual expenditures to be within $5.00 of the true mean for all active customers with 95% confidence. First, he has to estimate the standard deviation of expenditures. He has no data yet, so there is no way to determine this value except by estimation. The easiest way to do this is to estimate the likely mean and the likely minimum and maximum values that would account for roughly 95% of all active customers on the ACME Direct database. Once estimated, he will take the absolute value of the largest difference between the estimated mean and minimum value and estimated mean and maximum value and divide by 2. This will give an estimate of the standard deviation in the data likely to be observed.

For example, if he estimates the mean to be approximately $100.00 and the minimum and maximum values to be $25.00 and $200.00, respectively, then the absolute differences between the mean and the minimum and maximum values are $75.00 and $100.00, respectively. The largest of these two differences is $100.00. Dividing this figure by 2 yields an estimated standard deviation of $50.00.

In this example,

E = $5.00
S = $50.00 (as just determined)
z = 2.575 for a 99% confidence level

Plugging all known data into the formula provided yields the following sample size estimate:

$$n = \frac{[(z^2)(S^2)]}{E^2}$$

$$n = \frac{[(1.96^2)(50^2)]}{5^2}$$

$$n = \frac{[(3.8416)(2,500)]}{25}$$

$$n = \frac{9,604}{25}$$

$$n = 384.16$$

The market research director needs to obtain information from 385 customers in order to guarantee, with 95% confidence, that his estimate of direct marketing expenditures will be within ±$5.00 of the true mean expenditures.

Assume the survey is complete and the market research director surveyed 385 customers. Also assume that he was right on the mark in his estimate of the sample standard deviation at $50.00. If he now constructs a confidence interval around the sample mean based on the information provided in Chapter 13, how wide will the interval be? Under these circumstances, the width on either side of the mean should be ±$5.00, just as he desired.

How would the resulting confidence interval be affected if the actual observed standard deviation of the sample is *greater* than the estimated value of $50.00? The resulting 95% confidence interval will be *wider* than ±$5.00 on either side of the mean estimate.

How would the resulting confidence interval be affected if the actual observed standard deviation of the sample is *less* than the estimated value of $50.00? The resulting 95% confidence interval will be *less* than ±$5.00 on either side of the mean estimate.

To determine the appropriate confidence level, the market research director will go through the steps outlined in Chapter 13 for determining the appropriate confidence level for confidence intervals and hypothesis tests.

Sample Size Determination for a Sample Proportion

When you are interested in ensuring that a sample proportion will be within a certain range of the true population proportion, employ the formula provided in this section to determine the required sample size. For example, you are interested in closely approximating the response rate for a new product offering or new list of prospects based on a test.

To calculate the sample size required when concerned with the reliability of a sample proportion, you need the following information:

- The maximum allowable error variance E
  This measure represents the maximum allowable error you are willing to accept in your sample estimate. For example, the test response rate must be within ±0.0025 (0.25%) of the true response rate that will be achieved in rollout. In this example, 0.0025 is the allowable error variance.
- An estimate of the sample proportion p
  Estimate the response rate (sample proportion) you expect to receive in the test. This can be based on prior information or a best guess.
- The desired error rate α% and confidence level $(1 - \alpha)$%
  If, for example, a test yields a 3.00% response rate (as expected) with an allowable variance set at 0.25%, a 95% confidence level will guarantee that the interval 2.75%–3.25% will include the true population response rate with 95% probability. We recommend that all sample size calculations be performed at a 90% or better confidence level. Employing lower levels of confidence drastically increases the risk (error rate α) of obtaining misleading results, which could lead to incorrect and costly decisions.

Once all the information is known, the required sample size is calculated as

$$n = \frac{[(z^2)(p)(1 - p)]}{E^2}$$

Where
p is the estimated sample proportion
E is the maximum error you are willing to accept
z is equal to 1.645, 1.96, and 2.575 for 90%, 95%, and 99% confidence levels, respectively (z values associated with other confidence levels can be found in the Appendix).

Note that if you are unsure of the response rate you will achieve in test, it is best to err on the side that places the proportion closer to 0.50. In other words, if you believe the sample response rate will be somewhere between 2.5% and 4%, use 4% as your estimate, because it is closer to 50%. If you believe the sample response rate will be somewhere between 82% and 90%, use 82 because it is closer to 50%. Doing so will yield the most conservative sample size estimate and help guarantee that the sample error variance of your test will be no greater than what you set as the maximum desired error.

For example, the senior product manager at ACME Direct is prepared to test a new source of names from a list broker to determine the list's viability as a source of new customers. On the basis of past experience, the senior product manager believes the response rate for this list will be no greater than 4.75%. If she requires the test response rate to be within 0.25% of the actual response rate to expect in rollout with 90% confidence, how many names should she test?

In this example,

$$p = 0.0475 \text{ (the estimated response rate to be achieved)}$$
$$E = 0.0025$$
$$z = 1.645 \text{ for a 90\% confidence level}$$

Plugging all known data into the formula provided yields the following sample size estimate:

$$n = \frac{[(z^2)(p)(1 - p)]}{E^2}$$

$$n = \frac{[(1.645^2)(0.0475)(1 - 0.0475)]}{0.0025^2}$$

$$n = \frac{[(2.706025)(0.0475)(0.9525)]}{0.0000062}$$

$$n = \frac{0.1224306}{0.0000062}$$

$$n = 19{,}747$$

Therefore, if the senior product manager tests 19,747 names, she will be guaranteed, with 90% confidence, that the test response rate will fall within $\pm$ 0.25% of the true response rate she can expect in rollout. Once the test is final, this sample size will give her the confidence she desires to assess this list as a viable source of new names.

If the senior product manager decides to increase the confidence level of her sample response rate (from 90% to 95%), how many names must she test?

For a 95% confidence level,

$$z = 1.96$$

$$n = \frac{[(1.96^2)(0.0475)(1 - 0.0475)]}{0.0025^2}$$

$$n = \frac{[(3.8416)(0.0475)(0.9525)]}{0.0000062}$$

$$n = \frac{0.1738083}{0.0000062}$$

$$n = 28{,}034$$

To have more confidence in the results of her list test, all else being equal, she needs to sample 28,034 names. Obviously, this is a major increase in the number of names to test—a 42% increase, to be exact. In general, the higher the confidence needed, the more names are required to sample.

If the senior product manager decides to keep the confidence level at 90% but reduce the allowable error in the estimate from 0.25% to 0.20%, what is the impact of her decision on the sample size?

$$n = \frac{[(1.645^2)(0.0475)(1 - 0.0475)]}{.002^2}$$

$$n = \frac{[(2.706025)(0.0475)(0.9525)]}{0.000004}$$

$$n = \frac{0.1224306}{0.000004}$$

$$n = 30{,}608$$

To have less error variance in the results of her list test, all else being equal, the senior product manager will need to sample 30,608 names, again, a large increase in the number of names to test. The less variance desired in a test estimate, the more names are required to sample.

So, how do we decide what is the appropriate level of confidence and tolerable error variance (E) when planning test sample sizes? There is clearly a trade off. The smaller the amount of error you can tolerate in your estimate or the higher the level of confidence you need, the larger the required sample size. It depends on the importance of the test and how accurate the test result needs to be.

Determining the tolerable error variance. To determine the tolerable error variance, the senor product manager must take into consideration how close the expected response rate for the new list is to the "rent/no-rent" response rate level. The closer the expected response rate of the new list is to this cutoff level, the more important it will be to have a test estimate with little error variance.

Assume the senior product manager in our example will promote any new prospect list as long as it meets her break even response rate of 4.50%. If the senior product manager truly expects the list test to yield at least a 4.75% response rate, then for decision-making purposes she only needs to test enough names to ensure that her resulting confidence interval is no wider than ± 0.25% (4.75% minus 4.50%). There is no need to ensure a narrower confidence interval results. All that is needed for decision making purposes (rent the names or not rent the names) is to be certain that the response rate of the new list in roll-out will not fall below the break-even mark. Testing more names to yield less error variance and hence a narrower confidence interval is not necessary. She needs only to test enough names to yield the level of precision required to make her decision.

Determining the appropriate confidence level. To determine the appropriate confidence level, the senior product manager will go through the same steps outlined in Chapter 13 for determining the appropriate confidence level for confidence intervals and hypothesis tests. For example, if we assume the new prospect list costs $5.00 less per 1,000 names rented than most other prospect lists, a 90% confidence level would seem appropriate. It is a less risky proposition to make an error in this scenario than if the list costs the same or even more than others.

Sample Size Determination for the Difference Between Two Sample Proportions

When you want to measure the difference in response rates between two test panels in order to be able to accurately determine if one test has beaten another test, employ the formula provided in this section to determine the required sample sizes. This is one of the most commonly used formulas when designing format, creative concept, pricing, and offer tests while needing to compare the results against the control offer.

To calculate the sample size required when you are concerned with the reliability of the observed difference between two sample proportions, you need the following information:

- The proportion for one of the samples (p_1)
  An estimate of the response rate of one of the test panels is required. This can be based on prior information. However, you need a fairly good estimate for one of the test panels to use the formula. Typically, a new package or telemarketing script is compared against a control package or script. In all likelihood, the response rate for the control will be known, based on historical information.
- The minimum difference to detect as significant ($d = p_1 - p_2$)
  You also need the minimum difference (d) between the two test response rates (p_1 and p_2) you require to read with certainty. For

example, a control package is expected to yield a 4.00% response rate. The addition of a new premium is being tested, and at least five additional orders per 1,000 names promoted are needed to break even (or a 4.50% response rate). Therefore, the minimum difference of interest is 0.50%. In other words, the sample sizes for these two panels must be large enough to ensure that a 0.50% difference in response rates is considered a significant difference (i.e., not 0).

♦ The proportion for the other sample (p_2)
This will be calculated as p_1 plus (or minus) the minimum difference to detect (d).

♦ The desired error rate α% and confidence level $(1 - α)$%
For example, a 95% confidence level allows you to state that the observed difference between two test results of size d or greater is statistically meaningful with 95% probability. We recommend that all sample size calculations be performed at a 90% or better confidence level. Employing lower levels of confidence drastically increases the risk (error rate α) of obtaining misleading results, which could lead to incorrect and costly decisions.

Once all the information is known, the required sample sizes for the two test panels are calculated as

$$n_1 = n_2 = \frac{[z^2][(p_1)(1-p_1) + (p_2)(1-p_2)]}{d_2}$$

Where
p_1 and p_2 are the estimated sample proportions for the two test panels
  $d = (p_1 - p_2)$ represents the minimum difference to be detected
z is equal to 1.645, 1.96, and 2.575 for 90%, 95%, and 99% confidence levels, respectively (z values associated with other confidence levels can be found in Exhibit 13.1).

Note that, as previously mentioned, to use this formula reliably you must have a good estimate for at least one of the two test panels being planned. Typically, when employing this formula, you are preparing to test a new format or creative concept against your control package. If this is the case, in all likelihood you will already know the expected response rate for the control. Keep in mind, if the response rate for this control panel is not close to what was actually achieved, you may not be able to successfully detect the difference d in response rates between the two panels as being statistically significant (i.e., not 0).

To further illustrate, the marketing director of ACME Direct is testing the addition of a new scratch-off card to the current control package. Suppose the control format is known to yield an order rate of 3.40% (or

34 orders per 1,000 names promoted). If four additional orders per 1,000 names promoted (or a 3.80% response rate) are required to cover the additional costs of the scratch-off card, what sample sizes should the control and test panels be to ensure that the marketing director will be able to read at least a 0.40% (3.80%–3.40%) difference in response rates as significant and meaningful with 95% confidence?

In this example,

$p_1 = 0.034$ (the estimated response rate to be achieved)

$d = 0.004$

$p_2 = 0.038$ (the value of $p_1 + d$)

$z = 1.96$ for a 95% confidence level.

Plugging all known data into the formula provided yields the following sample size estimate:

$$n_1 = n_2 = \frac{[(z)^2][(p_1)(1-p_1) + (p_2)(1-p_2)]}{d^2}$$

$$n_1 = n_2 = \frac{[(1.96)^2][(0.034)(1-0.034) + (0.038)(1-0.038)]}{(0.004)^2}$$

$$n_1 = n_2 = \frac{[(3.8416)][(0.034)(0.966) + (0.038)(0.962)]}{0.000016}$$

$$n_1 = n_2 = \frac{[(3.8416)][(0.032844) + (0.036556)]}{0.000016}$$

$$n_1 = n_2 = \frac{(3.8416)(0.0694)}{0.000016}$$

$$n_1 = n_2 = \frac{0.266607}{0.000016}$$

$$n_1 = n_2 = 16,663$$

In order to conclude that 3.40% and 3.80% response rates are significantly different with 95% confidence, the marketing director will be required to test 16,663 names per panel.

What will happen to the required sample sizes per panel if the marketing director wishes to detect an even smaller difference as significant? The required sample sizes would increase.

So, how do we decide what is the appropriate level of confidence and the critical difference (d) in response necessary to detect with certainty when planning test sample sizes? The smaller the difference to detect as significant or the higher the level of confidence, the larger the required sample sizes.

Determining the tolerable error variance. To determine this, the marketing director must ask himself the following question: What is the minimum difference in response that *must* be detected in order to make a reliable marketing decision? In this example, the difference of concern is 0.40%. There is no need to ensure that a smaller difference can be read with statistical significance. He only needs to test enough names to yield the level of precision required to make a decision. Doing otherwise would be wasting testing dollars.

Determining the appropriate confidence level. To determine this, the marketing director will apply the same steps outlined in Chapter 13 for determining the appropriate confidence level for confidence intervals and hypothesis tests. In our example, the new test with the addition of the scratch-off card is more expensive. As such, a 99% or 95% confidence level seems appropriate. Because 99% is typically used only for the most extreme and risky tests, a 95% confidence level seems appropriate.

Marketing Test Planning Software

With the use of The Plan-alyzer©, as mentioned in Chapter 13, you can also determine appropriate sample sizes for given variances and confidence levels. It will assist you in determining the appropriate sample sizes when you are interested in the accuracy of a single test result or being able to accurately measure the *difference* between two test results.

Alternative Testing Approaches for Small Direct Marketers

Most major direct marketers test between 10,000 and 20,000 names per panel for format, copy, and pricing test. Smaller direct marketers typically test 5,000 or fewer names per panel. As you can probably guess, on the basis of the information in Chapter 13, testing 5,000 or fewer names per panel will not yield meaningful results from a marketing point of view. However, if you have a small test budget, there are steps you can follow to help increase the odds of making correct decisions based on your test results.

If you are a small direct marketer and simply cannot test enough names to yield significant results from a marketing point of view, consider the following guidelines to help you make the best decisions possible. For example, you are testing a new and more expensive format. On the basis of a cost analysis, you determine that in order to break even on the new format, it must generate an additional 2.5 orders per 1,000 names promoted over the control. The required sample sizes that will allow you to read such a difference in response as significant are too great. So what do you do?

- Evaluate the test versus the control at the 90% significance level via hypothesis testing. If the test is *not* significantly different from the control at 90%, evaluate the lower and upper bound of a 90% confidence interval around the difference in test response rates. Then examine the upside and downside potential in terms of the difference in response for this test, taking into account cost and revenue figures. If the upside potential appears promising compared to the downside potential, retest to a larger sample. If the downside potential looks too great compared to the upside potential, drop the test and consider it a loser.

- If the test *is* significantly different from the control at 90%, based on a hypothesis test, check to see if it is also significant at 99%. If it is, you definitely have a winner and are advised to roll out with the winning test (assuming that the result of the test meets your marketing requirements).

- If the test *is significant* at 90% *but not* at 99%, based on hypothesis tests, retest the panel to a larger sample unless,

  - On the basis of an assessment of the lower and upper bounds of the difference in response rates, you determine the risk of switching to be minimal, compared to the upside potential and, for example, you do not have any other options available for a new format. If this is the case, then roll out and skip retesting. However, we advise you to conduct a back test to ensure that the decision made was a correct one.

  - On the basis of an assessment of the lower and upper bounds of the 90% confidence interval for the difference in response rates, you notice that the test does not meet your minimum required difference from a marketing point of view. That is, the difference in response based on the lower bound does not even come close to meeting your minimum required to break even on the test. If this is the case, don't bother retesting. Use the money saved here to test a different package with better potential.

When retesting is required, based on the above guidelines, test enough names to read a significant difference from a marketing point of view. Follow the sample size determination guidelines outlined in this chapter. At this stage, you should not test too few names. You have determined the test to be potentially promising, based on a small sample, and you are now ready to confirm, based on a large sample.

For example, ACME Direct tested four new formats versus the control format. Each test was based on samples of 5,000 names selected at random from the primary customer segment. The results of each test panel are shown in Exhibit 14.7.

First, ACME Direct will conduct hypothesis tests at the 90% and 99% confidence levels to determine which new format is significantly different from the control format. The results of these tests are shown in Exhibit 14.8.

Exhibit 14.7 ACME Direct Format Test Series Results

Test Panel	Sample Size	Response Rate
Control format	5,000	3.00%
New format 1	5,000	3.75%
New format 2	5,000	3.45%
New format 3	5,000	3.29%
New format 4	5,000	4.24%

Exhibit 14.8 ACME Direct Format Test Series Significance Results

Test Panel	Sample Size	Response Rate (%)	Significantly Different? @ 90%	@ 99%
Control format	5,000	3.00	—	—
New format 1	5,000	3.75	Yes	No
New format 2	5,000	3.45	No	No
New format 3	5,000	3.29	No	No
New format 4	5,000	4.24	Yes	Yes

ACME Direct will then closely examine each format, based on the guidelines given to determine the appropriate actions to be taken.

New Format 1. This format is significantly different from the control at the 90% level of confidence but not at the 99% level. On the basis of the guidelines given, ACME Direct will assess the lower and upper bounds of the 90% and 99% confidence intervals to determine the true upside and downside potential of switching to this new format. A 90% confidence interval reveals that the difference can lie anywhere between 0.16% and 1.34%. A 99% confidence interval reveals that the difference can lie anywhere between -0.18% and 1.68%. If this new format is no more expensive than the control format, and ACME Direct desires a new format for simply a change of pace, they should feel comfortable in rolling out with this new format. The maximum downside potential is minimal (-0.18% in response) compared to the upside potential ($+1.68\%$ in response). If they do roll out with this new format, a back test is advised. Otherwise, they should retest to a larger sample.

New Format 2. This format was not found to be significantly different from the control at the 90% or 99% level of confidence. Had ACME Direct conducted this test to a larger sample size, they could stop at this point and consider this test a loser. Because they did not, they are advised to take a closer look at the response rate received. On the basis of the guidelines given, ACME Direct will assess the lower and upper bounds of a 90% confidence interval to determine the true upside and downside potential of switching to this new format. A 90% confidence interval reveals that the difference can lie anywhere between −0.16% and 1.03%. On the basis of this examination, they should retest to a larger sample. It does show potential, but not enough to warrant a rollout like that of New Format 1.

However, if this new format is more expensive than the control format, and, for example, an additional three orders per 1,000 names promoted or a 0.3% increase in response would be required to break even, they should not retest. The bounds of the very liberal 90% confidence interval for the difference suggests high odds of never meeting this requirement.

New Format 3. This format was not found to be significantly different from the control at the 90% or 99% level of confidence. On the basis of the guidelines given, ACME Direct will assess the lower and upper bounds of a 90% confidence interval to determine the true upside and downside potential of switching to this new format. A 90% confidence interval reveals that the difference can lie anywhere between −0.28% and 0.86%. When comparing the upside potential to the downside potential, they can easily determine that this test is not worth retesting and it should be considered a loser.

New Format 4. This format is significantly different from the control at both the 90% and 99% levels of confidence. On the basis of the guidelines given, ACME Direct will assess the lower and upper bound of the 90% and 99% confidence intervals to determine the true upside and downside potential of switching to this new format. A 90% confidence interval reveals that the difference can lie anywhere between 0.63% and 1.85%. A 99% confidence interval reveals the difference can lie anywhere between 0.28% and 2.20%. If this new format is no more expensive than the control format, ACME Direct is advised to roll out. With 99% confidence, it is guaranteed to beat the control by at least 0.28% in response.

If the new format is more expensive than the control and requires something less than +0.28% in response to breakeven, ACME Direct should roll out. If the new format is more expensive than the control and requires something significantly more than +0.28% in response to breakeven, they should retest to a larger sample.

Regarding your most expensively created test panels—such as new formats that may cost you up to $10,000 or more to have designed—you should always test enough names the first time around. This is true whether you are a small or large direct marketer. By doing so, you will be lessening the risk of misreading the results. Don't blow reading such test results. It will be quite an expensive mistake to make compared to misreading other test panels. The bottom line is this: If you are spending significantly more money on the creative development of a new format compared to other test panels, test it right and do not risk misreading the results. Test enough names to truly gauge the response correctly from the start. Not doing so could cause you to make a costly mistake.

Chapter Summary

Testing is the foundation upon which direct marketers build and grow their business. There are many important test design rules that must be considered before implementing any test series. In this chapter, we discuss five such rules. In addition, we discuss test design considerations regarding outside list testing, including full factorial test designs. We also discuss the importance of proper sample size determination. Without proper sample sizes, your test results will have error variance so great that the results will be unreliable. We reveal several formulas for determining the appropriate sample sizes. Finally, we discuss alternate testing approaches for smaller direct marketers with a limited budget.

Review Questions

1. Discuss the five rules that must be followed to ensure that marketing test results will be readable, reliable, and projectable.

2. Explain the advantages and disadvantages of full factorial test design.

3. Why is it important to determine appropriate sample sizes prior to any test execution?

15

Marketing Databases and the Internet

Ever since Keri first logged on to a bookstore Web site and was given suggested readings, she has been intrigued with the possibilities of Internet commerce. Over the years, she has registered on a number of sites and has received targeted e-mail about a number of products. Like many Web users, Keri occasionally receives unsolicited, nontarget e-mail that she finds annoying. Keri finds e-mail messages from direct marketing news services and Internet service venders particularly valuable for her work. These messages are oriented to providing customers with information and developing relationships rather than focusing on a hard sell. Keri hopes that any e-mail programs she develops will provide value to her customers.

Keri wants to understand the advantages and limitations of Internet marketing and determine which strategies and tactics would be most beneficial in helping her reach her objectives. Immediately, she recognized a potential cost savings. Not only was e-mail less expensive than paper mail, but she also saw potential savings in order processing and customer service. She thought of various forms of e-mail communications such as newsletters, personalized messages, and messages with links and attachments. To develop e-mail campaigns, she would have to link the house file to the Internet. Furthermore, to develop e-mail campaigns for noncustomers, she would have to explore the sources of e-mail lists relevant to her product category.

Sophisticated data analysis and Web data mining would have to wait until she and Inside Source's analysts understood more about the systems and tools available to them. Keri's immediate objective was to establish an ongoing contact with existing customers through e-mail and test some alternative communication strategies.

In earlier chapters of this book, we presented information about Internet database applications whenever appropriate. In the next two chapters, we focus on Internet database techniques and applications. This chapter covers basic database concepts as applied to the Internet, and Chapter 16 delves into data analysis and mining.

Developing a strategy for Internet database marketing is fundamentally similar to developing strategies for other direct marketing media. Focusing on customer relationships and repeat business is more profitable over the long term versus focusing on single transactions. Cross-selling is also an important strategic option that applies to all direct marketing channels. Internet marketers such as Amazon.com are attempting to implement these strategies. Amazon.com is building a large database that uses customer information to develop e-mail promotions that remind customers about products in categories in which they have demonstrated an interest. Furthermore, Amazon.com uses the database to cross-sell products ranging from books, CDs, electronics, health and beauty aids, and patio furniture. For example, book customers receive package inserts with discount codes for purchases at a drugstore Web site. Cross-selling tactics also include using electronic coupons sent in **opt-in** (opt-in is a policy requiring individuals to give permission before an organization sends offers to them) e-mail. Therefore, collecting and analyzing data effectively and efficiently is critical to evaluating Internet marketing programs as it is with other direct marketing channels.

Database Integration

As Internet marketing evolves and marketers understand its advantages and limitations, we anticipate that the Internet and other forms of electronic communication will be considered a component of an integrated approach to database marketing rather than a separate entity. Indeed, some companies are already taking an integrated approach. Customers are able to communicate and receive communications from a number of sources. An integrated database allows multiple communications and transactions to be tracked, regardless of whether by phone, mail, Internet, wireless devices (**m-commerce, or mobile commerce**), or at a physical retail location. Indeed, the integrated **clicks and mortar** (aka **clicks and bricks**) approach is more common than single-channel marketing on the Internet. A study by the Boston Consulting Group of 400 online retailers showed that the clicks and mortar retailers accounted for 62% of online revenues, whereas pure online retailers accounted for 38%. The multichannel retailers have an advantage over the single-channel Internet marketers. They spend less to acquire customers, have lower marketing expenses, and have more repeat business (Book, 2000). The successful trend for these multichannel marketers held for the 2000 holiday season (Davis, 2001).

A critical component in developing a responsive, customer-focused, multichannel marketing system is integrating or synchronizing databases. Although it is not the domain of this book to discuss the technical aspects of database integration in any detail, it is worthwhile for the database marketer to understand the general concepts behind the integration and its implications for developing marketing strategies and programs. Exhibit 15.1 is a simple schematic diagram of the possible inputs into the database for a multichannel marketer.

As we discuss the analysis of online data in the next chapter, you will see that the ability of an organization to access data from multiple sources provides a competitive advantage.

An organization that does not integrate databases (e.g., using a separate database for mail, the Internet, telemarketing) loses efficiencies and valuable information about customers. This might result in marketing programs that are not only inefficient but also may break down customer relationships. For example, calling or mailing an offer for a product that a customer has already purchased on the Internet may undermine the relationship with the customer. ("Why are you bothering me with this? I already purchased one.")

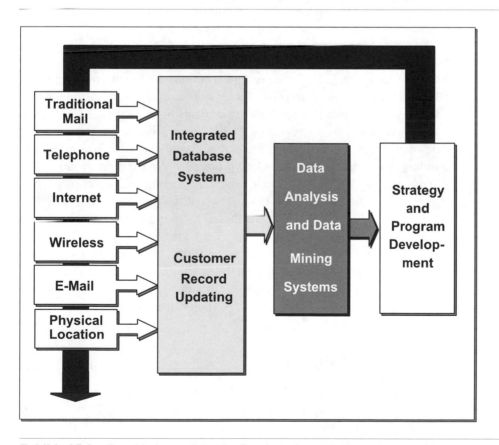

Exhibit 15.1   Possible Inputs Into the Database for a Multichannel Marketer

There is speculation that the higher level of abandoned shopping carts (shopping carts that are left when the customer leaves the Web site after making a selection but before finalizing the transaction) for multichannel marketers results from problems associated with integrating legacy system (older mainframe systems) databases with e-commerce applications. Efficiencies can be enhanced further if supplier databases are also integrated. With this level of integration, customer order levels can automatically trigger inventory replenishing systems.

One solution for database integration is to convert from the older legacy systems to newer systems with a centralized database that can accept real-time inputs from a number of sources. This is not a feasible alternative for many organizations that have large databases with millions of records stored on the legacy systems. In addition, legacy systems still work well, and for many organizations other alternatives offer no advantages. However, most legacy systems were developed for batch processing rather than real-time processing (i.e., there is not an immediate change in the database as an order is processed or a promotion is sent; the changes are made at periodic intervals). Technology companies such as IBM, Siebel, Kana, and Cayenta have developed software and systems to integrate databases, making them responsive to changing consumer channel preferences and organizational objectives for analysis and marketing program development.

An example of an integrated multichannel marketer is Payless ShoeSource Inc., one of the largest footwear retailers in the United States. Payless established a Web site to offer customers more options for purchasing shoes. The Web site transactions are integrated with store transactions. Customers may return or exchange online purchases to any one of more than 4,300 Payless ShoeSource stores in all 50 states. Payless even allows items that are not carried in a store to be returned there, and they also offer free shipping and handling for online purchases when products are picked up at any stores ("Customer Service," 2001). Other companies such as the GAP, Costco, Rite Aid, Williams-Sonoma, Wikes Lumber, and Ethan Allen have also moved to integrate online and offline databases to increase the effectiveness of marketing programs and enhance customer relationships.

Despite the movement toward integration, the Internet has unique characteristics and potential and deserves specific attention. We address these distinctions in the following sections and consider how databases are used to implement marketing strategies and programs on the Internet.

Growth in Internet Commerce

Internet commerce is experiencing a dynamic growth at this time. Growth predictions vary widely. eMarketer (2001) summarized data from various sources for both consumer and business markets. For 2002, in the b-to-b market, estimates vary from \$543 billion (Ovum) to \$6.8 trillion (Computer Economics). eMarketer predicted \$841 billion. For 2003, the estimates range from \$858 billion to \$9.9 trillion. eMarketer predicted \$1.5 trillion for 2003.

In the consumer market, the estimates are also quite variable. For 2002, they range from \$81 billion (Ovum) to \$870 billion (Goldman Sachs); eMarketer predicted \$167 billion. The predictions for 2003 range from \$133 billion (Ovum) to almost \$1.4 trillion (Goldman Sachs), and eMarketer's prediction was \$250 billion. Although there is variability in e-commerce revenue estimates, all analysts predict consistent growth over the next several years.

We should emphasize that Internet commerce is still a small part of the overall economy. For example, in 2000, revenues of one large retailer like Wal★Mart exceeded the total of all online consumer sales. However, many businesses are changing the way they conduct business because of the Internet. There are still numerous questions and challenges associated with the new Internet economy. Some of the business models are not solidified, and many of the current Internet businesses will disappear or consolidate as the industry evolves. Some initial approaches to developing an Internet business have been questioned. For example, an approach used by several Internet start-ups is to build large customer databases without an immediate concern for profitability. They hope that the company will carry its large customer database into other business areas. This strategy is dependent on customer loyalty and the capability of the company to cross-sell products to current customers. Therefore, an essential component for the success of this model is the ability of the company to use the database to develop loyal relationships with customers. It is uncertain whether strong customer relationships can be developed for commodity-type products that can be purchased from a number of sources. If the product is the same, only price and service can differentiate products from the customer's perspective. Indeed, if low price is the most important differentiating factor for consumers, then it will be difficult to establish brand loyalty. Consumers can easily move from one Internet retailer to another and purchase on the basis of price.

Service, however, does seem to be an important aspect of Internet commerce for consumers. More women are now online than men, although men spend more time online (Pastore, 2001). More important, according to the Ernst & Young 2001 Global Online Retailing Report, online shoppers in the United States are 60% female and 40% male. As the driving force for online growth, women will be demanding the service they have come to expect from other direct marketing media and brick and mortar retailers. Therefore, online companies are making customer interactions with service representatives immediately responsive. A high percentage of Internet shoppers abandon their shopping carts. Consequently, successful companies selling online need to be immediately responsive to questions or concerns of potential buyers on their site. Research conducted by Harris Interactive indicated that customers who contact customer service spend more than three times as much on average as those who do not contact customer service. Customer service is particularly valuable to new online shoppers. Buyers who made their first online purchases in the previous year made about half of the customer service contacts ("LivePerson and Harris Interactive," 2000).

Responding hours later by e-mail is no longer considered good customer service on the Internet. Instant messaging through pop-up dialog boxes or voice technology are ways companies are attempting to become more responsive to consumers. A number of companies such as LivePerson, eGain Live, and Cisco provide live customer service on the Internet. These companies provide services to companies with e-business sites such as QVC, Lands' End, Neiman Marcus, Godiva Chocolate, and Block Drug.

Online customer service usually works in the following way. Customers needing assistance click on a text hyperlink or icon. A window pops up, alerting a customer service rep. Customers are then prompted to input their name so that the customer service rep can refer to them by name. The chat session begins and customers ask questions and receive responses in real time. The customer can still keep the Web site window open and to refer to particular products or terms of an offer.

The customer service rep can respond to the customer's questions through the use of either common preformatted responses or a customized response. This method allows one customer service rep to handle several customers at the same time. Performance indicators (e.g., call length and interval between question and answer) are available. Some of the live customer service software allows customer service reps access to a customer's history that can facilitate service in some situations.

The Internet Versus Other Database Marketing Media

Businesses have already recognized several potential advantages to conducting business on the Internet. Cost savings are an important advantage for Internet marketers. Online catalogs are much less expensive than paper catalogs that are delivered to customers. The cost of e-mail is also much less than delivered paper mail. Online transactions eliminate the cost of hiring order takers and reduce errors if orders have to be transcribed from paper forms. E-mail costs have been estimated to be as low as $0.05 per contact, depending on content development and list costs. Direct mail can cost several dollars per contact, and telemarketing contacts can exceed $10.00.

Many more items can be cataloged on the Internet than is feasible with paper or other media. For example, QVC, the television shopping network, has a Web site that allows customers to select and purchase products online. It would not be feasible for most customers to watch extended hours of QVC programming to be exposed to all these products. The Internet is an important supplement to QVC's marketing because customers can examine products that they missed when the products were featured on television. The customer can also access a product that they saw in the past on television but only recently decided to purchase. In general, the Internet is more information rich compared to other direct marketing media. Marketers can provide potential customers with additional information that would not be practical for other media. For example, business customers requiring more information could click on a white paper, case study, or technical diagrams.

Speed is another advantage of Internet marketing. E-mail offers can be sent to thousands of recipients in a matter of minutes. New catalogs and updates of existing catalogs can be put online without the need for the extensive production and mailing processes that can take weeks or months. Testing offers can also be expedited over the Internet. Promotions associated with Web catalogs or e-mails can be tested in real time as customers click through to a site and place an order.

As technology advances, more e-commerce sites will have multimedia capabilities, including giving customers the opportunity to view three-dimensional representations of products. Saturn allows visitors to their Web site to take a virtual tour of the inside and outside of models of their cars (Saturn Corporation, 2001). Virtual tours are also used to market real estate, vacation destinations, and college campuses. Visitors to music commerce sites can hear samples of CDs they are interested in purchasing. These multimedia options are not possible or very costly with other direct marketing media and allow customers to have a more personal contact with a product.

Customer service has potential advantages on the Internet if it is conducted properly. E-mail is less expensive than mail or phone calls for providing customers with order status information. Some Internet marketers allow customers to check their order status online. This customer service advantage is significant for b-to-b marketers. Not only does this save the cost of a human contact, but it is also a more rapid method for many customers. United Parcel Service, for example, allows customers to input tracking numbers to determine the status of their package deliveries. Gateway also allows customers to check the status of their order by entering an order code or phone number. Customers can see whether the order has been received, is in production, or has been shipped. An estimated or actual shipping date is also provided, depending on the status of the order.

Cisco Systems, a marketer of hardware for Internet applications, has extensive customer service and support facilities on its Web site. Customers can download technical documents and software, register for technical workshops, manage service contracts online, and order products online. Cisco cites the following benefits of online ordering:

♦ It improves your company's productivity by have customers order products and service online anytime, day or night.
♦ It knows where a customer's order is in the manufacturing and shipment process and how soon to expect delivery.
♦ It provides up-to-date product quotes to your company's clients by accessing the most current price lists.
♦ It stays current with your company's accounts payable and measures how expenses are tracking to your budgets.
♦ It reduces the time it takes from submitting an order to receiving the product

Cisco's objective is to build customer relationships by providing responsive service and support systems. Because the majority of Cisco's customers are technology savvy, the most effective and efficient method to maintain relationships is through the Internet. In general, many businesses find the Internet an excellent tool for conducting transactions and maintaining relationships with customers and suppliers. The dramatic growth in b-to-b Internet commerce is probably due to the cost efficiency and responsiveness of the Internet for both business customers and suppliers.

In contrast to the b-to-b market, consumers usually do not have the same technical skills or purchase requirements as businesses. Therefore, consumer marketers have to develop different methods for Internet commerce. Good product graphics, easy navigation, and immediate customer service response are becoming more prevalent on consumer commerce sites. When customers contact a service representative, the service representative will have an advantage if a database can be called up that contains detailed information on that customer. For example, if customers have a question about a new product they've seen on a Web site, customer service representatives may be able to respond better to the customers if they have access to the customers' previous purchases and other information. The service reps could use the customers' previous purchases as a reference point for the new product under question, comparing colors, sizes, dimensions, content, and so on. Knowing where customers live can be helpful for a number of types of products such as clothing, garden supplies, and automotive parts. As we discussed previously in this chapter, the use of live text or voice online customer service may reduce the abandoning of shopping carts, and automatic queries and Frequently Asked Questions databases could facilitate the customer service interaction by providing customers with a quicker response and more options.

Another potential advantage to Internet marketing is the initiation of the contact. With telemarketing and mail, the marketer usually initiates the contact. But with e-mail marketing, the customer has initiated the contact by registering on a site and often allowing the marketer to send additional information. In many circumstances, the customer initiates the contact by visiting a Web site through the use of search engines or ads from other media. Customers who visit or return to a Web site are good prospects, because they have moved their interest to the next level of examining products offered on a Web site. In other direct marketing media, offers are usually self-contained and require less effort by consumers. In consumer behavior terms, the customer is often more "involved" in the process of purchasing online, and higher levels of involvement are associated with increased purchase probability and brand loyalty. The Internet can give the customer a greater degree of control over the purchase process relative to other direct marketing channels.

The Internet also provides the opportunity for real-time analysis of data. The marketer could evaluate critical factors such as the time needed for customers to find a product, the number of abandoned shopping carts, the pages that customers take as they move through the Web site to purchase, and sources—e.g., Web address (URL) or Internet service provider (ISP)— of the customer. Managers could be alerted immediately when certain problems are detected (e.g., a high percentage of people clicking past a new product rather than placing it in a shopping cart).

Testing can also be facilitated on the Internet. Several variations of offers can be tested and the results evaluated quickly, allowing poor offers to be eliminated as soon as possible. With other direct marketing media, the development of alternative offers for testing (e.g., mailer modifications, catalog changes) would be more costly and time consuming. We should emphasize at this point that all the advantages of Internet marketing that we have presented in this section are dependent on an efficient and effective database system.

Limitations of Internet Marketing

Although marketing on the Internet has distinct advantages, it also has potential disadvantages. Some marketers are concerned about the control of offers and promotions on the Internet. Pictures and graphics are limited by customers' equipment and their Internet connection. In contrast, for mail, catalogs, and television, the marketer usually has more control over reproduction. Because of download time, the resolution of pictures of products on the Internet is lower relative to printed pictures in the catalog industry. In addition, customers might attribute long download times or access problems with a site to the marketer, regardless of the source of the problem. Sometimes the problems are due to sources beyond the control of the marketer such as the customer's equipment or their ISP. In the future, as customers move to faster broadband technologies (e.g., digital, cable), these problems will be minimized.

Although many consumers find nontargeted mail (junk mail) a nuisance, nontargeted e-mail (**spam**) is often considered an invasion of privacy. Therefore, marketers must be extra cautious when developing e-mail campaigns. As we mentioned previously, many marketers are adopting an opt-in only policy for e-mail lists to minimize the chances of alienating consumers. When marketers do make a mistake and e-mail offers to customers who do not wish to receive the information, the customers should be able to immediately have their names removed from the marketer's list. In some cases, even marketers who are sensitive to customers' preferences have made it difficult for customers to remove their names from a list. Sometimes e-mail recipients have to click through several links and wait for several pages to load before they can request name removal from the e-mail list.

Target appropriateness is another factor and potential disadvantage. Not all potential customers for a product have access to the Internet. For example, marketers who target older consumers may still need traditional direct marketing media, because this target group has less access to the Internet. Furthermore, according to a study commissioned by the American Association of Retired People (AARP), older U.S. citizens have serious concerns about Internet commerce and don't feel they have appropriate computer skills. This is another problem with Internet marketing that will probably be resolved over time. Technological advances will make Internet access easier and safer. Furthermore, today's Internet savvy younger and middle-aged consumers will be the older consumers of the future.

Previously, we mentioned that in many circumstances, the customer initiates the contact in Internet transactions, whereas in other direct marketing media, the marketer initiates the contact by calling or mailing an offer to the prospect. There is also a downside to customer-initiated contact. Marketers must make their Web sites easy to find with search engines. In addition, many marketers don't want to wait and attempt to drive traffic to the site with ads in other media or through partnerships with other Internet sites such as portals. Marketers are still attempting to work out the best methods to drive traffic to their Web sites. Recently, marketers have had to reevaluate the effectiveness of using banner ads and television commercials. According to Nielsen/NetRatings May 2001 data, click rates are a meager 0.49% for banner ads. Furthermore, many companies have abandoned mass television advertising as a means of making customers aware of their Web sites. At the core of the issue of driving traffic to the site are basic premises of good marketing communications—that is, find alternative media that are viewed and attended to by the target group. Does it make sense to use banner ads or television commercials to drive traffic to a site if the intended target group does not click on banner ads or pay attention to television?

Which is the best way to drive traffic to a Web site? Citing data from Andersen Consulting, Weaver (2000) concludes that banner ads are better

(25%) for driving customers to shop online compared to newspapers and magazines (14%). Television had the lowest ability at 11%. Weaver claims that the effectiveness of the banner ads increases when they are targeted using technologies such as Double Click or Engage.

Consumers have some generally negative perceptions about shopping on the Internet. The results of a study conducted by Drozdenko and Cronin (2001) indicated that consumers rated physical stores as having higher product quality and service quality for several product categories compared to online stores. In addition, consumers in the study rated a lower purchase probability and safety for online versus physical stores.

In a second study, Drozdenko and Cronin (2001) found that marketers could improve the perceptions of Internet shopping by providing additional information to consumers. Reassuring consumers about the security of personal information, safety of credit card transactions, easy return policies, and responsive customer service not only can improve confidence in purchase safety but also improve the perception of the product's value, quality, and purchase probability.

Consumers, public interest groups, and legislators seem to be more concerned about the privacy of data collected on the Internet than to data collected through other direct marketing media. Privacy on the Internet is a complex issue even for the U.S. government. There are concerns that government Web sites are inadequate in protecting consumers. A number of privacy violations were cited in a report submitted to Congress by 51 inspectors general. These included violations of establishing privacy policies for specific government Web sites and violations of the Children's Online Privacy Act (Bremner, 2001). We examine privacy issues in more detail in Chapter 17.

Personalization: The Great Promise of the Internet

The great promise of the Internet is for one-to-one marketing and personalizing relationships with customers. Customers can receive personalized information on the Internet in several ways. E-mail can be tailored to the personal preferences of customers based on past transactions or other customer data such as demographics and psychographics. Web pages (portals) can be personalized with news and information that an individual prefers. For example, Yahoo! earns revenues in a number of ways, such as by accepting advertising, developing and hosting Web sites, and charging merchants a revenue share on sales driven by Yahoo! Therefore, it is important that Yahoo! entices people to come to their site often. Yahoo! allows people to develop personalized Web pages with My Yahoo! Content and layout can be customized to personal tastes. Sports, business, entertainment, headline news, and health are some of the categories that can be selected. Updates on certain stock prices, sports team scores, weather, and breaking news in specific categories can be presented when the page is called up.

Cookies are another means to personalize a customer contact on a Web site. Cookies are files placed on a person's computer disk by a Web site's software when that person visits the site. Cookies contain information about a repeat visitor to the site, thereby eliminating the need to reregister or sign in on Web sites. When the browser connects to a site, a cookie is read from the disk of the visitor to the site. If the cookie is not there, the visitor has to reregister or sign in. Furthermore, any Web pages that the visitor has personalized (such as My Yahoo! discussed previously) would no longer retain the custom settings.

Cookies can also be used to track browsing patterns of individuals. This is currently a controversial area, and some public interest groups are concerned about organizations planting cookies and then retrieving them in such a way that allows them to build detailed profiles of the interests, purchasing patterns, and lifestyles of individuals. It appears that how Internet data on individuals is collected and used will continue to be an area of concern for years to come.

Technological advances in wireless communications include Internet-enabled cellular phones that provide the possibility to engage in mobile commerce. According to the Strategis Group, mobile device use in the United States will grow from its current 2% to 60% by the year 2007. Jupiter Research estimates that by 2005, worldwide m-commerce revenues will reach $22.2 billion. However, predictions about m-commerce are questionable because of many unknown factors of the new medium, according to eMarketer analysts (Blank, 2001).

The new wireless technologies promise to bring another level of personalization. Using a database containing an individual's shopping preferences and global positioning satellite (GPS) systems, retailers have the potential to drive traffic to brick and mortar locations. GeePS.com, for example, can send promotions, product information, price comparisons, and so on to owners of Internet-enabled cellular phones as they move into the proximity of a retailer (Dana, 2000). IBM anticipates that m-commerce will expand to the global level. Using an enabled cell phone, consumers will be able to make purchases at locations in other countries without the need for currency or credit cards.

Privacy will also be a key concern of wireless Internet marketers. If consumers receive unwanted or excessive promotions from marketers, they are likely to turn off the wireless device or complain to the service provider. Some wireless advertising placement companies are removing identification information (names, e-mail, address, etc.) from personal profiles using only a randomly generated number to identify the wireless device.

Although privacy, device limitations, and slow networks are barriers to m-commerce, consumer apathy may be the greatest threat to its growth, according to Jupiter Communications. Fewer than 0.1% of 110 million U.S. wireless users purchased products using wireless data services in 2000, and just 7% of these users intend to try mobile shopping in the next year.

E-Mail Marketing

According to an eMarketer study, expenditures on e-mail marketing in 2001 are expected to increase 110% to $2.1 billion (Tomasula, 2001). Although the availability of e-mail lists is growing, there are fewer e-mail list providers compared to mail and telemarketing list providers. Mail and telemarketing list providers also have a wider range of **response lists** relative to e-mail list providers. Furthermore, fewer names tend to be on e-mail lists as compared to mail lists. Some traditional printed mail list companies have 100 million households in their databases that can be segmented by a number of demographic and psychographic variables.

In 2000, most e-mail list providers had less than 10 million names on file. However, the number of names and categories on these e-mail lists is expected to grow rapidly in the next few years. For example, as of 2001, XactMail has a database of about 50 million opt-in names, and PostMasterDirect.com has 30 million opt-in names in more than 3,000 topical lists.

E-Mail Applications

A number of e-mail tactics can be used to strengthen relationships with customers or acquire new customers. These include

- Informing customers of new products
- Offering incentives (e.g., discounts, special offers) to customers
- Contacting a targeted group of noncustomers who have some similar characteristics to current customers
- Providing periodic (daily, weekly, monthly, etc.) information to customers in the form of newsletters, news briefs, or other relevant information
- Following up contacts to people who have visited your Web site, trade show booth, and so on
- Updating customers on order status

As you can see, e-mail applications are similar to applications for other direct marketing media. The goal is to make them relevant to the recipient and elicit interest, purchase, and brand loyalty.

It is important to differentiate between opt-in lists and lists that do not have the permission of the e-mail recipient to receive messages from list users. Nonpermission e-mail lists can also be acquired. Some e-mail list providers use computer programs that harvest e-mail addresses from Web sites. The term *spamming* refers to e-mail campaigns that are sent to recipients who did not specifically give permission for commercial e-mail of a specific type to be sent to them. For example, people may have given permission (opted-in) for their e-mail address to be shared with companies that sell products related to skiing. These people are interested in receiving information in that product category. However, these same individuals may have registered on a nutritional Web site but did not give permission for their e-mail address to be shared with marketers selling nutritional products. If these people receive e-mail from a marketer selling nutritional supplements, it is considered spam mail. The owner of the nutritional Web site may have shared the e-mail addresses of people registered on the site without their permission, or another company may have used software to extract e-mail addresses from the site. We discuss the ethics of e-mail marketing techniques further in Chapter 17.

E-mail campaigns are believed to yield response rates that are higher than the average 1% to 2% response levels for mail campaigns. Response rates for e-mail campaigns have been reported to be between 5% and 10% (Priore, 2000). Higher e-mail response rates are commonly reported. For example, Kawasaki Motors said 28% responded to their sweepstakes e-mails (Cruz, 2001).

Although these response rates for e-mail marketing are impressive compared to traditional printed mail, they may not represent an accurate comparison. Many companies that e-mail are adopting an opt-in list policy, but most printed mail lists are opt-out lists. Opt-in lists have a higher probability of containing good prospects in a particular product category. Furthermore, "response" to an e-mail campaign is sometimes defined as a "click-through," whereas response to traditional mail or telemarketing often refers to placing an order.

E-Mail Formats

A number of formats are used for e-mail marketing. At a basic level, the same e-mail message can be sent to all recipients on a list. This is the cheapest and quickest method. However, because of the lack of personalization, software filters set up by the recipient or the ISP may screen out this type of message.

Personalized messages are also possible. Information from a database such as first name, product ordered, inquire date, and so on can be inserted into the message to make it more relevant to the recipient. Personalized e-mail messages are shown in Exhibits 15.2 and 15.3.

Exhibit 15.2   Personalized E-Mail That Uses Past Purchase Data

---

To: jxg01@qnet.com

cc:

Subject: "A Traitor to Memory" by Elizabeth George

As someone who has purchased books by Elizabeth George, you might like to know that her newest book, "A Traitor to Memory," will hit the shelves June 26, 2001. You can pre-order your copy by following the link below:

http://www.zzzzzzzz.zzz/exec/obidos/ASIN/0553801279/ref=mk_pb_sbr

Classical music, cybersex, and vehicular homicide figure prominently in this sprawling epic, the latest in the bestselling Thomas Lynley series that has won Elizabeth George an enviable following on both sides of the Atlantic. This can only add to her growing reputation as doyenne of English

mystery novelists. —From Publishers Weekly

To learn more about "A Traitor to Memory," please visit the following page at:

http://www.sssssssssss.sss/exec/obidos/ASIN/0553801279/ref=mk_pb_sbr

Happy reading,

Editor, Mystery & Thrillers

PS: We hope you enjoyed receiving this message. However, if you'd rather not receive future e-mails of this sort from ssss.com, please use the link below or click the Your Account button in the top right corner of any page. Under the Your Account Settings heading, click the "Update your communication preferences" link.

http://www.ssssss.sss/your-account

In addition, e-mail messages can contain attachments such as document, picture, or sound files, and links to Web sites that the recipient can use to place an order or obtain more information.

E-mail marketing can also be in the form of individual offers, newsletters, or periodic interest pieces. Some trade publications such as *DM News* have daily e-mail updates of news relevant to direct marketers. These e-mail messages contain advertisements from companies in the industry that the recipient can click on for further information.

Other companies offer daily e-mails to consumers on a topic of interest such as word of the day, recipes, trivia, or quotes. The objective is to keep the organization that is sending the e-mail accessible to the recipient. The e-mail recipient may click on a link embedded in the message and be sent to a Web site that in turn may contain offers or banner ads relevant to the interests of the e-mail recipient. For example, a foreign language site offers an e-mail that contains a word and phrase of the day. In addition to the word and phrase, links are also included in the e-mail. The links might take the e-mail recipient to a site selling language or culture CDs.

Exhibit 15.3   Using E-Mail to Confirm Order Shipment

To: jxg01@qnet.com
cc:
Subject: Shipment Confirmation

Dear Ralph,

Thank you for shopping at ZZZZZZZ. Please keep this email invoice for your records.

On January 26 we shipped your order number 3333333335 for the following item:

Santana : Supernatural

Format: CD Quantity: 1 Price: 12.58 to the following address via U.S. Postal Service:

 Ralph Wakely
 78 Main St.
 Anytown, CL 07777

Total number of items: 1
  Subtotal: $12.58
  Shipping: $ 2.99
  Sales Tax: $ 0.00

Shipment Total: $15.57

Your order was billed to Ralph Wakely. This shipment completes your order and is paid in full.

Most orders arrive within 4-8 business days. However, in rare instances it may take up to 2 weeks.

30% OFF Music by the Artists on Your Custom CD!

For complete information about your order (number 3333333335) or to confirm the status, click or copy/paste this link into your Web browser:

http://zzzzzzz.com/myorder/otid=3333333335

You can also access your Order History directly from our home page.

Please do not reply to this email. If you have questions about your order that are not addressed in your online Order History, please visit our Contact zzzzzzz page using this link: http://sssss.com/service

Thanks again for your order.

Sincerely,
Customer Service

Chapter Summary

The rapid growth of Internet commerce has been fueled by a number of factors, including cost savings, increased efficiencies, and greater customer control. As more traditional database marketers move online, there is increased pressure to develop integrated database systems that allow customers to access an organization from a number of media. Integrated databases have advantages for both customers and marketers because customers are able to obtain product information, order, pay, pick up, and return merchandise from a number of locations. Marketers increase their value to their customers by providing them with these shopping options and at the same time gain additional insights into their shopping patterns with the integrated database. However, integrated database development can be complex, especially when the integration involves legacy systems. Personalized communication is a key advantage of Internet marketing. Compared to other direct marketing media, Internet personalization can be dynamic, changing as customers access various types of information and make new purchases. Furthermore, personalization on the Internet is expanding into the development of real-time customer service systems that utilize the database.

Review Questions

1. Discuss the advantages and limitations of Internet marketing.

2. Explain the concept of integrating databases across direct marketing channels.

3. What are the customer service possibilities on the Internet?

4. What methods are used to personalize communications on the Internet?

5. What are some of the customer variables that are collected on the Internet?

6. What are the differences between traditional print and e-mail lists?

16 Analyzing and Targeting Online Customers

After attending a workshop on basic online marketing, Keri wants to understand more about the similarities and differences between online and offline database marketing. She realizes that there are different types of data that can be collected about online customers such as tracking visits to a Web site. Keri is also interested in software and services that track customer behavior online. Now she wants to take the next step and start to implement some of these techniques on the Web site of Inside Source. In particular, she is interested in testing offers and driving her current customers to the Web site.

Maximizing the use of e-commerce customer data employs the same principles and techniques as for offline enterprises. We covered these techniques in Chapters 6 through 14 on data mining and market testing. In this chapter, we present techniques and strategies unique to online businesses and their customers.

In particular, in Chapter 15 we noted that online customers initiate their contact by visiting a site and providing an e-mail address. This permission to communicate and the economies of communication afforded by e-mail have created a revolution in the direct marketing business. In this chapter, we investigate how Internet communication changes the marketing dynamic and how information can be leveraged to exploit this new dynamic. We discuss the similarities and differences between online and offline customers, the nature of the data available from online and offline communications, and how to effectively leverage the data to gain marketing efficiencies.

Data Collected via the Internet

Just as the Internet allows customers to initiate a dialogue with the marketer, the Internet also allows customers to state their preferences and provide a profile of information. Many sites have registration areas in which visitors are invited to outline their interests and their demographic profiles. All reputable companies also have their privacy policy clearly stated on their Web site wherever they collect customer information. Many Internet customers understand that by providing information regarding preferences and interests, they will receive offers tailored specifically for them. They further understand that if they decide in the future that they no longer wish to receive communications, they can express that preference at that time.

Individual-level customer data that are collected from a Web site can be classified as either registration, behavior, or source data.

Registration Data

Many e-commerce sites require consumers to register before they can make purchases, get information, or enter the Web site. The type of data collected varies from site to site. Examples of Internet registration data typically collected include

- Name
- Title
- Business title (if the site is a b-to-b site)
- E-mail address
- Postal address (business or home)
- Phone number
- Fax number
- Age
- Income level
- Gender
- Competitive product usage
- Current consumption level
- Product attributes

Some examples of e-commerce registration pages are shown in Exhibits 16.1, 16.2, and 16.3.

Exhibit 16.1 shows the Clairol registration page (www.clairol.com). The most comprehensive of the three pages displayed, questions on their registration page contain many product usage questions, including brand preference, usage frequency, and loyalty questions.

Exhibit 16.2 is a registration page from Saab USA (www.saab.com). This page asks only for name, address, and e-mail information. To help them better understand their visitors' intent, Saab should ask about their driving habits, if they ever previously owned a Saab, what type of car they currently

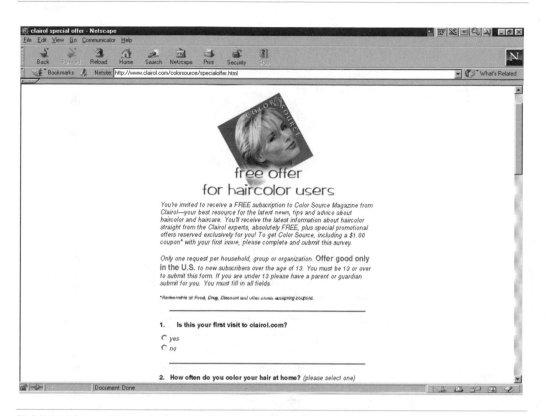

Exhibit 16.1   Clairol Registration Page

drive, how soon they are looking to purchase a new car, if they plan to buy or lease their next car, and what other makes of cars they are considering. With such information, Saab could direct the visitors to the appropriate dealer or provide a more targeted offer. However, as most direct marketers are well aware, there is a trade-off—the more questions asked, the lower the response. If this is the reason Saab is not asking more questions of the registrants, we hope they are at the very least gathering some valuable **clickstream data** based on where the visitors go within the Web site (a **clickstream** is the sequence of clicks or pages requested as a visitor explores a Web site). Doing so, for example, Saab could capture the fact that registrants click on the page that discusses the details of the new 2002 Saab convertible models. In this case, Saab would have very valuable information to help them properly communicate with the new registrants.

Exhibit 16.3 is the registration page for Club Med (www.clubmed.com). Club Med, like Saab USA, only asks for the visitors' name and address. However, they do offer a newsletter. Again, if they cannot ask questions on the registration page due to a decrease in response, they can still collect valuable information via clickstream data. This would provide Club Med with very valuable information about the different vacation packages the

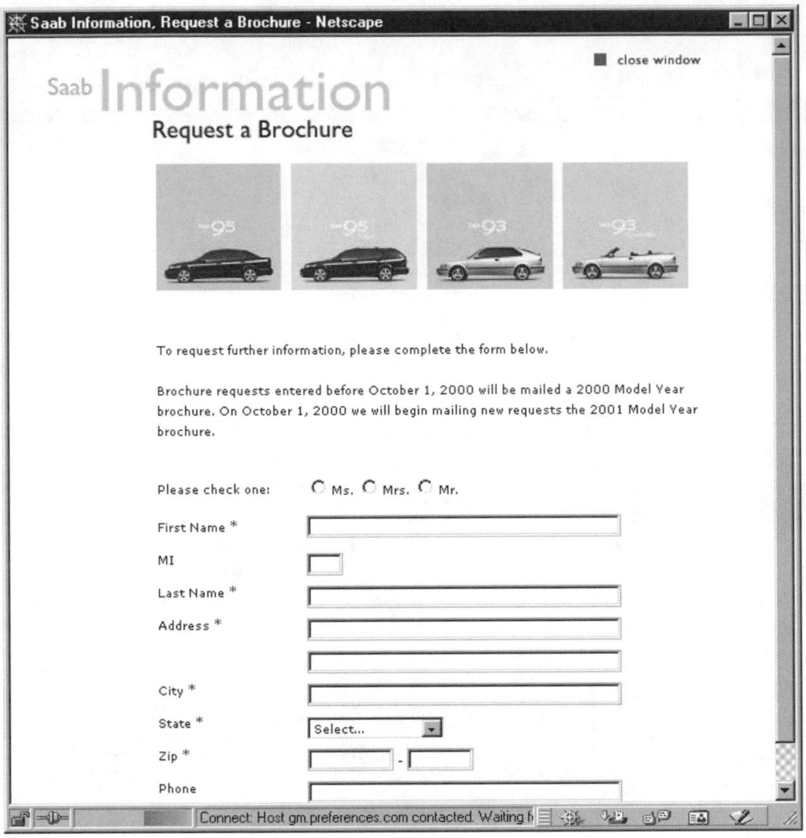

Exhibit 16.2   Saab Registration Page

registrants read about while they are on the Web site. With this information, Club Med would be a strong position to send targeted offers.

Behavior Data

In Chapter 15, we discussed the use of cookies as a means of personalizing
a Web site. Cookies can also be used to track the parts of a Web site that
are visited. As we also discussed in Chapter 15, a cookie is stored on the
Web visitor's hard drive with an identifying number. The cookies and their
identifying number are passed by Web servers to Internet browsers, so that
each time a visitor returns to a server that delivered a cookie, the visitor can
be recognized.

Besides the identifying number, other information stored in the cookie
includes previous pages visited and expiration date. In addition to recording
visits, cookies also permit a record of behavior to be stored so that a

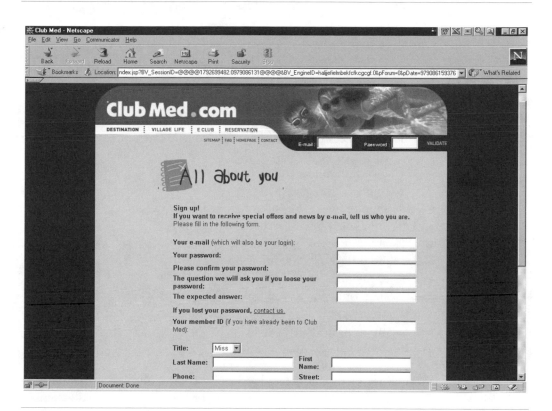

Exhibit 16.3   Club Med Registration Page

customer's page views can be identified. This record can be aggregated by the unique identifier found in the cookie to establish patterns of behavior for each online customer. The clickstream data can be valuable in many respects: A direct marketer can determine the most popular pages viewed by each visitor, segment customers for offers, or use it to predict a likely response to offers.

When a registered Web visitor becomes a customer through a purchase at an e-commerce site, additional behavior information is available in the form of product preference, delivery choices, frequency of access to account information, usage of online discounts, "wish lists," and other loyalty devices.

Types of customer behavior data that can be captured includes

- ◆ Visits
- ◆ Total page views
- ◆ Specific page views
- ◆ Time spent at the site
- ◆ Products purchased
- ◆ Customer service requests
- ◆ Access to personal account information
- ◆ Discounts used

Source Data

The importance of source information for proper evaluation of any acquisition effort cannot be stressed enough. The marketer needs to know what media convinced a customer to visit the site.

In their "Holiday Shopping Exploration" report, Digitrends quantifies the various influences that contribute to a consumer shopping online:

- 42% of online buyers shop on the Internet as a result of a promotional e-mail
- 41% shop online as a result of an article or site link
- 39% are guided by a search engine
- 38% are influenced by word of mouth
- 29% are directed by an online ad
- 27% are familiar with a site's offline store
- 21% shop online as a result of a magazine article
- 19% are influenced by TV or radio commercials
- 17% are moved by print ads
- 12% are persuaded by direct mail

Most offline direct marketers routinely track the source of a customer to evaluate the effectiveness of various media or lists and to correlate member quality by source. The source of a customer is just as important on the Internet for the same reasons. The method of collecting source will involve one of the following:

- Construction of unique URLs for each link or online ad
- Construction of unique URLs for specific e-mail lists or direct mail lists
- Evaluation of log files to identify search engines referring customers.
- Collection of survey data at registration for customers who were driven by print or broadcast ads, magazine articles, or word of mouth.

Understanding Internet Users and Online Buyers

Before proceeding, we must make a distinction between Internet users and online buyers. An Internet user is anyone using the Internet for purposes of conducting research or making purchases or both. An online buyer is a subset of Internet users. So what does an Internet user look like, and how many are there? An Internet user is younger, has a higher income and higher education than the general population. In particular,

- The number of Internet users aged 18 or older has been estimated to be approximately 93.2 million by the U.S. Census Bureau as of

August 2000. Other research suggests a higher number of users in this age group: Harris Interactive sizes the 18 + market at 114.2 million as of June 2000, Pew Research Center estimates 113.8 million as of August 2000, and MRI estimates 112.9 million as of spring 2000.

- ◆ MRI estimates the number of adults (aged 18 or older) active in the last 30 days at 86.3 million as of their spring 2000 survey.

- ◆ Estimates of numbers of Internet users who access the Internet from work range from 26.8 million by Media Metrix to 34.8 million by Nielsen/NetRatings in August 2000. Morgan Stanley Dean Witter's estimate was 36 million at midyear 2000.

- ◆ According to Forrester Research in January 2000 and the U.S. Census Bureau in August 2000, Asian Americans account for 3.8% of the population but comprise 6.1% of the Internet population. Hispanic Americans represent 11.6% of the U.S. population and 12.7% of the Internet population. African Americans represent 12.2% of the general population but only account for 9.4% of the Internet users. Caucasian Americans represent equal numbers in the general population and the online community at 71.1%.

- ◆ According to Pew Research in August 2000, 57% of Internet users are under the age of 34. Only 17% of individuals over 60 years of age have access to the Internet.

- ◆ According to Media Metrix in June 2000 and the U.S. Census Bureau, roughly 58% of Internet users have household incomes of $50,000 or more. This is in contrast to 46% of the general population of U.S. households with incomes of $50,000 or more.

- ◆ The UCLA Internet Project reports from their spring 2000 survey that Internet penetration is greatest among well-educated, high-income households. Eighty-six percent of individuals with a college degree or an advanced degree have Internet access. Seventy percent of individuals with some college have access to the Internet. Among individuals with no college education, the Internet penetration drops to 53%.

How do online buyers differ from Internet users and the general population? Online buyers are younger and more affluent individuals who have been active Internet users for many years. Their unique characteristics in contrast to Internet users and the general population are as follows:

- ◆ According to the Gartner Group in midyear 2000, the percentage of individuals with an income level of $50,000 or more who have purchased on the Internet is 51.2%. Only 39% of individuals with incomes less than $50,000 have made purchases online.

- ◆ Also according to the Gartner Group in midyear 2000, 36% of Internet users aged 55 and older have purchased something on the Internet. This contrasts to 49% of Internet users in the 35 to 54 age group who have made a purchase online and 46% penetration of online purchasing in the 18 to 34 age group.

- ◆ The UCLA Internet Project found a correlation between tenure of Internet use and online purchasing penetration: 71% of individuals who were Internet users for 3 to 4 years had made a purchase online, whereas online purchase penetration was 26% among individuals who had been using the Internet for less than a year.
- ◆ Estimates quantifying the dollars spent online in 1999 vary widely. The Direct Marketing Association estimates that the average online purchaser spent $559, the Boston Consulting Group estimated online purchasers averaged $460, but Ernst & Young estimates the average value of online purchases at $1,205.

Web Site Reporting

More and more direct marketers are establishing their presence online. Surprisingly, not all gauge the effectiveness of their Web site. The Direct Marketing Association commissioned a study on the state of the interactive e-commerce marketing industry in January 2000. Key trends in Internet usage among direct marketing companies include the following:

- ◆ About 96% of respondents reported the use of the Internet for marketing and sales applications in 2000. Sixty-two percent reported the use of e-mail marketing in 2000.
- ◆ About 97% of respondents reported that their companies have a Web site. In 1998, 87% of respondents reported that their company had a Web site.
- ◆ Regarding the primary function of their company's Web site, 80% of survey respondents indicated their sites were used for marketing or information, 60% reported their sites were used primarily for lead generation, and 55% reported their sites were used for sales or e-commerce.
- ◆ In 2000, among the companies with Internet sites, only 69% reported measuring their effectiveness. For those companies measuring Web site effectiveness, 77% measured the productivity of their site by the sales generated, 62% evaluated the effectiveness in terms of the leads generated, and 60% used home page hits as the key measure of effectiveness.

When you establish your Web site, the first thing you want to do is measure its effectiveness to determine if it is meeting your requirements. Currently, there is not a single standard for measuring the effectiveness of an e-commerce Web site. Traffic and revenue generated by a Web site can be reported in a variety of ways: number of page hits, dollar sales, time spent at the site, source of traffic, returning customers versus new visitors, and so on.

The ways in which reports are generated requires a means of tracking and managing the data so that it can be extracted into reports Web traffic is usually tracked by traffic analysis and monitoring software, of which various software packages are available. Most analyzers first compile the data into a **data mart** from which they can run reports. Packages differ in the process in which the data mart is built. Some build the data mart in real time and others build it by loading the log files during off-peak times.

Some examples of various e-commerce reporting and analysis tools that build data marts and analyze information in real time include the following:

♦ Accrue Insight builds the database in real time and can collect and store data on more than 1 million hits per hour. The data are stored in the lowest level of detail, and the resulting database can provide the maximum number of options on sorting, analysis, and report generation. This is a good choice for large commercial sites stored over multiple servers.

♦ Aria works in real time with separate components to monitor, record, and report the data. The monitor intercepts the data, the recorder processes the data, and the reporter provides the data in chart form. The data are stored in an object-oriented database.

♦ Webtrends has the ability to monitor server statistics almost immediately. It uses background processing to gather the data it needs. It doesn't import log files into a database but instead creates reports on the fly as the files are being read in. If capturing log file data in a database for later analysis is of interest to you, Webtrends will not provide a complete solution.

For a more complete report on available reporting and analysis tools, read *Data Mining Your Website* by Jesus Mena (1999).

The purpose of reporting can be to measure the relative popularity of various areas of an Internet site, the popularity of specific pages to a particular population, dollar sales generated overall, or by a particular population, the proportion of repeat visitors, and so on.

For example, At Home Online, an e-tailer of home-related products, rebuilt its Web site in October 1998 to be more user friendly and informative. The following exhibits are examples of reports designed to track relevant consumer information, by week, from their new Web site.

Exhibit 16.4 shows the total number of visitors and the number of visitors by specific pages (home page, the product search engine page, the garden page, and the cooking page).

Exhibit 16.4 Example Report Showing Visits and Specific Page Hits by Week

Week	# Visits	Home Page	Visits to Home Page (%)	Product Search Engine	Visits to Product Search Engine (%)	Garden Page	Visits to Garden Page (%)	Cooking Page	Visits to Cooking Page (%)
10/12/1998	42,400	40,564	96	19,318	46	29,680	70	24,168	57
10/19/1998	44,171	42,139	95	19,576	44	30,919	70	24,294	55
10/26/1998	46,015	44,032	96	19,747	43	32,211	70	26,689	58
11/2/1998	47,937	41,561	87	18,207	38	26,365	55	27,683	58
11/9/1998	49,939	46,576	93	22,181	44	25,574	51	28,964	58
11/16/1998	52,024	47,647	92	22,136	43	24,807	48	36,937	71
11/23/1998	54,197	48,542	90	21,769	40	24,063	44	39,027	72
11/30/1998	56,460	51,529	91	22,574	40	23,341	41	40,092	71
12/7/1998	58,817	54,457	93	25,934	44	22,641	38	41,760	71
12/14/1998	61,274	53,901	88	25,041	41	21,961	36	44,123	72
12/21/1998	63,832	60,877	95	27,301	43	21,303	33	47,242	74
12/28/1998	66,498	61,695	93	27,027	41	20,664	31	47,214	71
1/4/1999	69,275	64,126	93	30,538	44	20,044	29	49,885	72
1/11/1999	72,168	65,866	91	30,599	42	19,442	27	41,136	57
1/18/1999	75,182	71,941	96	32,263	43	18,859	25	41,350	55
1/25/1999	78,321	74,930	96	32,825	42	18,293	23	45,426	58
2/1/1999	81,592	78,546	96	37,406	46	17,745	22	47,119	58
2/8/1999	84,999	81,336	96	37,786	44	17,212	20	48,450	57
2/15/1999	88,549	83,738	95	37,553	42	16,696	19	48,702	55
2/22/1999	92,247	86,036	93	37,690	41	16,195	18	53,503	58
3/1/1999	96,099	88,975	93	42,372	44	48,049	50	55,497	58
3/8/1999	100,112	91,669	92	42,587	43	50,056	50	58,065	58

Exhibit 16.5 shows the dollar sales associated with specific product affinities and overall sales generated by the Web site. The last column shows average sales per visitor.

Exhibit 16.6 shows the time spent by visitors in specific areas of the Web site as well as the total time spent by all visitors. The last column provides the average time per visit.

Exhibit 16.7 shows the net visitors by a referring source. The last column reflects visitors who reached the Web site directly by typing the URL into their browser. This data could also be reflected as percentages.

Driving Customers to Your Web Site

For some traditional direct mail marketers, converting current customers to online communications may not be easy. After all, a customer who responds to a mail order offer is different from one who responds to an online offer. Despite the efficiencies to be gained in converting customers from traditional mail to e-mail, a loyal direct mail customer may resist doing business over the Internet for many reasons:

+ Technology. Doing business over the Internet requires, minimally, a computer, a modem, and an e-mail account. Some markets, such as the seniors' market, are lagging far behind the average in Internet penetration.
+ Preference. Some customers have a comfort level with doing business by mail or over the phone and will never feel comfortable providing credit card information over the Internet.
+ Convenience. Some catalog shoppers make their selections while waiting for appointments at the doctor's office or at night in their beds. For these people, the computer does not lend itself to the convenience of shopping when their time permits.

Still, the effort to identify the segment of customers sourced offline for conversion to online communication is worthwhile. The immediacy and efficiency of the Internet medium permits the development of a personal relationship with your most valuable customers. E-mail marketing provides marketers with the ability to increase conversion and retention rates by being able to deliver timely and powerful individualized messages to the various customer segments in ways that were not feasible with conventional direct mail.

For example, Fingerhut Companies Inc., recognizing that intelligent interaction with customers is the key to building a successful business, announced in April 2000 its plans to begin launching a series of targeted e-mail messages to their catalog customers ("Fingerhut to Launch New E-Mail," 2000).

Exhibit 16.5 Example Report Showing Dollar Sales and Page Hits by Week

Week	# Visits	Product Search Engine	Garden Page	Cooking Page	Sales of Garden Products ($)	Sales of Cooking Products ($)	Sales of Other Products ($)	Total Sales	Average Dollars per Visit
10/12/1998	42,400	19,318	29,680	24,168	28,000.85	9,858.73	5,093.50	42,953.08	1.01
10/19/1998	44,171	19,576	30,919	24,294	28,244.13	12,251.20	5,161.73	45,657.05	1.03
10/26/1998	46,015	19,747	32,211	26,689	22,614.89	14,537.19	5,206.62	42,358.70	0.92
11/2/1998	47,937	18,207	26,365	27,683	24,873.60	10,808.81	4,800.65	40,483.06	0.84
11/9/1998	49,939	22,181	25,574	28,964	22,516.22	12,370.08	5,848.42	40,734.72	0.82
11/16/1998	52,024	22,136	24,807	36,937	23,403.57	18,508.02	5,836.48	47,748.07	0.92
11/23/1998	54,197	21,769	24,063	39,027	16,082.01	15,743.16	5,739.95	37,565.12	0.69
11/30/1998	56,460	22,574	23,341	40,092	19,814.70	18,241.06	5,952.03	44,007.79	0.78
12/7/1998	58,817	25,934	22,641	41,760	17,843.92	22,746.59	6,838.03	47,428.53	0.81
12/14/1998	61,274	25,041	21,961	44,123	20,719.01	18,370.36	6,602.48	45,691.86	0.75
12/21/1998	63,832	27,301	21,303	47,242	16,071.24	22,812.38	7,198.50	46,082.13	0.72
12/28/1998	66,498	27,027	20,664	47,214	18,875.65	25,716.92	7,126.24	51,718.81	0.78
1/4/1999	69,275	30,538	20,044	49,885	17,598.01	20,769.23	8,052.07	46,419.31	0.67
1/11/1999	72,168	30,599	19,442	41,136	18,342.39	18,715.91	8,068.10	45,126.41	0.63
1/18/1999	75,182	32,263	18,859	41,350	17,792.12	21,378.71	8,506.82	47,677.65	0.63
1/25/1999	78,321	32,825	18,293	45,426	16,710.47	19,501.18	8,655.01	44,866.67	0.57
2/1/1999	81,592	37,406	17,745	47,119	12,458.31	21,438.32	9,862.77	43,759.41	0.54
2/8/1999	84,999	37,786	17,212	48,450	16,238.39	25,049.34	9,963.10	51,250.84	0.60
2/15/1999	88,549	37,553	16,696	48,702	14,699.40	20,276.63	9,901.72	44,877.76	0.51
2/22/1999	92,247	37,690	16,195	53,503	15,278.70	24,342.75	9,937.80	49,559.25	0.54
3/1/1999	96,099	42,372	48,049	55,497	32,113.03	29,578.20	11,172.28	72,863.51	0.76
3/8/1999	100,112	42,587	50,056	58,065	42,493.69	25,678.73	11,228.90	79,401.33	0.79

Exhibit 16.6 Example Report Showing Length of Time Spent by Page Visits

Week	# Visits	Home Page Hits	Time Spent on Home Page	Product Search Engine Hits	Time Spent Using Product Search Engine	Garden Page Hits	Time Spent on Garden Page	Cooking Page Hits	Time Spent on Cooking Page	Total Time Spent on Site	Average Time in Seconds per Visitor
10/12/1998	42,400	40,564	202,820	19,318	656,801	29,680	296,800	24,168	604,200	1,760,622	41.5
10/19/1998	44,171	42,139	210,694	19,576	665,600	30,919	309,194	24,294	607,346	1,792,834	40.6
10/26/1998	46,015	44,032	220,160	19,747	671,389	32,211	322,106	26,689	667,220	1,880,875	40.9
11/2/1998	47,937	41,561	207,306	18,207	619,039	26,365	263,652	27,683	692,087	1,782,584	37.2
11/9/1998	49,939	46,576	232,881	22,181	754,148	25,574	255,743	28,964	724,109	1,966,881	39.4
11/16/1998	52,024	47,647	238,236	22,136	752,608	24,807	248,070	36,937	923,426	2,162,341	41.6
11/23/1998	54,197	48,542	242,711	21,769	740,161	24,063	240,628	39,027	975,673	2,199,173	40.6
11/30/1998	56,460	51,529	257,646	22,574	767,509	23,341	233,409	40,092	1,002,302	2,260,865	40.0
12/7/1998	58,817	54,457	272,287	25,934	881,757	22,641	226,407	41,760	1,044,011	2,424,462	41.2
12/14/1998	61,274	53,901	269,503	25,041	851,384	21,961	219,615	44,123	1,103,080	2,443,582	39.9
12/21/1998	63,832	60,877	304,385	27,301	928,240	21,303	213,026	47,242	1,181,060	2,626,712	41.2
12/28/1998	66,498	61,695	308,474	27,027	918,922	20,664	206,636	47,214	1,180,341	2,614,373	39.3
1/4/1999	69,275	64,126	320,629	30,538	1,038,306	20,044	200,437	49,885	1,247,124	2,806,496	40.5
1/11/1999	72,168	65,866	329,328	30,599	1,040,374	19,442	194,423	41,136	1,028,394	2,592,519	35.9
1/18/1999	75,182	71,941	359,707	32,263	1,096,947	18,859	188,591	41,350	1,033,748	2,678,992	35.6
1/25/1999	78,321	74,930	374,650	32,825	1,116,056	18,293	182,933	45,426	1,135,658	2,809,297	35.9
2/1/1999	81,592	78,546	392,731	37,406	1,271,795	17,745	177,445	47,119	1,177,984	3,019,954	37.0
2/8/1999	84,999	81,336	406,679	37,786	1,284,733	17,212	172,122	48,450	1,211,239	3,074,772	36.2
2/15/1999	88,549	83,738	418,689	37,553	1,276,818	16,696	166,958	48,702	1,217,545	3,080,010	34.8
2/22/1999	92,247	86,036	430,178	37,690	1,281,470	16,195	161,949	53,503	1,337,574	3,211,172	34.8
3/1/1999	96,099	88,975	444,875	42,372	1,440,655	48,049	480,494	55,497	1,387,425	3,753,448	39.1
3/8/1999	100,112	91,669	458,347	42,587	1,447,957	50,056	500,559	58,065	1,451,621	3,858,483	38.5

Exhibit 16.7 Example Report Showing Number of Visits by Referring Page

Week	# Visits	Referred From Banner Ads On			Referred From Search On				Other Links	Direct Visits
		Yahoo!	Lycos	Excite	Yahoo!	Lycos	Google	All Other		
10/12/1998	42,400	9,879	8,056	4,155	3,816	3,180	3,345	7,509	1,272	1,187
10/19/1998	44,171	10,292	8,392	4,329	3,975	3,313	3,485	7,823	1,325	1,237
10/26/1998	46,015	10,722	8,743	4,509	4,141	3,451	3,631	8,149	1,380	1,288
11/2/1998	47,937	11,169	9,108	4,698	4,314	3,595	3,782	8,490	1,438	1,342
11/9/1998	49,939	11,636	9,488	4,894	4,494	3,745	3,940	8,844	1,498	1,398
11/16/1998	52,024	12,122	9,885	5,098	4,682	3,902	4,105	9,213	1,561	1,457
11/23/1998	54,197	12,628	10,297	5,311	4,878	4,065	4,276	9,598	1,626	1,518
11/30/1998	56,460	13,155	10,727	5,533	5,081	4,234	4,455	9,999	1,694	1,581
12/7/1998	58,817	13,704	11,175	5,764	5,294	4,411	4,641	10,417	1,765	1,647
12/14/1998	61,274	14,277	11,642	6,005	5,515	4,596	4,834	10,852	1,838	1,716
12/21/1998	63,832	14,873	12,128	6,256	5,745	4,787	5,036	11,305	1,915	1,787
12/28/1998	66,498	15,494	12,635	6,517	5,985	4,987	5,247	11,777	1,995	1,862
1/4/1999	69,275	16,141	13,162	6,789	6,235	5,196	5,466	12,269	2,078	1,940
1/11/1999	72,168	16,815	13,712	7,072	6,495	5,413	5,694	12,781	2,165	2,021
1/18/1999	75,182	17,517	14,285	7,368	6,766	5,639	5,932	13,315	2,255	2,105
1/25/1999	78,321	18,249	14,881	7,675	7,049	5,874	6,180	13,871	2,350	2,193
2/1/1999	81,592	19,011	15,502	7,996	7,343	6,119	6,438	14,450	2,448	2,285
2/8/1999	84,999	19,805	16,150	8,330	7,650	6,375	6,706	15,053	2,550	2,380
2/15/1999	88,549	20,632	16,824	8,678	7,969	6,641	6,986	15,682	2,656	2,479
2/22/1999	92,247	21,493	17,527	9,040	8,302	6,918	7,278	16,337	2,767	2,583
3/1/1999	96,099	22,391	18,259	9,418	8,649	7,207	7,582	17,019	2,883	2,691
3/8/1999	100,112	23,326	19,021	9,811	9,010	7,508	7,899	17,730	3,003	2,803

One way to determine which customers are likely to be qualified online buyers is to overlay enhancement data on your database regarding a person's online behavior. But remember, just knowing that someone uses the Internet is not sufficient, because not all online users are purchasers. As we previously stated, many Internet users are not buyers until they have been online for several years. You can employ regression modeling techniques to determine those customers most likely to be wired *and* responsive. Once identified, you can send offers inviting them to visit your Web site and register for a free gift or to enter a contest.

The Reader's Digest Association recently tested sending a postcard to their offline customers offering a free gift (camera or frequent flyer miles) in exchange for their e-mail address.

In June 2000, Experian and FloNetwork announced a service that will allow clients to use the extensive information in the Experian database to target customers online. Providers such as AccuData America and Donnelley Marketing offer assistance in straight appending of e-mail addresses (both personal and business) onto a postal list, but the match rate and coverage are relatively low. A good match rate ranges anywhere from 4% to 25%. But remember, once the e-mail address is appended, it may not be yours to promote until the names go through an opt-in campaign. Check with the vendor supplying the e-mail addresses. They may have already prequalified the names, which means you can begin sending solicitations immediately.

You may also want to consider the use of Abacus e-Direct service to help you find which of your direct mail customers will be good online customers. Or you might consider InfoUSA's e-ShareForce database, which is an enhanced version of its long-standing ShareForce database, which now includes Internet and telephone response data.

Retailers also are trying to encourage in-store shoppers to visit their Web sites. CVS/Pharmacy in May 2000 launched its first major online and offline integrated promotion. CVS stores handed out cards steering customers to their Web site with a chance to win a Palm Springs getaway vacation. Staples Inc. has also been highly promoting its Web site by launching its "Hey, you don't have to run out" campaign using in-store signage, its catalog. and stand-alone direct mail advertisements ("CVS Launches," 2000).

Targeting Online Customers

Targeting online customers is very similar to the offline world and consists of two major steps: defining the target markets and executing a contact strategy. Your strategy dictates the offer and message and the manner in which both are extended. E-commerce data can be used just as effectively to acquire, retain, reactivate and cross-sell online customers as traditional direct mail.

In this chapter, we discuss a number of marketing innovations precipitated by the Internet and the data acquired by these innovations. Customers interacting with a direct marketer's Web site or customers of a **pure play e-commerce site** can be segmented on the basis of their attributes and their historical clickstream behavior.

Just as customers are segmented by demographics, source, product affinity, or RFM for traditional direct marketing applications, they can be similarly segmented by these attributes and more for e-commerce applications. For example, consider our direct marketer ACME Direct. A customer who ordered offline recently and registered at the ACME Direct Web site for order fulfillment information can be classified in a segment of recent ACME Direct orderers and also be segmented as an offline orderer with a potential to convert to an online orderer.

For direct marketers conducting business both offline and online, segmentation analysis, as described in Chapter 8, will take on a new dimension. This is because the RFM data elements can be considered in the context of online or offline customer activity or both combined. The appropriate definition of segments will be driven by the specific needs of the marketer and the strength of the data to predict customer behavior. For example, suppose a direct mail cataloger has just begun to operate in the online world. Up to this point, the cataloger considered a primary direct mail customer to be anyone who made a purchase in the past 18 months. Now that they are in the online world, should the cataloger also include anyone in this primary direct mail market definition who placed an order via the Web site too? The cataloger may decide to include some, but not all, online orders in the definition. They may decide to include only recent online orders in their primary direct mail market definition if and only if the customer had at least placed one direct mail catalog order in the past. In addition, they may decide to exclude recent online orders in their primary direct mail market definition if the customer had never purchased via a direct mail catalog promotion. As you can see, it becomes very tricky and requires testing and analysis to determine the best way to segment the market. By not carefully planning the integration of both online and offline data in your customer segments, you risk telling customers via an e-mail message that you miss them, when in reality they just placed an offline order.

Web marketers also desire to maintain relationships when customers become inactive or if their product or service is associated with long purchase intervals (e.g., high-ticket items such as home furnishings, cars, or appliances). Segmenting the customer file based on the last Web site visit date or last online purchase date allows direct marketers to effectively execute a reactivation or retention program. And if they are also conducting business offline, they will need to determine how to integrate any offline customer activity into these segment definitions. By not doing so, once again, direct marketers risk telling a customer, via an e-mail message, that they miss them, when in reality they just placed an offline order.

You can even append enhancement data (as described in Chapter 3) to your online customer data (registration, behavior, and source). Looking Glass Inc. has developed 27 unique market segments describing online customers. These segments are similar to the modeled data described in Chapter 3 but for the online world. Direct marketers can append such data to their file for purposes of more targeted messages and offers. Examples of some of their segments include

- "Jules and Roz": affluent couples with kids
- "Kelvin": techie guys
- "Alec and Elyse": empty nesters, average age 53, income > $100,000
- "Jason": male students and graduates, average age 22, income < $20,000

Segmentation allows marketers to maintain a personal relationship with (a) active customers between purchases, (b) those who visited the site but never ordered, (c) those who have been inactive for 6 months, and so on. Some marketers send their inactive customers e-mails highlighting free shipping offers or percentage discounts available within a specific window of time. These offers may be sent via e-mail or traditional mail.

MotherNature.com segmented its file by those customers who registered and ordered versus those who registered and did not order. In an attempt to convert nonordering registrants, MotherNature.com e-mailed them a special offer ("MotherNature.com Streamlines," 2000).

For a consumer who is highly active over the Internet and browses and shops at many e-commerce sites throughout the year, these offers, though valuable, may be ignored due to clutter in the e-mail box and a lack of differentiation from other marketers. Sometimes to reactivate a relationship, it pays to send a reminder via traditional mail. This is a strategy commonly used by Amazon.com.

Ashford.com, the luxury jewelry e tailer, invited its best customers in 1999 to a preview party to view new, exclusive merchandise in advance of the 2000 holiday season. Customers meeting a dollar threshold of payments in 1999 were allowed to preview new collections prior to the new merchandise being posted on the Ashford site. Invited customers were allowed a 20% discount on the new merchandise. The invitation was sent via first class mail and required an RSVP. Receptions were held in several large metropolitan areas at exclusive hotels, at which Ashford.com corporate officers were also in attendance.

It is doubtful that the attendees of the reception or even those who RSVP'd in the affirmative were recorded on the Ashford.com database. Generally, receptions to specific customer groups are a public relations function, and no thought is given to updating the database with attendance information. Thus it is impossible to answer the question, "How much did a customer's reception experience affect his or her purchasing behavior?" The database may have recorded which customers were invited to the reception, but in all likelihood it did not capture those who attended. If a company routinely stages special events such as the one described above, then it is imperative to capture attendance data to gauge the effect on customer behavior.

You can also define your online target markets with regression modeling. You can use Internet data to predict the customers who are likely to click through and order via a unique e-mail offer just as effectively as you can predict order behavior for your offline customers. You will employ the same regression modeling techniques learned in Chapter 10. The only difference with online applications is the ability to isolate and identify key predictors of information to use in the modeling process.

The challenge for the analyst is to identify relevant variables in the constant stream of information stored in the e-commerce database. Factor and cluster analysis (as described in Chapter 8) is of value to identify dimensions of behavior in data and to reduce many correlated variables into linear combinations of a few important variables.

However, in most cases, the application of modeling for the Internet will not lie in identifying those most likely to respond, as is the case with traditional direct mail. Given that the economics of messaging a customer electronically are so low, the benefits of such modeling will never outweigh the costs of building the model. But modeling can be used to identify the right prospect or customer for the right offer.

For example, with the use of regression modeling, neural networks, and other mathematical algorithms, online publishers and retailers are maximizing their retention of customers by delivering targeted and personalized product offers, page content, and advertising based on real-time online customer behavior data and individual preferences. Most software vendors offering such services to online publishers and retailers use proprietary technology for capturing and analyzing the customer information. Some software packages, when evaluating a customer, will examine every Web page displayed, the sequencing of pages, and the time spent on each page.

A company like America Online also has a great opportunity to do this evaluation because of the vast amount of customer data they have on their subscriber base. All subscribers regularly receive various offers each time they log on to AOL and during an active session. Ideally, these offers are unique to each customer's observed AOL behavior in addition to any customer-provided information about likes and dislikes.

In 2001, Predictive Networks developed an ad targeting system that analyzes Internet users' keystrokes and mouse movements to differentiate quickly among household members using the same computer and account. Then they target ads to those individuals within the household.

Conducting Marketing Tests in the E-Commerce World

Just as was the case in the offline world, testing is also the foundation on which a direct marketer builds and grows an online business. When you are preparing to implement an online marketing test program, you need to plan it properly to ensure that the results will be readable, reliable, and projectable. Exactly the same appropriate testing principles should be employed as is discussed in Chapter 14:

- Use of appropriate sample sizes
- Observance of the "one change" rule
- Leveraging test winners to the same universes in rollout

In addition, once testing results are final, you should assess those results using the same tools as listed in Chapter 13: confidence intervals and hypothesis tests.

We next consider the two types of online tests for planning and analysis purposes: banner ads and e-mails.

Banner Ads

Online banner ads can be priced on the basis of the number of impressions, number of orders, or number of responses, depending on what you are offering. An impression is the exposure of a banner ad to a Web page visitor. Typically, direct marketers specify the number of impressions they desire. Once that number is reached, the banner ad is pulled. A click-through on a banner ad is analogous to someone opening the envelope in traditional direct mail. In both cases, the individual is looking for more information about the offer.

Those placements where your banner ads yield the most impressions and the highest order conversion rates are considered winners. You will continue to run banner ads on those Web sites.

For example, Vita-Protein wants to test several banner placements to determine which one provides the best click-through rate for a new women's hair care product. The banner ad will highlight a free sample and coupon offer. When prospects click on the banner ad, they will be taken to a page where they provide their name, address, and e-mail address in exchange for a product sample and a coupon in the mail. Vita-Protein has decided to test this banner ad on Excite, iVillage, and Drugstore.com

The marketing director at Vita-Protein, with the assistance of his media planner, determined that the expected click-through rates for Excite, iVillage, and Drugstore.com will be 0.003, 0.0045, and 0.004, respectively. Assuming that the marketing director wants the click-through rates received from the Excite, iVillage, and Drugstore.com tests to be within 3% of the actual click-through rate to expect in rollout with 95% confidence, how many impressions does he need to order for each site?

Using the sample size formula from Chapter 14 (Sample Size Determination for the Difference Between Two Sample Proportions), the marketing director set up the Excel spreadsheet as shown in Exhibit 16.8.

To gauge click-throughs at this level of accuracy would require 18,247,600 impressions of the Excite ad and would potentially yield 52,918 to 56,568 click-throughs.

Assume the marketing director contracts through his media buyer for 18.3 million impressions on Excite, 10.1 million impressions on iVillage, and 12.7 million impressions on Drugstore.com. The order went into effect on April 14, 2000. At the end of 3 days, he receives the report shown in Exhibit 16.9 from his media buyer.

Should the marketing director adjust the number of impressions contracted to ensure that he maintains the desired reliability in test results? It appears that the click-through rates are on forecast and that no adjustment to the number of impressions required is necessary.

Exhibit 16.8 Sample Size Determination Calculations

Placement	Estimated Click-through Rate	Acceptable Error Rate	Error Rate as a Percentage of Click-through Rate (%)	Sample Size Required for 95% Confidence Level	Expected # of Click-throughs @95%	Lower Bound for # of Click-throughs	Upper Bound for # of Click-throughs
Excite	0.003	0.0001	3	18,247,600	54,743	52,918	56,568
iVillage	0.0045	0.000135	3	10,012,401	45,056	43,704	46,407
Drugstore.com	0.004	0.00012	3	12,671,944	50,688	49,167	52,208

Exhibit 16.9 Click-Through Summary Report

Placement	Click-through Rate	Contract Impressions	Impressions as of 4/16/00	Click-throughs as of 4/16/00	Percentage as Click-throughs of 4/16/00	Percentage of Impressions Delivered
Excite	0.00293	18,300,000	3,244,018	9,505	0.28	17.73
iVillage	0.00446	10,100,000	1,189,473	5,305	0.44	11.78
Drugstore.com	0.00389	12,700,000	1,094,856	4,259	0.40	8.62

Once the test results are final, the marketing director will compare the results via hypothesis testing (as described in Chapter 13) to determine which were the winning sites.

It should be noted, however, that the banner ad cost model is changing due to the slowdown in the Internet business world. It is now becoming more common for search engines and Web sites to offer banner ad placement to other e-commerce businesses on a per response or order basis versus on a per impression basis. In other words, it is becoming much more competitive. Direct marketers no longer want to pay for impressions; instead, they want to only pay for responses or orders.

A new benefit being offered by many media buyers in the Internet arena is the capability, via optimization software, to shift media dollars on the fly, based on the performance of all media in a campaign. Consider an example of a product targeted to women: The media plan is to run test and control ads on women's interest sites and general interest sites. If the test ads on the general interest sites seem to be receiving more click-throughs, the optimization software would alert the media buyer to pull advertising on the women's sites and add more exposures for the test ads on the general interest sites.

If your media buyers use such software, you would be well advised to ask them the following questions:

♦ Are decisions to pull ads based on statistical significance?
♦ If so, at what level of confidence are the tests conducted?
♦ Is the level of confidence appropriate, given the specifics of the offer advertised and the associated profit impact?

E-Mail

Designing e-mail marketing campaigns is analogous to designing direct mail campaigns. To ensure a certain level of confidence in your test results, apply the appropriate rules given in Chapters 13 and 14 to all e-mail list, offer, and copy tests.

When you conduct e-mail response list tests, realize that the rules are different from traditional direct mail response list tests. In e-mail marketing, a list is rented and copy is provided to the owner for approval. The execution takes place by a vendor designated by the list owner or a third-party vendor who conducts broadcast e-mails. Some arrangements involve a stipulation that the copy contains an endorsement by the list owner. In other cases, the list owner has a maximum message length requirement. Many e-mail marketers don't bother to merge/purge, because some list owners rigidly control the access to their names and there is little monetary benefit in ensuring that each individual receives only one message.

The various arrangements that list owners require to communicate with their names may make the management of a test more difficult. However, as long as the responses are trackable by each specific treatment, marketers should be able to cope with the new rules. In fact, the rewards to marketers are great if they can get e-mail marketing to work for them. The costs are lower, and the response time is immediate. With proper test planning and analysis, online marketers are in a strong position to make the best decisions regarding offers, treatments, and communications.

Chapter Summary

Many of the data mining techniques discussed in previous chapters can also be applied to online databases. However, some unique aspects of online databases need to be treated differently. In addition to customer contact and demographic and psychographic data collected during registration, marketers can track customer behavior on the Web site. This information can be valuable for customizing the site to the customer and also delivering more targeted offers. Because there are cost and other benefits of doing business on the Internet, organizations are attempting to drive their customers online. Although not all customers will convert to online purchasing, database enhancement and modeling techniques may be useful in segmenting those customers most likely to convert.

Review Questions

1. What are some of the types of data collected from online customers that are different from data collected from offline customers?

2. Discuss the characteristics of online buyers.

3. How is Web site effectiveness measured, and which of these measures are most important to online marketers?

4. Discuss the advantages of real-time databases.

5. Discuss the process of online testing.

6. Why are marketers attempting to move their customers online, and what are some of the methods marketers are using to do so?

17

Issues in the Marketing Environment and Future Trends In Marketing Databases

In Keri Lee's new role as corporate vice president of Inside Source, her decisions are more strategic in nature and undoubtedly have a longer-term effect on the organization. Her decisions in her previous position might involve segmenting the database to select names for a mailing or testing a new promotion. These decisions were short term. In her new position, she also is responsible for strategic decisions such as deciding to enter new markets or setting policies that would have a long-term effect on the database.

These decisions also include expanding into global markets and establishing policies for the acquisition and rental of databases. Keri had already started to examine international markets and saw an immediate potential for her product in Europe and a growing potential in other global markets. It was not a question of whether to expand into global markets—it was a question of how and when. She now had to develop strategies and tactics for moving into global markets. Much more information was needed on culture, language translations, local competition, distribution channels and laws, and especially laws related to direct marketing. She realized that other factors would also come into play as she moved through the process of introducing the product into global markets. Keri anticipated that she would need to include consultants' fees in the budget, because the company was inexperienced in international marketing.

The second issue—developing policies for data acquisition and database rental—is easier. One thing she has to decide is whether to have customers opt-in or opt-out on renting or trading their names to other marketers. With the opt-in policy, customers had to specifically indicate that they want to receive information from other marketers; otherwise, Inside Source would not sell the customer's name. With the opt-out policy, Inside Source would be able to sell names to other marketers unless their customers indicated that they did not want this to happen.

For e-mail marketing, Keri was almost certain that she would implement a strict opt-in policy. There was a growing movement, supported by several business and consumer groups, to eliminate unsolicited commercial e-mail. Personally, Keri did not like receiving commercial e-mails unless she specifically requested them. She knew that broadcast e-mail was relatively cheap, but she did not want the future of e-commerce to be a battle by consumers of filtering through possibly hundreds of e-mail messages. Although unsolicited broadcast e-mail might yield profits for the company, Keri was concerned about the social implications of this action.

Keri was leaning in the opposite direction on a policy for regular mail. Inside Source had purchased lists in the past from a number of sources, and Keri was sure that very few of the customers on those lists opted-in. Inside Source also rented lists of their customers. Inside Source's current policy was to assume that the customer's name could be rented unless the customer made a specific request to opt-out of other mailings. Even though some public interest groups are opposed to unsolicited traditional mail, there are not as many strong feelings against it as there is against unsolicited e-mail. Personally, Keri did not mind receiving unsolicited offers in the mail. Before making a final decision, Keri was going to again review information from consumer advocacy groups and industry organizations.

Marketers have to consider more than potential profitability when developing, maintaining, and utilizing databases. Global, social, and legal factors also need to be considered. Larger companies have long used databases for marketing to customers on a global level. More recently, smaller companies have been able to use databases to facilitate global marketing. Factors like increased accessibility to technology and the Internet have thrust these smaller organizations into the global arena. Although the implications of global marketing are complex, in this chapter we examine some of the factors that are particularly relevant to database marketers.

Database marketing has come under close public scrutiny in recent years. Public interest groups and governmental agencies have examined the database policies used by various organizations. This has come about because the growth of Internet commerce has raised concerns over how customer information is accessed and used. The security of databases is a concern sparked by the unauthorized access and use of personal information and credit card numbers. Traditional direct marketers who use mail and phone solicitations have also come under increased scrutiny. In particular, marketers who use sweepstakes promotions and target older consumers or children have become the focus of public advocacy, legislation, and litigation. In response to potential legislation, many in the industry have called for self-regulation. The Direct Marketing Association (DMA) has established a Privacy Promise for its membership. In this chapter, we examine privacy concerns from different perspectives.

The final section of this chapter is dedicated to future trends in marketing databases. For example, it is apparent that marketing on the Internet will show significant growth in both consumer and b-to-b markets. Because the marketing database is a fundamental element of Internet commerce, we examine the evolving role of the database in Internet marketing. In addition, database marketing has been expanding in a number of different business areas. We therefore examine the challenges database marketers face in these areas.

The Global Business Environment

As markets become saturated in the United States, companies must look to the **global business environment** and evaluate markets in other countries. Continued growth is dependent on global expansion, and for many organizations, significant revenues often come from multinational operations. For database marketers, global marketing means a database system that is integrated and synchronized across all countries in which companies operate. Dell Computer Corporation, for example, markets products directly to consumers and businesses in 170 countries and maintains sales offices in 34 countries. More than 30% of Dell's revenues come from other countries. Because 40% to 50% of sales are Web enabled, Dell requires an integrated database system that transcends national borders (Dell, 2001).

Inter-Continental Hotels and Resorts also uses a database that goes beyond U.S. borders. Inter-Continental tracks customer information from more than 100 hotels located in more than 60 countries. In an effort to build customer loyalty, Inter-Continental built a central data warehouse. One of the problems they have is matching data from customers as the data enter the database from different locations. For example, in an English-speaking location, a hotel employee would enter the home address of a particular customer as "London, England." However, the same customer's address entered in a hotel in a French-speaking country might be "Lundres, Angleterre." Because of the cultural/language factors, Inter-Continental relies heavily on numeric identifiers like credit card numbers and phone numbers to match guests correctly ("You say London," 1997). Inter-Continental currently has several programs that use the customer database to build relationships, including travel mileage and accommodation upgrade programs (see www.interconti.com). These relationship programs also transcend U.S. borders. Database marketers face unique challenges in global markets. In particular, the legal, political, and cultural environments in other countries may differ drastically in the area of consumer privacy. In many cases, the organization must radically change the way they do business as they move into other countries.

Exhibit 17.1 shows some of the factors that challenge database marketers in the global business environment.

We present a brief overview of each of these factors.

Culture includes values, customs, rituals, symbols, roles, language, and other aspects of society that are generally accepted by people in a country. The database marketer has to consider several elements of culture. On a general level, the marketer has to consider how consumers with a particular cultural background perceive database marketing. Privacy is more highly guarded in some countries; for example, countries of the European Union (EU) have more restrictions on how consumer data are used by organizations.

Numerous nuances of culture can affect database marketers. Latin Americans, for example, may be more serious and formal than people from other cultures, particularly when it comes to work. Therefore, using humor or cartoons in direct marketing communications to Latinos has to be done carefully or not at all. But with Latinos it could be beneficial to focus on status. A mailing that looks official or expensive is likely to receive more attention (Haegele, 2000).

Because some Asians feel that debt is a disgrace, credit card marketers have to be careful to communicate properly to them. Positioning the card

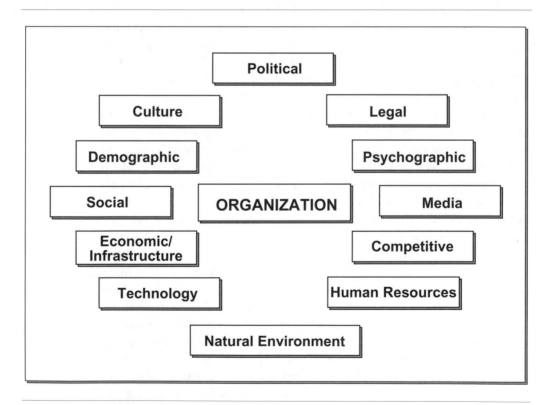

Exhibit 17.1   Forces in the Global Business Environment

as being safer than carrying cash or for use in emergency situations may overcome the initial negative attitudes. Because Asians in general like to read, a direct mail campaign might be appropriate. In addition, building relationships with Asians through multiple contacts is important. Marketers also have to be careful about overgeneralizations. Just as not all Latin Americans are alike, neither are Asians. The Chinese from Hong Kong are more savvy when it comes to credit cards than people from major cities in the People's Republic (Shermach, 1998).

Marketers also should consider whether shopping customs are consistent with direct channels that database marketers use. U.S. consumers have long embraced catalog shopping and are finding that shopping on the Internet is a logical transition. Credit cards are the common denominator in these transactions. Many Asian consumers, on the other hand, deal in cash sales, are less familiar with catalog shopping, and are worried about potential problems with credit card transactions. Furthermore, the social interaction of shopping, especially haggling, is more important in many countries than it is in the United States. Therefore, database marketers, who depend on credit card transactions and not face-to-face selling, have particular challenges when moving into some Asian countries (Schmit, 1999).

The *social* and cultural environments are interrelated. Societies have varying degrees of demarcation for individuals on the basis of heredity, wealth, education, occupation, and other factors. In some societies, social classes may be clearly defined, and social mobility (moving to other social classes) may be difficult because of prescribed class standing. Furthermore, it may be inappropriate for an individual to interact with people of a different social class. The roles of men, women, and children also vary from society to society, along with the influence of family members in purchase decision making. Therefore, it might be improper to target females in certain countries with offers for products that are considered primarily the responsibility of males (e.g., financial services and insurance).

The *legal* environment includes the laws and legal practices of a country at several levels—countrywide, state or regional, municipal, and religious. In addition, economic communities such as the EU have laws and regulations that affect database marketing in several European countries. At a very basic level, database marketers must comply with all relevant laws. In Mexico, for example, rental lists are sometimes acquired illegally from voter registration rolls and income tax records. Marketers must be sure that any list they use was obtained legally and that they have the right to use it (Sutter & Mandel-Campbell, 1998).

At another level, database marketers must be careful to avoid practices and policies that might move political action groups and legislatures to enact laws. The EU's Privacy Directive is currently a primary concern of many U.S. database marketers. The directive stipulates that companies may not transfer data from European citizens into countries that do not have privacy laws that are compatible with EU laws. The United States is currently not considered a safe harbor for data from customers in EU countries. Individual U.S. database marketers are hoping to negotiate safe harbor status with the EU pending their conformance to EU privacy standards.

One of the fundamental premises of EU privacy laws is to acquire specific expressed permission from consumers before data are used for other purposes. The favored policy in the EU is opt-in. In the United States, most marketers follow an opt-out policy, and it is assumed that marketers can use customer data for marketing purposes (e.g., rent a customer's name to another company) unless the customers request that their names not be given to other organizations. With the current political and social environment in the United States leaning toward more consumer control of personal data, some people in the industry are calling for database marketers to move to an opt-in policy before laws are enacted and there is no choice. (Orr, 2000).

In some countries, laws restrict access to consumer information that is important for efficient database marketing. In the United Kingdom, for example, access to the electoral roll is restricted. This roll has been valuable to direct marketers as a data-cleaning tool, because it contains updated records of personal details. Without access to this database, direct marketers have difficulty keeping databases up to date (Gordon, 2001).

Direct marketers must also be aware of legal processes and procedures especially as they relate to gray areas in the law. A foreign organization may not have the same flexibility in certain legal processes as would a domestic organization. This often means obtaining legal representation or consultation in the country of concern.

Demographics includes a number of variables that we have discussed throughout this book such as gender, age, income, family status, and residence. As in the domestic market, the database marketer has to determine the fit between a country's demographics and potential market offerings. In contrast to other countries, the United States has a population with a higher percentage of older people. In some developing countries, most of the people are under 20 years of age, but in the United States there are more people over the age of 35 than under 35. The database marketer should be aware that nonsegmented demographics may be misleading. For example, countries such as China, Brazil, and India with low median incomes may have sizable affluent segments that may be potential customers for higher-priced products.

Although culture refers to generally accepted values, customs, rituals, norms, and so on, *psychographics* refers to activities, interests, and opinions (AIO) of segments of a country's population. Psychographics may be more important than culture or demographics in evaluating marketing potential.

The AIO of a segment of a society may be in conflict with culture. For example, nonmaterialism may be a cultural component of a country such as India. However, as we just mentioned, sizable segments of the population may be more oriented to Western consumerism and luxury products. Database marketers should consider the potential of these segments but may have to adjust the positioning and pricing of luxury items consistent with the culture (Mistry, 1996).

There are obvious implications of activities and interest variables. A database marketer who offers gardening tools and supplies should look at the number of people in a country who report that interest. AIO may be derived from a number of sources. For example, if direct reports of interest in a particular area are not available for a particular country, the marketer may be able to estimate interest based on membership in interest groups or subscriptions to publications in the interest area.

As with the domestic market, evaluation of the *competitive environment* in global markets is essential. Does an existing company currently have a firm hold on a market in a foreign country that you are considering? For example, in Germany, the retailer Galeria/Kaufhof is a division of Metro AG, one of the world's largest retailers. Galeria/Kaufhof sells directly to consumers and through brick and mortar locations. Their product assortment is very broad, ranging from wine to watches. Direct marketers considering selling watches in Germany would have to evaluate the challenges that a competitor like Galeria/Kaufhof would impose on their marketing efforts. On a strategic level, marketers have to consider factors such as company resources, product assortment, target markets, positioning, reputation, and customer loyalty of the competitors. On the tactical level, a native competitor may have strong relationships not only with customers but also with suppliers. For direct marketers, establishing relationships with list brokers, mail shops, fulfillment centers, and other suppliers is important to operate efficiently. Native competitors often have an advantage in these areas.

The *economic environment* includes a number of elements, including employment levels, cost of living, exchange rates, inflation, and poverty levels. The infrastructure component encompasses communications and transportation. A country with economic data that is inconsistent with domestic economic data (e.g., extent of infrastructure development) may still be a reasonable candidate for market entry. However, database marketers need to make appropriate adjustments (e.g., alternative distribution systems) when approaching these markets. For example, adjustments need to be made if transportation channels are inadequate. Some more perishable items may require packaging changes or may not be able to be sold at all. In the United States, a responsive distribution system can move products across the country in a matter of hours if necessary. This is not the case in many developing countries.

Political environments and forms of governments vary widely. In particular, political instability (e.g., Pakistan, Russia) can offer an unknown element to the marketer. The legal and political environments are interrelated. Although certain practices may be technically legal in a country, government policies may make them impractical to implement (e.g., obtaining appropriate permits). Direct investment in a country, as compared to less risky operations such as exporting, should be evaluated in terms of political and economic stability. Setting up database facilities within a country can constitute a substantial investment. The database marketer must evaluate how current and potential future governments might react to the organization's initiative in the country.

Human resources include employee expertise, employee recruitment, and employment policies. Database marketing requires technical and marketing expertise. If these experts do not exist in the country, the organizations must consider alternatives such as employee relocation, training, or operating the business from another location. Companies like Allstate Insurance have established international technology centers in Ireland because of the available pool of well-educated programmers and computer technicians ("Allstate Unit," 1998).

The *technological environment* involves all aspects of technology (hardware, software, communication links, peripherals, etc.) related to database development and maintenance. Human resources are also involved in the technology area, because trained professionals are an essential component of database technology. The cornerstone of direct/interactive marketing is the computerized database. If access to database technology is limited within the country of concern, then the organization will need to make adaptations. Competent servicing, repair, and maintenance within the country are necessary. If they are not available, the organization must make adaptations. Sometimes the adaptation means housing the technology in another country and using only minimum services in the target country.

Although the *natural environment* has less of an effect on businesses in developed countries, it may have a significant impact on businesses in lesser-developed countries. Weather conditions, topography, pollution levels, and so on can affect business. Technology may interact with the natural environment and infrastructure. Sophisticated computer systems often require controlled environments. If weather conditions are extreme (e.g., high temperature, humidity), the environmental control systems must be reliable enough to avoid major system failures. In addition, the marketer must determine if media and distribution channels are susceptible to seasonal disruptions (hurricanes, floods, snow, etc.).

Media for database marketers are the means of communication such as mail, print, telephone, TV, radio, and the Internet. In some developing countries, mail delivery is inefficient and telephone service may be inconsistent. Even if mail and phone services are adequate, it may be difficult to find appropriate lists. Database marketing is growing significantly in Brazil, but direct marketers face several challenges. The quality of the names on list rentals is poor, mail service is inefficient, and phone service is inconsistent (Sutter & Mandel-Campbell, 1998). Despite these problems, companies like Lloyds and Citibank invest in direct marketing programs in Brazil. These companies believe that the risk is outweighed by the strong potential growth (Molloy, 1997).

Cultural and lifestyle characteristics interact with media. In the United Kingdom, for example, a majority of the population read national daily and Sunday papers. The weekly reach for all commercial radio there is 60% of the population. Free-standing inserts are popular in Europe and Japan. Radio and TV are significant media channels in Germany (Yorgey, 1998). The key questions regarding media and global marketing involve the appropriateness of available media for reaching targets, the organization's compatibility with the media, and how the database interfaces with the media.

Social Concerns and Ethics in Database Marketing

Database marketers must be concerned with how their actions affect various segments of society. These segments include not only customers but also prospective customers, public interest groups, regulatory bodies, and lawmakers. There are long-term implications if the actions of organizations elicit a negative response from these segments. For example, the way in which some companies used sweepstakes promotions elicited a negative public reaction and legislation that affected the entire industry.

Exhibit 17.2 shows areas of concern for database marketers.

At the base of the pyramid, marketer have more concrete guidelines for marketing actions. For example, according to FCC regulations, there is a ban on the use of fax machines to send an "unsolicited advertisement" (47 U.S.C. ß 227 (b)(1)(C); 47 C.F.R. ß 64.1200(a)(3)). If direct marketers violate laws, the penalties are a clear motivation to keep company practices within the legal boundaries.

As we move up the pyramid, the motivation for avoiding or implementing a particular practice becomes less clear. When the political situation is prone to enacting legislation, direct marketers are often motivated to change their practices. Most of the time, an industry organization such as the DMA spearheads efforts to have the industry regulate itself before laws are enacted. The DMA's Privacy Promise, which we present later in this chapter, is a self-regulation effort. Certain practices can have negative effects on some segments of society. These segments may not have the size or political power to directly affect the political environment. However, over time, public policy groups may adopt the cause of this segment.

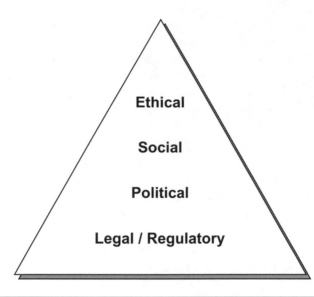

Exhibit 17.2   Areas of Concern for Database Marketers

Children, for example, don't have direct political power, so children's groups have adopted the cause of protecting children from certain types of database marketing.

Legislative action may have been taken on sweepstakes promotion because of the political power of a social group. Older citizens have higher voting rates than other groups, and therefore legislators are more likely to heed their concerns. The American Association of Retired Persons (AARP) has taken on the cause of protecting its members from fraudulent marketing practices and viewed certain sweepstakes practices as a major problem. Legislators heard testimony from directors of AARP and eventually enacted laws that are intended to protect older citizens and others from practices that were interpreted to be deceptive or misleading.

The Honesty in Sweepstakes Act includes the following provisions:

- There must be clear and conspicuous statements in the mailing, rules, and order forms indicating that no purchase is necessary to enter the sweepstakes and a purchase will not increase the odds of winning.
- The mailing must not claim that someone is a winner unless the individual is actually a winner.
- The rules must contain a description of the prizes and the odds of winning.
- An address or toll-free number must be included in the sweepstakes mailing, allowing a recipient or their assignees to prevent future mail sweepstakes promotions.

In an effort to strengthen relationships with consumers, governmental agencies, and public interest groups, the DMA established a Sweepstakes Helpline. The purpose of the Helpline is to educate consumers about legitimate versus fraudulent sweepstakes and offer assistance in directing complaints and name removal requests to marketers. From the perspective of database maintenance, these laws require a higher level of vigilance to ensure that consumers who do not wish to receive mailings are properly flagged in the database.

It might be beneficial in the long term to become responsive to the feedback from social groups before the issue moves into the political arena. This is a much more difficult task for the direct marketer, because the concerns of these groups have not been clearly represented. On the top of the pyramid are ethical concerns. Marketing practices exist that might not elicit social, political, or regulatory actions, but these practices might be questionable from another perspective. For example, direct marketers have made mail pieces look like official government documents. Although there is nothing illegal about this practice and it is not currently eliciting a large public reaction, some people think the practice is deceptive. Consumers open the mail because it looks like an important document, and when they realize it is an offer for a product, some consumers become angry. These negative sentiments do not help the image of the industry.

As times change, issues can shift downward on the pyramid. For example, questionable (deceptive) sweepstakes techniques that were once used with little controversy evolved through social, political, and legal arenas. These techniques are now susceptible to legal action.

The issue of ethics in direct marketing is complex. Most legitimate organizations emphatically state that they do not fraudulently take money from consumers, but there are some gray areas. For instance, is it ethical to deceive people into thinking that an envelope contains a check or is from a governmental agency so they will open the envelope and review the offer? Is it ethical to give consumers the impression that their subscription is about to expire so that the company can get an early renewal and hold the consumer's money longer to gain interest earnings on it? Is it ethical to use a contrived "survey" to solicit donations by attempting to manipulate attitudes with biased questions? Is it ethical to send e-mail offers to prospects and make it difficult or inconvenient for the prospects to remove their names from the mailing list? These are practices that are used by direct marketers that some people would argue are unethical.

In addition, something that may be considered negative by a particular group would not be considered a general threat to society. For example, because credit risk classification is often based on aggregate rather than individual data, some direct marketers restrict offers to people in certain zip codes. An analysis of their house data indicates that there is a higher likelihood that people within the zip code will default on payment. Therefore, these people are not given the same credit terms that people in other areas receive. Although this practice makes good financial sense for the business, some people believe the practice is discriminatory, because "bad risk" zip code areas can have a high proportion of certain minority groups. Furthermore, an individual consumer in a bad risk zip code with a good credit rating will be lumped in with others. Some would argue that this practice is unfair.

Industry Organizations

Industry organizations perform important functions within an industry. For example, the DMA helps in these ways:

♦ Represents the interests of industry members to the public and to governmental agencies
     A key goal is to promote self-regulation through the establishment of guidelines for accepted practices.
♦ Promotes education in the industry by sponsoring conferences and workshops
     The Direct Marketing Educational Foundation specifically services college students and professors.
♦ Conducts research on the state of the industry.
♦ Acts as an intermediary for the collection of names of consumers who do not wish to be contacted by direct marketers.
♦ The DMA's Privacy Promise (see Exhibit 17.3) was developed as a means to promote the adherence of members to certain privacy practices and applies to both consumer marketers and suppliers.

Industry organizations are concerned about privacy protection for a good reason. A study conducted by Voter/Consumer Research for the Association for Competitive Technology (Bremner, 2001) indicated that 76% of the consumers polled said privacy protection is a priority with them. Relative to other social issues, privacy protection ranked seventh out of nine in the following group: education, crime, health care, energy, social security, Medicare, privacy protection, national defense, tax cuts.

Without industry initiatives, legislation is more likely, but in some cases, industry initiatives are not considered adequate. For example, Congress is considering more legislation to protect the privacy of students; the legislation would have an impact on direct marketers who target families with school-age children (Campbell, 2001).

Another industry organization, the Electronic Retailing Association (ERA), has set guidelines for telemarketing. Members of the ERA, including organizations such as J. C. Penney and QVC, are asked to adhere to

Exhibit 17.3   Direct Marketing Association Privacy Promise

Privacy Promise Member Compliance Guide

Consumer Marketer's Promise

I certify that my company:

(please initial)

Provides customers with notice of their ability to opt out of information rental, sale or exchange. _____

Honors customer opt-out requests not to have their contact information transferred to others for marketing purposes. _____

Honors consumer requests for in-house suppress to stop receiving solicitations from our company._____

Uses The DMA Preference Service suppression files, which now exist for mail, telephone lists, and e-mail lists. _____

Supplier's Promise

I certify that my company:

(please initial)

Encourages our Consumer Marketer customers to comply with the DMA Privacy Promise. _____

Business to Business, Resident/Occupant, International

I certify that my company is exempted from the Privacy Promise. _____

This certifies that the below named company is in full compliance with the Privacy Promise, as described in the Privacy Promise Member Compliance Guide, receipt of which is hereby acknowledged. By my signature, I certify that I have personally reviewed the company's practices that are subject to the Privacy Promise, and that I am my company's designated contact authorized to make this certification of compliance on behalf of the below named company.

Source: © Direct Marketing Association. Used by permission.

guidelines on billing practices, disclosure of information to consumers, privacy, and the use of certain communication technologies.

Sometimes industry organizations advocate different positions on issues. For example, the Internet Direct Marketing Bureau (IDMB) developed guidelines for e-mail marketing that identify spam as being rude and irresponsible. IDMB endorsed a strict opt-in policy for compiling mailing lists. For example, a consumer who has recently made a purchase on the Internet would have to check a box on a registration form before marketers could send marketing information to the consumer or share the consumer's e-mail address with other marketers.

The DMA, on the other hand, currently advocates an opt-out policy for e-mail marketing. However, all DMA members who wish to send unsolicited commercial e-mail are required to purge their e-mail lists of individuals who have registered with a DMA service called the E-Mail Preference Service (EMPS). EMPS puts individuals on a list if they do not wish to receive unsolicited commercial e-mail.

Industry organizations in various areas of database marketing are facing substantial challenges in light of public and legislative attitudes toward consumer privacy and marketing fraud. On one hand, these organizations do not want to place unreasonable burdens on the businesses of their members by establishing policies or guidelines that require substantial resources or restrict productive business practices. On the other hand, if the public and legislatures do not feel that the self-regulation efforts are sufficient, the possibility of more stringent legislation increases.

Exhibit 17.4 is a letter to Congress from NetCoalition, an industry organization that seeks self-regulation of the Internet in the areas of privacy and database protection.

As you can see from the letter, if legislation is necessary, NetCoalition is seeking narrow versus broad approaches to strike a balance between public concerns and restrictions on companies in the industry.

Evolution and Trends in Database Marketing

Throughout this book, we have attempted to provide examples of marketing databases that reflect a wide range of industries and product categories. With the advent of new technologies and markets, the application of marketing databases will grow. Although it is not feasible here to review all applications of marketing databases, we summarize below some of the key trends of the major categories. Note that the categories are not mutually exclusive, that is, an organization in the b-to-b or not-for-profit market can offer services.

Consumer Databases and the Internet

The growth of consumer databases for Internet marketing will be substantial as more consumer purchases come from Internet sites. Analysis techniques will have to be developed to respond specifically to this emerging market. At least two categories of analyses are emerging, one for identified customers and another for unidentified customers or visitors to the Web site. Many Internet databases have a unique characteristic not found in databases built for other media: customers directly enter data into Internet databases. The data entered sometimes include psychographic data in addition to contact information. The advantage to these **customer-initiated databases** is that the databases may reflect a stronger affinity to the brand or product category relative to databases (lists) that are derived from other indirect sources.

Exhibit 17.4   Political Action Letter

February 7, 2000
United States House of Representatives
Washington, DC 20515
Dear :

In the coming weeks, you may be asked to cast a vote on H.R. 354, the "Collections of Information Antipiracy Act." As the House of Representatives contemplates the issue of database protection, the members of NetCoalition.com—an Internet industry trade group whose members include Amazon.com, AOL, Inktomi, Yahoo!, Lycos, and Excite@Home—ask you to only support legislation that balances reasonable protection with the equally important objective of allowing the free flow of information and the legitimate access to information that are the cornerstones of the Internet.

We are concerned that H.R. 354 does not strike the appropriate balance and therefore poses undue risks to the future growth of the Internet. NetCoalition.com has endorsed an alternative, H.R. 1858, the "Consumer and Investor Access to Information Act of 1999," as introduced by Representatives Bliley, Dingell, Tauzin, Markey, Oxley and Towns and would prefer strongly that Congress support this approach.

NetCoalition.com includes some of the largest creators and publishers of databases. These companies recognize the concerns of database proprietors who object to theft and dissemination of their databases.

However, we also recognize that one of the Internet's greatest values lies in its ability to provide efficient access to information gathered from a multitude of disparate sources. Consumers can use the Internet to find airline fares and schedules, music and movie reviews, sports statistics and results, stock quotes, research and analysis, and restaurant information. Overly broad protection for compilations of information could lead to claims that Internet data collection is unlawful, threatening the very Internet activity that consumers have found so beneficial.

In considering this issue, it is worth noting that current law already provides effective means to prevent database theft. Copyright law provides remedies against those who engage in the copying of databases. Contract law allows proprietors to impose limitations on the misuse of information. Technologies exist to prevent unlawful access to collections. Further, federal and state laws prohibiting unauthorized access to servers linked to the Internet are already on the books. If Congress decides that additional database protection is needed, that remedy should be narrowly crafted to address specific problems. We believe that H.R. 1858 meets this test, achieving the necessary balance between protection and availability of information. Unfortunately, other database legislation pending in Congress will not achieve that critical balance.

We appreciate your attention to this matter. Please let us know if we can provide further information or answer any of your questions.

Sincerely,
Daniel Ebert
Executive Director

Source: Reprinted by permission of NetCoalition.

A challenge for many direct marketers is to integrate the database across media, so that transactions can be tracked regardless of where they originate (e.g., mail, telephone, Internet, brick and mortar). The benefits of integrated databases to the marketer are substantial; one of them is being able to track changes in how the consumer wishes to receive information from the company. From the consumer's perspective, the integrated database allows consumers to buy on the company's Web site and pick up or return merchandise at a local store.

Another trend in consumer databases is the promise of better data analysis. Advances in statistical methodology and computer technology should help marketers, using a broad range of direct marketing media, to develop more efficient and effective marketing programs. Data and reports should be easier to access, and newer analysis techniques may be able to uncover and categorize meaningful complex behavior patterns on the Internet.

B-to-B Databases

In the business market, marketing databases fall into the area of customer relationship management (CRM). CRM software is a growing product category, and some estimates predict a continuation of a 50% annual growth rate (Trepper, 2000). Compared to consumer databases, b-to-b databases are usually smaller and require different analysis techniques. Some of the challenges for b-to-b databases are in the area of real-time access to the database by multiple people within the organization. For example, an account manager on the road needs to have access to the database to offer a customized proposal to a customer. At the same time, a reorder of a standard component needs to be recorded in the database at the home office by inside salespeople. Furthermore, with the enormous growth in b-to-b Internet transactions, an order or inquiry placed on the Internet needs to be recorded on the database.

Not-for-Profit Databases

In an increasingly competitive environment, not-for-profit organizations will become more dependent on good database development, maintenance, and analysis. Organizations such as hospitals will use database segmentation techniques to develop targeted relationship programs with groups of patients and prospective patients. Not-for-profits that are targeting donors may have to develop new analysis techniques to maximize communications with likely donors. Techniques that have proven valuable for consumer product marketing such as RFM (recency, frequency, and monetary value) may have to be modified for the not-for-profit market. For example, recent major donors may feel that the charitable organization is overly demanding or unappreciative if they receive numerous solicitations during the year. This approach might negatively affect the long-term relationship with these donors.

The challenge for not-for-profit organizations is to develop relevant analysis techniques within tight budgetary restrictions. Because of the unique relationships that are established between charitable organizations and its constituents, new models may need to be developed to maximize the effectiveness and efficiency of marketing programs. In the case of most charitable organizations, the offer leaves the "price" open for the donor to decide. Therefore, response to offers in yes or no terms may not be the best way to analyze the data. Charitable organizations may need to use survey data to a greater degree in order to explore a variety of issues or approaches that would maximize donation levels.

Retailer Databases

Retailers have been collecting an enormous amount of data for a number of years. In particular, store cards used by supermarkets allow retailers to track shopping patterns of individual customers. Translating the data into meaningful information for marketing programs has been a challenge for retailers. Many retailers don't have the capability to successfully mine the scanner data, but a few applications have emerged. For example, a South Carolina supermarket chain is using the customer database to reward customers for past purchases. Customers swipe their card at a kiosk, check their balance, and receive certificates for free products. A Wisconsin supermarket chain uses transaction data from store cards to personalize shopping lists mailed to members of a loyalty program (Lach, 1999).

Service Organization Databases

The U.S. economy is becoming more service based. Most new businesses are services. Because many service organizations must be responsive to individual needs of customers, databases have become a critical element for developing customer relationships. Databases for service organizations may include a unique set of customer preferences and requirements (e.g., room and service preference for a hotel chain, style characteristics for a home designer's customers, patient illnesses and medications).

Databases with these types of variables that are more qualitative than quantitative may require different analysis techniques. Software is available to examine the unstructured data (e.g., open-ended questions about service needs) that might be collected from customers seeking customized services.

Chapter Summary

Database marketers have to be attentive to a variety of issues in the marketing environment. Few organizations can ignore the globalization of markets, but the challenges of global database marketing are substantial. The organization needs to be aware of all the implications of using databases for marketing purposes in other countries. In particular, marketers have to be responsive to the legal and cultural environments in the target country.

In recent years, database marketers have become the target of public interest groups, legislators, and litigation. Within this environment, it is not sufficient for marketers just to adhere to the letter of the law. They have to examine how public interest groups and legislators are going to respond to their actions. Industry organizations such as the DMA have established guidelines in a number of areas that have an impact on consumers. The goal of industry organizations is to maintain a code of conduct through self-regulation rather than through legislation.

In the final section of this chapter, we examine some of the trends in database marketing. With advances in technology, more organizations will be collecting customer data. The growth of commerce on the Internet will fuel the development of many of these databases. In addition, because of the need for organizations, including not-for-profits, to become more effective and efficient, marketing database development and analysis will increasingly be a mechanism to achieve that goal. The challenge for organizations is to transform the data into information that assists business decision making.

Review Questions

1. Why are organizations moving into global markets?

2. Discuss the variables that database marketers have to consider in the global environment.

3. With regard to ethics and public perceptions, what are the internal and external influencing groups?

4. What is an industry organization, and what are their primary goals?

5. What are some of the current public policy concerns of database marketing organizations?

6. Discuss some of the future trends that will affect database marketing.

Glossary _____

address standardization   The process by which direct marketers clean up the addresses contained on their database. This process uses CASS-certified software, which is required to qualify for certain postal rate discounts.

aggregate marketing   A method to reach customers through mass media and traditional retail distribution channels that does not depend on data from individual customers but rather aggregated level statistics and information.

analysis sample/data set   A portion of the sample of customers on a database upon which the analysis for determining the target market is performed. Typically, the portion of the sample upon which the analysis will be conducted represents two thirds of the total sample. The other one third is held out for validation (see validation sample).

attributes   Customer information relating to purchase, promotion, demographics, and psychographics. Attributes are also known as data fields or variables.

banner ad   Online advertising that usually appears as graphic images. When banner ads are clicked on, the user will often be taken to another Web location.

batch processing   A method of data processing usually used by organizations with large databases on tasks that require substantial computer memory and processing capabilities. Batch processing occurs offline, and therefore the changes are not made immediately to the database but rather are made at periodic set schedules (e.g., biweekly, weekly, monthly).

binary data   Data that are discrete and only take on two values. For example, the variable "own home" can either take on the value of yes or no.

block groups   Subdivisions of census tracts formed by grouping blocks (streets). There are approximately 225,000 block groups.

bootstrapping   A method of building a stable regression model when adequate sample sizes are not available. This technique is also referred to as bagging.

breakeven response rate   The response rate required in which all promotional costs are covered and no profit is realized.

brick and mortar retailing   Retailers who have physical locations.

cannibalism   A situation that occurs when sales of a company's current product base are taken away by the introduction of new products.

CASS   U.S. Postal Service Coding Accuracy Support System-certified software used in the process of standardizing addresses on a database.

categorical variables   Data that take on a finite (countable) number of values and are descriptive in nature with no meaning relative to one another. For example, "car type" is categorical and may take on values such as 1 = Sedan, 2 = SUV, 3 = Compact.

census data   Data gathered by the government every 10 years that includes average or median income levels, home values, and so on, within each zip code, block group, and/or census tract.

census tracts   Subdivisions of counties as defined by the U.S. government. Today there are approximately 50,000 census tracts.

CHAID (Chi-squared Automatic Interaction Detection)   A statistical method of determining statistically meaningful splits in various data fields or variables. It is also sometimes referred to as a tree algorithm.

clicks and bricks   Organizations that have traditional physical outlets (retail stores) and are also involved in Internet commerce.

clicks and mortar   See **clicks and bricks**.

clickstream   The sequence of clicks or pages requested as a visitor explores a Web site.

clickstream data   The data collected by organizations to determine the sequences or paths that visitors take as they explore a Web site.

clone models   A regression model that is built for the specific purpose of identifying prospects on an outside list who look like your best customers. Such models are also called best customer models or match models.

coefficient of determination   With respect to regression modeling, it is the measure between 0 and +1 that tells you the percentage of variation in the response variable explained by the introduction of the predictor variables.

coefficients   The weights associated with each of the predictor variables in a regression model.

compiled list data   Lists of people or organizations gathered from telephone directories, voter registration files, membership rosters, department of motor vehicles, surveys, and so on.

computer network   A system of connecting computers and peripheral devices together with software and hardware. Networks can help improve the effectiveness and efficiency of marketing activities by allowing quick access to relevant data.

confidence interval calculation   A statistical technique that reveals, based on a test, a range in which the true response rate in rollout is likely to fall.

continuous variables   Variables that can take on any value within a range of values. Typically, the values of the variable have some meaning relative to one another. Examples include age, ratios, product paid counters, average cellular minutes per month.

cookie   Computer code that is placed on the visitor's hard drive by a Web site so that each time the visitor returns to that Web site, they can be recognized and tracked.

correlation analysis   A statistical procedure used to determine the strength of association between any two variables.

correlation coefficient   A value between −1 and +1 that reflects the strength and direction of a relationship between two variables.

cross-tabulation   A tabulation displaying two or more data elements in combination, highlighting interrelationships among variables.

customer contact data   The data necessary for a company to reach a customer (e.g., name, address, phone and fax numbers, e-mail address).

customer-initiated database   A database in which the customer has initiated the relationship by contacting the marketer, rather than the marketer attempting to initiate the relationship through mail or telephone contact.

database   A collection of information related to a particular subject or purpose that is usually maintained on a computer for easy search, retrieval, and analysis.

database integration   Systems for synchronizing and coordinating databases across different media (e.g., mail, Internet, retail).

database management system   Software and hardware that allow information to be created, modified, and accessed more efficiently.

database marketing   Marketing activities (e.g., selecting prospective customers) that use a marketing database.

data enhancement   A process by which external data are "overlaid" or appended to an existing database such as a house file for the purpose of understanding more about customers and increasing the effectiveness of marketing programs.

data fields   See **attributes**.

data mart   A repository of data designed to serve a particular community of knowledge workers. In scope, the data may derive from an enterprisewide database or data warehouse or be more specialized. The emphasis of a data mart is on meeting the specific demands of a particular group of knowledge users in terms of analysis, content, presentation, and ease of use. Users of a data mart can expect to have data presented in terms that are familiar.

data mining   The process of identifying previously unknown relationships and patterns in data, in particular customer databases, in order to solve a business problem.

decoy records   Owners of databases often include names in the file that are not real customers (decoys) to check how the mailing files are being handled by outside service bureaus or renters of a list.

deduping the customer file   The process by which direct marketers identify duplicate customer records and combine and eliminate them from the database or mailing file.

demographics   Characteristics such as gender, age, income, family characteristics, and occupation that are used to describe and segment customers.

dependent variable   In regression modeling, this is what we are trying to predict (e.g., response, payment). This variable is also called the response variable.

direct marketing   An interactive system of marketing that uses one or more advertising media to effect a measurable response and/or transaction at any location, with this activity stored on the database.

Direct Marketing Association (DMA)   A professional organization that serves the direct marketing industry by providing educational programs, research about the industry, privacy and other guidelines, political support for critical issues. They can be found at www.the-dma.org.

discount rate   The net present value (NPV) of an investment adjusts returns on that investment by a certain percentage rate (discount rate) to reflect its true value in today's money.

discrete variables   Similar to categorical variables in that they take on only a very finite and countable number of values, but in this case the values themselves have some meaning relative to one another. Examples include number of children and number of cars owned.

diversification strategy   The process of moving into new markets with new products. Testing the new products on a selected database of potential customers may be a way to reduce diversification risk.

DMA Preference Services   A voluntary program used by many direct marketers to purge their files of individuals who requested that their names be removed from direct marketing databases. There are preference services for mail, e-mail, and telephone databases.

dry testing   Making a mock offer to determine the extent of the demand for a product prior to finalizing product development. There are legal constraints on how the mock offers can be worded to make consumers aware that the product may not be available.

e-commerce (electronic commerce)   Business activity (e.g., buying, selling, communicating, servicing) that uses electronic media such as the Internet.

e-mail (electronic mail)   Used for communicating on the Internet.

E-Mail Preference Service (E-MPS)   A list of names maintained by the DMA of people who prefer not to receive promotional offers via e-mail.

encryption   Data-coding techniques used to protect files and individual records from unauthorized use. Almost all e-commerce companies use encryption as a means of protecting sensitive customer data.

enhancement data   Customer information gathered by outside sources such as compiled, response, and modeled data. Also known as external data.

expected profit   A value derived by combining one's likelihood of ordering and paying with the dollar values associated with such actions.

external data   See **enhancement data**.

factor analysis   A statistical analysis method that determines the factors or constructs that underlie the data and reveals relationships that are not easily observable. It is also know as principal components analysis or PCA.

factors   The unique groups of customer data elements determined by factor analysis based on patterns observed.

frequency data   Customer data related to a customer's total number of promotions, orders, payments, and so on.

frozen file   A sample used to determine the unique characteristics that distinguish responders from nonresponders. On such a file, the characteristics of each customer is reflective of how they looked at the time the promotion was sent.

fulfillment data   Data relating to the fulfillment of a customer order or other activity (e.g., "date of product shipment" is a fulfillment data element).

fulfillment file   The file containing all customer fulfillment data. All direct marketers must have a fulfillment file or database to conduct business.

full factorial test design   When conducting marketing tests with several package elements, sometimes a direct marketer is interested in assessing every possible package configuration. Doing so is called a full factorial test design.

gains chart   A table or graph showing the expected response of groups of customers to an offer based on a predictive model. Individual customers are scored according to the predictive model, and the file is sorted, usually into 10 groups or deciles, each representing 10% of the total sample.

geo-demographic data   A classification of customers based on where they live. Where a customer lives may be predictive of purchase patterns.

global business environment   The process of evaluating potential markets in other countries.

hardware   The physical equipment that holds the database. Hardware includes processors, storage devices, input and output devices, and components that link devices together in networks.

hot-line lists   Lists of customers who have recently responded (e.g., within the last 90 days) to some type of offer.

house data   Internal or house data is data obtained from sources within the organization. For example, customer contact data, past purchase records, product returns data, and customer services data all constitute house data.

house file   A database of existing customers that usually contains extensive house or internal data regarding responses to past marketing programs. External demographic and psychographic data may also be included in the file.

householding the customer file   The process by which a direct marketer identifies individuals on the customer database residing at the same address for purposes of obtaining promotional efficiencies.

hypothesis test   A statistical technique used to determine if a particular test response rate has beaten the control response rate.

independent variables   In regression modeling, these are what we call the variables or data elements that are being used to predict response, payment, and so on. Such variables are also called predictor variables.

interactive marketing   Often used interchangeably with direct marketing.

internal data   Customer data collected internally on customers, including all contact, promotion, order, and monetary data. Also see **house data**.

Internet service provider (ISP)   An organization that provides customers access to the Internet.

key codes   Codes that indicate which individuals received particular marketing programs. Key codes allow marketers to evaluate the performance of each marketing program.

legacy systems   Database systems that are many years old, often spanning decades. These systems are updated on a regular basis, but they are not state-of-the-art database systems. To convert the entire system over to a state-of-the-art system would be either too expensive or too disruptive for the business.

lifetime value (LTV)   The value today of future profits from customers. LTV is used to determine the return to the company for making an investment in gaining new customers, specific marketing programs, and product lines.

lifetime value (LTV) analysis   The methods used to determine the return to the company for making an investment in gaining new customers, specific marketing programs, and product lines.

logic counter variables   A variable that represents how many of a certain criteria are met by each customer. For example, a count could be created representing the total number of music genres each customer checked on a survey.

logistic regression   A different form of regression modeling that yields a true probability of the customer taking a specific action (e.g., respond, pay, renew).

longitudinal or time series variables   Variables that allow direct marketers to view a particular data element for each customer across time. For example, one way to estimate a customer's action on the next promotion sent may be to examine the customer's response (order, pay, silent, etc.) to the last three promotions sent to them.

LTV   See **lifetime value.**

Mail Preference Service (MPS)   A list of names maintained by the DMA of people who prefer not to receive promotional material by mail.

manual selects   A simple definition of the target market typically based on two or three key customer characteristics. For example, selecting customers from the database that are single, female, and age 30–50 would be considered a manual select.

market development strategy   The offering of existing products to new markets. A database of customers in other markets could be acquired to test the potential of a product in those markets.

marketing data   Any piece of customer information such as past purchase information used by marketers for the purpose of increasing the effectiveness or efficiencies of marketing activities.

marketing database   A file or group of files containing information about customers that enhances the marketing process. With current technology, the database is stored, manipulated, and analyzed on a computer.

marketing objectives   Quantitative and time-specified targets for business and marketing activities. Objectives may be specified for sales volume, profitability, market share, brand awareness, intensity of distribution, and so on.

marketing planning   A process that includes performing a situational analysis of markets, specifying marketing objectives, developing marketing strategies, implementing tactics (marketing programs), and monitoring and controlling the process.

marketing strategy   The longer-term direction to influence customers and achieve marketing objectives. It involves developing products to meet customer needs and positioning products (i.e., communicating about benefits) to target segments.

marketing tactics   The specific actions (or programs) to implement the marketing strategy. Each element of the marketing mix (promotion, price, distribution, product) should be considered in the development of tactics.

market penetration strategy   Increasing product use for existing customers or noncustomers with similar profiles. A database may assist in reaching existing customers in a more efficient and effective manner.

match code   A number and letter code that uses elements of a name and address to develop a unique identifier of an individual or household on a database.

match coding   The process by which match codes are assigned to each customer record for purposes of deduping or householding the customer file.

m-commerce (mobile commerce)   The marketing of goods and services through wireless handheld devices such as cellular telephones and personal digital assistants (PDAs).

merge/purge processing   The process of deduping mailing lists associated with an outside list campaign and purging the duplicate records.

modeled data   Data generated from statistical analysis such as customer clustering according to demographic, psychographic, or past purchase data.

monetary data   Customer data related to a customer's total dollar value of orders placed, payments made, and so on.

monitor and control   Comparing actual performance with marketing objectives and making adjustments to aspects of the marketing plan as needed. If performance does not reach objectives at specific milestones, the program or strategy may be modified.

multicollinearity   Problem that occurs when building a multiple regression model in which strong correlations between the predictor variables exist. Such a problem can lead to an unstable model.

multiple logistic regression   A different form of regression modeling that yields a true probability of the customer taking a specific action (e.g., respond, pay, renew).

multiple regression   A statistical method that builds a predictive equation or model based on the "best fit" between a dependent and one or more independent variables.

multivariate analysis   A statistical technique that reveals unusual and not readily apparent relationships in the customer data. Types include factor analysis, cluster analysis, and discriminate analysis.

NCOA (National Change of Address)   A U.S. Postal Service-approved service that updates address changes and removes nondeliverable mail from direct marketing files. NCOA maintenance must be conducted for certain special postal discounts.

negative correlation   A relationship in which higher values of one variable are associated with lower values of another variable.

net present value (NPV)   The net present value of an investment adjusts returns on that investment by a certain percentage rate (discount rate) to reflect its true value in today's money.

neural networks   A statistical method that "learns" the data by examining patterns. This technique is most common in credit fraud detection.

nixies   Nondeliverable mail that should be removed from a database to eliminate unneeded expense.

nth selects   A method by which marketers sample the database to ensure random selection of customers. For example, to test a new format to 5,000 names from a database of size 100,000, the direct marketer begins by selecting 1 name on the database, choosing every 20th (100,000/5,000) name thereafter.

opt-in A policy requiring that individuals give permission before an organization sends offers or information through a direct marketing medium (mail, e-mail, phone). With this policy, no solicitations or communications will come to individuals without their expressed permission.

opt-out A policy in which individuals have to request that no offers or information be sent to them through a direct marketing medium (mail, e-mail, phone). With this policy, solicitations or communications will be sent to an individual unless they take a specific action (e.g., filing a form).

outsourcing Using external organizations or individuals for various services such as database maintenance, analysis, mailing, and order processing.

point-in-time data A sample comprised of point-in-time data is used to determine the unique characteristics that distinguish responders from nonresponders. On such a file, the characteristics of each customer reflects how they looked at the time the promotion was sent. (See **frozen file**.)

positioning The process of establishing and maintaining a certain image of a company's product, relative to competitors, in the customer's mind.

positive correlation A relationship in which higher values of one variable are associated with higher values of another variable.

predictor variables In regression modeling, these are what we call the variables or data elements that are used to predict response, payment, and so on. They are also called independent variables.

product development strategy The process of developing new products for existing customers. The database can help in product development through the use of systematic testing paradigms.

prospecting database A database comprised solely of noncustomers. Typically, names and addresses found on such files come from compiled lists.

psychographics Activities, interests, and opinions of individuals such as hobbies, recreational activities, and political and social opinions, and so on that are used to describe and segment customers.

purchase behavior These data include previous purchases by product category, payment history, purchase frequency, and amount. This information is often predictive of future purchases.

pure play e-commerce site A company that only uses e-commerce as opposed to multichannel marketers.

purge The removal of certain records or data items from a database or list.

random sample A sample in which every member of the sample is equally likely to have been chosen, ensuring a composition similar to that of the population from which the sample was drawn.

ratio variables A variable derived by dividing one data element by another. For example, an estimate of the average payment rate for each customer could be derived by dividing total products paid by each customer by total products ordered.

real-time processing   A method of data processing in which task requests are entered into the system immediately and processed according to user or task priorities.

recency data   Customer data related to the recency of a customer's last promotion, order payment, and so on.

reconciliation   The process of comparing forecasted to actual campaign statistics such as response rates, payment rates, and profit.

regression analysis   A statistical method that builds a predictive equation based on the "best fit" between a dependent and one or more independent variables. It is also known as regression modeling or response modeling.

regression modeling   See **regression analysis**.

relational databases   Databases that have no predetermined relationships between data items. Information is contained in tables that can interact with each other. Relational databases are more flexible for data access.

representative sample   A sample accurately reflecting the population of interest from which direct marketers draw inferences. For a sample to be representative, no members of the population of interest are purposely excluded.

response lists   Lists of people or organizations that responded to offers such as mail order catalogs, subscriptions, or solicitations for donations.

response modeling   Methods (e.g., mathematical or statistical) used to select customers most likely to exhibit a particular characteristic (e.g., ordering, paying, renewing). It is also known as predictive modeling.

response variable   See **dependent variable**.

reverse test   When rolling out with a new format or creative concept, direct marketers often retest (reverse test) the old promotional package. Doing so provides valuable information regarding the performance of the new test package in rollout.

RFM (recency, frequency, and monetary) data elements   These variables are used to predict future purchases.

RFM analysis/scoring   A method of assigning certain values and weights to past purchase activities (recency of purchase, frequency of purchase, and the monetary amount of purchase) in an attempt to rank customers from those most likely to order to those least likely to order. One can choose from several scoring algorithms.

rollout   A large-scale direct marketing campaign

salting   Owners of databases often include names in the file that are not real customers (decoys) to check how the database is being used by outside service bureaus or renters of a list. This process is known as salting the file.

sample A sample is a subset of customer records. In most cases, it is taken randomly and is representative of the universe of interest on direct marketers' databases.

sample size estimation When planning a test of marketing programs, analysts should calculate the required sample sizes for the tests to ensure a certain level of accuracy in the results.

SAS Statistical analysis software commonly used by database analysts developed by the SAS Institute.

scoring The process of attaching a value onto a customer record based on a predictive model such as regression or a formal RFM analysis.

segmentation A process of dividing a market into smaller pieces based on demographic, psychographic, or behavioral (purchase) patterns. Segmentation is necessary to develop marketing plans that are more responsive to a specific group of customers.

SIC (Standard Industrial Classification) codes Four-digit numerical codes assigned by the U.S. government to business establishments to identify the primary business of the establishment. The classification was developed to facilitate the collection, presentation, and analysis of data and to promote uniformity and comparability in the presentation of statistical data collected by various agencies of the federal government, state agencies, and private organizations.

simple linear regression A regression modeling method that uses one independent variable and one dependent variable.

situational analysis An evaluation of environmental factors (cultural, economic, legal, political, social, demographic, technological, and so on), present and future markets, target market characteristics, competitors, and so on.

snapshot A file used to determine the unique characteristics that distinguish responders from nonresponders in which the characteristics of all the customers on the file reflect how they looked at the time the promotion was sent. (See **frozen file.**)

source A code that indicates how an individual record (i.e., name, household) first entered the database. Sources include lists purchased by the marketer, response to advertisements, cards filled out at retail, and so on.

spam Unsolicited or unwanted commercial e-mail. Spamming refers to the process of sending unsolicited commercial e-mail.

SPSS Statistical analysis software commonly used by database analysts developed by SPSS Inc.

stepwise regression A particular method of building any multiple regression model in which each variable must meet a specific threshold prior to entry into the final model.

structured database A database that has defined relationships and paths. Data in structured databases come from a single source. Items on the database are linked one to one: only one item relates to another.

structured query language (SQL)   A computer language used for database management.

summary/aggregate data   Data that provide marketers with information on how marketing programs are performing by totaling or averaging data from individual records. Total orders placed in response to a specific mailing is an example of aggregate data.

target market   The exact definition of a customer group deemed most appropriate for a particular product/service or promotional offer at hand. Database marketers often define target markets via analysis of past promotional tests.

Telephone Preference Service (TPS)   A list of names maintained by the DMA of people who prefer not to receive promotional offers via the telephone.

transaction data   Variables that relate to product purchase or other responses such as buyers versus nonbuyers, recency and frequency of purchase, amount of purchases, brand loyalty, position in adoption cycle, and product attitudes.

univariate tabulations   Tabulations produced on analysis samples and display the percentage responders and nonresponders to the offer for the various categories of each data element.

validation sample/data set   A portion of the sample of customers upon which the analysis is validated prior to using such findings for selecting names for promotion. It is also called the hold-out sample. Typically, the portion of the sample upon which one validates the analysis findings represents one third of the total sample.

variables   See **attributes**.

zero correlation   A relationship in which higher values of one variable are associated with all values of another variable and vice versa. Zero or near zero correlations indicate that two variables are not related to each other.

Additional Readings
in Database
and Direct Marketing

_____ **Database and Direct Marketing**

Beyond 2000—The Future of Direct Marketing, by Jerry Reitman

The Complete Database Marketer: Second-Generation Strategies and Techniques for Tapping the Power of Your Customer Database, by Arthur M. Hughes.

Customer-Driven Marketing, by John Frazer-Robinson

Customer Relationship Management: A Senior Management Guide to Technology for Creating a Customer-Centric Business, conducted by Price Waterhouse Coopers, commissioned by the Direct Marketing Association, Inc.

Database Marketing: The New Profit Frontier, by Ed Burnett

Database Marketing: The Ultimate Marketing Tool, by Edward Nash

Data Mining Your Website, by Jesus Mena

The Data Warehouse Lifecycle Toolkit: Expert Methods for Designing, Developing, and Deploying Data Warehouses, by Ralph Kimball, Laura Reeves, Margy Ross, & Warren Thornthwaite

Desktop Database Marketing, by Jack Schmid & Alan Weber

Direct and Database Marketing, by Graeme McCorkell

Direct Marketing: An Integrated Approach, by William J. McDonald

Direct Marketing Management, by Mary Lou Roberts & Paul D. Berger

Direct Marketing: Strategy, Planning, Execution, by Edward Nash

The Engaged Customer: The New Rules of Internet Direct Marketing, by Hans Peter Brondmo & Geoffrey Moore

How to Find and Cultivate Customers Through Direct Marketing, by Martin Baier

Integrated Direct Marketing, by Ernan Roman

Mastering Data Mining: The Art and Science of Customer Relationship Management, by Michael J. A. Berry & Gordon Linoff

The New Direct Marketing: How to Implement a Profit-Driven Database Marketing Strategy, by David Shepard Associates, Rajeev Batra (Ed.)

The New Integrated Direct Marketing, by Mike Berry

The Next Step in Database Marketing—Consumer Guided Marketing, by Dick Shaver

Power of Your Customer Database, by Arthur M. Hughes

Strategic Database Marketing, by Robert R. Jackson & Paul Wang

Strategic Database Marketing: The Masterplan for Starting and Managing a Profitable Customer-Based Marketing Program, by Arthur M. Hughes

Successful Direct Marketing Methods, by Bob Stone

Statistics References

Applied Linear Statistical Models, by John Neter, Michael Kutner, Christopher Nachtsheim, & William Wasserman

Applied Regression Analysis and Other Multivariable Methods, by David Kleinbaum, Lawrence Kupper, & Keith Muller

Data Mining Cookbook, by Olivia Parr Rud

A Second Course in Statistics: Regression Analysis, by William Mendenhall & Terry Sincich

References

A better supermodel than Kate Moss. (1999, November 15). *Direct*.

Allstate unit establishes information technology center in Northern Ireland; notes lack of U.S. computer programmers. (1998, October 24). *Insurance Advocate*. *109*(42), 26.

Ansoff, I. (1988) *The new corporate strategy*. New York: Wiley.

Baier, M., & Stone, B. (1996). *How to cultivate customers through direct marketing*. Lincolnwood, IL: McGraw Hill-NTC.

Beardi, C. (2001, April 16). CRM. *Advertising Age*.

Belfer, S. (1998) IT are from Mars, and marketing are from Venus. *Direct Marketing, 61*(5), 52.

Blank, C. (2001, March 5). Studies say m-commerce market is unpredictable. *eMarketer*.

Book, J. (2000, June 2). A multichannel effort yields the best results. *iMarketing News*, 25.

Brenner, K. (2001, June 25). Report: Privacy inadequate on government Web sites. *iMarketing News*, 3.

Brenner, K. (2001, July 9). Poll: Privacy not top social issue for consumers. *iMarketing News*, 4.

Campanelli, M. (2001, June 25). Joint congressional panel to weigh difference in privacy legislation. *DM News*. 3.

Cluster analysis helps Proflowers personalize email, increase profits. (2001, May/June). *1to1 Magazine*.

Cruz, W. (2001, March 21). Kawasaki gets big response from rich media e-mails. *iMarketing News*.

Customer service (2001). Retrieved from www.payless.com

CVS launches first integrated promotion. (2000, April 11). *dmnews.com*.

Dana, J. (1999, September 13). HIT the bricks. *Marketing News, 33*(19), 1.

Dana, J. (2000, July 17). New technologies in marketing. *Marketing News*, 25–28.

Davis, J. (2001). This year may become the year that bricks-and-clicks achieve their revenge. *InfoWorld. 23*(3), 70.

Dell corporate information (2001). Retrieved from www.dell.com/us/en/gen/corporate/factpack_003.htm

Direct Marketing Association (2000). Economic impact: U.S. direct marketing today (6th ed.) (chap. 1). Retrieved from www.the-dma.org/library/publications/libres ecoimp1b1a.shtml

Drozdenko, R., & Cronin, J. (2001) [Consumer perceptions of multi-channel purchasing options]. Unpublished.

eMarketer. (2001). Retrieved from www.emarketer.com

Fingerhut to launch new e-mail, database marketing program. (2000, April 11). *dmnews.com*.

First Union banks on fibre optic expertise from Amdahl. (2001). Retrieved October 1, 2001 from www.amdahl.com/success/mm002891.html

Full-size sport utility market import vs. domestic = status vs. utility. (1997, January 6). *PR Newswire*.

GoldMine. (2001). Retrieved from goldmine.com/support/care/isolutions/case-study.cfm?caseid = 22

Gordon, C. (2001, June 11). Establishing a Web presence in the UK. *DM News*, 32.

Haegele, K. (2000, March). Hispanic Americans, a crash course in culturally sensitive marketing. *Target Marketing. 23(3)*, 97.

IBM (2001). IBM zSeries (formerly S/390) solutions for business intelligence. Retrieved from www-4.ibm.com/software/data/bi/s390/solutions/index.htm

Jackson, R., & Wang, P. (1997) *Strategic database marketing*. Lincolnwood, IL: McGraw Hill-NTC.

Krol, C. (1998). Weber segments customers to keep its grill sales sizzling. *Advertising Age. 69(36)*, 17.

Lach, J. (1999). Data mining digs in. *American Demographics. 21(7)*, 38.

Levey, R. H. (2000, August). Pleasantville, NY: Pop. 30 million. *Direct*.

Levey, R. H. (2001, July). Just for you. *Direct*

LivePerson and Harris Interactive unveil the post-holiday customer satisfaction report. (2000, February 10). *Business Wire*.

Long, C. (2000, May). You don't have a strategic plan?—Good! *Consulting to Management C2M, 11*(1), 35–42.

Mena, J. (1999). *Data mining your website*. Boston: Digital Press.

Mistry, S. (1996, April). To succeed in India, marketers must look beyond the numbers. *Advertising Age International*, 16.

Molloy, C. (1997, November 3). Lloyds, Citibank take dead aim on Brazil. *Global Fund News. 1*(11), 1–2.

MotherNature.com streamlines its e-mail efforts. (2000, May 19). *dmnews.com*.

Orr, A. (2000, February). Count me in—opt-in, that is. *Target Marketing. 23*(2), 5.

P & G makes AOL debut with mouthwash ads. (1999, March 1). *Marketing News*, 1.

Pastore, M. (2001, June 18). Women maintain lead in Internet use. *CyberAtlas*.

Porter, M. (2001, March). Strategy and the Internet. *Harvard Business Review*, 63–78.

Priore, T. (2000, September 7). Improving e-mail response rates. *DM News*.

Regression modeling turns CareerTrack's DM campaign from static to dynamic. (1998, March 12). *dmnews.com*.

Roberts, M., & Berger, P. (1999). *Direct marketing management* (2nd ed.). Upper Saddle River, NJ: Prentice Hall.

Saturn Corporation. (2001). Retrieved from www.saturn.com

Schmit, J. (1999, February 16). Asia's culture hampers Internet commerce. *USA Today*, p. 6B.

Schultz, R. (2001, May 15).CRM cynics. *Direct*.

Shermach, K. (1998, June). Zen and the art of marketing cards to Asian consumers. *Card Marketing*. 2(6), 16–17.

Stone, B. (1996). *Successful direct marketing methods* (6th ed.). Lincolnwood, IL: McGraw Hill-NTC.

Surowiecki, J. (1999, February 1). The return of Michael Porter. *Fortune, 139*(2), 135–137.

Sutter, M., & Mandel-Campbell, A. (1998, October 5). Customers are eager, infrastructure lags. *Advertising Age International*, 12.

Tiffany & Company strikes gold with AS/400 business intelligence solution (2001). Retrieved from www-1.ibm.com/servers/eserver/iseries/casest/tiff2.htm

Tomasula, D.(2001, May 10). Study: $2.1 billion to be spent on e-mail marketing in 2001. *iMarketing News*.

Trepper, C. (2000, May 15). Customer care goes end-to-end. *InformationWeek, 786*, 55–61.

Weaver, J. (2000, August). New economy lies. *Smart Business*, 103–8.

Wunderman, L. (1998, October). Keynote address to Direct Marketing Association of Washington.

Yorgey, L. (1998). Global media choices. *Target Marketing, 21*(4), 29.

You say London, I say Londres. (1997, May). *Marketing Tools*, 12.

Name Index

Subject Index

About the Authors

Ronald G. Drozdenko, Ph.D., is Professor and Chair of the Marketing Department, Ancell School of Business, Western Connecticut State University. He is also the founding Director of the Center for Business Research at the Ancell School. He has more than 25 years of teaching experience. The courses he teaches include Strategic Marketing Databases, Interactive/Direct Marketing Management, Product Management, Marketing Research, and Consumer Behavior. He is collaborating with the Direct Marketing Educational Foundation to develop a model curriculum for universities pursuing the areas of interactive or direct marketing. Working with an advisory board of industry experts, he codeveloped the Marketing Database course in the model curriculum. He has codirected more than 100 proprietary research projects since 1978 for the marketing and research and development departments of several corporations, including major multinationals. These projects were in the areas of strategic planning, marketing research, product development, direct marketing, and marketing database analysis. He also has published several articles and book chapters. He holds a Ph.D. in Experimental Psychology from the University of Missouri. He is a member of the American Marketing Association, the Society for Consumer Psychology, and the Academy of Marketing Sciences. He is also the coinventor on three U.S. patents.

Perry D. Drake has been involved in the direct marketing industry for approximately 15 years. He is currently the Vice President of Drake Direct, a database marketing consulting firm specializing in response modeling, customer file segmentation, lifetime value analysis, customer profiling, database consulting, and market research. Prior to this, Perry worked for approximately 11 years in a variety of roles at The Reader's Digest Association.

Perry's initial position at The Reader's Digest Association was as a statistician in the quantitative analysis department, applying segmentation, response modeling, test design, and multivariate techniques. Later, moving into a product line role as Associate Director of Magazine Circulation Marketing, Perry assumed full strategic responsibility for all acquisition efforts, including mailings to house and outside lists as well as renewal and billing efforts. More recently, Perry assumed responsibility for creating a new marketing services division in preparation for the new marketing database, systems, and procedures being implemented at The Reader's Digest Association. As Director of Marketing Services, Perry was responsible for a staff of over 40 marketing database professionals in support of marketing efforts for the entire U.S. business.

In addition to consulting, Perry has taught at New York University in the Direct Marketing Master's Degree program since Fall, 1998, currently teaching "Statistics for Direct Marketers," "Database Modeling" and "Advanced Database Modeling" to future direct marketers. Perry was the recipient of the Center for Direct and Interactive Marketing's "1998-1999 Outstanding Master's Faculty Award." This honor was awarded to Perry in recognition of performing at a level above and beyond NYU's standard of quality by providing exceptional academic services to both students and the program. Perry also lectures on testing and marketing financials for Western Connecticut State University's Interactive Direct Marketing Certificate Program. Along with Ron, he is collaborating with the Direct Marketing Educational Foundation to develop a model curriculum for universities pursing the area of interactive or direct marketing.

Perry earned a Masters of Science in Applied Statistics from the University of Iowa and a Bachelor of Science in Economics from the University of Missouri. He is a member of the Direct Marketing Association, the Direct Marketing Club of New York, and the American Statistical Association.